Gaia Speaks

SACRED EARTH WISDOM

GAIA THROUGH PEPPER LEWIS

Gaia Speaks

SACRED EARTH WISDOM

GAIA THROUGH PEPPER LEWIS

Light Technology Publishing

This book has been compiled from articles previously printed
in the *Sedona Journal of EMERGENCE!*, a monthly magazine
published by Light Technology Publishing.

Cover art by
Rebecca Richman Flint
www.studiodune.com

ISBN 1-891824-48-1

Published by

800-450-0985
www.lighttechnology.com

Printed by

PO Box 3540
Flagstaff, AZ 86003

Acknowledgments

*L*ong before this book existed as it does now in its printed form, it still existed. It existed in my heart, in my mind and in my future timeline, which Mother Earth would reveal to me once in a while when life seemed particularly hard. As validation for its eventual birth, I felt both empowered and at peace whenever I would so much as sit with or add to the pages that Gaia had written through me.

Never has there been a time when I have been unsupported, unloved or alone, except by my own choosing. I have always been guided and assisted, not only by Mother Earth, but also by the wisdom of those who now read these words. I humbly thank you for helping me to hold the vision of an awakened, conscious, sentient and healthy planet Earth who is both our Mother and our partner in evolution.

I would like to express my deepest gratitude to a few very special people who have encouraged and supported me throughout this endeavor, especially when the task at hand seemed bigger than I. My words to you are simple ones, but the depth of the well of feelings from which they emerge is limitless.

To Albert and Betty Keen, my mom and dad: Thank you for allowing me to unfold and develop my life in my own way, no matter how different it has been from your own. Thanks for letting me keep the rose-colored glasses I wore as a child. As you can see, I am still wearing them, and they have made all the difference.

To Bryce and Keenan, my two sons: You are my greatest loves and are a continual source of inspiration. Your unique interests have allowed me to explore and celebrate my own. Thank you for teaching me the meaning of unconditional love and reminding me that the child within each of us continues to be our greatest hope for the future.

To Rob: Your trust, patience, love and support mean the world to me. Long ago I dreamed that I would share my life with someone whose vision was similar to my own: the vision of a whole and healed planet where compassion and partnership were the norm rather than the exception. You added the words "best friend" to that dream and then made it come true.

To Isis, my spiritual mom: Thank you for prodding, pushing, cajoling, reprimanding and loving me into accepting my role as a channel, writer, speaker and teacher. To my dearest friend, Bob Resnikoff: Thank you for teaching me the kind of wisdom that only a spiritual curmudgeon can know and for sharing the joys of a fellow bibliophile. To Lee Carroll, my friend and adept companion in the field of channeling: Thank you for pointing the way and for holding the door open. Thank you to Kahu Fred Sterling for creating a warm and inviting inner and outer environment in which smiles and laughter are always spiritual. To Ronald Ross, my friend and mentor: Thank you for helping me to see that the baby steps and the giant leaps all come from the same source. To Melody Swanson of *Sedona Journal of EMERGENCE* and Light Technology Publishing: Thank you for encouraging me to take the next step in channeling whenever it seemed that I was hesitating on the threshold. Thank you to Beth Black for encouraging me to seek sanctuary at Mt. Shasta and for offering her friendship and her resources. To Sharon, Lynette and Donna: You are the best friends any woman could hope for. Thank you for being such a significant part of my journey.

And to Mother Earth: Thank you for awakening all that was dormant within me and for teaching me to marvel at the wonder and diversity of life. You taught me to hold my vision before the criticisms and cynicisms of the world and to stand tall against seeming adversity. Thank you for your endless faith in me as a partner and channel for your words and for the finest education anyone could hope for, including a course in grace and courage. Your gentle reminders have helped me to look beyond what is readily apparent and see beneath the surface. Most of all, thank you for making sure that every path I chose, no matter how remote, always led back to my heart, to you and to Source.

—Pepper Lewis

Contents

Preface:
The Art of Channeling

An air of mystery has always obscured the art of channeling, shrouding it with mists that lie between the known and the unknown. Channeling is a metaphysical art, meaning that to explain it, one must look beyond the physical realm. Unfortunately, this label has managed to render the entire subject somewhat "hands off," especially for those who reside outside metaphysical, or New Age, circles. Although venerated long ago, today channeling lies somewhere along the dubious outskirts of reality, toggling between the believable and the forgettable. But those whose lives have been touched by this art know otherwise, and I place myself proudly among them.

Channeling, also referred to as mediumship, is both timeless and ageless. It is best described as the ability to become aware of and translate higher frequencies and dimensions of understanding, as well as to benefit from them in some measurable way. A channel, or channeler, is someone with the ability to access and focus this experience. Although a more simple process could not exist, the veils that separate the dimensions can be quite dense. Layers of thought forms as well as various belief systems lie between what we are able to respond to and what we can only imagine. These can easily interfere with and even prevent us from receiving the full benefit of multidimensional awareness. They can make the distance between realities span even farther. If we could simply release anything that stands between our reality and its illusion, channeling would quickly become obsolete—but until such a time, it serves a splendid purpose.

Channeling is possible because everything in the universe exists first as energy and then as form. Some forms of energy vibrate slowly, and other forms vibrate more quickly. This rate of vibration determines what dimension the energy will be expressed in, because density, or slower vibration, creates matter. A slow, or lower, vibration might be expressed physically in the form of a table, a chair or an automobile. Higher vibratory energy might express nonphysical things like creative ideas or thoughts. Beyond the comprehension of the human mind, energy continues to vibrate until it becomes finer still. We cannot see these vibrations and our minds cannot logically comprehend them, but we can perceive them because they are there; they exist. These finer vibrations are just as available to us as any other resource.

Channeling is an art not a science. It is objective in intent but subjective in form. Both the subtle environment of the heart and the not so subtle environment of the mind influence channeling. The mind's child, the ego, sees the process as a game whose outcome would benefit from its involvement, so we must acknowledge that even the most adept and devoted channels are subject to both inner and outer influences. One can never become an "expert" channel. Those who take pride in proclaiming themselves the only, the truest, the original or the first and last authority on the subject do so from a biased and personally subjective point of view. This immature stance is often tempered by life itself and later surrendered. Even within the ranks of trusted, world-class channels, the diversity can be stunning. The best channels are those who have a deep and abiding trust in Spirit and are aligned with the path they have chosen.

Adept channels consistently and accurately represent rather than interpret what Spirit offers. It is the channel's responsibility to remain an observer of the process. Detached yet aware, the channel moves her awareness into the background, allowing higher wisdom a wide spectrum within which infinite potential can be expressed. A good channel is able to set aside personal issues and concerns by aligning body, mind and spirit with energies that transcend the lower self. Because channeling takes place at deep levels of awareness that exist beyond the reasoning mind, there is no need for channels to surrender the ownership or authority of their bodies. Trust and true partnership guide the process from beginning to end.

Everyone has the ability to channel, to a certain degree. We send and receive messages all of the time, even when we are not consciously aware of doing so. In fact, we often take our own intuition—which is also a form of channeling—for granted. Anyone with a sincere desire to develop this ability can do so. There are only a few prerequisites, the most important one being the ability to trust and surrender to the process. Not everyone, however, is naturally adept in this regard. Just as there are gifted artists, writers and musicians, there are also gifted channels, who excel in their field. Although a positive interaction with channeling can lead to a wonderfully fulfilling experience, a less than favorable experience can quickly sway a neutral mind. Such an outcome is often the result of an unskilled intention gone awry. It is best to allow each experience to remain independent of the rest.

Channeling offers us greater awareness and deeper wisdom than our normal waking reality provides, but it would be a mistake to assume that it is a quick fix for solving our problems or resolving life's disappointments. Most often channeled guidance offers simple, uncomplicated and unrestrictive answers to our direct questions. What we do with these answers is between our own free will and us. As humans, we have a tendency to complicate the simple and to hear what we want to hear rather than what is being said. It is important that we accept the guidance we receive in the spirit of good will in which it was expressed. Remember that guidance will shelter you from indecision, but it will not remove the decision process altogether. Ultimately, your life is your own.

There is as much to learn from the guidance we receive as from the process itself. With so many different spiritual teachers and guides to choose from, it is good to develop your own moral and spiritual compass. There are a variety of schools of thought to discover, libraries to access, halls of records to visit, angels from every order to consult, and there are helpful higher beings who can impart wisdom from any number of dimensions and disciplines. The path of service does not end when our physical lives end; usually, it only begins there.

Approach every channeling experience, including this book, with an open heart and an open mind. When we remove our self-imposed limitations and restrictions, self-love and well-being are often revealed. If we allow this, it can open the door to peace, joy, abundance and fulfillment. Set an intention to receive the highest and best that Spirit can offer. Ask that specific and pertinent guidance continue to flow into your awareness long after the experience has ended. Do your part by recognizing and appreciating the intent behind the guidance that is being offered. Realize that there are some things you must discover for yourself and that it may not be in your best interest to receive these from any other source. Be open to receive wisdom and positive reinforcement at all times and from all sources, including your own self. Give full credit to the subtle, indirect nuances of life as well as the synchronicities that present themselves moment by moment.

Allow yourself to receive the many benefits that channeling can offer, including a revitalization in health and well-being, specific guidance, unique discoveries, a sense of peace and answers to issues and concerns. Never forget that you are one with All That Is/Creator/Source. As such, you are entitled to all of the wonders of the seen and the unseen worlds. Channeling can bring the best of all worlds into your own—it has into mine.

—Pepper Lewis

Introduction

Welcome to your book. I say your book, because indeed that is what it is. The words printed on the pages of your book may at first glance seem identical to those found in additional copies of the book by the same title, but I can assure you that your copy is unique and original. In fact, it has been written with you in mind and has been specifically dedicated to you. You will hear and respond to the words herein differently than any other reader. If need be, the words will rearrange themselves on the page in order to call attention to what is most important for you to know at this time. Reading on different days and at different times will yield different results, as will reading in different environments.

It is proper etiquette for an author to make appropriate introductions whenever possible, but perhaps especially before embarking on a journey of such magnitude. A passenger on a ship should know something about its captain. As a reader, you also deserve to know something about the background of this author as well as how these words came to be.

I am the nonphysical sentience of this planet. Simply put, I am the planet Earth. I am the body and the soul of the planet you currently inhabit. My sentience is conscious and aware of itself and its purpose. That being said, the Earth's physical body, which includes her resources and functions, is not the author of this work. By comparison, the physical you that authors your daily thoughts and words is not the same as your soul, which authors your life's purpose. You call the physical planet "Earth," but she is also known by other names. Today you are familiar with terms such as Mother Earth, Gaia's Voice, Mother Nature and Terra Firma; other civilizations have had names of their own. My sentience guides and enlivens all that surrounds the planet as well as all that is upon and within her. My sentience animates the air you breathe, the energy you burn and the water you drink. All of the elements are under my care and direction, as are the seasons and the weather. I am a devoted companion and trusted friend to all life forms, including the animal, plant and mineral kingdoms that share the planet with you.

My sentience, the most aware, advanced and attuned aspect of my being, is that which directs these words. This endeavor is not the first attempt on the part of this (my) sentience, and many other works that are still in existence could easily claim my name. History, more often than not, recognizes and endorses those who least merit it, hence my namesake is of least importance. It is only as relative as the wisdom you discover within these pages. On the other hand, great effort has been expended by the physical vehicle, our channel [Pepper Lewis], who has been receiving and transcribing these transmissions for over a decade.

Although many believe in a sentient or feeling Earth, not all are attuned to her. Channeling offers a unique advantage in this respect, because it allows the transmission of vibrations and impressions to be communicated as language. The advantages of this tool far outweigh the obvious drawbacks, which include unconscious obstruction and conscious distortion. In this forum, composed for use by the public domain, my words are offered through a clear and receptive channel, one whose duty and devotion has been tempered by time, sacrifice and service. A deep and constant yearning to communicate with each of you urges me to depend upon this ancient art and the service of a trustworthy medium, my companion in numerous incarnations.

Those who work in the name of Spirit do so because their personal journey is aligned with their soul's path of service. The path of service is two-fold and encompasses both service to self and service to other than self, or world service. Although humanitarian work can indeed be called selfless, it is not the same as the path of world service. For instance, one who is devoted to humanitarian efforts may very well have sworn such an oath in a previous life, for a variety of reasons. The path of service is a long one, spanning many lifetimes. It is rigorous and severe, and although the rewards are many, it may be several lifetimes before they are experienced. To be clear, the path of service is not a selfless one but is that which leads to self-fullness.

Our scribe, on the occasion of this life and for the purpose of this work, which shall be expressed in various volumes, is the aforementioned Pepper Lewis, a name which hardly suits her but has adhered itself to her nonetheless, for reasons she can best explain. From time to time and during the course of our journey, I will make reference to her using various expressions and names. These will include scribe, channel, medium, author, partner, companion and Elizabeth or Eli, a name that is a much better fit, at least by account of this unbiased opinion. All are considered terms of respect and endearment by this sentience, who has known many past close associations with this channel, perhaps more so than with others. Details of these experiences will be revealed as they become relevant to the subject at hand. The chronology of these events is of little importance at this time.

To be accurate, the process by which this material is made available to you is called automatic writing and is a form of mediumship. This method was placed into active service just after the fall of Atlantis. Prior to then, your mind was not separate from that of your brother or your neighbor. Your memories were individual but also collective. Although the process by which impressions are received by our scribe is not a difficult one and the relaxed state of awareness is fairly easy to achieve, appropriate and devoted candidates for this work have never been large in number. A surrender of at least a certain amount of personal identity is required, as are authorship and any claim to fame that may ensue from such an endeavor.

Over time much has been said and written about the Earth, yet little has been accurate. As you rediscover your origins, you will also rediscover mine. I have been the sentience of this planet from the beginning and before then as well. I was here as it was but a thought in Creator's infinite mind. When the fires were at last extinguished and the molten rock began to cool, a dynamic combination of elements emerged. Many forms of life have come and gone over eons of time, and humanity's existence upon the Earth is but a drop in the cosmic ocean. Still, the greatest potential has always existed with humans, because they are the product of both creation and evolution.

Your cosmic origins give rise to possibilities beyond what you now imagine. My ability to communicate with humanity has waxed and waned over time, although it has always been my creative directive to do so. Our communication has been influenced by many factors, including individual and collective consciousness, religious and spiritual fervor, planetary evolution and upheaval, genetic mutation and manipulation, as well as alterations and aberrations in how time is expressed.

Today two priorities guide my sentience. The first is to erase the perception of separation that seems to threaten the planet. Assumptions, suppositions and misinterpretations have given rise to fear and distrust. Soon separation will be disarmed and falsehoods will be dispelled. Consistent communication between all forms of life will return, and a true language that speaks with one voice and is heard by all hearts will again be the norm. The second priority is to awaken and expand the collective consciousness that has immobilized the hearts and minds of many.

Long ago access to knowledge and wisdom was unlimited. An ever-present field of awareness made memorization obsolete. Telepathic thought made the field available, and intent allowed your mind to extract the desired knowledge. Much later, after the fall of Atlantis, true knowledge was much more scarce, so it was kept secret and protected from all but a few. Wisdom was taught first-hand and passed between generations of initiates by spoken words and formulas that were laced with alchemical wisdom. This was difficult to memorize, as you might imagine, so after a time, the wise ones encoded stories, puzzles and games with mysteries that could be discovered by the most adept.

Today the electronic media presents many new opportunities. Communication travels so quickly and effortlessly that important messages are often mistaken for common jargon. Information has given birth to its offspring, misinformation, which has proliferated faster than anyone could have imagined. Wisdom is still plentiful; it abounds in every language and on every continent. True masters of wisdom still stroll among the common citizenry, just as long ago fools hid secrets that are only now being revealed.

The words I speak are also not new, but you will hear them as if for the first time. They are represented in the first person rather than in the second or the third, where they would seem even further removed. You will receive my words both within and without, because they are not separate from you. I am an extension and expansion of that which you are. Those who hear my words do so above and beyond other voices and demands that clamor for attention in the busy modern world. You will find that my words are most present in your life when you are most present in your life. Your experience of my sentience may be emotional or intellectual, depending upon your own makeup. You will find that my communication is compassionate, yet precise. Together we will explore obstacles, solutions and opportunities.

I have no interest in chastising humanity for the problems that currently face the world. My message is not intended to save you or the planet, and it will not prevent the occurrence of any upcoming calamity. There is no adverse condition that cannot be righted with the power of intent and the right use of will. Beyond that we are both eternal beings and as such will continue on regardless. What you embrace or reject today will have a significant effect upon the outcome of the next several years, and my messages are but one of many resources from which to choose. Where the will is established, a way will present itself that is clear, concise and forthcoming. As compassion and authenticity continue to increase, humanity will discover the courage and willingness to heal the environment and the world. Abundance, health and joy will replace scarcity, poverty and fear.

This book will first be offered in English, a somewhat generic language whose meaning is often misconstrued, but one that is also common throughout much of the globe. It is my sincere desire that my choice of words will be descriptive, yet practical and concise. Soon after, this work will be published in other languages as requests come forth and opportunity abides.

It is my hope that you will find my message meaningful and that you will continue to develop an appreciation for who and what you are. Your quest for truth and knowledge did not begin here and it will not end here. This is but one of many paths that crisscross your heart and mine on the way to Source/All That Is.

A Thousand Points of Light

May 2002

I have heard of Indigo children, but can you tell me if they are the same as or part of what is called the "violet race"? Can you also describe holographic beings?

Indigo children, and Indigo adults for that matter, are humans who are arranged differently from what most would describe as the norm. They are predisposed to individuality and to leadership, though not all will express themselves in this way. They perform poorly in confinement and isolation; classrooms, think tanks and meditative postures are anathema to them. Indigos are carriers of a dolphinlike frequency and perform best in podlike situations. An Indigo's pod becomes his or her family for life, even if the pod members are not actual relatives and regardless of any time sequences that might separate the pod. Indigo beings respond best to direction when it is presented with a natural, open and creative approach. Indigos are extremely loyal to those who befriend and understand them but can become easily agitated and insecure when questioned regarding their loyalty or fidelity. They are aware that differences exist between themselves and those who are unlike them but believe for the most part that these differences are due to societal demands above and beyond those required of others. Indigo beings are unique in a variety of ways and, depending upon the individual, the differences can be pronounced and even astounding.

INDIGOS: THE FORERUNNERS OF FUTURE GENERATIONS

Indigo beings are the forerunners of the race of beings most humans (not all) will evolve into. They will assist in elevating the higher aspects of societal response but will ignore or destroy the lesser aspects. For instance, Indigos are less apt to condemn others (regardless of injustice, crime or violation), and they are/will be less than willing to conform to a forty-hour work week simply because it is the norm. Injustices work against their personal sense of balance and rhythm, and their frequencies cannot abide this. The thoughts and conclusions drawn by Indigos will not often concur with those of others, regardless of what peer pressure might be brought upon them. They will argue, but not fight, and will most often quit rather than succumb.

The brilliance and intelligence of Indigos lie in their ability to create and live in an abstract reality rather than one born of logic or linear thought. Let us say that a linear/logical, reality-based experience finds a person's direct path blocked by a mountain. Logic would dictate that the mind contemplate and then execute a new direct path, perhaps one that goes through, around, over or beneath the boundary or obstruction. An Indigo would evaluate the same choices as the logical thinker but not often choose a solution based upon a logical conclusion. An abstract, reality-based experience will find the Indigo denying that the mountain is a block to the direct path. Much to the frustration of a logical thinker, an Indigo will force another reality to manifest. The new reality might—or might not—offer better choices, but to an Indigo, that is not the point. The Indigos' intelligence lies in their ability to create based on new and abstract ideas that exist beyond the third dimension, the dimension of logic, mind, form and density. Their brilliance allows them to make use of another reality while existing in this one, which is the very reason that they are the forerunners of future generations. Indigos are closest to becoming fourth- and fifth-dimensional beings. This can be most exasperating for teachers, parents, employers, spouses and others who can interact with them only in the third-dimensional plane.

Indigo beings respond differently to sunlight and to patterns of sleep as well as to all space and time considerations. They are often early or late but rarely on time (which would be logical). Their interests are varied and can therefore be turned on or off at a moment's notice. Their health cannot be measured by antiquated devices such as food pyramids or caloric intake. Their eating patterns might be unusual or erratic, because their physiological vitamin and mineral content is unique. An Indigo's physiology has a propensity for sugar, which assists him or her to turn on or adjust (lower) his or her frequencies to an alignment more consistent with the balance of humanity at this time. As humanity continues to evolve and adjust, so will the Indigo's dietary requirements.

Indigo children are sometimes diagnosed with deficient attention spans. In this time frame it is called attention deficit disorder, or ADD. Indigo children find current societies in disorder and their corresponding educational systems in deficit; therefore, they will offer little of their attention in support of them. It is likely that, of necessity and by the sheer increase in their numbers, they will cause new schools with new methods of education to emerge.

Eventually, these will become the norm rather than the exception.

Indigo beings are agents of change and as such, they are a part of every walk of life, within every societal venue and occupation. They continue to be born upon all continents and to all races and cultures. Their energy and frequency will serve as a bridge between realities and dimensions. They are equally at home (or not) in a variety of situations as long as they can access their pods or support systems. These will often consist of an unlikely grouping that, not surprisingly, will not seem logical to the observer. Indigo children will raise themselves with the assistance of their pods as well as with the assistance of their families. A parent or friend of an Indigo child or adult would do well to celebrate what is likable and acceptable regarding the Indigo individual while honoring with humor what is not. Guidance is best offered in abstract or indirect ways that do not impinge on the courageous Indigo.

VIOLET RACE INCARNATES AGAIN ON EARTH

Violet beings are part of a race that is once again choosing to incarnate upon the Earth. These beings have lived both upon and within the Earth at various times throughout Earth's history. Their lineage can be linked to the violet frequency or ray of expression which—perhaps more for them than for other races—has served them both in and out of body. Because of this, their health is typically better than that of the average human citizen, even though they are subject to the same environmental influences as other races and beings. The violet race can more easily identify, react and adapt to Indigo beings, because they are both catalysts, agents of change.

The violet race has lent its seed, or essence, to other races but has not received the same in return. Violet beings' vibration has been violet upon violet upon violet, adding to, rather than diminishing, their frequency. They do not hold themselves apart from other races or beings; on the contrary, they offer their friendship, honor and respect whenever possible. The violet race is a peaceful one; these beings do not condone maliciousness, use of force, weaponry or aggression of any kind. Can you see why some of them have been asked and others have volunteered to return to physical Earth? The violet race walks among you daily. It is one of many races that will make their presence known as the vibratory frequency of the Earth allows.

Long ago, the first conscientious objectors came from the violet race, during a time when ills similar to those that face present-day Earth were considered and evaluated. Violet beings gave voice to their concerns and complaints when an open mind was present and held silent when not. Their objections were presented peacefully, and even those who made their home at opposite ends of the energetic spectrum found little fault in what was proffered. While not in physical body, they have continued to offer support to humanity in ways and waves

honored by the natural realms. Perhaps one of the finer and most recent examples of the effects of the violet race are the words, energies and support lent to
well-known civil rights leader, Dr. Martin Luther King, who took to heart the
visions and dreams that were shown to him. Other citizens have also been
offered the same assistance, which requires a step toward unity rather than separation, but not many have yet been able to move in this direction.

The violet race is generally more attuned to nature than other races of beings.
This attunement will bring about changes in chemistry, botany and all fields relative to the use of land and that which it cultivates. The violet race also carries
an understanding of architecture based upon geometric principles that will make
housing more ergonomic and naturally climate controlled without the need of
fuels and gases as is common today. These beings are attuned to the partnership
and cooperation of all elements, even though they do not always enjoy physical
interaction with them. In other words, they are interested in clearing air pollution but do not, for the most part, like to fly. They are fine gardeners but will do
their best not to get dirty; they will go to great extremes to find or develop clean
water but do not often like to swim or frolic in water. Likewise, they enjoy the
company of crystals, rocks and minerals but will not go far out of their way to
seek them out, preferring instead to have the specimens themselves find their
way into the environment of the violet beings.

The violet race is here to stay as far as can be presently seen. Violet beings
are here to assist and participate and can be found in small and large cities alike.
Their numbers are currently small but are growing consistently. They must find
and partner with others of their own race in order to continue their lineage here.
A small segment of violet race beings will intermarry or link up with other beings
of complementary frequency, but these arrangements do not often produce a
child. For this reason, those of the violet race must seek out one another.

HOLOGRAPHIC BEINGS ARE ENERGIES

Holographic beings are best described as energies that can manifest a body.
They are not a race of beings but could be considered a race of energies. They,
more than other beings, are able to arrange and rearrange themselves in different patterns in order to serve themselves or others. They are primarily a
race of caregivers or service providers, though a loose interpretation of this
must, of necessity, be invoked. Holographic beings could, for instance, manifest a body within a certain circle of governmental intelligence in order to
impart important information. They are never perceived as being out of place
in a given situation, because they match their energy with the highest and
best use of their gifts of service, and that is how they are perceived. Only the
manifested body is a hologram; their energy in the form of a message or assistance is quite real. Service is offered and almost always accepted, on all lev-

els and in all places. Imagine someone asking you if you need help carrying a heavy box or bag at a time when that assistance is of most use to you. Would you stop to question whether or not that person is real or only a hologram or would you simply accept the assistance? Later on you might realize that the person came out of nowhere and departed the same way, but most likely you would still simply be grateful that the person was there when you most needed help. As you begin to relax your views and definitions of reality, you will see and experience much more!

Holographic beings are also able to create holographic experiences designed to serve you or a greater cause, as the case may be. For instance, they can create or orchestrate a reality (hologram) in which you are able to experience yourself at a higher level, thereby giving you the confidence to continue to do the same for yourself. They can create a reality (hologram) in which you are able to experience and then release a fear that has burdened you, thereby assisting you to overcome a different hurdle. Many have had wonderful encounters with holographic beings but remember only the experience as wondrous and not the being.

On certain levels of reality, your physical life can also be called a hologram; certainly, at times it has been referred to as an illusion. Holograms are constructions, basic or complex, based upon living matrices of light. They are compositions, art forms and expressions. Holographic beings are guided by an intelligence that can permeate and participate in all worlds—and in many ways—where it is welcome. Humanity has been most appreciative of the role this intelligence has played thus far, with more to come.

THE HUMAN BODY'S GRID SYSTEM HAS INTERSECTING LINES

Can you explain in detail the difference between the grid system and the meridian system of the human body?

The grid system is part of the original (divine) blueprint. It is divided into several quadrants and supports many intersecting coordinates. Each coordinate represents a specific point of light or vibratory expression, depending upon how that coordinate is viewed. The grid system, as defined by human orientation, is similar to the Earth's grid system, which is supported by axiatonal lines (also called ley lines). These lines also intersect and interact with one another in order to create and stimulate uninterrupted well-being, maintenance and communication. When operating optimally, this system is designed to promote the expression of perfection. Each coordinate or intersecting point of light is unique unto itself even while it also relates to the body and the beingness, which supports its purpose. In other words, each point of light is sentient, aware of itself as well as the grander purpose or being it serves. This is important to note, because it reveals that there is both perfection and a plan even for the smallest points of light.

Grids vibrate or pulse according to each individual's own code. No two codes are ever alike; at best, they can be described as similar. Twins can be said to have almost identical codes. This is how they are aware of each other's thoughts and feelings. Conjoined twins share the same vibration but express their frequency differently, often an octave or so apart. If conjoined twins are separated, the frequency will change, often substantially so, because the reference point has also been changed.

If a medical emergency causes one twin to be spared and another to be sacrificed, both frequencies will remain within the surviving twin, and he or she will continue to feel his or her partner throughout the balance of his or her life. Only the physical vehicle will have been sacrificed; the original energy will still remain. The same holds true for walk-ins. A walk-in is a being who, by agreement, takes over the soul's contract and the body of a being who cannot complete the terms of his or her own contract for one or more reasons. This is more common than most would believe and is quite prevalent today, given the difficult choices that face many individuals. A walk-in must honor the original contract as well as his or her own. It is a decision that cannot be made idly or without forethought or good counsel. The walk-in being must carry both frequencies, however different or mismatched. The original contract must be honored, but it can be expressed in a variety of ways and carried out concurrently with one's own.

THE HUMAN BODY'S MERIDIAN SYSTEM IS LAID OUT VERTICALLY

The meridian system rests lightly above the grid system. Meridians are energetic (charged) lines laid out vertically (for the most part) over the human anatomic structure, although they extend well beyond the physical boundaries of the body. Each body is unique, and it is not uncommon for these energetic lines to reach as far as twelve to thirty feet. If you doubt this, think about a time when simply entering a room altered your entire structure or perhaps challenged your sense of well-being. While the grid system offers support to the northern, southern, eastern and western hemispheres, the meridian system is responsible for the north and south poles. For instance, whether or not one responds in a grounded manner is a function of polarity registration. Likewise, a dualistic or opposite nature is the result of an unbalanced meridian system; this applies to all physical and nonphysical imbalances.

Meridian systems are as unique as grid systems and, here again, no two are alike. However, there is a correspondence between the two that generates a unique energy resonance, which can be recognized by gifted healers as well as those who practice acupuncture, acupressure and other forms of energetic healing. Although most meridian systems run energy from north to south, this is not a hard-and-fast rule and there are many exceptions. In certain places and for specific purposes, the meridian system and the grid system touch, creating channels designed to open, shut or redirect energy as needed. The joining created by the intersection of the grid system and the meridian system at unique times and specific places can bring about brilliant light (enlightenment) and miraculous healing. Likewise, if these important energetic matrices are clogged or damaged, discomfort, dis-ease and even illness may result.

ENERGY MUST BE ABLE TO TRAVEL FREELY

Healers and adepts are particularly susceptible to imbalances in these areas, because they offer themselves openly, completely and without reserve. Although valiant and unrestricted, they often facilitate not only the universal energy (ch'i) designated for their recipient but also some of their own for added good measure. It is their way of offering a guarantee or insurance policy to their client. Balance cannot be achieved or maintained if one's personal energetic chalice is repeatedly depleted. The intersecting points where the grid matrix and the meridian matrix touch are sacred. These points act as gates or thresholds for energy that is designed to pass easily and undisturbed. As the energy travels through these gates, it receives new encoded information that must also be carried throughout the entire energetic being. Let us say that you have a desire that you wish to manifest or bring into physical form. How do you believe the instructions for the manifestation of this desire are made known to your beingness, to the whole? The partnership between desire and manifestation is more successful if the message can be carried easily and swiftly to all points of light and beingness within and without you. If the gates are clogged or stripped of the energy that supports them, the energy and the manifestation might be delayed or partial, do you see?

If the energetic matrices that support the organism become overtaxed, the physical body might respond with a lack of energy, strength or will, and the emotional body might feel stressed and overwhelmed. Headaches, backaches, flulike symptoms and even the common cold can be attributes of these energy blockages. This is how humans at times create their own illness—inadvertently or purposefully. Even the healthiest of humans can create adverse conditions within their bodies that do not support or complement what the heart and mind desire. Must every imbalance and condition be treated? Not necessarily, no. Stresses and other conditions can be automatically released by the body's own intelligence system. A simple pause inserted in one's day can be extremely beneficial in supporting the energetic flow of the body, yet this vital and simple remedy is often ignored or left for the remains of the day. Prayer and meditation also automatically allow mind/body/heart/soul to settle, reset, rejuvenate and reignite. Unnoticed by the participant because of the simplicity of the moment, the positive effects are felt later on and not always attributed to the original moment.

It is just as easy for the body to heal itself as harm itself. It depends upon what an individual will choose and on which level of consciousness the choice will be made. Awake or at rest, the body's intelligence system will always seek to enhance itself for your benefit. Only in extreme cases, when an individual completely neglects the body, the mind and the path, will the meridian system begin to falter and eventually shut down. Your energy is your own and is of little use to others. Rather than surrender your own energy, vitality and health, remind others of their own unique and divine patterns. Treasure and nurture yourselves, replenish what is missing or in lack, rejuvenate what is depleted by redirecting, opening and expanding energetic channels to the infinite.

EARTH'S PARTNERS INADVERTENTLY CREATED IMBALANCE

I recently read that Mother Earth and Father Sky are reuniting as Mother/Father Earth. Although I do not doubt this, I would feel better if you would validate this information as well as add your own comments on the subject.

Mother Earth/Gaia, as the sentience that now directs these words, will, yes, confirm the accuracy of the message as well as the sincerity of the messenger. So that you will be well at ease, I will add these additional comments:

My sentience has never been separate from what we will call the masculine attributes of heaven and Earth. Shutting down the divine masculine could cause injurious results to the divine feminine. Grains could not grow, reproduction of healthy cells would slow and the planet would become confused, to say the least. The Earth has been mandated, since its inception, as a planet of choice, a plethora of diversity, a myriad of possibilities and a cornucopia of creation. Achieving and maintaining balance, however, was placed into the hands of Earth's partners. Is this not what even now you are attempting to do?

Balance is not heavy or solid; it does not weigh upon backs or shoulders. Balance is not liquid, which is always endeavoring to pour more or less of itself into the next vessel or being. Balance is not gaseous or air, floating ever higher and becoming unattainable, dissipating when it is most needed but least available. Balance is light; it is everywhere in equal measure. It exists in a wide spectrum of color, frequency, vibration and design.

Long ago Earth's partners desired to understand frequency and light, in order to harness and distribute it, but in so doing a great imbalance was created. This imbalance eventually permeated all realities, all kingdoms and all elements. Humanity was affected, as was my own sentience. Before the time of imbalance, many species shared the ability to procreate, and both the male and the female of the species were able to bring forth the next generation. Parenting responsibilities were evenly distributed between two or more adults. Balance also allowed different species to mate, creating new and unique varieties and splendor for the Earth to call its own.

IMBALANCE SLOWED DOWN EVOLUTION

After the time of imbalance, variety ceased to be the norm, evolution slowed and some species became extinct. The youthful face of nature was craggy to look upon and tired in appearance. Everything seemed to come to a stop. Earth's partners did not wish to create this imbalance. Their desire was to create accountability and order, but their methods were antiquated and from another world with less diversity, beauty and originality than this one. Their protocol was authoritarian and dictatorial. The physical Earth responded first by shuddering, then by shrinking back and shutting down certain areas; my sentience was deeply affected as well.

For a time, I felt numb and constrained. I could not move or stretch. My ability to create new landmass by pushing up on the ocean floor so that new species could flourish was curtailed and limited. I felt tired and sleepy, and my body ached. I desperately wanted to respond to the calls and the pleas that found their way to me but found it nearly impossible to do so. My last attempts to provide for the Earth set into motion a few events that still remain active today. These include the delicate harmony that exists between the species who make their home in the Great Barrier Reef, the unique diversity and balance of the indigenous species of the Galapagos Islands, the silvery pristine quietude of the Alaskan preserve and the volcanic biological miracle that is the continual growth of the Hawaiian Islands. All of these are threatened today; once again the Earth hangs in the balance, along with its partners. Other attempts were made as well, but my sentience cannot account for them even now.

THE DIVINE FEMININE BECAME DORMANT

My sentience became dormant during the time of the imbalance; the desires of the few outnumbered the wellness of the many. I felt powerless to advance evolution or to assist in rebalancing what had been ripped from my sentience and my body. I left the reins to the devas to manage as best they could. I endowed them with my consciousness and left explicit instructions to be awakened when and if my consciousness could once again make a difference. Even as the tides were retreating and leaning toward the masculine I asked my constant companion, the Moon, to assist in my absence. So it is that the Moon, although structurally masculine, became attuned to the divine feminine. What could not be altered in waking time would at least be influenced in the dream state.

This was many yesterdays ago, more than many will remember. It is not unkind to block one's memories when they are painful, and this is no different. It is important to remember that the divine feminine did not die, neither did it depart. It became dormant; it slumbered as I slept, leaving it open and exposed. The feminine remained, but it was no longer divine, do you see? If the feminine was no longer divine, the masculine could not be divine either, for where was the balance? The masculine, therefore, also lost its divinity. Without divinity, masculine energy remained awakened but unbridled and usurptive. Societies within all species suffered, and humanity suffered that much more.

Yesterdays eventually give way to the possibility of tomorrows, and that is where the Earth and humanity find themselves today. The divine masculine has not yet returned, but indications are that balance is being restored. The divine feminine has not found its complement yet, but the return of hope and faith has opened the door to the unification of the two into the bond of the one. What separates masculinity or femininity from its divine complement? Balance; as always, that is the key.

A glance at world news as well as economic, political and social agendas would seemingly confirm that a present imbalance will only give way to further imbalance, but that is not true. Imbalance will give way to balance, and those who seek otherwise will take their toys and go home; as the saying goes, so they will. Balance will bring order, which, in turn, will inspire creativity. Do not fear those who speak of a New World Order. Their confusion will be at the forefront of the creative charge that is to come. Creativity is born of chaos reordering itself. Chaos is a requirement, an integral part of the formula. Allow the light and the dark to once again find balance, for your own balance rests within them.

BALANCE, REINTEGRATION, RESTORATION

The marriage of the divine feminine and the divine masculine is an alchemical process. It involves all of the elements of the Earth and those of heaven as well. Alchemy is not always a quiet activity, performed behind closed doors. It is fusion at its very best; it is the big bang. The big bangs that currently make such an impact upon and within the planet are the inevitable death throes of the less than divine coupled with the birth cries of the divine. It is balance reemerging even if it wears a garment different from the one you had expected or that is familiar to you.

What of Earth/Gaia sentience? Is Mother Earth no more? Is a new name present within the new dawn?

No, dearest partners. It is not my gender that is changing, but my awareness. In balance, my beingness becomes more aware of greater possibilities even as yours does the same. Limitlessness rather than limit, open thought rather than thoughtless boundaries, do you see? My sentience is still Gaia, but my divinity will be expressed in your very nature.

The restoration of balance between the divine feminine and the divine masculine will heal the rift that currently exists between the sexes. Both will be honored and revered as living examples of the divine. Balance between the sexes will allow more choices for each. Modern inventions will require less physical strength. Strength will be a measure of intelligence and endurance rather than of physical prowess. In other words, firing sequential codes within one's awareness in order to achieve optimum results might become a new comparative measure, an Olympic event in which both sexes can participate evenly. Balanced integration of body, mind and heart, as well as equilibrium of being, will eventually allow either sex to become pregnant and carry a child to term. Though this might sound distant to you today, I assure you that it will come to pass—and sooner than you think.

Balance, reintegration, restoration—these words as well as the concepts they espouse will be guideposts and indicators of what is to come. Look for them and see if they do not become visible in your own environments. Look to the many faces of nature for validation and support. See if rejuvenation is not also an aspect of balance for you to welcome and enjoy.

My sentience, Gaia, is available to you now and always. You can count upon the feminine, the masculine and the divine balance that exists between the two to guide and support you. Where you are present, I am there as well. Where your thoughts are, mine will find you also. Where you invest your heart, the return will be plentiful.

A Climate for Change

June 2002

I have written to you repeatedly, asking you to address the air we breathe and how it is being manipulated beyond our control. Far from simple weather anomalies, we are under attack! Our skies are polluted and sprayed with chemically engineered weapons daily. Our atmosphere is in decay and subject to collapse. Why have you allowed this and why have you not addressed this important issue?

Ah, it seems that often I am as chastised for what I do address as for what I do not. Such is the life of a mother, perhaps it is not unlike your own. Do you believe that your concerns are not my own? Do you believe that my not addressing your issue in this column is an indication of my thoughtlessness or indifference? I am sentient, aware and fully engaged as a representative expression of that which I am. I am a demonstration of peaceful reform. I am a physical and nonphysical manifestation of living truth, a mirror of human experience and awakening desire.

My sentience is not encoded to disallow that which humanity has created, even in folly, but yours is. My awareness will not disallow humanity's free will, but it will educate, demonstrate and mirror a different approach. My responsibility to humanity and to all other beings who make their home here, whether temporarily or permanently, is to absorb, reflect and support the love of All That Is to all who accept and welcome it.

I will honor your questions and respond to them in the fullness of my ability and the merit they present, but other questions beg to be asked as well. Why have you allowed that which both angers and frightens you to take hold of your reality? Why have you surrendered the quality of the air that you breathe? A frank discussion must, in all fairness, acknowledge your own power as well as my own.

EARTH IS PATIENTLY WAITING UNTIL HUMANITY UNDERSTANDS THE WORLD

Okay, I guess that's fair.

With so much going on in the world right now, how do you decide which topics, issues or concerns to address? For the most part, you do. Consciously and unconsciously you magnetize your concerns to you. Sometimes you study, resolve and dismiss your concerns, and sometimes you do not. Some of your concerns are of a personal nature, whereas others affect societies, cultures and the world around you. Currently, humanity is beset with issues of global proportion. Your world no longer seems recognizable or acceptable. Stability has been replaced by an erratic, unfolding reality that threatens to topple lives best described as illusory. How you see yourself is not an accurate representation of that which you truly are, because you have outgrown the outmoded definitions of self that are offered to you daily.

A question that cannot be dismissed and cannot be answered by your own reality creates a unique frequency, one that touches upon an awareness we will call the new paradigm. Such questions leave a nagging, unsatisfactory, distasteful feeling within you when you try to dismiss them or nullify their importance. They are meant to do so! They are triggers offered by aspects of you that are here to effect a difference in one or more realities. These questions call upon you to take note of what has caused your concern or imbalance. When a cursory search for a reasonable explanation or plausible solution does not net the result you would wish, the frequency bands that surround you expand the search. Your alignment with self and soul will guide you to a level of experience in which you can receive an answer that will help you to grow; in this case, I am the response to your question or frequency. These issues and concerns interest me as much as they do you, because within every question is an answer that will satisfy you and others like you. Your issues need not be of global proportion to garner my interest; they can be as simple as a mindful concern about your mother, daughter or neighbor. It is the sincerity of the asking that empowers the frequency, and it is the vibrational quality of the answer that empowers you.

I have seen no greater vision of art than an empowered, divine human, but if it is necessary for humanity to participate in unconsciously polluting its skies in order to fully understand the world it has created, then I will wait patiently while humanity does so. If, on the other hand, humanity tires of the folly that destruction offers and becomes more interested in creativity, revitalization and the wellness that oneness/wholeness will bring, then I also stand at the ready to respond with empowerment, instruction, discovery and support. If my sentience launches a full-scale rescue now at the request of the few rather than the many, it will remove free will and choice from many more beings than you now imagine. It will remove the choice from your generation and from subsequent generations as well. In my place, I know that in good conscience, you also would not allow this.

I can't say that for sure. Maybe I would save the Earth and those who feel about it as I do.

Then your agenda would be no different from the one that is offered to humanity today. You believe that your decision would be equitable, a trade-off as you say, one that would benefit many, including my own sentience and physicality, but I disagree. I am a sentient representative of your (and others') empowerment to do, be, state, ensure, claim and radiate all that you are. This is a more accurate representation of our merging; this is what I patiently and lovingly await. Though you are presently harried and hurried, I am not. My wealth and my health are as renewable as my resources, and yours are no different.

HUMANITY IS PURE POSSIBILITY AND POTENTIAL

Can we talk about your (our) resources now? I would like to know who wants to ruin them and why?

The beautiful blue sky that surrounds you is your legacy and that of future generations as well. Throughout history, humanity has looked to the skies for answers and for portents of what the future would bring. The skies have long appeared fathomless, beyond understanding or reach. Humanity has seen both beauty and danger in the skies. All that has been deemed important has either ascended or descended from the sky. When my physical body was forming and not yet stable in its present orbit, all manner of phenomena and experience was drawn close to or within its magnetic pull. All possibilities existed then; there was no dictate or plan that Earth should develop into a world that would later sustain third-dimensional life. The big bang proposed by science was one of many. Birth is like that, rarely a quiet and uneventful experience. My birth was a delight to Creator/All That Is, who desired a grander and fuller experience of Itself. The instability of the Earth's orbit, along with its strong gravitational pull, magnetized and invited experience to within its boundaries.

The sentience that now directs these words was not yet a part of that experience. That came later on, in the form of an invitation—one whose acceptance has been a constant source of joy and an unlimited source of pleasure. Never has my sentience experienced a moment's regret or an untoward thought. The same is true of you, but the veiled field of limited experience keeps you from remembering this in the present moment.

At the time of the Earth's physical creation and subsequent evolution, space navigation was already prominent upon many worlds. Many races of beings who made their home elsewhere within the space of this galaxy and this universe traveled extensively for reasons of discovery, exploration and trade. During this time, the Earth was off-limits, not because of today's law of noninterference, but because the Earth's magnetic field was unstable and dangerous even for the most adept pilots and crafts. An unstable planet with an erratic gravitational field can easily destroy or wreak havoc on any and all spacecraft, regardless of origin or construction. The space that surrounded the Earth was also unstable and large amounts of what you would call space debris obstructed and distorted all forms of instrumental navigation and control.

The Earth was left to create itself, a canvas of unlimited creativity and possibility. Raw essence composed of potential life force coursed through my being. Veins and arteries carrying rich and nourishing minerals raced to create the interior, then the exterior of the planet. Primordial essence created an element similar to lava, which sculpted and planed all that would later become solid. The rich, naturally occurring elements of the universe were pulled into the Earth's magnetic field. These were spun at alarming speed until they were eventually pulled into my body, creating a solid core. This core contains every element and essence known in this universe, which is why the Earth can regenerate and re-create itself in whole or in part.

Source/Creator does not create that which is incomplete or less than whole. Later on, humanity was born of this same primordial universal essence whose physicality is called matter. You also exist as a field of pure possibility and potential. This simple but profound fact often eludes humanity. It is overlooked or abandoned in favor of more dramatic win-lose possibilities, but infinite Source is interested in win-win experiences, and ultimately, so will you. Think on this: If you were All That Is (which you are) and you were the originator of all thought, experience and possibility (which you are), would you not design a game/experience/reality in which you would ultimately win?

The Earth remained unstable for a very long time. It shook and shuddered and sputtered as if attempting to thrust some invisible force off of itself. This thrusting created mountains and valleys both inside and outside the Earth. Deep chasms created secret pathways, which still exist today, from surface to core. These enforced that life on the surface would mirror life within the planet. Oceans flow deep and undisturbed within the planet, and marine leviathans still make their home there today. Time was not measured then, and so it did not exist. All calculations as to the age of the Earth are incorrect; at best they are approximations, because, if time does not exist, it does not pass at a measurable rate. If you did not measure your age, you would not age at the same rate. If you pretended, for instance, that one year lasted twenty-four months, you would age at that rate.

MANY ARE VYING FOR YOUR VOTE OF CONFIDENCE

Many stories, histories and debates describe what happened next. For my part, I will say that there is truth and fiction in all accounts that have been

offered to date. All That Is/Source created an ever-evolving field of pure potential in which to discover Itself. That being said, it is inevitable that a variety of
expressions and representations of Source in Its different forms would eventually be drawn to the Earth. That is exactly what happened. Who arrived first
is a matter or conjecture and interpretation, as is who first decided to claim the
Earth as their own. Today you are bombarded with more "truths" than your
human psyche is able to process, and many beings wish to impress you, assist you
and reestablish their interests here. Currently, those who are able to express
themselves in your languages and who best understand how humanity responds
to suggestion (manipulation) have your attention. Others are working in different ways to impress their own interests upon you and to enlist appropriate support. The Earth is presently the platform for the grandest political campaign it
has ever known, and each vote (each individual consciousness) is paramount to
those who wish to push forward their agendas.

Your skies have become part of a worldwide campaign to promote ignorance
and restrain awareness. They are as giant billboards, and you need not even
look up in order to be influenced by them. What do these billboards say? In
essence, they are an invitation, a promise in exchange for a vote of confidence.
What kind of promise? One that allows the eyes to remain sleepy, that offers
many channels to watch yet nothing to see; a promise that makes the status quo
seem inviting and interesting. In order for a world (the Earth) to belong to a
race, a nation or a being, its inhabitants must agree to it—consciously or unconsciously, the approval must be unanimous.

How can there be unanimous approval if our consciousness is being unfairly influenced?
Most of the planet is not even awake yet. Can our approval be coerced from us?

Yes, because consciousness and unconsciousness are both states of being; they
are choices. Influence is also a choice. One chooses to be "under the influence," whether the choice is one of fact or fiction; narcotic or chemical; psychic, esoteric or even political. A vote is a vote is a vote. In essence, the rules
of engagement state that every physical being present upon the Earth at this
juncture in time who is capable of manifesting a third-dimensional body or
beyond, is entitled to a vote. Borrowing from your own electoral systems, it
would be valid to say that the primaries have ended, and you now find yourselves embroiled in a full-scale battle for your vote of confidence.

THE NATURE OF INFLUENCE

Humanity is well accustomed to the influence offered by television, radio
and the print media. It knows it is being influenced, and its expectations are
duly met. Influence is a matter of perception. Some see it as assistance. Divine
guidance can also be called influence—it influences you to discover deeper
truth and awareness, but it is still influence. Your body influences you to con-

sume foods that will benefit it. Your intuition influences you to act in your own best interest. Influence can be the answer or the solution to uncertainty; the more vague the uncertainty, the more effect influence has upon it. The sky is layered and littered with influence.

Is everyone affected? What else can you say about the nature of this influence?

Yes, to a certain degree, everyone is affected. The theory behind this practice is similar to that employed in crop-dusting techniques. Using this example, let's say that a field of next season's crops is not responding as those who manage the field would like. The crop is weak and impoverished, because the nourishment it receives from the soil is poor, and the water it receives via the irrigation system has a low oxygen content. The managers of the field have enhanced the soil and the water many times in a variety of ways in order to influence the crop to respond in the desired manner. This has only led to turmoil because the soil no longer recognizes the elements within the water as natural or vital to the crop, so it does not absorb the water as it once did. The water now sits atop the soil, creating a drowning surplus in some areas and dryness near desiccation in others. This triggers an imbalance in what used to be a symbiotic relationship between the elements and the vegetable kingdom. The crop, which is already subject to stress from a variety of sources, is now also under attack by a parasitic invasion due to a new imbalance with the animal kingdom. The managers of the field decide that something must be done in order to net the desired results. They devise a plan to saturate the air surrounding the field with a chemical solution that will influence the crop to respond to their will.

Do the crops respond in the desired manner?

Yes, for a time, because the introduction of the new chemical into the crop's sphere of influence has the entire field abuzz with curiosity. The crop does not immediately recognize that the new ingredient is artificially designed to undermine its natural intelligence and the divine relationship it has with the soil and with the water. Without knowing it, the crop has become separated from its own divinity. Its intelligence is now guided artificially rather than naturally. Once friends, crop, soil and water are now adversaries, struggling to move beyond the boundaries now firmly in place and unable to reestablish the communication they once had. As their language is no longer the same, they now depend upon an intermediary, the managers, in order to understand and relate to one another.

What happens next?

The crop adheres to the instructions encoded in the chemicalization process that has been injected into the airspace. The managers are pleased with the results and vow to introduce this same process to fields everywhere. They publish their findings and receive accolades and awards for their discoveries and for helping to advance technology in a modernized world. They turn their attention elsewhere, forgetting about the original field, and focus their awareness on solutions to problems that include where nature falls short of meeting their expectations.

What happens after that?

The crop becomes ill and discontented because it can no longer sustain itself in a toxic environment. The managers have already turned their attention elsewhere and don't yet notice that the entire field is ill. It is wilting under the stress it has been subjected to. No longer able to respond to the natural world, it begins to disassociate itself from the physical casing that has been its home; realities begin to blur, and bridges to grander truths seem nonexistent. Eventually, the chemicalization process no longer affects the crop, because it has surrendered its identity and released its form from its previous obligation. Its DNA has been restructured and transformed, its matrix converted from a natural essence to an artificial one.

You mean after all that, it dies?

No, it does not die, but it surrenders its form and identity. It replaces original thought with a *belief* in original thought. The intruder chemical created an imbalance of injurious proportions. The crop, no longer able to identify itself or relate to the world around it, has withdrawn its cooperation from all realities, pledges, obligations and relationships. It can no longer define itself, so it simply chooses not to.

Does the story end there?

No, it does not, because the crop is but one of many, the field is only one in terms of awareness, the chemical only a sample of the varieties available and the managers only representations of agendas already proposed.

Can we speak in "real world" terms now? Can we talk about you and me, humanity and Earth?

Yes, of course, but you must understand that the "real world" facts are not as different from the story as you might imagine. My words have engaged your thoughts in storybook fashion, because no precedent existed within your thought patterns to confront or rebuff what has been gently offered. Your reality is not much different from that of a snowflake, a teardrop, a grain of sand or a crop in a field. Slumbering consciousness separates, and awakened consciousness unites. Words and language speak loudest, but in the end, it is truth that speaks dearly to the heart.

Here are the "real world" facts relative to the skies that surround you. Deeply shaken by worldwide acts of both cruelty and courage, humanity continues to awaken in great numbers. Awaken to what? Awaken to the sounds and sensations of Creator/All That Is speaking and working through it! Hearts that long for peace are no longer quiet in their longing. Minds that yearn to express themselves no longer wait for others to do so in their stead. Disillusionment from lack of answers and an unsatisfactory outer environment have caused many to look inward for answers to yet unasked questions. A common ideal throughout many cultures states that each subsequent generation will make a contribution to its society, to its culture and to the world that surrounds it. Parents from all over the world have high hopes that their children will experience more peace and prosperity than they have known.

Three Schools of Thought Define Earth's Population

The world today is one of chaos, with a propensity to destroy bridges rather than build them. Humanity can no longer account for what the next generation will contribute, because it can no longer account for its own generation. Currently, three schools of thought define the population of the Earth.

The first one, which we will call the mind of man, believes that the Earth is in decay, that it is in an unstoppable downward spiral, on its way to death and destruction. The beings who subscribe to this mind have surrendered their power to those who have purchased it wholesale on the open market called "fear." This aspect of the population or school of thought has separated itself from others, because it has become separate from itself. It finds it difficult to rejoin others, because it has relinquished its faith and hope and no longer sees the possibility. It lives quietly on the sidelines of life, awaiting confirmation that the situation is indeed hopeless and giving up the only option. These beings go about their business as usual, but the light in their eyes has been dimmed, and the spark that once guided their souls is all but extinguished. They have little hope for future generations and pity them more than anything else.

The second school of thought, which we will call the mind of rage, is easily angered and instigated into action of any kind. It will battle itself or others in order to avoid accepting a life of servitude and status quo. These beings care not about the decisions made by past generations, and they care even less what the future might think or record. They are insistent upon making a statement that decries the present as absurd and the future as a waste. They hold little value for human life and see the Earth and its resources as already having been bought and paid for. With little to contribute and nothing to gain, they often find themselves on the offensive, for they have nothing of their own to defend other than an ego or a point of view.

The third school of thought is called the mind of peace. It is where hope and faith still reside. It is the home of the heart, even if it is currently in despair and uncertain of many things, including itself. This school understands that change is inevitable and permanent—surprisingly to others, it finds peace even in this.

It sees the world around it as a mirror and an expression of itself. It knows that reflections change daily and finds peace in this as well. The mind of peace is just as easily swayed as the other minds, but because it knows that change is inevitable, it knows that it will inevitably be swayed back to its own center. Thus it knows peace. It is the mind of peace that is most subject to attack by the havoc that currently reigns in the skies and rains upon you from the skies.

CHEMTRAILS ARE CONTRAILS WITH AN AGENDA

Called contrails by some and chemtrails by others, they have become one and the same. A contrail is the aftermath or effect upon the sky of a jet's inter-action with the space it has traversed. Although aircraft can be designed to pass effortlessly through space, currently they do not. They pierce, tug, pull and drag the space around them, consuming more fuel and creating instability in the air currents that surround them. Today aircraft are subject to more turbulence than ever before. The air is too dense in some areas and too thin in others. As air-craft crisscross the skies, they drag one kind of air into another, creating a tur-bulence for themselves and for the planes that will follow. Airline travel fol-lows similar routes day after day, hour after hour, marking and polluting these routes, filling them with soot and man-made chemicals. Many airplanes choose to jettison their fuel in the sky rather than chance a landing with heavy fuel tanks. This practice has created a toxic, unbalanced waste field in the sky. The sky is now falling, as one of your nursery rhymes appropriately predicted. The sky is no longer up there; it is here. It is the air that you and all the other kingdoms breathe, and it is polluted.

A chemtrail is a contrail with an agenda. The chemical content of a chem-trail is such that it is detrimental to human health and well-being; for some it is detrimental to survival. Chemtrails consist of chemically altered and manipu-lated fuels and gases. These chemicals are jettisoned, emitted and injected into the air as the planes that carry them traverse the airspace on their appointed routes.

Where did chemtrails originate?

In God/humanity's mind, where all other thoughts originate. You and God could never conceive such a thought? Not so. Humanity lays claim to my heart and my soul, but it has traveled far in this past millennium. It has traveled to the furthest reaches polarity will allow, and here it has discovered how to create life as well as how to destroy it. Currently, both paths are being examined in close detail.

Was humanity influenced or coerced by outside forces into cooperating with or accepting this wholesale destruction of the planet?

My sentience has not detected the imminent destruction you fear, but yes, humanity has been and continues to be influenced by both inner and outer interests. I have called these agendas, for lack of a better word in your language.

In this case, you are being influenced by those who would benefit from having a smaller, well-managed population on the planet. The chemicals in the chemtrails are designed to weaken those who are already a detriment to the future proposed agenda. The chemicals weaken the immune system. A strong, well-balanced immune system is less susceptible to this form of influence, but a weakened immune system opens the door to the emotional body and to the subtler energies that make up your beingness.

HOLOGRAM: A REACTIVE REALITY

You bring up so many points that I don't know what to ask next. I guess first I would like to know more about the agenda behind chemtrails, like who is promoting them?

They are promoted by a collective consciousness that desires to own, not merely control, the Earth. Long ago these beings believed that humanity was an asset to the planet—after all, good employees are always needed in order to run a company efficiently. Humanity's collective consciousness did not question or object to the job when it was offered. As a matter of fact, the nature of the required activities allowed humans to develop at both an individual and a collective pace. Humans delighted in advancing the causes of others, because they believed that in doing so they also advanced their own. Humans believed that the rewards would be equal to the task they were given. Only recently have they realized that this might not be the case. This realization has been gradual but is now quickly accelerating. Soon the evolutionary leap in humanity's collective consciousness will be evident.

In their zeal to explore and experience, humans often bypass the present moment in their attempt to anticipate the future. In sharp contrast, beings from other worlds seek to understand the present moment (reality) in order to better participate in it. Because humans' participation is still mostly at an unconsciousness level, the future still takes them by surprise far too often, causing them to react to reality rather than create it. Another name for a reactive reality is a hologram. A hologram is a semireality that allows for programmed participation and a probable outcome. A hologram is a story line that is created for a cast of characters known for offering a predictable response. Probable responses can be programmed into holographic environments that take every sequential possibility into account.

The most current example of a collective holographic experience are the still clouded details surrounding September 11, 2001, and the events that have followed that unforgettable day in humanity's history. They were designed to be unforgettable and as such have programmed your thoughts and environments. This was a successful attempt to influence or polarize the entire population of the Earth into enthusiastically embracing an agenda that otherwise would have been shunned.

Is an illusion different from a hologram?

Yes. An illusion affords a conscious or unconscious choice. It has no polarity, no agenda. An illusion exists within a reality, whereas a hologram is a substitute reality. For example, illusion allows you to play at poverty until you discover your unlimited potential. In a hologram, your experience is polarized so that poverty becomes your reality. Illusion is a third-dimensional game; it is child's play compared to a holographic reality. The veils that shadow illusion have become almost transparent now, but the veils that shelter the holograms are the shadow.

HOLOGRAMS HAD TO BECOME MORE SOPHISTICATED

If we are awakening and accelerating so quickly, why can't we step outside of these holograms and see them for what they are?

You are. That is why the holograms have become more sophisticated. That is why their agenda now involves a greater segment of the population. Humanity's constant and consistent awakening is the very reason behind chemtrails; they are a second-phase attempt to reinforce the perimeter of the hologram. If humans are consumed with orchestrating health, job, home and money while at the same time guarding against the next possible invasion of terror, they will have little time or energy left to find their way out of the hologram. This is the central and pivoting role of the programming; it has been well designed.

So first we have to step out of the illusion we created. Then, if by some miracle we manage to do that, we will still discover (or not) that we are in a hologram and have to find our way out of that, is that right?

No, not exactly. You give more power to both the illusion and the hologram than you give to yourself, and certainly more than they merit. The only thing that keeps you believing the illusion and participating in the hologram is that something or someone outside of you and more powerful than you is forcing you to participate in it. It is true that the holograms have been well designed, but so have you. As you have lent your support to its creation, so do you also have the power to dissolve it. Even if you have forgotten how to dissolve it, you can still choose to destroy it. Remind yourself again, when necessary, that you and All That Is are one. The hologram is also an aspect of All That Is, although its origin seems foreign to you now. All that is a part of All That Is; it cannot be otherwise. This is the fail-safe key that will always unlock the door.

The door to the hologram seems impermeable; it is not. Every program contains at least one flaw, even this well-designed program is heavily flawed, as you will soon see. If humanity had not already taken an evolutionary leap forward, chemtrails would be unnecessary. Humanity's evolutionary leap has for the most part gone unnoticed by its semiconscious mind. No matter—your self-realized God consciousness has recorded all the details, and your history will reflect each moment. No adventure will go forgotten or be left untold.

YOU CAN REJECT THE HOLOGRAM OF THE CHEMTRAILS

What effect, if any, does all this spraying have on the elements that make up our atmosphere?

It is detrimental to the atmosphere, the air and all who breathe it, as you might imagine. Not all chemicals or aspects of chemicals drift down. Some of the elements are caught up in great currents and carried loftily to other destinations. Some do not come down at all. They become attached to pockets of air, filling holes here and there with an energy that is harmful to those pockets. Energy is another word for purpose—it is how nature uses and responds to purpose. Energy pockets are not empty vacuums that float here and there; they are patterns of response that relate to weather conditions. They can, for instance, absorb or couple with energy that would otherwise become a hurricane or a tornado. Have you not wondered why ideal hurricane conditions do not always cause hurricanes? It is because nature's intelligence directs and guides these energies appropriately. It is not prudent to avert all such occurrences, but certainly some can be avoided. If these energetic pockets become filled with energies unlike their purpose, there will be an increase in weather anomalies and natural disasters. Artificial manipulation of the sky and the air has already created atmospheric changes. These changes will be difficult (but not impossible) to reverse.

Is the whole world subject to the chemical effects of the chemtrails, or are they localized events?

The entire population of the Earth is being influenced by more than one campaign. Chemtrails are localized events; that is to say, the aircraft involved must make various passes and fly at certain altitudes in order to release their influential gaseous cargo. Once released, the chemtrails are attracted to or repelled by the energies, frequencies and vibrations they come in contact with. Again, not all beings are subject to the full effects or harm the chemicals are capable of inflicting. For example, many humans smoke or otherwise ingest tobacco, but not all of them contract cancer. It is not by casual accident that this is the case, but by causal agreement. Do you see the difference?

The airspace within other countries is not as wide open as within the boundaries of the United States. In other countries, smaller private planes, jets and helicopters are not as plentiful. Still, the missives of these chemicals, coupled with the intent with which they have originated, will see to it that the effects are worldwide.

Can you offer us some practical suggestions that will help avert or deflect the effects of chemtrails upon our physical and emotional bodies? Can we avoid becoming controlled or influenced by them?

You cannot avoid being influenced by chemtrails, but you can avoid being controlled by them. Earlier in this discussion, it was said that you were being invited to participate in a holographic experience and that your vote of confidence was needed in order for the campaign to be a success. This is true, and I emphasize these words now. Influence is not demand, even when you are presented with a demanding influence. The chemical content of the chemtrails causes you to see the world through chemical-agenda-colored glasses. This by itself does not cause distress. It is the attempt to remove the glasses that is distressful. Removal of the glasses causes an imbalance of the equilibrium and of all other vital fields. Physical discomforts, side effects and illnesses are a result of nonacceptance of the campaign. Physical and emotional symptoms are a vote of discontent and no confidence. They are a rejection of the hologram and a statement of self-awareness.

In other words, if we don't get sick, it means that we approve of the rape and ownership of the Earth?

Not entirely, no. But physical recognition or identification of an intrusion into your personal space is also an acknowledgment of an awakened consciousness, do you see? It is an indication that you are not asleep relative to the events in your reality; it is a confirmation that it is indeed your reality. As such, you are free to change it or to influence it of your own accord. You are not as susceptible to interference from others as you now believe, but you must grasp hold of your reality and make of it what you desire, for if you do not, others surely will. As you can see, they are awaiting your decision with bated breath.

Not all humans are subject to the effects of the chemtrails, even though chemicals have now been released into 90 percent of the world's skies. In the past, we have spoken of the variety of beings who populate the Earth at this time, and we have noted their dimensional planes and places of origin. Currently, the chemicals contained in the chemtrails affect only those of human lineage, not those whose home world is elsewhere or whose physical lineage has not been consistently human.

Chemical spores breathed into human lungs currently cause the highest degree of distress. The spores circulate throughout the body and into the brain, which requires steady and constant amounts of oxygen in order to remain clear and focused. That is why the most reported side effects are headaches, nausea and clouded or unclear thoughts. Smaller spores remain in the lungs for a time and are then exhaled or absorbed into the bloodstream. Secondary side effects include flulike symptoms, suspended breath and, in worse cases, discomfort in and/or shutdown of primary organs. Spores that are exhaled by one person can later be inhaled by another.

METAMEDICAL TREATMENTS FOR NEW ILLNESSES

All this because we won't go along with an agenda that threatens to destroy us in the long run anyway? What about modern medicine? Isn't there an antidote or something?

There is no medical antidote, because the medical community has not acknowledged the existence of the condition. For the most part, it is unaware of the severe though isolated cases that have been reported. The medical community is not prepared nor was it designed to respond to the effects of biological influences upon the body. In order to combat a poison, one must know what that poison is. If not, the treatment will be of little consequence or worsen the original illness. The medical community has been alerted to this and other maladies, such as Gulf War Syndrome. It has, in some cases, acknowledged a preponderance of the symptoms described within a locational radius on given occasions. It cannot treat the offending spore, because it is unaware of its existence and cannot identify it. Eventually, some of the spores will morph into other identifiable but incurable diseases. Health insurance companies are already at work reworking and rewording their contractual offerings and obligations. Soon they will insist that medical treatment must be for reasonable, treatable, identifiable, known and understood, curable and survivable illnesses. Terminal illness and other syndromelike distress will be disallowed.

If (when) this happens, what will become of the ill and uninsured?

Secondary and tertiary medical programs and clinics will emerge in response to the needs, demands and outcries of those who stand outside the perimeters of perfection. Metamedical treatment will be offered to those who do not or cannot receive assistance elsewhere. At first, the insurance and health care industries will offer financial backing and support. Later, federal and state government programs will be created. Ultimately, though, these will be withdrawn. It is likely that private funding will step in to bridge an important gap.

How will these clinics be able to treat a chemtrail syndrome if hospitals and doctors can't?

They will be staffed by awakened beings who understand and employ light (crystal laser) technology and other metamedical treatments. Medical teams able to acknowledge not only the anomalies within the human race and its many cultures but those of other species as well, will staff the clinics. They will have access to unproven, untested and illegal tools, medicines and procedures.

Is this why they will lose their funding?

It is one of the reasons, yes. Evidence will accumulate when the time comes. Not all beings will benefit from the procedures—the ones who do not will be held up as examples of malpractice. The clinics will come under scrutiny and will be called "euthanasia clinics" by those who oppose them. An attempt will be made to link or otherwise attach treasonable offenses such as smuggling or spying to these programs and to those who back them. Some of the claims made will be legitimate in the eyes of those who make them, because those who are untreatable in these clinics might yet be cured elsewhere.

Where? Will they be taken somewhere else?

If the offending weapon remains in the sky, then it stands to reason that its cure might remain elsewhere or in the sky's opposite.

Underground? Do you mean that underground facilities will be there to cure and combat the effects of the sporadic syndromes? If so, do you mean "underground" in the literal (physical) sense or figuratively?

Both.

AWARE BEINGS ARE A THREAT TO THE AGENDA

Are humans really such a threat to this agenda? Why?

Humans are not a threat, but aware and awakened, spiritually conscious beings of all kinds and from all places are. A self-realized, self-actualized, God-conscious being will not allow the ground underneath and the sky above to be claimed by others of selfish origin. Technology or tomorrow's trinkets and toys do not as easily sway awakened beings. They are more interested in creative resources of planetary and universal origin. Their joy comes from seeing the sky adorned with the jewel that is this planet, rather than seeing this planet's jewels adorning them.

Who or what is to gain if humanity becomes ill and some of us die? Doesn't the agenda need humans?

The agenda needs docile, controllable, easily influenced humans. It needs physically strong workers who are loyal to a purpose and an undertaking not their own. It requires a race of unquestioning, unwavering, faithful service.

Who would do that? Who would be crazy enough to offer his or her life for that purpose? Wouldn't everyone rebel against that?

It is not a question of crazy, but a matter of influence. Are not those who are today called "suicide bombers" crazy enough to perpetrate unthinkable deeds because they have been emblazoned with a stamp of influence? All life is precious; the all rather than the few must again be embraced. Balance must reign above and below, now as well as later.

Are you (the Earth) also subject to the effects of the holograms and chemtrails?

The Earth, which includes my sentience, is a multilayered, multifaceted awareness just as you are. Therefore, certain aspects are affected, whereas others are not. The Earth's physical resources have been depleted by approximately 72 percent, and the elements—air, water, earth, fire, thermo-heat—now offer themselves at a substantially reduced capacity. By agreement, as humanity approves and subscribes to these numbers, so will my physical body. Beyond that, my sentience is eternal.

The physical Earth does not ensure the survival of my sentience; my sentience ensures the survival of my physical body. The Earth is not doomed and neither are you. My physical body—and its physical resources—will regenerate itself, as will yours. Civility aside, human nature is free, and its spirit is wild.

My sentience exists outside of the hologram and apart from the illusion; my body does not. The same is true of you. Your divine nature exists beyond the hologram, but your physical life currently exists within it. Long ago I tethered humanity deep within my heart. Here you are well guarded from the imaginary monsters that frighten children in the middle of the night. Remember that the best stories always begin with "Once upon a time . . ." and end with " . . . and they lived happily ever after." Ours will be no different.

Your words feel good but sound contradictory. On the one hand, we seem to be more lost and vulnerable than ever. But on the other hand, all is well and will turn out just fine.

Yes, that is exactly how it is. Isn't that wonderful?

Is there anything that hasn't been said regarding this subject? Is there anything else you can offer us?

Much is still unspoken on this topic, perhaps appropriately so. It cannot all be said at once, for it would not all be heard. Possibilities have been considered, and probabilities have been evaluated; now it is for you to decide on an eventual reality. The choice is yours as it always has been.

In closing, I offer a gentle reminder of the incentives inspired by the mind of peace. It is most like the face of nature, which subscribes to and honors the seasons of the spirit, even as it is carried aloft by the winds of change. Because a tree sways in the breeze, does it vacillate in mind or opinion? Does the breeze render the tree unable to make up its mind whether to stand or lean? If it bows to the breeze, does it surrender its will to that of the wind? Perhaps it understands its steadfast purpose and design, sometimes offering itself to the sunlight and at other times straining to kiss the Moon, sometimes standing fast and at other times leaning toward light or bending to shadow. Today's adversarial winds will calm, bringing tomorrow's warmth and peace.

I offer myself to you today and always, in shadow and in light. Illusion or holograms have no effect upon my love for humanity. Until the next moment brings us together.

Perspectives on War and Peace

July 2002

I grew up in the Middle East and made my home there until a few years ago when I left (for good, I thought). Since then I have lived in many places, none of which felt like home. I feel as if I have turned my back on my country and my people, but the decisions made by those in power today instill great fear and disagreement within me. I know that you abhor war and would prefer to address a more uplifting subject, but please Gaia, speak about war and the Middle East. I very much need to find my courage, my heart and my home . . .

In this regard, my heart is as heavy as your own, perhaps heavier. I offer myself to humanity unconditionally, now and always. In order to address this question fully, we must consider the spirit and vibration with which it has been asked. Be prepared to allow adjustments in your vibrational field, for these more than words spoken will both heal and cure. Be prepared to empty your heart and then fill it again, and you will find that there is ample room for decisions that must be made.

AGE-OLD BATTLES CONTINUE

Battles will continue to rage in this region; individual against individual, sect against sect, country against country and religion against religion. It is the age-old battle of the less than righteous seeking to become more than righteous. These battles provide no spoils and no victors, only undeclared losers, martyrs and followers of sorrow. The battles are no more than thought forms given exposure in an unstable reality, arcade games whose flashing lights and sounds create spellbinding effects that make participants forget all else until it is time to deposit more coins in the slot in order to continue the game. Over time this phenomenon has created distorted truths that rule over divinity. These distorted energies are dense but invisible, and because this geographic area has been a hotbed of discord for eons of time, they walk among those who make their home there just as if they were physical beings, though in fact they are not.

The Middle East region is densely populated with these thought forms, which are energetic patterns without hearts or minds. They exist because thoughts created them, and thoughts continue to direct them. They attach themselves to other energies, which makes them more dense and ensures their survival. Positive energies are of no interest to these energies, because their wholeness or lightness makes it difficult for them to attach and therefore survive. It is much easier for them to lodge themselves within negative energies, because their force and direction are most like their own. The presence of these thoughtless thought forms proliferates violence.

It is thoughtless to take the life of another, but this is forgotten when unconsciousness yields to thoughtlessness. Unconscious thoughts engage and enrage those who do not yet hear or heed their own heart. Unconscious battles serve unyielding enemies whose only gain is unrelenting resentment and retaliation. Alignment with these thought forms brings a steady chain of new, unseen and unproven adversaries. Thoughts without bodies or souls lodge themselves where closed hearts and minds exist, forming strongholds and barriers that lead to thoughtless actions and deeds. Heavy chains bind those who are compelled to acts of violence by unconsciousness; they are to be pitied, assisted and lifted whenever possible rather than thrown to the ravages that already rage within them or discarded and dismissed from possibilities that are open to all beings. There is a loving place within my heart for all beings and for the choices they make. The same is true of you. Find that place within you, and you will also find my sentience and that which is All That Is. This is the home you are searching for; an appropriate physical one will not be found until this one is acknowledged first.

How is it that the value of a human life has become so small, and if that indeed is the case, what then is greater in value? Land! Not just any land—this land, ancient Earth resplendent in both historic importance and future perspective. Hidden deep within what appears to be a regional conflict replete with age-old disputes over religion and ownership are agendas whose origins lie elsewhere. On the surface, there seems little to be gained; the area itself is arid and some consider it a desert wasteland. The sands of time continue to shift, but in the long run, it is still only sand. Why battle for a postage-stamp-sized piece of land with few resources to yield? Because the treasure is not the real estate but what lies beneath it.

FIRST VISITORS TO EARTH STAYED IN MIDDLE EAST

Afghanistan's caves were recently featured on the world's spotlighted stage. This strange and intricate network was investigated and later destroyed, when a search for a presumed outlaw criminal did not result in his capture. The caves and the network that hosts them are older than human civilization. They were formed at the direction of those who first came to Earth. These visitors were accustomed to living both above and beneath the surface of their own home world, and they thought it odd that Earth had not been similarly prepared. They were familiar with the instability of young planets and the erratic weather patterns they often produced. The longevity of their species had helped them to become excellent engineers and geothermal scientists. They understood the properties of most of the elements they encountered upon the Earth, because they had already traveled the universe extensively prior to their arrival.

The Middle East did not look then as it does today. It was rich in soil and vegetation, and the climate was mild in comparison to other parts of the globe. These visitors did not simply happen onto this land by chance. They surveyed many different areas and then chose the area you call the Middle East as the primary base from which they would come and go. For a long time their visits consisted of scientific experiments and studies. They came and went from the Earth, returning to their laboratory ship in the sky as often as possible. Eventually they found what they were looking for, but it proved more difficult to obtain than they had originally thought.

An extended stay was agreed upon, and their Earth base was expanded. In order to ensure their safety and that of their equipment, they excavated the Earth by means of a technology that blended a laserlike beam with a specific frequency attuned to the Earth's sound barrier. This frequency carried a template or code that spoke to the Earth in a language that yielded the desired result. In this way, a multilevel, complex network was created, and because of its unique construction, it exists virtually intact to this day. It is not the sand and stone that are unique and long lasting, or the region that is seismically stable, for that is not the case; it is the method with which this network has been asked to hold its form. The same is true of the great pyramids of Egypt and of other ancient structures throughout the world, though certainly not for all of them. Old does not always mean ancient, and solid is not always sacred.

While the visitors' stay was initially short in duration, it became prolonged and extended later on. There were no specific laws governing uninhabited planets then, especially ones whose sovereign sentience was not yet acknowledged, as was the case with the Earth at the time. Universal laws were given to interpretation, and while some species honored all laws, others honored none. These visitors from space were not plunderous villains as they are sometimes portrayed; they arrived with purpose and direction and abided by rules and laws of their own making. By contrast, those who today rape and pillage the Earth, its resources and its people, have more to be accountable for than these beings. I marveled at their engineering feats and easily surrendered what they wished, as I had no immediate need of any one resource.

OFF-PLANET RACES' INFLUENCE ON HUMANITY

As time passed, Earth was visited and later inhabited by a variety of races and beings. They were mostly indifferent to one another, which surprised me. They claimed different resources and made their home in different parts of the world, so conflicts were rare and easily resolved. Some beings made their home in the water, deep beneath the waves. They were able to breathe underwater, as their physiology allowed this, but the salinity of the sea shortened their physical life span. Many off-planet races have contributed to humanity's gene pool, though few would recount this today. Earth humans are the result of the cumulative effects of receiving the best and the worst that both heaven and Earth have to offer. It has been left to you to decide which traits you will keep and which ones you will forego. Further studies in genetics will assist this process, as will advanced knowledge from beyond the Earth that will soon be added to what is already known.

Humanity received knowledge and assistance from other races, but it would not be prudent to assume that what was received was the best that each race had to offer. Earth was a temporary home for engineers, scientists, scavengers, treasure hunters, renegades and more. For the most part, they were not ambassadors of peace who brought gifts of reciprocity in order to establish diplomatic relations and cultural perspectives. The same can be said of those who today venture forth in the tiny modules your governments send into space. Are they the very best the human culture can offer or are they simply humans on a purposeful and well-rehearsed mission? What might another culture expect to find if an encounter were to take place? What could be said or offered about the human race at this time in history. Do you see?

Humans learned many things from those who long ago interacted with them. Among these were how to do many things such as how to build, how to grow and cultivate; in essence, they learned how to work. Early humans did not learn how to be; they did not learn the value of *being*. Being leads to nurturing, and when one is nurtured, one is valued. Human value leads to human respect, and respect leads to friendship and rapport. This important step was omitted for a variety of reasons, some of which are obvious. Humans were taught how to do many jobs, and they were rewarded when they worked hard. Early humans worked hard to please those who they believed were more powerful and advanced than they were. Deeply ingrained within the human psyche is the desire to please and the need to work hard. How does a student earn good grades in school? By working hard! How does an employee earn a raise or keep a job? By working hard! How do humans earn rewards such as paper money, a home to live in, a vehicle to drive, a television to watch or a week of vacation? Work hard!

Visitors to Earth believed that human life was less valuable than other advanced life forms. Early humans did not resist or resent this, especially as it came from what they believed were their parents. As a matter of fact, they incorporated this very ideology into their own cultures. As they had no other species to look down upon, they looked to the differences within their cultures and to the variations in the color of their skin. What my sentience experienced as beautiful and bountiful variations and expressions within a species, humans experienced as vital flaws, and they responded with violations of unwritten disapproval. Social classes seemed to spring up almost overnight, carrying the same implications as they do today. As cultures and societies developed, beliefs and attitudes regarding worship and deities also developed, and these only served to further separate rather than unite humanity.

Eventually, humanity was left to fend for itself. Men and women continued to work hard at tasks that had become obsolete. Humans mined for precious metals and gemstones they had no need of, but they assigned value to them just the same. Crops were harvested and game animals raised, but these did not contain the nutritional content needed to maintain humanity's health. Physiology and biology has adjusted over a millennia of time, or humanity would have perished. To be was to be idle, and this was frowned upon then, just as it is today. Mothers nurtured their sons and daughters for only a short time before they were quickly taught how to work in order to serve the needs of family, community and culture. The lessons of long ago have not yet been unlearned, but they will be because they must be. Societies now teach their children from a very young age what is expected of them. They are taught to prepare for the rigors of life rather than for its bounty. The value is with the service or commodity provided rather than with the source of creative energy that provides it.

THE MIDDLE EAST: TICKET TO THE STARS

Deep within human cellular memory is the knowledge that those who long ago departed would one day return. Many of history's twists and turns have been designed to position certain beings and orders in such a way as to receive good favor upon this return. Humans have worked hard themselves or caused others to do so, and they have abided by laws that are skewed and fatally flawed in order to ensure this outcome. Today's power struggles and disputes will become tomorrow's overtures toward ownership of the Earth. Descendants linked to beings from long ago believe the Earth and other worlds can be owned and are busy attempting to make that a reality. Why the hurry? Because at this moment, they believe that they are on the top rung of the ladder, but they are also well aware that things can change "when the stars fall from the sky," as the prophecy indicates. Some power mongers are eager to claim all or part of the Earth while they can, whereas others seek to impress and entice those who will return with riches, comforts and valuable commodities. Long ago it was written that these beings would return to the very same place from which they both arrived and departed. That place is the Middle East.

This embattled region might appear to be only a desert of sand, but to those who desire its ownership and control it is far more. It is the key to unfathomable wealth and power as well as a ticket to the stars. It is worth almost any price, of which the cost of human life and suffering is but a minor irritating component. Underground networks still exist beneath many cities in the Middle East. These networks are wonders of human and extraterrestrial history. They are halls of records as well as amplifiers of energy. Many who make their home in this region can be easily incited to react as directed, because they are unconsciously influenced by the energetic patterns that also make their home there. Encoded labyrinths of leftover power are the spoils of war desired by those who make suicide bombers of gentle warriors, in the guise of fathers and mothers, sisters and brothers. In a game that pits one life against another there are no winners, and even those who see this game as a success will soon know otherwise.

Humanity's Earth beginnings are in the Middle East, and humanity's divinity will be reborn there as well—but perhaps not as prophecy or the books considered holy foretell. The Middle East is genetically prepared for an alteration or translation in frequency. It is encoded with truths and recorded histories that will soon be revealed (revelation). Of the codes that are already understood, this much is known: Those from far away are due to return to the very place they consider their home away from home. Here they expect to find the reincarnated leaders of long ago, along with the progress they have made and the resources they have employed. Those in power today meet to discuss this very thing. They discuss how to promote people and resources to their advantage. They note how expanded the world has become and propose plans to reduce it to a more manageable size. They believe that fewer world leaders would benefit and support their agenda. They prepare themselves and their environment much as you do, but for a different outcome.

What of those who will return? Will they find what they are looking for?

Is it not common in your time to visit your history, to visit the homes you have lived in and the schools you have attended? Do you expect to find these as you left them? No, you understand that they belong to those who now occupy them; they belong to the present, not the past. Those who return understand this as well. It is certain that they will return to the Earth, but it is not yet certain whether they will honor the Earth or attempt to lead; you will both decide this. They wrote their histories that you would remember them, but they did not write their future—or yours. Why is that? Do you believe they left the future to chance? They did not; they left it to you.

Humanity has moved itself along a number of timelines in the thousands of years that have passed. Would the same not be true of these beings? They have set down their history, left behind a dowry devoted to their heritage and then moved on much as you will one day do. They have grown and learned and advanced their race; you have been their teachers more than their students, though you do not know this given your current frame of reference. Humans have discovered vast resources within the Earth and within themselves; could they not discover a new resource in these beings?

Many possibilities exist today, and in all fairness it must be noted that merit can be found in all possibilities, depending upon one's vantage point. That is why it is always advisable to heed your own inner voice first and the voice of all others second. Most of today's possibilities and tomorrow's probabilities were created long ago. They are based upon expectations and interpretations of a future that has not yet been experienced. It is as if an agreed-upon history was projected into the next modular moment, where it was promptly proclaimed your future and your destiny. Prophecy requires belief, which in turn creates possibility. Without believers (consensus reality), prophecy means little or nothing at all. The future belongs to all and so do all possibilities. If you judge yourself or your world by those who tell you about it, your experience will fall short. Evaluate yourself and the Earth by your desires and by what is reflected to you in the mirror. Of necessity we will acknowledge that the desired future is not yet the present. That being said, the following comments will address the situation as it is currently being experienced by a vast percentage of the population, remembering that it is but one reality of many.

WAR MACHINE PULLS MORE COUNTRIES INTO THE FRAY

The Middle East will continue to have its borders challenged on almost all fronts, making new enemies of old adversaries. It will be difficult to discern who is right and who is wrong, which is appropriate given that no side can be. Borders will quickly become barricaded boundaries, and moving about freely will not be easy. Levels of distrust are at an all-time high, with no signs of diminishing. Citizens have become pawns in a chess match that cannot be won. They will be moved from here to there and back again, each time losing ground and gaining nothing because human life is still of little consequence; it is considered collateral damage and as such is a foreseeable loss.

Proponents of the war-machine ideology will force neutral countries and leaders to join their battle cry by promise and power as well as by indulgence and intimidation. They know all too well all Achilles heels; they are well aware of the strengths and weaknesses of all concerned. For this reason, cooperation and support will be offered by less than likely candidates. It will seem, at least in the beginning, that diplomacy and good will have taken a giant leap backward. A variety of forceful measures will be put into place to ensure that policies and positions of authority do not slip.

The country with the largest war machine agenda [the U.S.] will step fully and completely into the limelight, leaving little to the imagination regarding what it desires to accomplish. It will critically overstep its bounds and fatefully expose itself, but this will not be understood for some time. Many nations will be pulled into the fray, because they will no longer be able to hide behind protective skirts that do little more than avoid issues of principle.

Israel will begin to lose worldwide favor in its attempt to institute the war-machine policies of its benefactor. Palestine will rise from its crouching position; it will lift its sword and blandish it angrily, but with little bravery. The heart and soul of a people whose vision once included peaceful liberation will be nearly extinguished; in its place will be an artificially transplanted heart that knows only retaliation and retribution . . . unfathomable acts in response to unconscionable provocations. The world's population will be bewildered. They will not know who or what to believe or how to anticipate what will happen next. The initial response will be to close doors and windows and minds to the atrocities and the bloodshed, but the borders and the boundaries have already been breached, and even hearts in seeming retreat will know the despair that others live. The people within this region suffer great injustice, but is any suffering just?

The battles will be of limited duration, but they will be ongoing, and the destruction and loss of life will be dear. The forces at work in this region will stir the destructive energies, and then they will stir them some more, bringing to the surface what has already boiled and is now ready to burn. Explosions will ring out in the countryside as well as in the hearts of men and women. Right and wrong are at polar opposites in the roller coaster called duality. Of necessity, a center point will be found, for if it is not, those who ride these precarious rails will find themselves clinging to a position they cannot maintain, and they will eventually fall. Right and wrong will no longer have meaning, and only the end of suffering will have true meaning and value.

SEE AND FEEL TRUTH BEYOND THE PHYSICAL

While many minds continue to rage, others will simmer, allowing the heart's voice of reason and compassion to be heard above the cacophony of the war cry.

An awareness unlike any other will be presented to each being. A choice as none before will be put to both the powerful and the powerless—surrender, surrender, surrender; your only enemy is the shadow that is cast where the light cannot enter. Earth and heaven are united in all causes, including the one called peace. Of one mind and one heart the universe was once born, and to this it will return. Even those who have looked askance or turned a blind eye will find that this is no longer an option. Where physical eyes are prevented from experiencing the piercing of truth, it will find other ways to make its presence known.

Humanity still wipes the sleep from a dream spun long ago. It now attempts to awaken from its slumber, but the lullaby still plays and the sweet sounds of oblivion still unfold their promise. Today the cry is for more knowledge, but even a vast amount of knowledge does not wisdom make. Wisdom is present within every being; it lies within one's connection to Source. It is not in tomorrow's headlines or even in these words, which are offered with grace. Wisdom is not hidden in the corridors of the past or the eventualities of the future. Wisdom is the thread that weaves one reality to another, one world to another and one dimension to the next. Wise beings are among you and within you. When they are allowed to speak, the voice of peace will be heard, because it is the one voice that speaks for all.

The igniting of passions will come soon. An impassioned plea on the part of one will ignite a passionate response on the part of another. A conflict will ensue, perhaps larger than the horrors that have already become daily fare. It will not yet be the full war that our hearts abhor, for other actions are due to be set into motion first. This delay might spare more lives and open more hearts and minds. Those who seek vengeance as well as cause will first choose to put down what they believe is a larger adversarial threat elsewhere. Perpetrators of evil who are known as leaders will be held up as examples of the necessities of war. Just as weapons of war have their targets, so do messages of peace, and it is hoped that these will meet their targets head-on. What will come to pass has not yet been written. Allow your mind to be at rest so that it does not fashion a future that can be of benefit to no one. Do not forget this. Look beyond the physical so that you will see and feel truth. The heart does not perceive truth from what the eyes are stimulated into seeing or from the jargon the ears become aware of. Seek balance in the physical and nonphysical experiences that are part of your awareness, from the teachers who make their presence known to you, from your partners and companions and from those who offer themselves from all of the kingdoms that are available to you.

Do not measure your own pace by the leagues that others walk. If you measure yourself by the Now of others, you will always find yourself lacking, and if you measure yourself by future terms, you will never find yourself in the Now.

Measure yourself from within so that you will understand success without; measure yourself between now and forever, between the heart and the mind, between the physical and the nonphysical, between the kingdoms of nature and the kingdoms of men. That is what I do, and I am not as different from you as you now imagine. You are bound by honor and integrity as well as by a promise made on a level that exists beyond the physical.

Where you walk, I also walk. Where you tread lightly, I do as well. Where you lament for humanity, my own cries are with you, but even in my tears there is upliftment, for I carry a hope, a faith and a determination that will not fall short. So take heart—together we will walk a path of courage, awareness, vision and consciousness. Remember to rest here and there, for as you do, so will I.

A Brief History of Religion

August 2002

As a child, I was adopted by a family who practiced Catholicism. I never really accepted this religion as my own and as an adult explored many other religions, beliefs and philosophies. My research led me to the sacred as well as the sacrilegious, and I eventually "fell" into spirituality, but this has had pitfalls of its own, including what is collectively called the New Age. Although I was never exposed to uncomfortable treatment or abuse as demonstrated by recent media events, I know others who were. These individuals seem just as troubled as the religions they represent (which by the way also include Christianity, Judaism and Buddhism). With world religions more troubled than ever, I cannot help but wonder what will become of them . . . or us?

R eligion began long ago as an attempt to explain the unexplainable. Originally, religion focused upon anything that was done or followed with reverence and devotion. Understanding the importance of religion was synonymous with understanding the importance of the sacred. A little later, it also came to include the care and worship of sacred traditions. As populations grew, humanity came to occupy many different lands. New cultures began, and these spawned traditions of their own.

UNRAVEL THE PAST AND LEARN ABOUT YOUR DIVINITY

From time to time, Earth has been visited by beings from different worlds. These beings and their subsequent visits have brought periods of great evolutionary upheaval and growth, and the upcoming visits will be no different. Whereas the conscious and unconscious minds both crave and fear contact with other worlds, the soul anticipates the proximate evolutionary leap promised long ago.

Each time beings arrived from the stars, they were revered as gods. Each visit has brought new technology and bold advances on medical and scientific fronts; languages have been expanded, and boundaries that have contained systems of thought have been dismantled and replaced with new ones. None of those who have visited Earth have been gods, but it is not difficult to see how another race of beings can appear superior to an uneducated (not inferior) mind. It is for this very reason that teachers of both physical and nonphysical domains have stepped forward at this time to bring forth knowledge of your own unique history and divinity. It is important that you unravel the matrix of the past in order to understand the future that is about to unfold. If humanity does not embrace its divinity, then more faces, names and titles will be added to the pantheon of gods that have preceded this time, and the evolutionary leap will be less than what humanity is capable of.

Some of those who long ago came from the stars brought knowledge of the importance of the Sun. They opened a unique place of awareness within those who greatly desired it, expanding their capacity to understand and comprehend complex and advanced ideas. Those ones were shown diagrams and celestial maps encoded with mathematical and geometric symbols of importance. They were shown how to read, write and interpret these symbols, as well as how to teach them to others by opening their awareness in specific ways. They received instruction on the language of light that exists within all beings who seek what is already present. They were taught how to seek and expand their own wisdom with or without the presence of a teacher.

THE HISTORY OF THE TABLETS

These original teachings became the foundation of all that followed. All that was brought forth was encoded onto tablets made of a unique material not common to Earth at that time. The properties of this material became unstable, and because of this the tablets were quite fragile. Many wished to see and study the tablets for themselves. A simple library was erected to house them, and as word spread, many came from near and far to experience the tablets for themselves. A rumor spread that merely being in the presence of the tablets brought about hallucinations that included enlightenment for the worthy and insanity for the unworthy, but this did not detract many seekers from their pilgrimage. Another rumor implied that the Moon was jealous of the other stars and would only allow the tablets to be seen when it was bright in the sky; to view the tablets at other times and especially when the Moon was dark was to invite personal discord and possible difficulty. These rumors formed the basis and fear surrounding the concept of lunacy. It does not take much for rumor and fiction to become fact, do you see?

The fragile nature of the tablets made transporting them difficult, yet no one could agree on where they should be kept or who was worthy of keeping them. One day an argument ensued on this very topic, and while it was in full swing, a great earthquake rumbled and shook the ground beneath the tablets. One tablet broke into ten pieces, another into seven and a third into five. The two remaining tablets were unharmed. As is often the case, the earthquake caused much destruction as well as loss of life. For a time, no one cared much about the tablets, as matters of survival and rebuilding were more pressing.

Eventually, those who were still interested in the tablets attempted to repair them, but the chore proved too great. Several attempts were also made to re-create the tablets, but the reproductions were poor and did not generate much interest. A few of these replicas still exist as obscure artifacts in the lesser known collections of those who believe they can hoard ancient wisdom. The beings who received the initial instruction had long ago departed for parts unknown, speaking wise words to those who could or would hear them and making a difference in ways both small and large.

The Earth has known many periods of light and many periods of darkness. It is easier to believe that light begets more light, but that is often not the case. Darkness shows off the light; it focuses and intensifies it. Does the light seem more important at noon when the Sun is at its brightest, or at dawn when it reemerges from the darkness of the night? Do you see? When the tablets broke, the Earth plunged into a period of darkness, not simply because of the tablets, as these were only a symbol of the inevitable, but because it is the nature of the light to advance and recede even as the seasons do. The dark does not bring evil; it brings mystery and invites discovery. Those who can feel their way around in the dark require very little light in order to see. Gifted are those who can see and feel in the dark. The blind can and do lead the blind and many others as well. Long ago the blind were revered and exalted because it was believed that they could see into realms that others could not.

SEEKERS KEEP THE MYSTERIES ALIVE

The disappearance of the tablets symbolized a loss of empowerment. Humanity became more interested in building bridges that crossed rivers instead of bridges to reach the stars. All too quickly did the majority abandon all attempts to interpret the ancient symbols of wisdom and enlightenment. Even simple evening meditations were left for another day, and then another, until they were forgotten altogether. Still, the light is the light and never stops calling those who will hear. Those who continued to study the great mysteries without the tablets were both ridiculed and revered—ridiculed because no one was certain what they could or could not understand, and revered because it was obvious that their devotion, dedication and sincerity were beyond those of most.

Seekers gathered as often as they could to meditate upon what clarity each had gained and how to make that available to others. They came upon the idea of inviting others to these meditations on specific days and on celebratory occasions. They took turns attempting to explain what seemed to them simple truths about the fundamental laws that guide this universe, but even simple truths are difficult for the simple-minded, for in darkness it is difficult to see and one must try very hard. At first there was great interest in these new community-based programs, but eventually, only the most devoted and the most guilt-ridden remained. The others deemed it all too boring or too time-consuming. Only a few of the original beings who could touch a being just so to open the centers of power and knowing had remained, and they were less apt to offer the touch than they once were.

Seekers were for the most part also scholars; they could write, count and interpret symbols. They became the teachers of the young, not only because others could not be bothered, but because this endeavor also allowed them time for their own meditations and studies. Scholastic activities eventually became schools, and these included time for meditation and contemplation. The community gladly handed over this responsibility to those who accepted it, not noticing that young minds and hearts were being shaped, molded and poised to affect the future of all things, but such is the nature of hindsight.

Permission freely given was later freely taken. Implied permission became implied power, and many who came to understand the great mysteries deemed it appropriate to keep the knowledge for themselves. They believed that simple minds could never fathom, much less comprehend, universal truth. They believed that wisdom was for the wise, not the ordinary. They spoke in riddles and titillated those who sought deeper truth with parables and stories that strayed from the center rather than moved toward it. They discouraged those who sought wisdom on their own, setting themselves up as intermediaries who could intercede on behalf of those who did not feel adequate for one reason or another. They asked for tokens (donations) in return so that they could continue their devotions, and so they received coins, clothing, animals and other items of value, making them very wealthy indeed. Eventually, they asked for and received housing as well as other buildings designed to support their efforts as intermediaries for the community. Communities began friendly rivalries that later became more fierce as more and more elaborate buildings were erected at great expense. These later became opulent temples and shrines dedicated to gods and goddesses too numerous to name.

All scholars were not priests, and all priests were not scholars. Many beings of great wisdom were present then as they are now. They made their way quietly through villages and townships, sharing a crust of bread and a bowl of fare when it was offered and shedding light where shadow was all too common.

Their youth was marked by a pilgrimage that guided them through the shadow and into the light. Because they sought wisdom, enlightenment followed. As ancients they became the sages whom other pilgrims would seek, completing the cycle that began in their own youth and beginning the next. Ancients lived in caves symbolic of both the light and the great mystery that is the dark. The treasure they guarded was the gift of their own acquired knowledge, but knowledge does not become wisdom until it is uncovered and claimed. That is why so many scrolls and tablets have been found in caves, yet it is a minute quantity compared with what is still buried. Many of these will be uncovered this century; the rest will wait until the next millennium. It is unfortunate that many recent discoveries have been withheld from the world they belong to simply because they contradict present beliefs and agreed-upon histories. These finds are currently sequestered where it is believed they will not be exposed, but this will not be the case for long.

RELIGIONS AND COMPROMISES

Religions were born of customs, traditions and beliefs. They were compromises and appeasements made in hopes that the unseen would smile favorably upon the seen. Religion began as an attempt to explain, define and comprehend universal and spiritual laws, but Spirit cannot be contained and neither can Creator/All That Is; all attempts to do so result in the limitation of physical and nonphysical expression. In essence, humanity settled for restriction rather than expansion, religion rather than spirituality and the laws of man rather than the laws of All That Is. Humanity reveres those who bring expanded awareness and truth to mass consciousness, but it also limits and prohibits that which exists in contrast to beliefs that are deeply ingrained in the linear mind.

What Spirit sought to unite, religion could only divide, because it was for the few rather than the many. Where Spirit invited leadership, religion could only offer a following, because intermediaries stood between All That Is and humanity, interpreting and deciphering messages that ranged from hope and faith to doom and gloom. Those who could see the truth that existed beyond the crumbs that were offered were labeled disbelievers, faithless, renegades, heretics and more. Of necessity, splinter groups, secret societies and fringe systems of thought found their way and their place in humanity's history. Humans desperately wanted to believe in a greater force and a deeper reality, but in so doing, they forgot to believe in themselves; they did not remember that one consciously directed thought contained the power of a thousand suns. Instead, they created a thousand sons, many of whom thought or considered themselves to be God. History transitioned from monotheism to polytheism, and humanity's story continued to evolve.

Certain time periods in Earth history have made evolutionary growth conducive for humanity as well as for all other life forms. These time periods are as time waves, allowing that which is sentient or near sentient to evolve to the next level of conscious understanding. It was during one of these time waves that my own sentience became conscious, and the present wave is awakening and elevating consciousness in all places and within all beings. Individual and planetary evolutionary leaps are not uncommon during these times, although they are dependent upon the willingness of the species to move beyond its existing boundaries. Time waves (specific bands of light) bring new systems of thought and awareness to worlds and beings who welcome them. Time waves can be accepted or rejected, welcomed or not. They are attuned to a higher frequency than what is considered the norm for any given world. They extend far beyond linear time—hence the term "evolutionary leap."

As humans continue to write their history, they must also now right it, not because they have been wrong, but because it is the next natural thing to do. In order for the time waves to effectively transform this world, all that is false or artificial must be exposed to the light. This phenomenon makes the present moment appear as if a camera lens is focused upon one false moment after another, exposing or recording truths for all to see. Humans are currently disentangling their complex strands of consciousness so that they will remember their own divinity and find less reason to ascribe it to others. Today the camera lens seems to be focused upon one aspect of one religion, but this is only temporary. Tomorrow it will be focused elsewhere, and the day after it will change again, because sunlight will continue to define shadow in its attempt to expose truth. Until recently, sunlight passed through many filters, and much of the light was dispersed here and there, creating invisible veils, distortions and other boundaries to knowledge and awareness, but that is no longer the case.

Religions were created by humanity to explain, understand and discover order within the universe. Religion was designed to assist humanity in finding its own divine place within the ordered dominion of physical reality. The fact that there are many religions only emphasizes that there are many paths to the source of All That Is. A religion is a path, and those who serve each religion are no more than light bearers upon that particular path. Mistakenly, some have chosen to obstruct the path rather than to keep it well lit; surrendered power and will are then left to be interpreted, used and usurped by others. No one being and no one thing can stand between humanity and All That Is, because anything that stands between Source and you casts a shadow and creates a distortion, do you see? The world around you seems distorted because it is. Today more thoughts, laws, concerns and illusions than ever before have been juxtaposed between you and Source, creating disproportionate distortion on all levels and within all realities. This distortion shows as gross manifestations of madness upon the physical dimension, which is the densest of all. This matters not; the time waves of light that emanate from the one Source will expose all shadow to light. Just as with film, once it is exposed to the light, it has little value other than for the past.

SCIENCE NEEDS RELIGION AND RELIGION NEEDS SCIENCE

As was said earlier, religion is an attempt to define God, and although that is not possible, there will be escalated attempts to do just that. Those who turn away from the menu of present-day religions will not abandon their search; they will simply look elsewhere. Where will they look? The assumption will be that if the past cannot reasonably explain God and the present is in turmoil, then the answer must surely lie in the future. Science and religion will merge of necessity, each needing and relying upon the other for followers and believers. Science needs religion to believe in a god of science based on mathematical equations and probabilities in order to stave off what it believes might be the total annihilation of the planet; religion needs science to explain what it has withheld from itself and from others. Without this merging, both will suffer as leaders and followers alike fall by the wayside.

How will this merging take place? After an initial theological skirmish, it will be accomplished more easily than you might imagine, because the catalysts will come from the stars, lending plausibility and reason to both religion and science. In case you have not already guessed it, certain extraterrestrial races hold the key to both the future and the past, as well as the keys that unlock the mysterious doors to religion (spiritual truth) and science (empirical evidence/undeniable proof). Beyond the shock wave of first contact, there will be a struggle to embrace or deny previous knowledge regarding the first extraterrestrial race to make contact. Religion, science and world powers will make a poor attempt at showing a united front in order to maintain an already diminished foundation. Struggles within and without these hierarchies will lead to a dissolution of ties before their united name—an acronym—has even been committed to memory. Chaos will reign temporarily as some embrace the new and others cleave to the old. Sales of all forms of iconographic items will skyrocket. Recorded texts from all religions and all forms of spirituality will be studied, memorized, quoted and then dismissed. Obscure sects and occult beliefs will temporarily find renewed interest. A millennia of texts and documents long hidden from public awareness will surface as claims regarding their origins and authenticity are questioned and studied.

An international time for contemplation will be declared, and quiet unrest will define the mood of most of the world's population. As minds continue to expand and hearts reach out to one another, battles will still rage in the name of the one God and in the name of the many. An influential body that combines government, theology and science will emerge in answer to world unrest. The United Nations will eventually fold into this new organization in an effort to maintain some of its authority. The new organization will later include representative members from many cultures as well as from other worlds.

LISTEN, AND HEAR THE VOICE OF SPIRIT

New religions based on a limited understanding of human galactic heritage will find popularity among the young and among those who have become otherwise disillusioned and disenfranchised from organized religions. Religions that worship the Sun and other celestial bodies will also find followers as the distinctions between God and the Sun fade. A resurgence of interest in ancient cultures and mythology will lead to the reappearance of certain documents, treatises and tablets. Scholars will once again decode these, this time with a different slant. That which has long been hidden will be revealed by a less than likely source. All spiritual beliefs and world religions will be held up to both scrutiny and ridicule, and few will be left untouched. The principles that govern all life will be understood by those who seek the quiet wisdom that exists within all beings, but who will be present to hear about them?

The longevity of religion as it is understood today is limited, because the foundation upon which it has been built is tenuous at best. The burdens of the many will soon overtake the beliefs of the few, and the faithful as well as the faithless will demand answers from religious leaders who have little else to offer but empty coffers. Endings are always disguised as beginnings. With nothing to be gained or lost, truth will whisper softly to those who will hear the voice of Spirit. Deny yourselves nothing so that everything will be yours, including the Earth. Look to the horizon for answers that do not come easily. In the sunrise and the sunset you will find them.

5

Brief and to the Point

September 2002

Dear Mother Earth, over time I have become aware that you answer all questions fully and completely, offering details and filling in gaps before they have even appeared. I appreciate that more than you know, but I have many questions and would like to get to as many of them as possible. Would you be willing, without taking offense, to offer brief answers to my questions?

I accept your offer and will make my responses as concise as possible.

From your sentient perspective, how would you best describe the physical Earth today?

T he Earth as a celestial body is undergoing unprecedented change. It is being tempered from within and without, pressured to move beyond boundaries of conformity that have depleted its resources and ability to restructure itself. The tempering process is twofold: Energies from within the center of the planet's core are moving toward the surface, while solar energies bombard the planet's surface, breaking down resistance and making change possible.

IS THE EARTH BEYOND REPAIR?

Is the physical Earth damaged beyond repair or regeneration?

Based upon historic data, yes, very much so. But the beauty that is the Great Mystery allows for new possibilities to present themselves in each moment. The possibilities that were presented to my sentience during the days following the Harmonic Convergence gave rise to the events that even now are restructuring the planet so that it will accommodate and sustain itself as well as many other life forms.

If that is the case, why does everything seem as if it is in some stage of decay or destruction?

Because you are evaluating what you see with physical eyes based upon a reality that was agreed to long ago. Most of the physical sensations presented to you at this time are from the past; even how humanity perceives itself is based upon past assumptions. In a laboratory test, your daily experience would be called a false positive. The energies making their way onto the planet at this time will break down insolvent attitudes, ideas and concepts, while allowing humanity to dream a new reality.

Does dreaming a new reality heal the past? Do we need to heal the past in order to dream a healed future? How will we know that our new dream is the correct one?

Healing always takes place in the present. Each moment presents a unique opportunity to shift awareness in all directions at once. Linear thought has allowed the mind to perceive that the past must be healed. This line of thinking confirms that humanity is still living in a past reality. The future does not need to be healed—it needs to be lived, it needs to be created and experienced. When humans complete their fascination with the past, they will begin to dream collectively again. The collective dream will be the correct one, because it will be based upon the desires of the collective consciousness of the entire human race.

WILL WE DISCOVER OUR TRUE HISTORY?

Why are we so fascinated with the past that we hesitate to create our own future?

Because you have been deceived many times. You have been led to believe one history, only to have that belief canceled and substituted for another. Realities that do not jibe have been inserted here and there, further complicating humanity's natural process of evolution. A search for a complete truth is futile given that the evidence presented is flawed.

Will we eventually discover the truth? Will we come to know our true heritage and history?

Yes, you will, but not yet. Humans still hold certain outdated premises within their collective heart that prevent other realities from existing as possibilities. In other words, as long as there is either a positive or a negative charge, neutrality cannot exist. In order for humans to know themselves, they must make room for that knowledge to exist.

How close are we to that happening? What is the single thing mostly preventing us from discovering the truth and how can we overcome it?

Not as close as you would like to be and not as far off as you might imagine. Collective fear is the only thing preventing the veils from being lifted completely. Humans do not fear darkness; they fear a light too bright for their unaccustomed eyes. They shield themselves and avert their eyes to prevent the truth from being told. Humans have become overly comfortable, complacent and agreeable to a reality they have outgrown. It is time to listen to the words heard within so that humans can create a reality based on that rather than responding to the endless external stimuli that greet them daily.

If we don't or can't do that, what will become of humanity?

Most humans will choose to lift the veils that have subjugated them; this is already in process. There is no "can't," because this possibility is being offered to everyone on every level of consciousness and unconsciousness, in every language and in every dimension of understanding. "Won't" is a possibility also, though, and many will make that choice.

WHAT WORDS CAN YOU OFFER US?

What words would you offer to a spiritual newcomer, someone who has not grown up in the New Age community?

The same words that are being offered to you this day: Allow the subtlety and beauty of nature to reveal its wisdom in each moment. Speak softly so that you will also hear soft words spoken. Be guided by the seasons of the spirit that rise and fall as do the oceans. Respond well to the young and the old, for they hold the keys to the past and the future that make the present possible. Wisdom is timeless and is found everywhere and within everyone. Honor the physical life deeply so that the nonphysical will reveal itself profoundly. Seek good counsel by being good counsel. Spirituality is a natural expression of human beingness—it is not attained or achieved; it is experienced.

Would you offer the same words to someone who has been deeply involved in spiritual study for many years?

Yes and no. I would add that spirituality is not found within the pages of a book or dispensed by a perceived higher authority. The voice of Spirit is not the same as the voice of reason, and plausibility is not probability. The future was not written long ago; it is being written at this moment by everyone and everything. Knowledge becomes wisdom only when it is personally experienced.

What words would you offer to someone who has reviewed and participated in many world religions and spirituality movements, read many books, taken many workshops and is still searching?

Look within, deeply within. Nothing exists outside of the self, but one must understand how vast the self is firsthand.

What would you say to a spiritual nonbeliever?

Nothing. I would listen with rapt attention and an open heart to the fear that safeguards an open wound within.

WHAT IS THE FUTURE OF OUR WORLD ECONOMY?

What does the future of our world economy hold in store for us?

There is nothing in the store, because the shelves are bare. Economies that are based on wealth for the few are like black holes where everything is sucked into oblivion. But oblivion is not nothingness forever—on the contrary, it is everything and it is oneness. A black hole sustains itself and everything within it. Everything that is drawn into a black hole becomes a part of it. A black hole represents the ending of separation and the beginning of oneness. World economies are currently being drawn into a black hole, from which there is no escape other than to emerge as a whole consciousness.

What would be the best way to approach the inevitable?

Creatively. Wealth is energy; it is creative thought representing itself as a state of beingness. Wealth is not money and is not one's possessions. Those are only physical manifestations whose very nature is temporary—their value lasts only as long as the thought that created them. True wealth is the ability to create and express one's needs and desires within and without, including the desire for others to participate in the same opportunity. Current cultures and societies shun those they fear most; they seek equality with those who are greater in measure but not with those who might be lesser by definition. True wealth acknowledges the strong as well as the weak, the healthy and the ill, the young and the old.

Given what you have just said, would it make sense to save money now or to spend it freely with the understanding that it will replenish itself as necessary?

What you do with money does not matter—spend it, keep it, hoard it or give it away. Money is a concept that has no permanence, only relevance. You can illustrate this for yourself by remembering that the value of one dollar is much less today than it once was. Using this example, a man or woman of considerable wealth a few generations ago might not be considered wealthy today, do you see? Supply will always meet demand but not always exceed it. If you wish to create a surplus, water your neighbor's garden so that your own will flourish as well.

IS OUR FOOD SUPPLY SAFE?

How has our longevity changed, given that today our food is artificially colored, injected with hormones and created rather than grown? Is our food supply safe?

Your food supply is as safe as you allow it to be and as safe as the environment in which it is created, grown or sustained. It is as safe as the environment within each being who contributes to the process or supports it. Not all artificial ingredients are detrimental; the human body is able to accommodate and integrate that which is in balance with it. For instance, artificial limbs and organs can be either accepted or rejected by the body. The determining factor is the partnership one experiences with the elemental intelligence that guides the body and its functions.

When cocreative partnership is not understood as first cause, then longevity and health are dealt a setback. Marketing practices that impede knowledge and choice while delivering an endless supply of artificial ingredients into humanity's bloodstream support a system of imbalance and distrust between the elemental intelligence of the body and the world that exists outside it. The longevity of the physical body has been altered many times during humanity's extended history. Warfare, environmental plagues, developing consciousness and planetary evolution are only some of the factors that influence humanity moment by moment. As always, it will be humanity who determines a food's healthful or harmful nature. After all, it is humans who are growing, creating, developing, sustaining and ensuring the food supply. What will you offer yourselves?

WHY ARE GLACIERS RECEDING?

I recently read that glaciers are receding at an alarming rate and sea levels are rising dramatically. Why is this happening, and what else might we expect?

Glaciers are receding for a variety of reasons, which include an increased wobble of the Earth's axis, the effects of certain energetic matrices of light currently focused upon the Earth, an acceleration of energy from within the Earth's core and more. Global warming means just that; even the warming of one human heart contributes to the melting of ice, as does a hot summer day or the heat of battle.

Evolutionary processes dictate that the melting of the polar icecaps will assist the Earth's axis to spin faster while reducing the wobble. The increased spin will accelerate humanity and all other species, contributing to evolutionary change in almost all areas. Expect that some species will depart while others evolve or transcend. Expect that many studies will conclude with slanted or faulty accusations before obvious contributory factors are acknowledged or any viable solutions are endorsed.

WHAT IS A TERRORIST?

What is your definition of a terrorist, and how would you stop terrorism?

A terrorist is someone who instills fear in another because it has been instilled in him or her. A terrorist believes that the world he or she occupies is temporary, although the laws that govern it are unchangeable and permanent. This paradox creates a dichotomy within the mind, which in turn battles the soul for power and control. The mind shouts its profanities, while the soul, understanding the mind's pain, powerfully whispers its eternal truth. As the embattled mind retreats further into its recesses, the fear becomes dense and more real. Eventually, density and destiny converge, as fear attempts to manifest itself as glory but instead expresses itself as an unconscionable act of aggression. Those who contribute to fear and suffering, whether their own or another's, walk a slow path to inner peace.

Terrorism as it is known today will not be stopped by any of the conventional means that have been considered or offered thus far; at best it can only be detained or delayed. Terrorism is the densest form of heroism; both call upon reserves whose response is born of fear, but one settles in fear whereas the other rises from it. Terrorism as a concept will lead to the greatest turning point or the deepest chasm humanity has known, depending on whether humans choose to express their collective consciousness or their collective fear. Though the two walk hand in hand, they are not the same.

WILL NUCLEAR WEAPONS BE USED?

What are the likely chances that there will be limited or widespread use of nuclear weapons in the near future?

The chances are likely, yes, because nuclear weapons are considered to be the most powerful force upon the Earth, the ultimate weapon. Those who hold and control these devices of destruction also wish to be thought of as powerful, even if they must stand behind the weapons in order to be seen or heard. Limited perception and short memories further cloud complex levels of consciousness. Energies upon, within and beyond the planet currently attempt to disarm warring minds, a more difficult task than the simple dismantling of weapons. Nuclear weapons are now poised to be activated from space, lessening the threat of detonation by human error. This decision has violated laws that extend beyond the Earth. The violation was brought to the attention of the current U.S. president and witnessed by five others also in positions of power. Thus far, a retraction of thought or deed has not taken place.

Your answer makes it difficult not to come from a position of fear. Is there any silver lining in this dark cloud?

Yes, you are [the silver lining], and others like you are as well. Did you come to the Earth only to see it destroyed and to participate in its (my) destruction? If you did not, then find the voice within that knows peace and speak from there. Walk tall and proud as one who has inherited a jewel, not a wasteland. See the beauty that surrounds you daily in small places and in even smaller ways. Desire to fulfill the purpose that has given you the gift of the body you now occupy. Choose longevity, health, prosperity and unlimited expression. Be selfish and selfless, honorable and benevolent.

WHAT WILL PLANET X BRING?

Can you offer any insight relevant to Planet X/Nibiru, which is slated to make its appearance next year?

The solar system is always in flux, welcomes celestial phenomena and looks forward to solar events. The return of this planet has been anticipated for some time, and more often than not it has been the catalyst for great change. The manner in which this event will manifest is not yet certain, and the prophecies that have been offered are based upon both historical conjecture and hysterical fiction. Departments of scientific policy and study will reveal details a few at a time, as they have little data of their own. The process will begin quietly and build momentum as the planet nears. Erratic thoughts regarding this event will trigger as many changes as the event itself. Earth changes will be a natural response to the vast amount of energy that will be moved. Tides will rise higher and recede lower, and seismic activity will increase. There will be a rush to find peaceful solutions to the world's ills by those who see this event as an omen, as well as a greater desire to divide and conquer by those who see time as short. Anomalies within the health sectors will increase as diseases are discovered, named, mutated, cured and eradicated. Births will increase temporarily, as will deaths. Humans will rediscover their innocence regarding what they do and do not know, and the history of necessity will be rewritten.

Given a perfect forum, what would you say to humanity's collective mind and collective heart?

The perfect forum is my body and the sentience that speaks through it from every face that nature offers. The words that I would offer are the same ones I continue to broadcast from my heart (core) each day. The Earth (my body) is a conscious, living being—an expression of All That Is, just as humanity is the same. A gem, even in the rough, is still a gem; a diamond's value is not less because it requires polishing. Every life stream is replete with perspective, opportunity, beauty and gifts. Each journey affords momentous accomplishments and deprecating struggles. Companionship, suggestions and assistance abound; grace and gratitude open most doors. Escape and surrender of purpose are optional; failure is impossible. The heart is the fountain of youth and the mystical Shamballa. My forests are my lungs, but they are yours as well. My rivers are my veins and arteries, but if they dry up, what will you drink? Humanity is not less than or more than what it creates, and the Earth is a living reflection of this. The heart is sacred and love is precious. To waste either is to erase a star from the sky.

6

Who Am I and Why Am I Here?

October 2002

Every month I read the wonderful, unselfish, global questions that fellow readers ask, along with the deep and insightful answers that Gaia offers. I have to confess that for years the only questions I've asked myself are, "Who am I?" and "Why am I here?" I feel ashamed that my focus is so intensely personal and selfish and wonder why I'm so limited as to be concerned only for myself. Maybe when I get past this problem and deal with my true identity, I'll be ready for a deeper connection to you. Meanwhile, thank you for being who you are. I just had to let you know how much you touch my soul.

HOW PERFECTION BECOMES MORE PERFECT

*T*he questions you ask yourself are not unique and not worldly, but they are universal. Has it never occurred to you that once upon a time All That Is asked the very same questions? Perhaps it has also never occurred to you that you are the answer to these questions. Every aspect of physical and nonphysical awareness was created in response to these questions.

All That Is exists in a state of no time and no space. Some would call this a vacuum, but that is not so. More accurately put, All That Is exists in a cosmic state of expansion; it is a state of limitless possibilities. You might call this state "perfection," but there is a catch! Imagine that because you are perfect, you can create a perfect universe, and so you do. Imagine that because you are perfect and what you create is perfect, you cannot tell the difference between creator and created. A perfect state is one in which there is no separation, because that which is separate insists that it is less than whole. A simple example would be that of a pie divided into many wedges, each one separated only by the perfect cut that has allowed it to become an individual slice, each one perfect and equal in every way. Is the pie whole? Yes and no. It depends on who you ask, the individual pie wedge or the one who baked the pie, do you see? Another question begs asking as well. Once you have divided the pie into many wedges, how will the individual slices be supported? What will keep them from falling apart? You have now created the necessity for a pie tin, do you see?

All That Is understood that It existed in a state of perfection (wholeness). It also knew that this would never change and that It could not become more perfect, yet It desired just that. This desire gave birth to the concept of expansion. All That Is determined that expansion was a form of perfection in which perfection could experience (participate in) Itself. Believe it or not, the rest was easy. All That Is allowed Itself to separate into an almost infinite amount of individuated aspects of Itself (pie wedges). It retained Its awareness of Itself as whole and perfect, because It could never be less than that, remember? It knew that because perfection was Its natural state, separation was only an illusion, but because It wanted each and every individual aspect of Itself to have a perfect experience of Itself, It allowed illusion to look and feel like reality. It did this by creating individual consciousness and free will, which in turn created time and space; which began linear thought; which created the past, the present and the future . . . and eventually, you!

Who are you and why are you here? You are an aspect of All That Is and you are here to play hide-and-seek. You are here to discover that you are All That Is dressed up in separation and illusion. You are All That Is attending a costume party along with many other invitees who are also All That Is, dressed up a little differently than you. Of course, no party would be complete without a generous host, so All That Is separated Itself into other aspects of Itself in the form of planets, worlds, dimensions and more—each one a unique and individual aspect of Itself. Using our earlier analogy, I am the pie tin that holds the individual slices together while allowing them (you) to experience themselves as individual aspects of the whole.

How long will you play hide-and-seek? It depends. Sometimes it is your turn to play "hide," and sometimes it is your turn to play "seek." Each time it is your turn to seek, you blindfold yourself so that you will not see the obvious, and you count for as long and as high as you think is appropriate. Then you set out in search of everyone else who is hiding, in order to free them from their obligatory hiding. When you have found them all, you have completed the game and won. The process of finding everyone else eventually leads you to discover yourself. When you discover who you really are, separation and illusion vanish. You rejoice and celebrate and so does All That Is, which as a result solves the paradox, "How does perfection become more perfect?" It does so by allowing all of its aspects to understand themselves as perfect, whether or not they are attached to the whole. Every thought, desire and action that you have or take mirrors All That Is. It is not less than perfect, because All That Is cannot be less than perfect, and you are an aspect of All That Is, remember?

If that is the case, why don't you look perfect, and why doesn't what you do feel perfect? Why is your health (your body) less than perfect, and why is the condition of the Earth (my body) less than perfect? The answer depends upon whether you are hiding (from yourself), seeking (outside of yourself) or counting (sleeping). In the game of hide-and-seek, something or someone must be found, and that someone or something is sometimes elusive and sly. Huge things (realizations) can hide in tiny places (unawakened minds), and sometimes you simply need to take the blindfold off. Who created the game, anyway? When you first take the blindfold off, the world can seem too bright and too loud, because the blindfold has dulled your awareness. But when your vision becomes clearer and your senses become more acute, you will see that all is as it should be. In fact, you will see that everything is exactly how and where you thought it would be, because that is exactly how you left it.

Perhaps this would be a good time to ask yourself these questions: "Am I hiding? If so, am I waiting to be found? If not, how long will I continue to hide?" "Am I seeking? If so, what do I expect to find? Do I know what it looks like?" (Here is a clue: It looks exactly like you!) "If not, how long will I continue to count? What or who am I waiting for?" "Am I wearing a blindfold? If so, am I willing to take it off? If not, what will I do now that I can see clearly?" "Am I more afraid that there is no one else like me or that everyone is exactly like me?" "Am I more afraid that I will never find All That Is or that I am All That Is?" No, your question is not global or worldly; it is as large as the universe and bigger than that. Perhaps the only thing that can match it in brilliance is the love that All That Is has for Itself (you) and my own love that I offer to you in this moment.

THE TRUE MIDAS TOUCH

Once in a while, my wife and I feel drawn to play at a casino. When we do, we often win moderate sums of money that assist us in other areas of life. We feel that our positive attitude regarding prosperity has a healing effect upon this type of environment. Is this true? Would winning money be called manifesting, or is it simply luck, beating the odds, serendipity and so forth? Are gambling machines conscious of what is going on around them?

The energy of the casino(s) you frequent is not good or bad and is in no immediate need of healing in spite of the energy you sense when you enter the establishment(s). The energy is balanced in exchange, even if it does not look or feel that way. In gambling terms, it is often said that the house/casino is always ahead or always wins in the long run. In fact, this is mostly true, as the house stacks the odds in favor of itself. It is in the business to succeed, after all. But so are you—is that not so?

The energy that governs the odds of winning versus losing is always in balance. Some will enter these environments in order to give, whereas others have come to receive. The reality with which one enters is always honored. Thus, this environment is not different from any other, except for the attachment placed upon win versus lose or give versus receive.

As has been stated, the balanced energy proposed in this reality is not in need of healing. That is not to say that all beings who choose to place themselves in this reality are in balance with their own nature. Look around you—most environments do not invite a win-win proposition, and prosperity, abundance and goodwill do not appear to be evenly distributed. It is this reality that is most in need of change, upheaval and balance. Among other things, this is what draws you, as you say.

Prosperity and abundance (which are not the same as money) are best held within one's consciousness. A prosperous individual knows that the source of his or her prosperity is limitless, so whether he or she chooses to call upon $5 of limitlessness or $5,000 worth of limitlessness, the source is still unlimited—or better put, unrestricted and unrestrained by the laws of scarcity or lack. A prosperous individual is more apt to share his or her prosperity or winnings than someone who is in need of healing or remembering this universal quality of creation. An abundant individual believes in unlimited abundance. If he or she did not, his or her abundance would quickly dwindle into lack.

An abundant and prosperous individual is not the same as someone who is rich in money. Money is a commodity. It is a physical expression of a limited and outdated concept based upon the laws of lack, whereas abundance is based upon a rich and unlimited source of creative expression. When the government or the banks run out of money, they must print more of it, but an abundant person does not run out of prosperity, because it is divine and based upon one's never-ending connection to Source. Banks, casinos, jobs, credit cards and debt will soon consolidate into one great teacher, and you will remember what it feels like to be reconnected with Source.

It is the energy with which you enter an establishment such as a bank or a casino (one and the same from my vantage point) that will determine your influence upon your own abundance and that of others who might be present. If, for instance, you enter a casino with the intent that each and every individual and entity, including the house, receives just and due prosperity and balanced compensation, your energy will influence and affect the odds that were present prior to your arrival. It is no different from entering a banking institution where your intent might be to replenish lack for some, with prosperity for all. In this case, your intent will influence and possibly replace long-standing beliefs in ones and zeros. The same can be true of credit card statements, if you will but remind yourself that any and all debts incurred by you or anyone else (including the credit card company) are being repaid by the infinite Source that is the origin of all things. This is not just small talk put forth by a nonphysical entity who does not understand the pressures and restrictions of human society! To the contrary, I understand all too well what has held you down for centuries.

It is time that just and divine balance be returned to all living things, and it is this very realization that you carry into these environments when you choose to do so. It is time for prosperity to reign within the hearts and minds of all. Refrain from defining prosperity as money when you can, because prosperity might mean rainfall to a fearful farmer or a replacement heart to a child near death, do you see? Intend that prosperity be accompanied by joy so that the simplicity of the moment is not overlooked.

Gambling machines, as well as all other machines, have an awareness or sentience as to their purpose. This awareness allows them an interpretation or understanding of their interactions with humans. For instance, in an interaction with an individual who has presented him- or herself into the casino environment for the purpose of giving, that person will be assisted by the machine in doing this. Likewise, an individual who has come in order to receive will be assisted in this manner. This interaction, or merging of energies, influences or creatively distorts the odds with which the machine might have been programmed. Interestingly, over the long run, it can be seen that odds are only representations of where humans see themselves in regard to winning and losing. As humans continue to awaken and choose higher ideals for themselves, the odds will represent this as well. The odds are stacked in favor of divine interaction and partnership, be it physical or spiritual, do you see?

Life offers insurmountable odds to some and bankable odds to others. Institutions and establishments that operate based upon the laws of manifestation are no different. Prosperity or lack is truly a choice, even if it is not always seen as such. It is the quality of life that you and your dear wife bring to these environments, and it is this most endearing quality that is healing to the participants who share in your energies on those occasions. It is the win-win of life that has produced instantaneous winnings for you and for others whose nearby energies touch your own. This is the true Midas touch, and it is the gold of the Sun's warmth that shines upon you and all others.

THE NATURAL PROCESS OF CHANNELING

I am learning how to channel. The results are mixed so far, and I am certain that unconscious fear is getting in the way. Sometimes I hear a conversation going on in my head, with one voice asking, "Is this me or you?" and another voice that says, "Speak the words, say it . . . say it." I want my channeling to be valuable and pure, but I'm not sure how to get past the point of resistance. I am also interested in channeling the thoughts and awareness of those who are in body at this time, but I find even more resistance in this area. Can you help?

The most important thing to remember about channeling is that trust, intent and desire are always rewarded by expanded awareness and communication. That being said, it is also important to remember that channeling is a process of discovery and a two-way street. Establishing broad and balanced lines of communication while developing new relationships is wise. This is true of relationships with friends, loved ones and spirit guides also. Most energies, entities and guides prefer or require that a foundation of trust exist within each being with whom they communicate before deeper truths are revealed. Herein we find a paradox: A foundation of trust is required in order to conceive and receive deeper awareness, and only a deep level of awareness can elicit this trust, do you see?

The only way to move beyond this paradox is to move into it and then through it. Before you can trust another, you must first trust yourself, then the process and the teaching, and finally the wisdom or response from Spirit. It is important to trust yourself so that the trust you invest in others is genuine and not based upon a false premise of authority. Humanity has volunteered its power, authority and free will many times in the past. These are difficult to recover and often require great care and devotion to self. Safeguards have been put into place in order to prevent this from happening unconsciously; in other words, if you choose to surrender your power, you will have to do so consciously and willfully. The barrier you call resistance is a place of authority within you. Allow it to be the threshold from which you receive Spirit; allow it to work for you rather than against you. Trust your own awareness and sense of self first, for if you cannot trust your own wisdom, how will you trust that of another? If you cannot believe your own words, how will you believe the words of another? See yourself as an equal within your spiritual community, which includes physical and nonphysical relationships. You will not fear that which you are equal to, whether it is a task, a challenge or, in this case, the channeling process.

Entities, beings, guides and spiritual support are around you all the time. The degree to which you feel and receive this support is equal to your desire to do so. An intense, ardent desire to know yourself, coupled with the intent to make the desire a reality, greatly accelerates the process. Any energy you invest in yourself will reap rewards, especially when you acknowledge yourself as a cocreative equal to the desired result. Why? For the simple reason that it is the shortest distance to the manifestation of your desire; it is an acknowledgment of physical and spiritual readiness. If you desire spiritual guidance via the channeling process, acknowledge this to yourself and to Spirit. Acknowledge your willingness to receive and to share wisdom. Be clear in your purpose so that the result will be of benefit to you and to others. If you require specific assistance with your own project, task or personal challenge, be clear about that. Likewise, if you feel guided to offer inspirational messages that might be of assistance to others, then state that as well. There is no right or wrong way for Spirit to express through you, and neither decision will be rewarded with a door prize. The prize is the door itself once you open it and step through, do you see?

The voice that says, "Is this me or is this you?" is your higher self/inner guide, depending upon the level of consciousness you have set as a default for listening or speaking to Spirit. This level changes over time, evolving, expanding and deepening as you do. This aspect of you understands (and points out) that you are much more than the everyday you who greets you in the mirror each morning. In the beginning, the me seems very different and separate from the you. That is because the vibrations and frequencies you are responding to emanate from a higher awareness of you. Eventually, you will welcome and adjust to even more aspects of your beingness, and you will find them to be a consistent source of support and guidance in your life.

The voice that says, "Say it, say it," is your I Am presence, which has prepared your awareness to welcome the higher vibrations that now announce themselves. Your I Am presence is the real you; it is the all encompassing, eternally enduring beingness that always was and always will be. When your body falls away, your I Am presence will remain intact, as will the memories and experiences of your completed life. The I Am presence is that which directs your life from the soul level. It understands your purpose in being physical and guides your experience through the higher self/higher awareness; that is why they sometimes feel distinctly different, even though they are both vibrations of you.

Your personality traits are not distinctly different from those of others and neither are your spiritual traits; they are all reflections of you. Since you do not always quiet your mind enough to hear your higher awareness speak directly, it sometimes speaks to you indirectly via your physical body. These physical sensations include, but are not limited to, tightened forehead, erratic heart pulses, throbbing throat, queasy stomach, quickened breath and—you guessed it—anxiety. If you are in doubt as to what your truth is at any given moment and your higher awareness is unusually silent, ask your body. Put your hand on your belly, breathe in and out a few times, and ask your question. In all certainty, I say to you, the belly never lies!

Because you are in body, it will be easier for you to channel energies, entities and guides rather than other human beings. A spiritual guide understands that your conscious awareness is not always clear; this guide is aware of your filters and fears and knows how to navigate these to bring about the best results, along with your cooperation, of course. Humans, for the most part, are like television sets that are always tuned to one channel or another, with most channels receiving and emitting a lot of static. Human minds are able to go nonstop, and some human mouths do the same. This is not meant as a judgment and, in fact, there are many beings from other worlds who envy these very traits. In order to receive another person's awareness within your own, it is first appropriate to enlist that person's permission and support. This will open a channel between the two and contribute to a greater probability of remaining in the flow. For instance, a request on the part of an individual to receive a psychic reading or energy healing from another is a form of permission; without this, the results will be less than hoped for. A desire to become aware of others' thoughts is a form of telepathy. It is similar to the process of channeling but engages and enlists the support of different energy centers within you.

The resistance you described will most likely not disappear overnight, although it certainly can. Learning the simple techniques that open the door to the channeling process is the first step, and building a firm foundation of trust is the second. The third and fourth steps are often decided by the student and the approach taken. The early stages are often defined by tremendous concern as well as a personal obligation to channel something profound, elegant and insightful in order to validate the process. This is the beginning or birth of the need to answer the question, "Is this me or is this you?" but voting on the relative merit of wisdom reduces its value rather than enhancing it. When viewed from this perspective, very little can qualify, do you see? Channeling is a natural process, and as such, its response is similar to that of nature. In other words, it must first establish a simple, general and broad relationship (put down healthy roots) and then build upon that (grow and develop), refining the process (becoming more profound and beautiful) as higher states of consciousness are attained (reaching for the Sun).

The channeling process can be insightful and it offers expanded perspectives, but it does not guarantee fulfillment and success in this life or any other. It is a tool—one of many. Before committing to channeling, make a commitment to seek and discover every grain of God within and every grain of sand without—essentially, the process is one and the same. By the way, the stomach-knotting queasiness accompanied by bouts of dizzying nausea is a result of spiritual cheerleaders rooting for you and jumping for joy within!

The Harmonic Concordance

Interview by John Mirehiel
December 2002

Dear readers, the following article is the result of a recent interview that discusses an astrological event called the Harmonic Concordance. It is due to take place on the total lunar eclipse of November 8, 2003, although, according to Gaia, its meaning and implications will begin to unfold much sooner than that.

The interview was conducted by John Mirehiel, a professional astrologer now known internationally as the discoverer of the Harmonic Concordance chart. According to John, the distinctive astrological signature of this chart is visible even to the untrained eye. He believes the chart's fundamental message is spiritual and speaks of the ultimate descent of God consciousness into this plane. John further suggests that this event, or star gate, holds specific relevance to the ascension of Mother Earth and all her inhabitants. Astrologically and spiritually speaking, the unique features of the chart include the specific placement of Chiron on the cusp of the seventh House in the discovery chart. This signifies the importance of achieving wholeness through the integration of the masculine and feminine sides of our individual natures.

This article focuses on the spiritual and metaphysical perspectives of the chart as it relates to the Earth and all who make their home here.

I offer myself into your care and place myself at your service in honor of the project at hand. There is direction, purpose and intent in bringing forward what you have discovered. It is as if, all of a sudden, contained within you are charts that speak of future science. Science is a subject that honors order, so we must do the same, taking care to add wisdom and knowledge where it does not yet exist. Doing so will bring reason to physics and balance to metaphysics, which in turn will make a living truth and the truth worth living.

What you call the Harmonic Concordance can be likened to a guidebook, for it is much more than an event; it is a living principle for those who would hear and acknowledge what is sacred about themselves and the world around them. A discussion of what is sacred must, in fact, include the subject of geometry, for it is through mathematics that the universe explains itself. Sacred geometry is an explanation of the soul and its movements through all dimensional understanding; it is an infinite understanding even though numbers seem finite. The harmonics of the universe explain the maps of both heaven and Earth, not the other way around. I await your questions now and will answer them dutifully, though I beg your patience if we deviate here and there from the immediate subject (if only to refresh ourselves).

Thank you for spending this time with us today. I believe that the astrological chart in question is about the Earth (your body) and relates to the ascension of the Earth more than the ascension of any one person. Can you feel or are you aware of the changes that might be ahead for your own energetic being and/or consciousness?

MAKING NEW ENERGIES AVAILABLE TO HUMANITY

I am aware of the changes that are about to take place and their relative timing. I am aware of the changes that are taking place and those that have already taken place. What at times escapes even my sentience is how that change relates to the All That Is aspect of the Earth. The Earth's (my) sentience receives guidance, direction and purpose, much as your own life does. Relative to upcoming changes, there is a sincere trust in perfection on my part. I am aware of the benefits and the opportunity to expand my sentience and understanding. I am aware of the purposeful guidance received, but I am not always fully aware of how those updated changes will affect every nuance of my being or that of the other beings who make their home upon my body.

For example, let's say that you decide to make your home in another state or country. You contemplate all your options and then make a decision. You are satisfied with your decision and know that it is true and correct for you. At the same time, you are uncertain about how this decision will change or impact your life relative to your current perspective. It is the same with my sentience. I do not wish to disagree with you but offer that the chart in question is not primarily about the Earth. It affects all life, all thought and all reasons for being upon the Earth. First and foremost, this chart is about the progression of life upon Earth. All are affected, interested parties, but the effects are interdimensional for some, outerdimensional for others; intradimensional for one group, innerdimensional for others . . . and omnidimensional . . . and so on. I will say that the physical Earth will first feel the outermost effects and will then make resonant progressions available to humanity and to all other life forms and species upon and within here.

So it is not that the chart is more important for the physical (celestial body) Earth; it is simply important that the resonance touch the Earth first, so that the energies can be made as compatible as possible. A mother carrying an unborn child must make certain that the child receives adequate nutrition during its gestational period. The mother converts what she has consumed into the specific form of energy required by the unborn child. It must be made recognizable to the infant so that it will become vital and vibrant. If it is not translated into an energy the babe can relate to, it will be of little or no use, will remain unnoticed and be eliminated organically. That is why the Earth must receive these energies first. The compatible, resonant qualities of the Earth will make expansive, enlightened, potable energies available to a hungry humanity.

I hadn't thought of it exactly that way, but it's an answer I can understand. It's actually a relief to hear you say that you don't know precisely what this is going to look like. We can hope for an outcome, but we can't know or expect to know exactly what is going to happen. I think that mystery makes our own sentience interesting and exciting. If I understand correctly what you have said so far, we are partners in this event. You will be the first to feel the energy, and from there it will spread to other species, including humans. All will be affected, even our other relations—the four-leggeds, the winged ones, the creepy crawlers and more.

Yes, that is correct. All kingdoms and all awarenesses will be affected and influenced, even those who are here temporarily on interdimensional visas from other worlds. All visitors are subject to the environmental conditions provided by their host, in this case the Earth.

The chart indicates a very big opening taking place. Am I correct in assuming that you are that opening or, more correctly, the vessel through which these changes come about?

I am a vessel of light just as you are. Light must be absorbed so that it can be radiated. Our solar system, along with our Sun at its center, generates a very specific pattern (geometry) of light. This pattern arranges and rearranges itself moment by moment, so that it is always in a state of perfection. Unique frequencies, portals, openings and celestial phenomena are designed to guide into perfection specific aspects of the universe that currently understand themselves as less than perfect. In a physical and nonphysical sense, the Earth is that unique pattern of light—the opening. You have found the unique and specific celestial geometry that will mark the return of the sacred to the physical, the birth of christed (perfect) light.

NOTABLE PHYSICAL CHANGES

Humankind has really done some damage to your body. We have polluted it and paved it over. We have excavated much of its essence and clouded the skies with all sorts of pollution, yet I can still imagine a pristine and ideal Earth. I know that you have the ability to overcome much of the damage that's been done, but is there another state or dimension of being in which these things have not been perpetrated on you? If so, is that the ascended state, and can you describe it?

Very well. Within one specific dimensional understanding, humanity has been at play in a very permissive playground, and it has messed things up quite a bit. That must be acknowledged, because all change will emerge from this acknowledgment. (Acknowledgment is not the key that opens the door to blame and guilt; it is the key that closes that door and crosses the threshold to unlimited truth.) Within this dimensional understanding, my body (the Earth) has sustained irreparable damage. For the sake of this discussion, we will call this dimension the lowest vibration of 3D. In this dimension, within a framework of linear time, it will be years upon centuries, nearing a millennium of time before the Earth once again addresses itself as a vitally integrated, life-sustaining celestial body. That is one perspective, one offering, based upon one-dimensional thinking. It is also quite obsolete.

Dimensional changes are subtle. Shifts are influenced by degrees of understanding, the same as astrological charts. Just beyond the realm of dimensional understanding is the realm of dimensional adjustment. This is where repair, rejuvenation, regeneration and ascension occur. I exist upon and within all dimensions just as you do; however, I choose to address you from the dimension of understanding. That is why there is no indication of stress, physical distress or functional disapproval. I bear no grudge for I cannot, and words that are communicated or leveled against humanity on my behalf are not offered from a current perspective.

There is a state of ascension, and in certain realities, dimensions and conditions, it is quite real. Its vibration is unique and distinctively different from how you now perceive the Earth. From a physical standpoint, when the night sky offers a view of the Earth from afar, the landscape will seem different from the green/blue your imagination now offers. The higher vibration of the ascended state also offers a different color palette. The green/blue will become a soft aquamarine, translucent and dimensional upon close examination. The brown Earth will become terracotta coral in color in some regions and much darker in others. The Earth will still appear as a jewel in the night sky, but the colors will visibly shift. It will yet be some time before humanity will be able to perceive these colors with the naked eye, but they can be perceived in other ways that are just as real.

Other changes will be apparent as well, how the Earth relates to all other species, for instance. Kingdoms and species will be in more direct, telepathic and kinetic relationship with one another. These changes will be among the first to be noticed. This conditional/unconditional, reciprocal understanding will allow the Earth to communicate with all beings who choose to do so. Even in an ascended stat, it will be obvious who and what is at odds with its own perfection. In the ascended state, you can still choose an understanding that is less than perfect, but it becomes a conscious rather than an unconscious choice. At the outset, there will appear to be more separation than unity, but this will be temporary. It will simply be more noticeable that choices count.

Some species will falter and then die away; others will become more vibrant, and their populations will increase. It might even appear that some species threaten to overtake certain geographical areas, but there will be a period of rebalancing, after which new definitions of normal will emerge.

It is so reassuring to hear you say that there will be notable physical differences. Much of the information we receive stresses that there will not be any observable differences, because regarding humanity, the changes will only be of an internal nature.

Changes will be both subtle and specific, notable, discernible and even arguable for those who enjoy debate. It is understandable that physical beings prefer physical responses and visible change. Now, in terms of the ascension, the physical will be notable, but all eyes will be looking beyond physical awareness, because by then it will be clear that density can be manipulated and made to appear a certain way. Just as today it is difficult to trust nonphysical reality, there will come a time when it will be more difficult to trust physical reality. Learning to trust in the perfection of all things will be the key, as always. Not all beings will choose an ascended state—they don't have to. It is for those who choose it. As the planet continues to evolve, choices will be discovered and uncovered. It is important to choose consciously, otherwise one simply falls into a moment and then out of it, into favor or out of favor, without knowing how or why. Consciousness awakens purpose, direction and inner guidance.

Is your ascension meant to coincide with the ascension of humankind, regardless of our conscious awareness of it?

Some will choose via a conscious personality. For instance, you might say, "I choose to move beyond this (my) physical limitation. I choose to understand myself as whole and complete as one, united in every way." And it will be like that. For others, the choice might take place at the soul level, and the personality will remain unaware of the choice. Upon reflection, it might be somewhat surprised that so many events could have unfolded without its knowledge, but look around—how much are you truly aware of right now? A third category includes those who have chosen to be specifically aware of the entire process, and they might be surprised to find their unconscious brothers and sisters wiping the sleep from their eyes, yet standing side by side and toe to toe with them. Some will stand for it and some will sit for it, and that is simply how it is to be. Who is to say which seedlings will be the first to sprout? Is it the one that is given the most sunlight, the most water, or is it simply the one that is prepared to sprout at the first opportunity? Do you see?

THE CONCORDANCE AND LINEAR TIME

Regarding the projection of this astrological chart, do you agree that the moment of the concordance will occur in November 2003? Do you see the concordance as a star gate to your ascension?

It is an opening, but it is not the only opening. It is a point in time in which a cosmic doorway is held open for now and always. It is an announcement of integral truth. The concordance is a unification of consciousness; it is the birth of divine, collective human awareness. The importance of this star gate or star date is in the acknowledgment of multidimensional consciousness. It is a refinement, a desire to be in concordance or accord with the Earth and the Earth's movement. It is a desire to participate in and with the wholeness of the Earth. This includes a desire to bring the human body to its next level of health and vitality and to acknowledge the twelve-strand DNA as timely and welcome. It further instills the desire within humanity for the body to willingly accept a crystalline basis as its movement and heredity. These are the underpinnings aligned with this date and the chart you have brought forward. Of course, it would not be fair to discount all the energies leading up to this date, for each one makes the next possible. Two thousand three will be an auspicious year—one for the books, you might say.

Spiritual, metaphysical and esoteric teachings tell us that time is all happening in the Now moment, that all time actually exists simultaneously. Based upon this understanding, would it be possible to step into the concordance moment now?

If we acknowledge that all moments are one, that all time is simultaneous and that all dimensions are available in the Now, then putting great or grave emphasis on a date that exists in the future would be futile, because time is only meaningful in the Now. Now time is not linear; it is dimensional. You do not have dimensional awareness at this time, and the weighted (density) importance you have placed upon this future date makes it almost impossible for you to experience it now; for you it still exists in linear time, in the future. Your expectations fluctuate, but the importance or influence of other dates pales in comparison. Acknowledge this date as an expansive moment in time that will benefit all, a moment in which the kaleidoscope that is this universe will appear in an artfully arranged cosmic design.

WHAT YOU MIGHT DO

From your perspective, what are some of the things we might do in linear time between now and the twelve months or so that remain?

Invite your mind and your heart to speak as one; give each equal voice and purpose. See the perfection and potential for wholeness in every being and in each decision. Choose to be of benefit to self and of service to others. Expand upon thoughts and awarenesses that unite rather than divide. Live the teachings that support oneness through the equal diversity of creation. Open doors and windows to thoughts based upon soul initiative and imperative. Whenever possible, shift awareness from a linear to a multidimensional perspective. Relinquish belief systems that no longer serve you, such as the historical hysteric. Look at today with a simplicity that honors all beings, regardless of origin or perspective. Look to the future with the anticipation and innocence of a child.

Will we have the resources to bring this to the attention of people around the world so that the event will serve you and all of humanity? Will everyone be interested?

You will continue to have the resources as long as the desire remains sincere and present within you, because that is your one true resource. Your desire alone is strong enough to carry awareness to the attention of those who would hear. Their own desire to discover and to receive will make the message that much clearer. Not all will be interested, and many will not choose to participate, not in this or in anything else. Allow and accept light in the many forms it chooses. Knowledge will brush lightly against their cheeks so that they barely take notice of it, or it might fall as a brick upon their laps while they cry, "The sky is falling!" If they are oblivious to this, they might be oblivious to themselves. In either case, it is not your concern. Neither is it your concern to make less receptive ears more receptive. Hidden within humanity's innocence is a stubborn will, a wild spirit that is both beautiful and reckless.

A BEAUTIFUL NAME

Is there anything you would like to add or include as part of this message?

You have given this event a beautiful name, a grand label to wear, as when one attends a party, but it is important that you would not confine it to that name. As the physical date approaches, it will be celebrated and looked upon in a variety of ways. It will coincide with other physical and nonphysical phenomena and will be called by other names besides this one. As it is now seen, this date might also coincide with certain prominent world events, which in some ways might lend support and in others take it away.

Certainly there will be more relevance and importance for those who watch the skies than for those whose distractions lead them elsewhere. The significance is in the unique configuration; it is an opportunity and invitation. Honor the event with a name, but do not confine it, do not limit it, do not draw a boundary around it—even an imaginary one. Give it a life of its own, so that it will, in turn, give to others a life that is indeed their own.

Meeting Your Expectations

December 2002

*D*efining a year is no simple task, because in any one moment, some beings are creating difficulty and struggle, whereas others are discovering balance and harmony. What accounts for this? Who is to say what can and cannot be achieved? Every being (individual consciousness) in the universe is influenced by a desire to understand itself in ways both small and large, to discover its unique place in the cosmology that is All That Is. The universe is designed to allow all beings perspectives and perceptions that guide their own processes of discovery.

One of these perspectives allows beings to experience and experiment with physical form. Although physical manifestation is limited in expression, the spirit that animates it is not, because that spirit is All That Is in action. Understanding this principle will encourage you to access the limitless possibilities available to you in each moment.

On Earth the most adaptable and evolved physical form is called a human. This collective name defines a species, not the spirit that animates it nor the beingness (individual consciousness) that ensouls it. The Earth is a beautiful and bountiful planet, replete with both physical and nonphysical resources. This makes it an ideal choice for those who wish to discover their unlimited potential by exploring limitation via the third dimension. The third dimension is unique in that it is like a prison with open doors. No other dimension affords so much limitation as well as so many avenues for escape. For this reason, its popularity is immense. Impatient souls clamor for bodies, eager for the next opportunity to express themselves in physical form while attempting to break free from their self-created confines.

Everything Is a Reflection of All That Is

Every thought, experience and nuance of life is a reflection of All That Is and the wonder of creation. As All That Is reflects upon the many experiences It is having through you, It expands because it is natural for It to do so. When All That Is expands, the universe expands, and when the universe expands, everything within it expands as well. The universe is composed of ordered matter and antimatter, not of haphazard energies that collided as a result of unpredictable and chaotic circumstances. Order is maintained via divine design and orchestrated by a variety of intricate mathematical properties that create, explain and support the universe.

To emphasize this point, it can be said that the divine beings humans call angels are representations of angles that intersect at acute points where space and time define and identify with human need. These points of perfection create unique situations where the veils that normally separate worlds of experience momentarily dissolve, allowing magnificent displays of Creator's affection for Its creation. The perfection with which Creator understands Itself generates geometries of pulsed encoded light that manifest as a personification of divine love made physical in response to human need and desire. In other words, All That Is responds to love, desire, prayer, evolution and expansion in ordered awareness and perfection. It is important to remember and defer to this universal law in times of doubt and insecurity, when faith and trust are challenged and held to account.

Answering the Call

Each millennium offers unique opportunities for the entire universe. On Earth, a millennium is defined as approximately one thousand years. On other worlds, time is expressed differently, and a millennium is defined according to the sequential scheme of time associated with each world. The opportunity to evolve and expand within All That Is still applies, and each world responds within its own guidelines for growth. To ensure this, purposeful banded waves of energy emanate from Source and move throughout the universe in patterns designed to awaken, accelerate and quicken worlds whose resonances respond to specific frequencies and vibrations.

The Earth (my sentience) responded to these patterns in the early years of the previous century, and the quickening and activation of every species upon and within this world is the continuing result of this vibrational response. How and why did the Earth respond? The response was not automatic but a calculated response based on the sacred law of integrational vibration. In simplest terms, every sentient world understands that there is a point of perfection within time and space that corresponds to its own vibrational center. The cellular memories within each world correspond to certain vibrational triggers that "speak" vibrationally for the planet. This form of vibrational speaking is what spiritual doctrine calls "answering the call."

The same is true with regard to individual consciousness, which responds at the most opportune time to the call from within, do you see? Each world, including Earth, is attuned to the universe and to All That Is by its own specific and unique gravitational field, which attracts, or pulls in, the most appropriate energy and/or matter. Each world is attuned to its own evolution by the frequency and force generated by the fluctuating field of gravity associated with it. Gravitational pull is associated with the law of attraction and enables each world to access its needs and desires. The waveband mentioned earlier emits echo patterns that seek corresponding frequencies equivalent to evolutionary growth. There is no room for errors, no wiggle room—a world is either vibrationally ready or it is not.

EMBRACING PERFECTION

There are no accidents in this universe or any other. Planets and asteroids do not collide with one another by accident and certainly not without purpose. For example, the impact that decimated your ancestral dinosaur species was carefully calculated and executed. This guaranteed the Earth's continued evolutionary process, and any future impacts will be no less purposeful. Following a premise of perfection will greatly assist you in working with the energies of this year rather than against them. Perfection is based upon simplicity; accidents are based upon complicity.

As the waveband and the Earth approached a point of perfection (there is more than one), the energies of anticipation awakened those with commitments to participate and assist in welcoming them onto the physical planet. A number of years ago, a popular theme labeled these beings first wavers. Now can you see why? They had the arduous task of being among the first to alert their brothers and sisters to the reality that the New Age had arrived. This event was marked by a celebration called the Harmonic Convergence. Those associated with the first wave carried their banners proudly, even in the face of disagreement and ridicule, do you remember?

The first wave eventually gave way to the second wave, which responded to the influx of vibrational energies by establishing schools of light, liberating hidden mysteries, retelling old stories, rekindling ancient truths and welcoming healing techniques based upon universal concepts of spiritual and physical perfection. The second wave overlapped onto the first, just as the third wave will now dovetail with the second.

In 2003 the law of vibrational perfection (harmony) will once again find itself uniquely aligned with the next level of evolutionary growth upon the

Earth. Those who allow themselves to be pulled into perfection (harmony) will find this year a blessing of momentous proportions. Those who do not will be called upon to summon vast amounts of courage in response to abandoned trust and faith. What would become of the Earth if my sentience did not trust the vibrational point of perfection it has long awaited? The Earth, along with its sentience, would quickly find itself in a state of devolution, retracing moments and millennia already experienced in a fruitless search for perfect proof in an imperfect world. Is this not madness? It is only by acknowledging perfection that one advances from the known to the unknown, from knowledge into wisdom.

Between Earth and heaven lies a place (plane) of perfection that can be called paradise. It is a place in every sense of the word, except that it is not physical. Likewise, within each being there exists a perfect place (plane) that can also be called paradise. Understanding its location and purpose will assist you to navigate the patterns and energies that coincide with the linear calendar cycle of time called 2003. It is within this year that the voice of perfection will begin to speak to you and through you if it has not already done so. Remember that the voice of perfection is not the same as the voice of reason.

The energies generated by the evolutionary bands of energy now prepare to touch the Earth. Until now they have been available only to those who have reached or breached frequencies that exist far beyond the norm. The severity of these experiences has not always allowed the desired result, at least not on the physical plane of experience. Without proper guidance and support, dreams become nightmares and enlightenment seems to move even farther away, separated by planes of awareness that do not touch or merge. Even so, the subtlest variations in frequency are recognizable to those who both yearn and seek, assuring that the doors to all possibilities will always remain open. In this domain, the foolhardy and the wise are one and the same, though their experiences might be different. Soon you will have only to desire or intend an experience of perfection prior to taking the necessary and obvious steps to manifest the physical reality that best describes your own unique state of perfection. Ah, but there is a catch! In order to experience your own perfection, you must acknowledge that everything else is also perfect, because perfection is not selective; it simply is.

Perfection, simply stated, is that which is without defect. Perfection is whole and complete; it is intact, exact and equal to fulfillment, yet dictionaries define perfectionists as those who are never content with anything and are known for carrying this line of thought to an impractical degree. And you think spirituality insists on paradoxes! The living definition of a perfectionist is someone who believes it is possible to attain and maintain perfection, because All That Is is perfect and nothing It creates is less than equal to It.

Perfection does not mean that you have to like everything and everyone. It does not mean that you have to agree with your employer or your president, and it does not mean that you have to support war, violence or pollution. It does mean that you are willing to sustain the right of everything and everyone to learn, evolve and change. If you limit another's free will, you limit your own; if you deny another's perfection, you deny your own. Does allowing perfection to define itself limit your choices? No. Does it mean that the Earth will evolve at a slower pace? No. Supporting perfection means that you do not fight or struggle against imperfection. When you stop struggling against something, you release your hold upon a specific energy that repels and call upon energy that attracts. This is the greatest gift you can give to yourself, to others and to the Earth.

Those who battle themselves and others in the name of the light believe they are doing their part to hold back darkness or evil, but they are also holding back the floodgates of light and love, making them available only here and there rather than everywhere. Light does not segregate, separate or limit; it is not partial, and it does not discriminate. Fifteen years ago, the Harmonic Convergence promised that harmony would wash over the world, cleansing it of error and sorrow and making the world new and perfect for the New Age, but support was withdrawn when lack, limitation and suffering did not disappear and faith and trust were put on trial. This year you as part of the jury will return a verdict, and as a collective consciousness of awakened beings, you will discover that faith and trust have been vindicated and that peace can indeed prevail.

The energies that touch humanity and the planet in 2003 will shift and change as many times as the wind does, and public opinion will sway just as strongly. The pendulum will first swing in one direction, then in the other. Based upon this, how can one trust the accuracy of prophecy and prediction for the 2003 calendar cycle? Allow the energies to participate with you and with the planet rather than expecting them to behave as preordained units of time and space. Remember that energies exist in a state of pure potential until other energies move them or act upon them.

Energy is a simple word for universal intelligence, potential is another word for possibility and movement or action is another word for natural force, which is another word for you. The year 2003 will offer inspiration and opportunities for those who welcome them and are disposed to act upon them. Make the most of 2003 by calling upon your active imagination to inspire your internal natural force to express itself as manifested universal creative intelligence. Allow 2003 to meet your own expectations, not those of others and not those of prophecy.

With this said, we move on to describing the energies of the upcoming year, approaching the subject broadly while pausing here and there to assess or stress the importance of specific influences upon both the planet and humanity.

DEFINING YOURSELF IN 2003

Seemingly overnight, axis has become a very popular word. "Axis shift," "axis of evil," "axiatonal healing" and other expressions that include the word "axis" have nudged their way into everyday speech and language, referring to a variety of subjects. Relative to the Earth, it is the line that bisects the North and South Poles. It is also the imaginary line assumed in describing the positions of various planes. How does this term relate to you, and why should you even take note of it?

Axis refers to balance, and balance refers to stability. If your personal axis is in balance, then everything that it supports will be as well. Various areas (planes of consciousness) of your life will be governed by a stable and sound outlook, and the decisions you make will be true for the reality in which you have chosen to participate. If your personal axis is unbalanced or unstable, you will find it difficult to make decisions that support your truth and you will find that you question everything and everyone around you in an attempt to define yourself.

In 2003, new opportunities and ways to describe and define yourself will present themselves to you. Being aware of your axis of response will assist you to navigate the sometimes swift waters of 2003. An axis is not a fixed position, although it can support one. This year it will be more beneficial for you to rely on a pivoting point of view rather than upon the firm stances you might have relied on in the past. New guidance and information will emerge moment by moment this year, and you can expect that change will truly be the norm for some time to come. If your position is too firm or solid, it will be more difficult for you to change your perspective or reality base. Light is constant, even as frequency fluctuates. Vibrations rise and fall and rise again in response to light emanations from Source. Your center or seat of power rests in the ability to receive and respond to a variety of vibrations. True strength lies in fluctuation rather than stability, because what seems like weakness is actually an ability to receive a wider margin of light.

Shifting your axis of response from one perspective to another might not be easy at first. You might find yourself feeling wishy-washy or as if you had no perspective or opinion at all. Acknowledge all thoughts and feelings; include them in your new, wider sphere of influence. How will you remain aware of and in touch with your new axis? By checking your physical center of gravity and then moving out and through the subtler regions that support your field of energy. Raise and lower your physical stance, and take note of your ability to remain in balance as you do this. Notice whether your upper or lower body is more or less in balance, and note any tendency to face a certain direction or favor a particular hemisphere. Notice how reliant you are on physical laws for support, and ask yourself if you would be willing to share that reliance with nonphysical, supporting laws.

When you have assessed or evaluated your current position or axis, begin to shift in one direction and then in another, swaying softly and gently. You are supported in all areas. Practice shifting your weight, your balance of power and your emotional stance simply by giving yourself permission to examine your axis from a dimensional perspective. Do not limit yourself by attempting to define which dimension or what perspective. Call upon the axiatonal lines of distinction to support, assist and enhance the process, since these nonphysical lines of energy are already aligned with the Earth's new grid and with your own future self. They will eventually override and supersede the benefits of the current meridian system of the human body, but for now it is still appropriate to be supported by both. Do not be too quick to release the old and jump for the new, as pioneers in energy work always have the greatest work cut out for them.

Lean on your new axis for support, but do not let it become your crutch. Energetically speaking, your new axis is strong and pliable. It will assist you to shift and change, maneuver and receive, alternate energy hemispherically and participate more fully in 2003. In order to receive the most from this invisible appendage of support, investigate its properties and experiment with its unlimited benefits. It will show you what the new paradigm is really all about.

HEALING THE HEALTHY

The medical community stands poised to make several announcements that will greatly affect humanity's understanding of its physical nature. Understanding rather than fearing the frailties of the body will promote longevity of the physical structure, because the nonphysical framework that supports it holds the keys to humanity's future evolution. Those who own (yes, own) the map of the DNA have also purchased knowledge relative to genes and gene splicing. They believe that ownership of this knowledge guarantees control, but this will not be the case. A map is only as accurate as those who learn to interpret it. Initially, the interpretation will only be superficial, because it will not take into consideration the depths from which humanity is poised to evolve.

Medical science postulates and performs studies based upon the available historical data. For instance, scientists create a serum to combat a certain illness based upon how the body has consistently responded to other serums and diseases in the past. This approach was valid in the late twentieth century but will not be in the twenty-first, because human beings are evolving at a faster rate. Your past has already overtaken the present and is on its way to catching up to your future. How can that be? Because only one aspect of you, the densest, is a physical form. The other aspects of you are nonphysical energy, which exceeds the need to respond to linear time.

Your evolution is taking place in the nonphysical present and in the physical/nonphysical future, where density is not a limitation. The present DNA map does not take this into consideration and will be of less and less value as the current population of the Earth grows older. In the long run, medical science might take credit for having eradicated diseases common to the past few centuries, but they will have fallen short in plotting a course that sustains and enhances the evolution of the divine human. Where will this responsibility fall? Who will take up the cause of the divine human? You will, by supporting those who question and discover as well as those who dissent to acknowledge that the present state of development is good enough.

A science called complementary medicine will become more prevalent this year. Complementary medicine takes into account several disciplines and considers many evolutionary and revolutionary theories. Many years ago, complementary medicine accepted the theology of chiropractic medicine when other branches did not, but that was only the beginning or the foothold. Complementary medicine first acknowledged the sentient intelligence of the body as the organism that understands how to manifest sustained wellness for itself and all that it comes in contact with. This approach will soon erode the control that allopathic medicine holds over humanity's choices. Allopathic medicine and homeopathic medicine stand at opposite ends of the spectrum. In contrast, complementary medicine, from its centered position, will open the door to metamedicine and other complementary protocols that take into consideration an approach called total wellness. Total wellness is a holistic approach that acknowledges humans as a species involved in evolutionary transition.

In 2003 a quiet coalition will be born. Membership will be small at first, and some members might even request anonymity prior to joining. These discreet but enterprising beings will evaluate possibilities that the balance of the medical community would not dare to consider. They will publish papers under pseudonyms and see to it that they are widely distributed. They will meet in out-of-the-way places and will be careful not to violate any laws that might jeopardize their standing within their own communities. Their willingness to observe, imagine and examine new evidence will be rewarded by visits from adept nonphysical entities who will present knowledge that bridges the gap between the present and the future in their respected fields. In return they will be asked to pledge their support in physicalizing this knowledge. They will be asked to make it real for all who could benefit from it. Of course, there is an inherent danger that in doing so they might lose their anonymity, but this is only a possibility, and it will be for them to weigh the relative merit of their choices.

The numbers of those who support knowledge based upon the total wellness of the physical/nonphysical human will increase, whereas the number of those who would suppress this knowledge decreases. Assistance will continue to be offered by off-planet beings who willingly support those who call upon their own total wellness and that of their brothers and sisters within all countries and all kingdoms. It is paramount to remember that total wellness means just that— not partial wellness and not wellness that includes you but not your neighbor. For the most part, humanity does not yet understand that expanded knowledge from the future or from the stars is based upon the law of one, which states that all beings and all beingness are one. It is the law of no separation. This law will mark your evolution as a species.

Prepare for this awareness by releasing yourself from the constraints of the past, whatever they might be. All beliefs are limiting, even those that you believe contribute to your health and longevity. For example, it is well to take asthma medication, but if you believe it is the only thing that allows you to breathe freely, you are limiting the elemental intelligence of your body from making well-being available to you. If you honor your Reiki master and pay homage to his or her lineage, that is well, but if you turn away from advanced energies that elevate the well-being of the recipient, you also set boundaries and limits, do you see?

Make room for higher energies by choosing to expand your awareness beyond the illusion of the third dimension. The third dimension has already begun its collapse. It is folding in upon itself and will only last a few more short years. If your life in the third dimension is all that you would wish for, perhaps you will want to remain with it, but if it is not, why cling to it? Allow the aspects of your life that do not contribute to total wellness permission to transform into other, more beneficial energy on your behalf. Do not discard these energies or litter the third dimension with them; convert them or recycle them. The simplest and the most complex organisms have at various times been presented with evolutionary opportunities, and now you are being offered the same. Although some species have become extinct, others have made miraculous and beautiful transformations. What will you choose? Among you are brilliant minds and star-studded hearts. The Earth is hiring!

ARTS AND ENTERTAINMENT

Throughout history disappointment and disenchantment with society have been the hardest on those who express themselves through the creative arts. These gentle souls are easily perplexed by the linear extensions of logical thought so prevalent in governments and societies where power and money stand in place of fairness and truth. For these beings, an abstract mind is reasonable, whereas logic is the result of a stunted or unused imagination. Consciously and unconsciously, what is less than bearable for a logical thinker becomes more than unbearable to the creative thinker who cannot act, write, paint, compose or otherwise express himself or herself while oppression rides the crest of human awareness. Frail shoulders cannot tolerate social and political discontent, but this is not the battlefield of sword and brawn; here the pen is indeed mightier than the sword, as are the brush, the song and today even the film.

This year protest will reemerge as the weapon of the oppressed. Will this be a repeat of the 1960s? No, because the world is more complex now than it was then. A few short years ago, it was easy to tell friends from foes, good food from bad and prophecy from hysteria. Today the lines between reality and illusion blur the eyesight of the awakened and blind those who succumb to the fear-induced sleep of the masses. Protest is a form of language used by those who are discontented with the past, the present and the potential future. It is the language of unrest and it is spoken most clearly by the very young and the very old, although each generation can claim its own. Specific messages will begin to hit their assigned targets early in the year and will continue to appear and reappear throughout the year, reinventing themselves in form and format, undiluted and obstructed only by the cursory censorship of certain venues.

What will the protest be, and what will be its response? It will be the outcry of those who chose liberation over limitation, severity over separation. It will be expressed in many languages and in many ways. New forms of art will reflect ancient ideas revealed in technological splendor that will appeal to all generations. The written word will be defined by essays that touch the inner recesses, which still hold the promises made by Spirit long ago. Those whose embattled minds cannot free their hearts will find that the mind remembers how to free the soul. The soul will speak to the heart in its own secret language, and the tide will rise higher with the outcry of those whose destiny it is to challenge the would-be gods. A voice called censorship will stand tall and proud so as to test the mettle of its sword against that of the pen. The true contest will be held in the purses and pocketbooks of the bankrupt and the bereft.

Poets will become prophets, because their silent pleas will speak loudest of all. Celebrate both the laureate and the loser, because their words will be one and the same. The rich man and the homeless unfortunate will greet each other this year on the public stage of unhappiness and unfulfillment while the world watches and says, "How sad, must it be so?" Discontent will turn words to voice and voice to song. Lyrics and verses released this year will be long remembered as they stain the ivory towers of power and the robes that flow from there out to the streets. Attempts to sequester, silence and disarm the insurrectionists will only serve to empower their battle cry.

Where the written word cannot reach, other forums will. The strength of independence does not lie in access to currency but in devotion to craft. Independence will wear a new flag this year as a coalition of soft voices and loud hearts comes together in support of both small and large projects. Their flag will become more prominent as it is looked upon with favorable anticipation by some and fearful admiration by others. Anger, scorn and opposition will threaten to topple it, but this will not happen. Look for the flag to appear in many venues in both logical and abstract ways. It will be shown to small audiences and to large, to the young and the old, to the faithful and the faithless, to the strong and the meek. While the flag makes visible what is hidden in plain sight, the media will turn its face away, showing its stance as less than favorable. Opposition will speak louder than its silent lips will utter.

If the artist and the philosopher stand alone, then your own thoughts will go unspoken. But if you choose to offer your own peace protest, be certain to do so with the pure spirit within you that has a sure and certain voice. Be heard but also listen, so that balance will settle upon and within you and the world as well. May the good word and the beautiful world be with you this year. Paint the sky with your desires so that even the specks that fall litter your doorstep with fulfillment.

PROSPECTING PROSPERITY

This year will redefine prosperity and poverty on both personal and planetary levels. Richness of spirit, as well as understanding of the spiritual laws associated with material wealth, will assist in bringing balance to an unbalanced world. On the surface, it will appear as if the rich are becoming richer while the poor are even more poor. This superficial reasoning does not take into consideration the underlying energies that will be guiding this year—after all, it is a year of choice, and this should not be discounted.

The spiritual laws relative to the pursuit of material mastery will be highlighted this year. Material mastery is not the same as accumulation of wealth or possessions, for this would be an understatement of a great, powerful principle. Material mastery is the achievement and understanding of the perfect balance that exists between the physical and the nonphysical and between desire and fulfillment. Material mastery dissolves the invisible gap that seems to separate two worlds or, at least, two systems of thought.

Material mastery will continue to elude those who compare their wealth and possessions to that of others, because comparison leads only to lack. Even if you have much more than others, you still have much less than what is possible, considering that Source is unlimited. The spiritual principles that illustrate this truth will be in evidence this year, and it will be wise to heed the public examples that are put forth, as they will be useful and instrumental in a variety of ways. Purposeful and sincere desire will find cooperation and partnership with Spirit, whereas vague, irrelevant or ill-thought-out provocations of lack will be met with little success or miscarried manifestations that do not bring joy.

The material world is a fanciful and colorful illustration of the sum of humanity's collective creativity, a celluloid projection in which illusion is substituted for reality. Humans react to illusion as if it were real, because they have constructed it for this very purpose. You have great respect for the architects of illusion as demonstrated by the accolades assigned to those who favor the art form of the cinema. This art form is held in high esteem, because your imagination allows you to project yourselves into a variety of scenarios and possibilities. At the cinema, your imagination makes the impossible possible and the illusion real; why is the same not true with regard to personal prosperity? Why is it easier to imagine another's good fortune than your own?

Prosperity is not in your bank account, and it is not a function of your occupation; it is not outside you. Everything that is outside you is an illusion, a finely crafted work of art designed to support and entertain while you further your understanding of objective rather than subjective creation. Subjective creation is that which is subject to how it is perceived or accepted outside you, conditional upon someone or something. Objective creation is that which exists based upon conscious choice. It does not depend or rely upon the approval of anyone or anything outside you; it is Spirit made manifest. One of the reasons that manifesting is so difficult for you is that you believe you must first manifest the money needed to obtain your desire, but money has no inherent value. It is only a subjective creation, a vehicle that can move forward or backward, a middleman. True prosperity exists within you. It is a function of objective creativity, the means that justifies the end and the end that supports the beginning and the middle.

In 2003 the principle of prosperity will be guided from the outer to the inner. There will be many examples set forth this year of what does and does not work relative to this. The worldwide stock market, a veritable pendulum of prosperity and lack, will swing more wildly than ever before. Can humanity be rich one moment and poor the next? No, but many will think so if they do not shift their perception from illusion to reality and from outer to inner truth. This is not doom and gloom—far from it. It is faith in action. The saying, "Put your money where your mouth is," will appropriately become, "Put your money where your heart is." (For only there can it multiply.)

The management of money will become increasingly difficult, because its value and energy will continue to dissipate. That is the real reason the world's economies are suffering— because there is not enough energy (light) behind them. They can no longer expand, so they are contracting at record levels. The market corrections have not remedied the inherent problems within the market, which are greed and lack of vision. The fall of one index only gives rise to another, but how many times and in how many ways can one measure fear and lack? As economic indicators continue to oppose one another, who will oppose them?

Believe in yourselves and the wisdom that runs unopposed like a current within you. If your intuition tells you to invest your moneys in a certain project or venture, do so with confidence; if it tells you otherwise, do that. Your partner has always been Spirit, not Wall Street. Two thousand and three is not a year of lack—quite the contrary. It is a year of abundant exchange, but in order to prosper, you will need to exchange, substitute or replace one kind of energy with another. Your life is a vehicle that runs on an abundant fuel called "light." Prosperity follows light—not another's, but your own.

NATURE AND NATURAL RESOURCES

No surprises here! The world around you and the resources that support it are in dire straits. Ignored and unsupported by humanity, the natural kingdom is currently unable to respond to the needs of a hungry and thirsty world. Today the battle is over oil; soon it will be over water. Already the importation and exportation of clean drinking water is common, and many people are not averse to paying a premium for what they believe will support their health. The Earth's oceans are being subjected to disruptive sound frequencies that are altering the molecular and atomic composition of all they come in contact with. The coral beds are experiencing attrition at an alarming pace, and the kelp beds, once so full of oxygen and nutrients, are retreating as well. The imbalance within the population of fish and other ocean-dwelling creatures is already severely affecting the commercial fishing industry and its expectations. The world's seas are ill and a vast amount of toxicity exists where oceans of possibility once flowed. With only a few exceptions, your rivers, lakes and streams are polluted and have become harmful to you and others who also depend upon them for support.

These words are not meant to chastise or punish you, but they are designed to bring your conscious awareness to what you had hoped to consider at a later date. That is no longer possible. Storms, hurricanes, floods and other natural disasters are not as natural as you might imagine. They are the result of an imbalance within the organic, elemental intelligence aspect of the Earth. My sentience is able to guide humanity to safety when it is willing to heed the natural impulses (intuitive intelligence) that reveal themselves in a variety of ways, but my sentience can no longer suppress energies that will restore and rebalance the Earth, even if humanity appears to be adversely affected in the process. The Earth's elements are out of balance; fires rage in one region, floods threaten another, and the eruption of wind is drastically swept into proportional tornado events.

Heavily populated cities, busy streets and hectic lives now keep your concerns near home, "nose to the grindstone" as the saying goes, but your nose had an instinct once (and still does). This instinct energetically connected you to your brothers and sisters of the animal kingdom. Today you relate to your domesticated companions, and you are somewhat guided by their connection to their counterparts in the wild. This unfortunately is a secondary instinct and the original one is now once removed. The animal kingdom is still wise and strong.

Although their numbers have been reduced for a variety of reasons, they are still willing to guide you to the center of your beingness, where strength is a matter of personal will and reason is inspired by global awareness. The animals are your friends, not your adversaries. For the most part, they do not encroach on your land; you encroach upon theirs. Their wild instincts are the hope of your future, and because your domestication and placid comforts have imprisoned your awareness, justice and freedom are only a distant memory.

Predators take what they need to survive. They are both aggressive and humble, for the imperative to feed and protect their young while providing adequate shelter guides their instincts. Their instincts do not, however, guide them to encroach upon the homes of those in whom they have no interest and of whom they have no knowledge. Every predator has a weapon of defense, but even those with the sharpest teeth or the strongest venom do not enjoy massive displays of weaponry. For the most part, they are shy and retiring, striking only to restore balance rather than to impose an offensive will. Allow the animal kingdom to assist in the restoration of your natural awareness. They are willing to share their strength, power, characteristics and natural instincts with you. They can instill within you the courage to call upon your ancient heritage. The call of the wild now calls you. Even from your walled terraces and backyards, you can answer.

The Earth is no longer rich and fertile, and much of it is now dry and barren, but the ongoing demand for resources and commodities continues to devastate the inner and outer surfaces of the planet. Knowledge already exists that can diminish or altogether eradicate the need for fossil fuels and coal deposits. This simple yet advanced technology could be put in place within five years' time, if it were not being suppressed by those who still stand to fill their pockets and fulfill their legacy. This legacy will not pass to the next generation, because the Earth will not support it. You are the generation of beings who will shift the present course so that the future will exist for generations to come. I have little to no concern for my body, as it is a manifestation of the will of All That Is, just as yours is; I am timeless and for all time, as are you. That being said, my body (the Earth) is a crystalline jewel and you are its star-studded crown. Must it perish?

Look to the thoughts, opinions and decisions you make this year. Are they supportive of who you are? Are they supportive of the Earth and its (your) future? I remind you in this moment that you are not separate from the Earth (from me); it only appears that way so that our experience is full and eventful. The elements, seasons and kingdoms of the Earth desire to restore balance as much as you do. Together, with integrity and partnership, miracles can be accomplished; alone, it is near impossible.

RELATIONSHIPS

Many relationships have suffered over the past few years. These are the victims and casualties of a collapsing third dimension. Relationships that were or are solely based upon third-dimensional agreements with no hope of transcending, transitioning or evolving have suffered the most. What is wrong with relationships that are based upon and within third-dimensional understanding? Nothing, because they are based upon absolutely nothing. The absolute is the *no thing*, but nothing (no thing) is absolute, except change. Relationships that were or are based upon an understanding that includes a steadfast unwillingness to change or evolve are not absolute; they are tenuous, uncertain and subject to collapse.

The third dimension is collapsing because it cannot evolve any more than it already has; its structure has been compromised. Most of humanity desires to continue the evolutionary process by which discovery of divine perfection leads to unity and oneness. The third dimension has carried this process as far as it can and is now ready to pass the baton. Third-dimensional relationships have structure but little purpose, agreement but not cooperation, understanding but not vision; a 3D relationship is a meeting of the mind but not of the heart.

If the third dimension is collapsing, why have we not moved beyond it? Because its collapse is a process, not an event. Opening or closing a door is also a process, determined by the size (expanse) and weight (density) of the door (threshold), as well as by how wide open it is held (angle of ascent) and for how long (time and space). Dimensions, densities and energetic doorways are subject to the same universal laws that govern structure and form. Higher dimensions are subject to the same truths as lower dimensions. These laws are applied in equal measure in every instance. In other words, the energetic doors to the higher dimensions open proportionately to both the hold and resistance to the hold of the third dimension. As long as there is energy invested in relationships and ideas with structure and without purpose, the third dimension is upheld. It remains in a continual state of collapse, contraction and contrition. Can you see why so many relationships appear to be in peril of collapsing but continue on for some inexplicable reason?

You cannot rid yourself of 3D relationships simply by dumping them on the side of the road on your way to the higher dimensions. Doing so will simply cause you to carry them with you, making your own load more difficult to bear. The higher dimensions are intended to lighten your density, not to make it more burdensome. The first step then is to lighten your relationships whenever and wherever possible. Loosen the cords and strings that bind you to others, especially in difficult and contractual relationships, be they personal, business or spiritual. This decision alone will bring a marked improvement to almost every relationship. Next, take an inventory of your relationships. Which ones are most stuck in 3D? Which ones seem to have the most potential for advancement? Which ones do you have the most energy invested in, for better or worse? Which ones have you already released? Where have you forgotten to remind yourself or the other party that there are no more strings attached?

An Energy Garden

Once you have taken a mental and emotional inventory, you can begin to choose where and with whom you want to place your energy. Think of your energy as seeds you would like to plant and each potential relationship as a garden. Will this garden welcome your seeds? Will you be free to come and go while the garden is cultivated? Can this garden be easily tended when weeds threaten it? Does it have the potential to grow and expand? This simple exercise will assist you to look beyond the immediate (present) and into the potential (future) of each relationship you have or are considering. Place your awareness where the Earth is most fertile, the elements most supportive and the sunlight the brightest. What about your other relationships? Yes, those. Accept them when you can, bear them when you are able, free them when you are ready, show them the way when they appear lost and release them when the light becomes so dim that you can no longer see one another's light and only shadow remains.

Of what consequence is mastery of relationships in 2003? Simply this: The third-dimensional threshold announces the way to the fourth and fifth dimensions this year as never before. Beginning with the month of February and each subsequent month thereafter, the shift becomes more pronounced, as will the collapse of 3D, which might manifest as a breakdown in communication between countries, distance between friends, anger within families and scorn where desire once existed. Read contracts carefully, as even strong pillars will crumble to dust this year. Seek permanence through commitment to compassion rather than in contracts that are only veiled in ignorance.

The third dimension will give way to the fifth dimension via the fourth. Dimensions are not linear and they are not solid; they are manifestations of light based upon expansions of energy. The lighter the density, the more expansive the energy. One dimension is not better than another, and each serves a purpose. The fourth dimension builds a stairway to the fifth; it provides the blueprints and the architecture for the fifth dimension. It is the planning, managing and support for the fifth. Devic energies, as well as many of your guides, direct themselves from the fourth dimension because they are most able to help you build your dreams and desires from there, do you see?

Soon you will move beyond the third dimension, through the fourth on your way to manifesting yourself and your desires in the fifth dimension. The fifth dimension is less glamorous and more down-to-earth than the third, even though the energies are finer. That is because the 5D energies manifest as crystalline rather than carbon-based light. This form of light is more fluid and balanced, and it requires less effort to maintain or sustain light frequencies. Lightbodies and light structures are an aspect of the fifth dimension.

The fifth dimension is your future and it is your Now. As an aspect of All That Is, you exist in all dimensions at once, although you only manifest yourself in some dimensions. Your awareness will assist you in placing your energies appropriately this year. Allow yourself to flow and float between dimensions whenever possible. It might be time for a spiritual yard sale, but resist the temptation to jettison all of your third-dimensional belongings. Even comets have stardust trailing behind them.

YEAR OF DIVERSITY

Relationships are defined by specific frequencies or currents of energy that describe different aspects of the One. Calendar cycles are subject to these same influences, and 2003 will not be an exception. Frequencies and vibrations are tools of reference that are based upon a common understanding, an unseen language of energy. Relationships that are unstable do not share common vibratory patterns, making it more difficult to speak the same language. When individuals with different customs and preferences do not understand one another, they often raise their voices, which lowers their vibration—making it even more difficult to communicate with one another.

Communication, or lack thereof, will be a central theme in 2003 for a variety of reasons, including many that have been enumerated throughout this text. How you choose to relate to this theme will, to some degree, affect many of your interests and concerns. You might find that your energy and vitality will be more stable if you are able to resist the urge to polarize your thoughts. Two thousand and three will be an energetic, outgoing year, and you will find that you have many thoughts and opinions about what is taking place. Some events will have specific relevance to you and some will not. Take care not to jump to a conclusion or an attitude that does not relate to you or the world you envision, because this will cause you to become polarized or attached to an outcome, do you see?

Imagine that you are dining at a restaurant and that guests who are seated at a nearby table are having an unpleasant experience. Does that unpleasant experience affect you, and if so, how? If you decide that it does indeed affect you, you must make a choice. You can choose to ignore the situation altogether, you can offer your assistance, you can join in the upset, you can leave the establishment or you can shift the energies via another expression of goodwill. All these choices are worth considering. You might also choose to participate in a different frequency altogether, instantly shifting your polarity and environment along with it. This choice allows you to remain compassionately detached as well as intentionally influential. Two thousand and three will highlight choice as it relates to intention versus intervention. Intention allows you to hold an energetic, impartial and enlightened worldview. It acknowledges that change is present, forthcoming and sometimes chaotic, but it does not call for you to become pulled into a melee of thoughts, concerns and fears that will bind you to polarity. Intervention is both a conscious and unconscious choice to participate in an event or a reality, based upon a polarization of one or more directions. It acknowledges that one thought, idea or act is better or more important than another. Neither choice is right or wrong and both are simply states of being, but even choice involves polarity.

Are you to ignore the ills of the world, the potential conflicts of war, the economies of doubt and so on? No, but you will find that you accomplish far more with intent to become, desire to serve, acknowledgment of presence and opportunity for being than you can by allowing yourself to be pulled into the lower vibrational matrices that will abound this year. When in doubt, choose forgiveness, forbearance and fortitude of spirit. This alone will sustain you. Support what you truly treasure and love the rest into oblivion. Nature is complex in its demonstration of variety, but it is the epitome of simplicity in its display of the majesty that exists within each individual moment. This year is but a moment, a simple truth that I leave you with.

Meet the Neighbors

January 2003

W hen was the last time you approached your neighbors with more than a cursory greeting? Do you really know who they are? They might seem no different than a passer-by, but what if they are? The universe is littered with stars and cosmic dust that will one day combine with other aspects of All That Is and form new worlds. This world (the Earth) is littered with energies, vibrations, frequencies, dimensions and beingness that are defining a new face for humanity and its future.

The Earth (my body) is home to many invited guests, of which you are one. Some are dignitaries from other worlds, while others are from the future or the ancient past. At face value, it is difficult to discern who is who, given the wide range of influence the Earth is fortunate enough to receive. This means that your unenlightened neighbor, your unworthy brother-in-law or your unconscious friend might not be exactly what you think. Given the diversity of the participating population, know that the sideways glances and astonished expressions you reserve for your neighbors are also reserved for you!

When Halloween (All Hallow's Eve) comes around each year, young and old alike dress in clothing designed to disguise their normal appearance. They play roles unlike their own, change their speech and generally show off aspects of themselves you would otherwise not see. Well, the Earth has now been decorated for a party such as has never been seen before. It is a masquerade ball, and most of the invited guests are in costume. The roles they now assume have been selected specifically and individually, and accommodations have been arranged for all players. Would you not assume that at least some of your neighbors are part of such a grand production?

Here I present to you a menagerie of folk much like yourself—except that they are different. How different is a matter of perception and given to personal interpretation. Perhaps you will find a bit of yourself in each category that I list and perhaps you will write your own category. I only list a token few, just enough to tickle your senses and expand your awareness. On the surface, it might be difficult to know who is who, but gods playing at being God will eventually reveal themselves to one another. In the meantime, I offer you this playbill, in no particular order, to both educate and amuse you.

SCIENCE BENDERS:
RENEGADES WITHIN THE SCIENTIFIC COMMUNITIES

Science benders are the self-acknowledged renegades within the scientific communities. They are scattered here and there and are defined by their less-than-scientific approach in their individual fields. They are less dependent upon empirical evidence than their academic contemporaries and are more apt to take things at face value. Their vocabulary rarely includes words such as "always" and "never," and they are not prone to rely upon the research of others. Their method of discovery is based upon the abstract future rather than the finite past. They often change direction abruptly, retrace steps from different perspectives and search for answers in places where others would not dream of going. It is their desire to undress the universe strand by strand in order to reveal its complex nature as nothing more than the simplest form of beauty.

As their name suggests, science benders bend the rules and laws by which advances of any kind are made. Most have access to higher knowledge beyond that which institutes of higher learning provide. Although the passions of some were born in other lives and other places, it is here and now that they will define themselves. They can be found in all frontiers, including the medical, social and scientific. These renegades will shift perceptions and allegiances if need be; the pursuit and advancement of an open society is their only goal.

Although their numbers vary by country, they are currently in the thousands. Most are well funded, even those whose ideas are far-fetched or seem to go against the grain. They are funded by the wealthy, the eccentric and by those who find investing in the future the greatest possible return on assets. They are supported by world governments and by financial institutions that do not wish to be left behind as the world continues to purge its dross.

What is their work? It varies by individual, by network and by area of concern. For some it is as simple as dispelling and disproving currently accredited facts—an easy task for these brilliant folk. Although, discovering avenues of expression where truth can flourish often proves more difficult. Most societies and cultures are content with their textbooks and their laws; few are interested in rewriting them, especially when it comes to history and science. Science benders have little interest or patience in the societal virtues of the few, preferring instead to busy themselves with expanding the local universe into one giant neighborhood advancement/beautification project. A scientist is someone who is more committed to the process of discovery than most.

Scientists are interested in revealing, participating in and partnering with universal law rather than local law. Science and limitation do not go hand in hand. A flower, a star, a universe and a paradigm can all be described even if they cannot be dissected or defined. Science benders do not depend or rely upon the acceptance or approval of their antiquated counterparts; they are too busy designing a sustainable future for generations to come. Their interests are both selfish and selfless, as many wish to return to the Earth at a later date. They do not evaluate or judge their work, and rarely do they allow others to do so. As long as they continue to find value in their work, they assume that others will do the same.

Not all science benders are currently working in their field; many are in support positions or awaiting specific guidance. Some are here to open doors for those who will walk through them. Even this is no small task, given the density that holds back or delays the slightest advancement. The world does not always welcome or embrace the new, especially when even the smallest contradiction can topple a career or an empire. Science benders support those who, like you, have a vision that transcends time, space, thought and dimension. They will continue to bring their discoveries to the public forum, for only here can they spring to life.

PEDDLERS OF FEAR: CLINGING TO THE OLD

Peddlers of fear cling to the old because they fear the new. They will tell you that the new world bodes no better than the old and see no reason to exchange one for another. Their fear is their safety net; it is a perceived form of security and they will continue to cling to it. Should all begin to fall, they believe it is their fear that will both protect and serve them. A life that is steeped in fear is a difficult one. It holds one prisoner in a mind with no walls. Fear is another name for boundary, limitation, belief and disbelief. True fear is stronger than any weapon known to humankind; it is the first and last line of defense. Its barriers are invisible and its power untold.

Fear peddlers cling to the old because they have not found value in the new. For the record—they are not backward, uneducated, irreverant or intolerant, and they are not close-minded. They embrace the old because it has embraced them. Those whose lives are steeped in fear see the surface of the past as smooth and well-worn and the surface of the future as rough and uncharted. If the surface is so unsafe, what can one expect from what lies beneath?

The process they undergo is not wrong, certainly no more so than your own. Their presence is necessary and dear; without them the doors to the past would quickly close and there are yet many things that must be reconciled. Their fear supports a slower passage of time, which allows for gentle change where others would insist upon radical change. Would you rather rebuild sandcastles while gentle waves lap at your ankles or have a tidal wave destroy your city so that you must begin anew? This contemplation is at the root of much fear. Neither choice is incorrect and both are supportive of both old and new paradigms. Fear is a mechanism and a guidance system. When understood as such, it can be used as a tool—a bridge between two or more dimensions, worlds or thoughts.

WISDOM WALKERS:
EXAMPLES OF LIVING WISDOM

Wisdom walkers are examples of living wisdom, whom others would like to emulate. They are teachers but do not think of themselves as such. When asked, they will reluctantly and with great humility share the many initiations that have led them to a place of wholeness, peace and continued self-discovery through self-reflection. They do not think of themselves as teachers, because they have a sense of many facets and experiences as yet unexplored. They live simply and smile often because there is no reason not to. Their energy is magnetic and appealing, especially to those who still rely upon the complexities of life to reveal the hidden secrets and the keys that will free them from their own bondage. By contrast, wisdom walkers have already attained their freedom, having realized that their prison cell always has been open, since prisons are self-imposed limitations whose locks are called beliefs.

Wisdom walkers teach by making their lives examples for others. Some are born leaders while others are not. They can be found in every field and walk of life. Although some choose careers in professional environments with accompanying levels of responsibility, they are more often found in common, mundane or even menial jobs where stress is not a determining factor. These beings have little tolerance for stress, seeing it as the prison from which they have already gained their freedom. They do not often need to be reminded of this lesson a second or third time. If you know people you greatly admire and perhaps even envy while at the same time thinking they are not aspiring to their full potential, take a moment to remember what it is you truly admire about them. What can you learn from them? Is it their aspirations or your own that you are more concerned with? Do they seem to be content and at peace? Do they seem to be more interested in being or in doing? Which of their qualities do you find most attractive? Do you enjoy spending time with them? Is there something you can learn from them?

As the third dimension continues to become less accommodating, the living example of the wisdom walkers and the choices they make will become more appealing. Simple attitudes will no longer be thought of as simple minds. Wisdom walkers are highly adaptable to situations and circumstances that others would find daunting. They will make good allies when your favorite comfort item is suddenly unavailable and the local coffee vendor cannot consistently support your favorite addiction.

FIRE WALKERS:
FIGHTING FOR WHAT IS RIGHT

Fire walkers are brave souls. Individually and collectively they undergo trials and tribulations that often make headlines. Their jobs are rarely easy, and their difficulties are many. Their unique purpose is to bring to light what others would sweep under carpets and stones. Fire walkers assist others and themselves in growth that involves trial by fire. A fire walker is most often found where the laws of man conflict with the laws of the universe. Fire walkers are pacifists, but they are not above breaking laws they believe are contrary to justice. Fire walkers sometimes practice law and sometimes practice going against it. They can be found in the political arena if they are strong enough not to be swallowed. They are activists, economists, environmentalists, mothers, fathers, sisters and brothers. These individuals are not content with believing in what is right; they believe they must stand for it or fight for it as the case might be. They do not know how to back away from a fight, especially from a good one. They will first lead the charge and only later look back to see if there was any additional support behind them.

How can injustice, inconsistent irrelevance and irrational nonsense be adjourned if not by first bringing it to light? If you are not aligned with the will to do it, then who will be? Fire walkers thrive in this arena, though they will most likely tell you that they do not. With a flair for the dramatic and a bit of local bravado, they will emerge as the social heroes of your time. Reform often beats a rather loud drum, but then again so does lack of reform. These individuals are tenacious and will continue to be so even to their last breath.

Fire walkers often find themselves embroiled in cultural conflicts where political doctrine and social injustice do not support the individual or the collective. They care as deeply about the environment as they do about their neighbor's personal difficulties. These individuals rarely know how, where or when to draw the line, which often makes for difficult decisions. Fire walkers carry a flag called justice; it is emblazoned upon their forehead for all to see, and as you might imagine, it is not their first time at this picnic! Fire walkers need no invitation to crash a party where injustice is served as the main course.

EARTH STEWARDS:
CARING DEEPLY ABOUT THE EARTH

Earth stewards sometimes seem more concerned with the condition of the environment and the world that surrounds them than with themselves. They care deeply about the Earth and the viability of its (my) future. They question and assess all that they purchase or consume and do not support or frequent that which does not in some way contribute to the planet and/or its inhabitants. These deeply thoughtful and introspective beings follow a lineage of past lives that has been equally devoted to the Earth; some simply return again and again to continue working where they left off.

Their devotion in terms of Earth stewardship is without compare, but they often sacrifice relationships and other passionate pursuits in favor of the work they believe is their passion. Their physical appearance is mostly youthful and athletic, but their health is often fragile because it is unsupported and taken for granted. When these individuals succumb to their delicate condition, it is most often through cancer and other debilitating diseases.

If Earth stewards are to assist in healing the Earth in this lifetime, they must also make a commitment to healing themselves. Balance in all things must be the rule of the day, and this must of necessity apply to these beings as well. In the past, their greatest allies have been the trees, because here they found the wisdom that often escaped others. However, the baton of wisdom is now being passed on to the mineral kingdom, and it is the crystalline beings who will guide future generations of Earth stewards. Are all beings Earth stewards? Yes and no. Most beings are committed to the regeneration and advancement of the Earth and its kingdoms, but ask yourself how many will go to great lengths to save a neighborhood tree or the ground squirrel and woodpecker who live there.

PLANET X, Y AND Z FOLK:
MISFITS OF THE UNIVERSE

Planet X, Y and Z folk sometimes look like the misfits of the universe. They do not seem to fit here, there or anywhere. It is difficult to describe these individuals, much less to catalog or stereotype them—a fact that seems to provide endless satisfaction to an otherwise ho-hum existence. They are interested in any form of underground news and information, particularly the kind that describes the covert activities of individuals, societies, governments and nations. No subject is too complex for these intelligent individuals, whose brain activity would be considered off the charts if measured appropriately. Planets X, Y and Z appropriately designate no planet and all planets, for these beings do not claim a specific home or heritage. Instead, they travel the local universe searching for intelligent forms of life or items of technological interest to be peddled elsewhere at a later time.

Although it would seem that these beings have little or nothing to offer in service to others, this is not true. Their vibration carries an omniuniversal quality that assists in dimensionalizing your world. For the most part, they are impervious to the brain-laundering activities of the later twentieth and early twenty-first century. They find these techniques laughable and quotable but not very useful. They wonder why you put up with it and suggest anarchy as a viable alternative, if for no other reason than that it would make interesting headlines. These individuals can easily become addicted to stimulants, especially coffee, although the relative effect of these drugs is sometimes the opposite of what one would expect.

For the most part, these are solitary individuals, although they can be said to belong to a much larger collective. As their brothers, sisters, cousins and colleagues begin to arrive via unconventional means, the majority of the population will look up in astonished wonder, but these individuals will simply say, "I told you so."

SHAPE SHIFTERS:
DEFYING CONVENTIONALITY

Shape shifters defy all conventionality. Rather than fix what is broken, they will destroy and re-create it. They see no reason to remain in the same form or live within the same format day after day, year after year. If they are not happy with their shape or their environment, they will change it. Isn't this true of everyone? No—and certainly not with the frequency and creativity that these individuals are capable of. They belong to an energetic collective that emphasizes and strives for transcendence via shifting attitudes, beliefs, relationships, careers and more. There is no limit to what these beings can accomplish once they tap into the source of their gift.

To be fair—they do not often begin life with such awareness. Their beginnings are often humble and their surroundings simple. They are born into circumstances that they must transcend if they are to survive. Dysfunction, limitation, fear and stress are but a few of the issues a shape shifter must confront early on in order to hone his or her specific skill. Where others make peace with difficult moments and situations, agreeing to live with or abide by them, these beings do not. They have an ability to transcend adversity, limitation and the oblique. Shape shifters do not often call upon an easy childhood, and their adolescence is often one of constant searching. By adulthood they realize that they cannot change their circumstances or adjust to a reality based upon varying degrees of discomfort. A nagging dissatisfaction will eventually promote looking inward, and here they will discover what they could not find elsewhere.

Shape shifters influence and are influenced by more than one world and one reality. They seek fairness, balance and equality in all things—obsessively so.

They are at home in a changing and changeable world, though they will most likely tell you that they both fear and abhor change. When the weather is bleak, they will either blow the clouds away or go elsewhere, in more ways than one. Unsatisfactory relationships are just cause for redecorating the soul and reinventing the environment. Should this option become impossible, they will sometimes offer their life for adoption; in other words, they might make their body available to a being who is willing to "walk in" to a life in order to further his or her own growth or that of another. This falls within acceptable parameters that honor all forms of life and all decisions within the uniqueness that is life.

These beings are not simply survivors; they are creators in a creative world. They are artists, writers, travelers, actors and weavers of lives fully lived. What they cannot physically experience, they will imagine into existence, making the unreal real—for a moment or a lifetime. They are here to help imagine and then create a new world. As this world begins to fade, they will engage the transcendent qualities of the universe and sprout the means to begin anew.

PILLARS OF STRENGTH: BRINGING STABILITY

Pillars of strength, as the name implies, are personal and planetary reinforcements who bring stability to an unstable world. They are the Rock of Gibraltar in your life. It does not matter how spiritual they are or even how awakened, evolved or dedicated to consciousness they seem to be. It only matters that they are here too. In an emergency, you might wish to be with them; surely, they would know what to do. And it's true. They understand how things are put together, so they know what to do when they seem to fall apart. These individuals are at home with both logic and emotion, and they know how to navigate the challenges inherent in each. They seem partial to the third dimension, because they have spent eons of time studying and participating in it. They will tell you this world will last forever; they will say that the most fit will survive. But when push comes to shove, it is the weak and the helpless they will be ready to assist.

These individuals are the warriors of times long gone. They are the chivalrous knights and the Joan of Arcs. Their traits are not gender-based, but they are righteous and forthright. They will not attack, but they will defend; they will not speak harshly, and they will not allow others to do so either. Pillars of strength will continue to support and uphold the laws of man until these no longer support humankind; then they will look to another authority, within themselves. Their true power lies not in their strength but in their ability to see clearly. Their past is littered with deception and illusion but their path is not.

Pillars are stalwart. They are dependable, faithful, sturdy and loyal. Do you know such people? It is likely that you do; in case you do not, be on the lookout for them. They are disguised in all walks of life and in every form imaginable. Often they come to the aid of those they fear or resist. Why? So they can learn to lean on others as well as to be leaned upon. Even a sturdy tree must learn to sway with the breeze. Their future will be like yours, only different. One day soon you will see with their eyes and they will see with yours. If you know such beings, do not hurry them into your dimensional tasks and beliefs; they will arrive in a timing based upon their own divinity.

EMISSARIES OF LIGHT: HEALERS OF TIMELINES

Emissaries of light are from your future—the future of the Earth and any other fifth-dimensional world you will come to know. They have moved backward in linear time in order to assist the reconstruction of a different outcome here on Earth. They are here to spare humanity many of the catastrophes that would otherwise prevail. What catastrophes? The ones the emissaries of light have already lived through—not once but many times. They are not catastrophe experts as much as healers of timelines, ascensions of planets and other multidimensional births of consciousness. You might say that if the catastrophe were an earthquake, for instance, these beings would know where all the faults are, what to shore up and when to evacuate. These beings are teachers and their wisdom is unparalleled at this time.

They are leaders, ambassadors, counselors and directors, but not in the traditional sense. You will not find these individuals rallying those around them to participate in public displays that mock the status quo or incite further discontent. These gentle and quiet beings instill confidence in those around them. They promote wellness by living it and inspire others to listen to their own counsel before seeking that of others. If they do make a suggestion, it will often be accompanied by a variety of perspectives as well as a glimpse into the past, present and future of any given situation. These beings are educators in the grandest sense, because their experience has been rich, varied and expansive compared to your own. They have nothing to teach you, and you have little to learn from their current life upon Earth, which has more than likely been simple and uneventful (this might not be the case with their current Earth relatives).

Emissaries of light propose the impossible and envision the improbable by current Earth standards. Those within earshot of their simple words often come away believing that these beings are out of step with reality and either a throwback to the distant past or a purveyor of an impossible and unrealistic future. These beings are from the future, so how could it be otherwise? They have seen what you have not and have lived to tell about it. Look for these gentle souls in your neighborhoods, precincts and parishes. They have no religion, no belief, no judgment, no political platform and only a smidgen of self-interest. Their interest lies within your heart, which is one of the reasons they speak so softly. They speak at a volume that is aligned with an aspect of your future and is found only in the heart.

CONSCIOUSNESS SEEKERS:
AWAKENINGS IN LARGE NUMBERS

Consciousness seekers are everywhere today. They are awakening at alarming rates—and not a moment too soon! Just like the storybook dwarves they come in several themes and varieties, of which Grumpy and Sleepy are all too common. Other varieties include Cloudy, Itchy, Angry, Troubled, Enchanted and Disenchanted, and more varieties awaken every day. These beings have been in human bodies for a very long time.

Density still rules the body and the mind because it is the heart that awakens first. When an unfulfilled heart cries out, the soul convenes a panel to see what can be done to ease the heart's pain as well as to promote growth, healing and experience. During this perspective, the soul often calls upon guides, angels, higher beings of light, healing energies and other forms of wisdom from a variety of paradigms and places in order to review the soul's code. Each soul is endowed with a panel or host of beings and energies to draw upon. Each soul's code is like a very specific map, and no two are alike. Scattered throughout this map are a variety of opportunities designed to propel consciousness and dispel unconsciousness. How, when and where these influences are inserted is up to the entourage of guidance provided to each soul as well as to the individual or group soul association.

Unprecedented numbers of souls are awakening now, because many other opportunities were bypassed for reasons of importance to the individual soul. "Wake me when it's over!" is not an uncommon statement among those who are now struggling to their feet. "It's not time yet," is another all too common response. But the heart is hungry now, and only an awakened soul can satisfy this type of hunger. Those who awaken now are like Rip Van Winkle, finding themselves in a new world and wondering how it could have eluded them this long. Be patient and tolerant with them; they will yet encounter many growing pains as they attempt to free themselves from the distractions that have captivated them.

THRILL SEEKERS:
ENJOYING THE RIDE

Thrill seekers are those who enjoy the physical and emotional roller coaster rides that most abhor. Are you one? Thrill seekers are here for the ride. They sit back in amusement while the world around them turns somersaults and attempts to right itself. They are not concerned with their retirement account or lack thereof and yawn when the conversation becomes too heated and opinionated. They are here to see how it all turns out, waiting for the imaginary moment when the roller coaster comes to a screeching halt. These individuals often upset others who feel pushed to the brink of diplomacy, but this only serves to invigorate them even more. They are here for the fireworks and they intend to have front-row seats. They have an important part to play, which will not seem obvious until it is almost too late.

Roller coasters by nature instill unreal fear; it is a thrill ride, after all. Illusion is another word for fear that is not real. A perception of impending doom triggers the imagination to stimulate the brain, which in turn produces adrenaline and other physical, chemical-like substances that perpetuate the event. Since the danger was never real but only imagined, the body relaxes and the mind celebrates the event. That is how these individuals perceive the present you share. They laugh in the face of fear while others quietly seethe at their unbelievable impertinence, and they believe they will have the last laugh. In the meantime, they extend their good humor to those who welcome it and thumb their noses at those who do not.

SPIRIT WALKERS:
ACKNOWLEDGING MIRACLES

Spirit walkers are ethereal beings, here one moment and gone the next. Who are they? Some are angels disguised as humans and others are humans disguised as angels. These beings seem to have little or no identity of their own, but they are quite interested in yours. They appear out of nowhere with the right words or the right job for a moment or for a day. They disappear as quickly as they appeared and rarely wait around long enough to be thanked. They are not here to perform miracles but are here to acknowledge them. A miracle is a creative moment that, once acknowledged, becomes physical. Many are not able to acknowledge miracles, and most do not know where they are or how to find them.

Spirit walkers are energies who have manifested bodies temporarily to suit a need or serve a purpose. They are not of this world—at least not any longer—but they are more than happy to participate in it for a time. They alone decide what brings them here and how long they will stay. A moment, a day, a month or a year are all appropriate, given the right motivation. If you are fortunate enough to have met such an individual, be grateful; these occurrences are few and far between and not intended for all. These individuals bring hope to the hopeless and rekindle faith in the faithless.

Do you have need of such individuals? Where can you find them? They exist out of time and out of place but within each of you. They are directors of fate and bringers of destiny, but they cannot replace that which you are.

Those who encounter spirit walkers have for the most part also had an encounter with themselves. Spirit walkers will not twist your arm or point you in a specific direction, but they will touch and inspire what was there all along, as long as you are willing to do the same. If you truly desire such an encounter, ask yourself if you are really willing to experience yourself as you are—in other words, to tell the truth about who and what you are. That is the only prerequisite, but it is unalterable and the aftereffects are permanent. What do you long for? What are you willing to be in order to manifest it? This is a good place to start.

WHAT WILL BE YOUR PART?

The world around you is much different than your physical perceptions often tell you. The nomenclature I have offered here is but a sampling of your surrounding environment. Would you be willing to look at it differently? The person who lives next door might be the extraterrestrial you have been longing to meet; the bank teller might be an angel in disguise and the acquaintance or friend you argue with might be a thrill seeker rather than the expletive that often comes to mind. There is something to learn and gain from each experience and from every encounter; if there was not, you would be having experiences elsewhere.

Watch carefully now as the scenery begins to change and the actors change parts. Award season quickly approaches and the nominations are many. What category do you best associate with? Where would you wish to be? What part will you play and how well are you willing to play it? Most of you have been auditioning your entire lives, but for whom? Who is the director and who has cast the role you play? Your fortune awaits and your destiny is assured—will you not then offer only your best?

The Earth
Kingdoms Speak

Gaia, the Plant and Vegetable Kingdom, the Animal Kingdom
and the Mineral Kingdom
February 2003

When I first encountered the channel [Pepper] many years ago, I did so cautiously, taking great care not to startle any of the delicate growth that was taking place within her. Above all, I desired to be understood and to collaborate on projects that would expand awareness worldwide of who and what Gaia sentience is. I decided early on to guide her through several steps in the discovery process by attuning her individually to each Earth kingdom. One by one we explored the plant and vegetable kingdom, the mineral kingdom and the animal kingdom. Later on, as she became acutely aware of the subtle nuances within each kingdom, we explored in great detail the responsibility that each kingdom carries, as well as the role that each has been assigned at this critical juncture for both Earth and humankind.

There were no lessons, only encounters and experiences; each being (when applicable) spoke for itself. I did not offer myself in my fullness as I do now, for fear of overwhelming or overburdening one who had as yet not consciously agreed to any responsibility or charge. Although the decision had already been made at the soul level many lifetimes ago, it was imperative to allow this lifetime's personality the freedom to renew its choice—for if not, what place would free will have in this or any other life? She was not immediately aware of the presence of more than one being. Her interactions and encounters were brief and childlike at first, nurturing moments with a grandfather tree and magical episodes with faeries disguised as hummingbirds and butterflies. Each offered a glimpse into another world or dimension as well as a view of the past, present and future. Each shared a vision of happier times as well as a path that led to the return of such times.

These experiences both saddened and gladdened her heart and helped form the foundation from which her commitment to bring awareness of a sentient, self-realized and self-guided Earth continues to this day. I share this brief history with you in order to prepare you for similar experiences. I can say with certainty that your experiences will more than likely be grander and fuller, because many years have passed since what I have related took place. Those years have been active and interactive, and much growth has taken place on your part and on mine. The Earth is not as it was or what it was, just as you are much different than you were a few short years ago.

The physical Earth and the (my) sentience that directs it both need and desire restructuring if they mean to transcend the dimension that would otherwise destroy them. Humanity will soon follow suit and claim its rightful place as a divine race rather than a forgotten one. While restructuring takes place at a submolecular level and a nonlinear pace, its results are observable at an experiential level. As I did long ago, I now bring you a direct, but not so subtle experience of each kingdom. Each offers its own collective voice, and I suggest that you receive it as such, as long as you do not perceive it as separate from the sentience that understands itself as whole. Your mind and your heart are unique and distinct from each other, yet the soul nurtures both as one.

The Plant and Vegetable Kingdom Speaks

Our words and our voices are collective. We seem to you so different from one another, because a tree is not a flower and a flower is not a vegetable. This is true, but we are not as different as you might imagine, and you are not as different from one another either. We choose to honor that which unites us and celebrate that which makes us unique. Humanity would do well to follow this example, and it is our hope that it will. It is with a little apprehension that we share these words with you, because we do not wish to be perceived as critical of another kingdom. We are as actors in a supporting role; we are here to benefit, assist and sustain the other kingdoms. We are a natural resource, a sentient extension of the physical planet. That is to say, we are self-aware as individual species and as the collective consciousness you call the plant kingdom. Our awareness allows us to be in communication with many other species, and we are vibrationally attuned to the needs of the other kingdoms, because this is aligned with our purpose.

SUPPORTING ALL LIFE ON PHYSICAL EARTH

Our purpose is to support the physical Earth and all life upon and within it. We understand ourselves to be a renewable resource, and we delight in the many and varied uses by which we are employed. For instance, we are pleased to offer ourselves medicinally when appropriate and necessary. Healing is of great interest to us, and many of our plant species have as-yet-undiscovered properties that we are eager to share with you. Interestingly, some of these properties would be considered controversial and most likely illegal within your cultures due to their narcotic influence. Still, these plants, or rather the fibers within them, would be of great benefit to you because they are self-healing, meaning that they are aware of the purpose for which they are being introduced into a system or body.

This kind of intelligence would make the healing process quicker and more effective, because communication between two or more sentient systems would take place and not delay or dull the process of healing as is common today. Toxic shock happens when there is an inability to send or receive healing communication messages by one or more aspects of physical beingness. An impasse is created when the body believes an invasion of grand proportions is about to descend upon the very system it has sworn to defend. When one kingdom is unable to recognize another as a mirror of its own perfection, difficulty, disaster and death often follow. This is true at all levels of experience—the physical, the superphysical and the supraphysical. Our experience has proven this over time, as has our interaction with all levels of matter and nonmatter within each kingdom and each Earth element.

FEEDING ALL WHO HUNGER FOR PLANTS AND VEGETABLES

As individual species we are guided and influenced to respond in one or more ways. We are influenced, for instance, to feed as many as hunger for what we offer. To that end, we allow ourselves to ingest the chemical formulations that are offered into our soil and water, although we would prefer to reject these. We do not possess individual will; that is to say, as individual plants we cannot choose to reject what we are fed. We are destined to allow nature to take its course; however, we trust in the longevity, rejuvenation and regeneration of this sentient planet (our home) to sustain and guide us through uncertain times such as these.

We don't mind that we are consumed or otherwise utilized to benefit humanity and the other kingdoms. This allows us to serve the purpose for which we were created (grown). We would prefer to be consumed completely so there would be less waste, though. In fact, if this were the case, there would be little or no waste, because most species have been organically designed to benefit the Earth in many ways that are still misunderstood. It has been our experience that the current mindset among those who study us slow our evolution and yours more than the deleterious environmental quality that surrounds all present-day kingdoms.

THRIVING WHEN HUMANS DO

Our kingdom, which consists of plants, trees, seeds, fruits, vegetables, roots, leaves, fronds, stems, flowers and all of the byproducts of these, including those released into the air, water, soil and consumed by fire, composes these words that now reach you. This same collective voice acknowledges our kinship to you and the other kingdoms. We thrive when you do, and our conscious awareness transcends when yours does. The most evolved within our species are those whose purpose is fully understood and implemented. There is little differentiation as to whether we are serving to cleanse the liver of carcinogenic toxins or delivering a fragrant sense of well-being to a stunned or lonely heart. Our simple desire is to be in communion with all life at a cellular, transformative level.

We exist only in the present moment. We are fully aware and sentient of our permanence in the present moment, but we have no awareness of the future as you do. A cabbage, for instance, is aware of its roots and every nuance of the soil that supports it. It is aware of its growth and its purpose, its neighbors in the garden and all of the elements that support it. It is aware that its purpose serves a greater good. Upon maturity, it experiences a transformation as it is taken from the garden and introduced into a different environment, and it experiences yet another transformation when it is consumed and experienced by another kingdom. All of these experiences take place as cellular sentience; they belong to the species and to the kingdom.

We are aware that you are concerned with your future, yet we wonder: If that is the case, why are you not concerned with the present? It is one of the many aspects about humanity we do not understand. For our part, we will continue to offer ourselves as we do—fully, completely and in unconditional service to that which we call "great wonder." We are content to be what we are.

The Animal Kingdom Speaks

We offer these words in one of your commonly used languages. We speak in many tongues and make many sounds, but our most common method of communication is what you would call body language. You also speak this language, more often than you think, but sometimes prefer to use words to say what you mean, even when your eyes and your body contradict them. In our language, there is no subtle misconception, no attempt to deceive. When we are hungry, our intentions are well known, and even under the cover of brush or darkness, our energy emits a frequency that speaks what words could not say.

COMMUNICATING AT AN ENERGETIC LEVEL

Many of us are predators, and many humans are too. But our methods of hunting and our attempts to feed our hungry families differ in many important ways. For instance, our body language and our vibration might say the following: "I am a mother, and I must feed my hungry children. I honor your life force and the choice you have made to place yourself before me. By taking your life, I further honor you, as I will place your life force into my own body and that of my young."

Does every species within our kingdom offer these thoughts prior to taking a life? No, because not all species are self-aware. Still, within what you call animal instinct, there is a communication that exists at an energetic level. Humanity does not like to think of itself as predatory, and it is likely that you prefer to call yourself a consumer.

We are considered the closest to the human kingdom in brain capacity and development. We understand that you consider some of our primate species a distant relative of the human race. We hope you will not take offense if we do not always think that is a compliment! Those who volunteer themselves into your experimental care do so by choice, and those who make attempts at communicating with you via symbolic language do the same. You believe that science is investigating nature, but of necessity nature must turn a wary eye toward science. Volunteers from every species participate in your experiments and live among you as you see fit. It is a collaborative effort on both our parts, though many times what is learned seems to be of little benefit or significance to either of us.

Our history is as varied as yours. Many of us are native to this planet, but some species were born elsewhere, genetically speaking. We find it interesting (and fortunate) that your predatory instincts find little interest in species that have origins elsewhere. It appears that what is not in your cellular memory holds little or no interest to you, so in some ways, our paths are parallel but do not intersect. We are interested in the present and the future but have no interest in reconstructing our past. This is not because we are only interested in the survival of our individual species, but because we understand that perfection has brought us to this moment and will carry us beyond it. Development within the animal kingdom takes place at a different level of experience than for humans. We understand this and do not begrudge the many paths humanity takes in its effort to understand who and what it is while expanding in awareness.

LACK OF CONCERN FOR ANIMALS CAN BECOME A CONCERN FOR HUMANS

What concerns us most as a species? The longevity of certain species, the departure of some of our companions, the encroaching of humanity into habitats that are precious and already few and the lack of awareness with which our game animals are seized and thought of as wholesale commodities. Are we advocating that you become vegetarians in order to save our numbers? No—we understand your needs because we understand our own, but a severe lack of concern for us could soon become a concern for yourselves. When one species or kingdom turns upon another, the result is often disastrous for both. Already there are viruses, infections and other anomalies within the game animals you consider a part of your food supply. This is not simply due to poor handling but to a true breakdown of communication between and within species. True respect and communication support interspecies and intraspecies wellness, whereas lack of respect and poor communication breed illness, which when ignored or unattended complicates issues further. We place no blame but simply offer this topic for your consideration as the opportunity to speak our truth has presented itself.

Species Are Debating whether to Withdraw

We know that you are concerned about our ocean-dwelling friends, and with good reason. Their good will toward humanity has not been met with much kindness in return. You marvel at the oceans—the depth, beauty and color and the myriad life forms found within—but you take their permanence for granted, and it is no longer guaranteed. Levels of awareness within each species allow them to make collective choices. The continued presence of certain species, even those who number in the thousands, is not assured. Historic precedence has little ground to stand upon, for never before have so many adjustments been necessary within so many species.

There is confusion within even the most sentient of species, and the choice to withdraw en masse is being debated at an energetic level. This choice could severely affect humanity and the rest of the Earth kingdoms. What if some of the integral cells of your body departed all at once? Your body would be forced to re-create itself—if indeed that were possible. Cells normally used for one function would have to be deployed elsewhere immediately, and a state of emergency would exist in your body. The same would be true of the oceans; after all, they are bodies of water. Collectively, we hope that this is not the case. It is our further hope that humanity's continued pattern of awakening brings up the care and concern that this subject deserves, for alone we can do nothing.

We have more in common with you than your daily experience would offer. Although our present-day circumstances may be very different, our future is more alike than not. We are both dependent upon the Earth for our survival, but beyond that we are dependent upon one another if we are to evolve in consciousness and awareness. You believe that your development as a species is tied to the chronology of the stars and what they will bring, but do not forget that viewed from space, the Earth also appears as a star. If you wish to learn, gain, grow and expand based upon what you hope to learn from others, would you not wish for something to share or demonstrate in return?

The Mineral Kingdom Speaks

We are the oldest kingdom of record. It is true that we are an Earth kingdom, but we are also much more than that. The diversity of our resources encompasses a vast part of the universe. Many of you are more comfortable living in one geographic area than another. Although you might believe that it is the breathtaking coastline, the open plains or the forest canopy that draws you there, it is more likely that the composition of what is underneath the ground (the support) is what keeps you there.

The Earth is a composite of universal particles of density that created its physical mass. This composite is not distributed evenly but in uniquely and strategically placed energetic vortexes. These seeming anomalies give the Earth the diversity with which to enrich itself. They also serve as passive/active receptive/conductive force fields of energy that channel universal energy to everything that exists upon and within the Earth. The radiation from the Sun maximizes these energies—intensifying, lessening and stimulating their effect in order to promote accelerated growth of all that is within the Earth's influence. These force fields of energy can influence an increase or decrease in the population of any species. They also influence how you relate to your environment, because as a sentient species, you "track" these energies everywhere you go. The reason for you feeling at home in one crowded city over another might therefore lie in what is underneath you, the substrate material of the Earth or the content and influence of the mineral kingdom.

ALIGNING WITH THE MINERAL KINGDOM FOR A SMOOTH TRANSITION

Our influence upon and between other kingdoms will soon be taking center stage. Each cosmic age ushers in shifts and changes. Just as humanity is experiencing an awakening of sorts, global warming and other environmental phenomena are awakening a purposeful call within the mineral kingdom to increase the flow of energy that it receives from the core of the Earth. This stimulation affects the entire kingdom, but most specifically the crystalline threads that weave specific energetic patterns throughout the globe.

It is no surprise that quartz movements govern your watches and timepieces and that organic and artificial silicon powers your computers. As the twenty-first century continues to evolve, one age will close and another will begin. Although these transitions are natural occurrences, how harsh or smooth they are upon humanity somewhat depends upon how aligned humanity becomes in relation to both its physical and nonphysical environments. The mineral kingdom relates to humanity in both physical and nonphysical ways. Our kingdoms are joined, and one is never far or separate from the other. Human bodies contain minerals that are also relative to the Earth; even the levels that support balance and well-being are in ratio with that of the Earth. It must be noted that as the Earth continues to have its resources depleted, humanity will as well. If the Earth falls out of balance, humanity will do the same. Evidence of this is already in your midst, so it is likely that these words will come as no surprise. If you wish to strengthen your bodies, it is advisable to supplement your diets with minerals; would it then not also make sense to supplement the Earth's reserves rather than deplete them?

What Is the Interior of the Earth Like?

A variety of theories have been put forth regarding the interior of the Earth. These theories have brought up more questions than answers and have stirred up a good deal of controversial rhetoric. In addressing this subject we hope to satisfy curious minds and allay ungrounded fears.

The Earth is hollow in certain places and quite solid in others. Although the Earth is perfect, perfect uniformity would not be an accurate description. Diversity has always been the guiding force in all decisions relative to evolution. Land mass is not evenly distributed throughout the Earth; it is in balance but not uniform. The same applies to the interior of the Earth; it is in balance within the framework of the universal laws that govern it. This means that there is biodiversity of all ecological Earth and universal matter, as well as purposeful development of all species and cultures that make their home within the interior of the planet.

At the very center of the Earth is its core. The core of the Earth is not hollow, but it is nonphysical. It is pure sentient energy that can be compared to the Sun's radiation as it moves outward from the core. It then enters a radiation field that amplifies, disperses, reflects and energizes all life. The radiation field begins the process of physicalizing energy. It has the ability to make the Earth's intent solid or dense. Nonphysical energy moves through and becomes solid energy in crystalline "beds" that grow energy.

This is one of the reasons that the human kingdom finds such attraction to crystals of every kind, magnitude, color and shape. At deep levels of consciousness, you are aware that this is the energy of creation. Your participation with this energy acknowledges your desire to be in balance and for well-being in heart and soul or in physical and nonphysical ways. Each species within the mineral kingdom attracts a very specific form of energy that it then "ensouls." This amplifies the healing and nurturing properties of the energy and personalizes them somewhat. This personalization makes them more or less attractive to you, according to need and desire.

Rocks, crystals, gemstones and precious metals all play a large part in your life. Why are you more interested in yellow gold than white gold, for instance, or less interested in copper than platinum? It is not based entirely on financial or aesthetic value as you might imagine, although heredity and culture certainly influence your societies. Your attraction is based upon polarity and soul origin more than any other criteria, and it is your body's duty as an extension of your soul to make you as comfortable here as possible.

PARTNERING WITH THE MINERAL KINGDOM

The mineral kingdom influences and assists you from within and without; its healing aspect is its nature, and its nature is to heal. Crystalline energy has been used to heal and power the planet before—as an idea it is not novel, though its approach certainly can be. Humanity is beginning to understand in just how many ways quartz can be used. Expanding upon these theories, you will soon come upon other ways to channel rather than harness energy and healing from the minerals.

What is the difference? One method partners the kingdoms, the other places them at odds. Humanity is still at odds with itself over many issues that it must resolve, but the crystals and the energy they will reveal will wait patiently until the time is right.

Crystalline energy will not allow itself to be used in the fashioning of weapons, since this has already proven to be detrimental to all aspects of the Earth. We will lend our efforts to technology but not to weaponry, which has already been tested and found to be true. A mountain does not hurry in creating its summit, because it knows its crowning is assured; there is no other waiting to take its place. The mineral kingdom was the first and it will one day be the last, but that time will yet reveal itself beyond the Now.

It is obvious that the mineral kingdom is the most dense or solid of all, but the properties that govern and direct it are also the subtlest. Humanity's growth has also been subtle in comparison to that of life on other worlds, but that will soon change. Assisted by its partner kingdoms, all will shift into places of higher awareness. It is the desire of the mineral kingdom to make your transition as smooth as possible. We hope you will continue to welcome the assistance we offer you from within, without and underneath. We will continue to make ourselves available to you until instructed to do otherwise by wisdom and intelligence beyond our own.

Gaia Speaks

A s you have welcomed the words of the kingdoms I have offered, one day soon others will welcome a new kingdom into their midst. The next generation of humanity is poised to become the first to be considered genetically divine. These beings will be born beginning in 2007 and will reach maturity in twenty-two years. Their agenda will be explicitly peaceful and their nature expansively creative. They will be engineers and architects, scientists and healers. They will be interested in healing the present and creating the future. You will exclaim and take note of the decidedly violet color of their eyes. Later you will take note of their deeds, which will positively influence your own and confirm the life you have been aspiring to live.

I can no longer offer you "dress rehearsals" in which you improve your costume but not your part, but I remain committed to the evolution of a conscious awareness that will spark your true nature now and always. I am always in your debt, heartfully present and hopelessly underfoot.

Walk Your Way or Walk Away

March 2003

A friend of mine recently joined an organization dedicated to saving the planet and its resources. I feel their work is important and compelling and I am considering becoming involved, but I have doubts and reservations about the methods it employs in getting its point across. For instance, destruction of property and civil unrest is not beyond its scope. I care for the Earth so very much, and there is not much I would not do on its (your) behalf. I would feel better if you would address this as frankly as you have addressed other subjects.

Very well. A candid and frank position on this subject is that I have no immediate need of being saved. The organization you have referred to and others like it have drafted a charter that represents their interests, not mine. Now you must decide whether or not your own interests are being represented. If you find that they are, joining this organization will be the right decision. If, on the other hand, you discover that your interests are not well represented, then other avenues of expression might prove more creative.

In an effort to assist you, we will explore the subject further. Contrary to popular public opinion, neither the planet nor the planet's resources are in need of saving. You cannot save the planet any more than you can save yourself. What would you save it from? Who would you save it from? Who and what would you save it for? Future generations? This is a very popular response, but it is an incomplete one.

The planet cannot be saved by humanity because it cannot be destroyed by humanity. This response might be difficult for you and others to fathom, but it is true. The celestial body called Earth and all that is a part of her continues to exist because she chooses to. There is purpose and intention in the continued existence of the Earth and all that is upon and within her. The Earth is part of something much greater than herself, just as you are part of something much greater than yourself. You and I are part of a universal cosmology that blends structure, form and purpose with free will and divine intention. When the Earth's purpose has been exhausted, other avenues of expression will become available, but until then there is much work and play to be accomplished.

HUMANITY IS IN SURVIVAL MODE

One of the reasons there is so much current emphasis upon saving the Earth is that its (my) resources are diminishing at an alarming rate. In addition, time seems to be racing against humanity rather than with it. This illusion creates a state of imbalance and unrest within various environments and species. When a being or species feels threatened, its sympathetic nervous system takes over in order to regulate and guide its pulse and other vital functions. The sympathetic nervous system is most active during times of stress and danger. The acceleration in time that humanity is now experiencing creates a false positive within the nervous system. In other words, you (your body and personality) are reacting from a level of stress, fear and danger. This reaction places you in a state of unrest where survival comes into question.

Survival is a natural instinct wherein the biological directive is to survive at all costs; this applies to all organisms, including the smallest cells, to all species and life forms and to celestial bodies such as my own. Sometimes survival involves engaging automatic and semiautomatic defense mechanisms such as natural protective responses to danger, predators, attack from outside forces or invasion by disease agents. Survival responses are also triggered when a threat or potential threat causes emotional distress, destructive impulses or a threat to self-esteem. In humans this is especially true if one cannot suppress unwanted thoughts or memories.

When the desire to thrive is replaced by a need to survive, creative processes are temporarily halted, because an imperative situation in which a reaction is necessary takes precedence over all other creative functions. Have you noticed how difficult it is to concentrate on a creative project when you feel concern and worry in other areas of your life? When a being finds itself in survival mode, it tends to apply the same philosophy to its environment. This is why a natural disaster, for instance, triggers humans and other beings to react with abnormal and erratic distrust of others who would otherwise be welcome within the same environment. If a natural disaster can trigger fear and distrust, what do you fathom an unnatural disaster such as war, a depletion in ozone or a reduction in resources associated with longevity can trigger?

Humans are battling an unseen foe. They are fighting in the dark, and because of this they are only fighting themselves. If you fight only to survive, you will most likely survive, but at what or whose expense? If you fight only to control, you will most likely control, but again, at what cost? What is the answer then? Can there even be an answer to this unnecessary paradox? Yes, and a solution as well.

Both the answer and the solution exist within the problem as with all things. The universe is mathematical, conceived in divine geometry and played out in angles and configurations. All That Is is the sum of Its parts and It is the whole; It is the absolute and the absolute is perfection. If a question is perfect, then its answer is as well. The same applies to paradoxical questions. A paradox is a situation that seems absurd or contradictory and is almost always contrary or in conflict with conventional or common opinion; but in fact, it is or may be true.

A paradox therefore exists in that the Earth is being systematically dismantled, denuded and destroyed, while at the same time this experience is quite impossible. Why is this experience impossible? Because you cannot destroy what you did not create, and you cannot be less a part of what you already are. In order to destroy the Earth, humanity would have to destroy itself first. Humans cannot and will not destroy themselves, because imbued within them is a divine imperative not only to survive but also to thrive. Your survival upon the Earth is dependent upon both your body and mine. In order to thrive rather than merely survive, humans can and will rediscover themselves and the Earth in the process.

A NEW EXPERIENCE OF TIME WILL EMERGE!

Why have they not done so yet? Because humans still see themselves as separate from themselves, separate from me (the Earth) and separate from All That Is. Lost in time, they have forgotten that they are timeless. Linear time suggests a beginning and an end, a birth and a death. Time and space are sequential but not linear. A sequence of events inserted into dimensional time and slowed down or stepped down to a frequency of personal and planetary experience would give the appearance of a beginning and an end. From this perspective, there is indeed an end, and it is near. Do I mean the end of time? Yes, the end of time as you currently understand it.

Time as you now measure it is short, and for this reason you are short of breath, your breathing is shallow and erratic, which in turn disrupts your sleep patterns. Because of this you breathe without depth or resonance. Without depth lives seem shallow and experience seems temporary. Time as it is currently experienced will come to an end because a new experience of time will emerge. Space will prevail upon time for a new method in which to balance the universe, and humans will be guided to reimagine themselves and re-create themselves within a new system of thought.

Before the dinosaurs were destroyed, they reimagined themselves as a different species within a different context of time and space, do you see? Humanity has a number of choices to make as time is currently measured, and it is doing just that—you can see it all around you if you look. Many possibilities are being contemplated, and many scenarios are being played out. These will lead to the evaluation, culmination and final matriculation into a higher echelon of education.

Do you remember when you were a small child and you took apart your toys to see how they were put together? In a sense, that is what is happening today, with the difference being that you are no longer tinkering with a toy and you will not be able to put it back together as it once was. Do you remember that distinct moment of panic when you knew it would never be as it was? Most (but not all) of you will have that feeling as well, because for the most part, it is only when you determine that you cannot go back that you discover how to go forward. And so you will.

Does this mean that you should live upon the Earth with disregard for its current resources until new ones are discovered? Should you turn away from those who cannot see tomorrow from yesterday? Should you ignore the struggles and hardships of those who impose them upon others or themselves? No, because you cannot ignore the reality you have chosen to participate in, and make no mistake—you have chosen this reality. You are here to actively participate in each moment of your life in both subtle and grand ways. The choices you make broaden or narrow your path according to the action that accompanies the thought. In terms of the activities selected by the organization you are currently considering, you must ask yourself: "If the Earth was not in need of being saved, what choices would we (I) be making today? If our choices determine the next moment and the one after that, what choice would we (I) make next?" Ask yourself if you would be willing to lead this organization rather than follow it, and if so, would the directive be the same?

Surround yourself with those who support your ideas and your ideals. If you do not, you will not be able to support those of others. The Earth needs partners, friends, allies, stewards and companions. Humanity needs the same. If you think in these terms, you will see that your creative awareness will open other avenues of expression that are more pleasing to you. If you wear the insignia or banner of an individual, group or organization, make certain that you are willing to call it your own. This applies to all relationships, including those that bind the heart by promise. If it is still your intention to save the Earth, seek clarity over conviction so that any guidance you seek (including this) will serve you well. Align with the highest truth you hold within you, the one you would swear to if push came to shove. Allow this truth to guide all of your decisions. If the harsh sunlight blinds you, allow your inner eyes to reveal a more subtle light, and if by folly you have fallen in the dark, be guided by the Moon, whose light is even brighter in the darkness.

THE ASHTAR COMMAND

Lately I have been attracted to or been called to the vibration of Ashtar. I have even thought about joining a discussion group associated with this vibration, but something seems to be stopping me from doing so. Can you tell me who or what "Ashtar" or the "Ashtar Command" is associated with? Is it part of the Great White Brotherhood? Is it part of the Galactic Federation? Is it associated with the planet's ascension? What is in my best interest to know about this subject?

The one called Ashtar is in actuality more than one being. This might surprise you and it may stand as contrary to what is offered in popular New Age thought. "Ashtar" is a name associated with a specific type of service, just as those who belong to a specific order of angels vibrate to the name associated with it. In terms of vibration, it is powerful and strong; it commands the respect of those who vibrate within its sphere of influence. For a variety of reasons, many call it the Ashtar Command.

Those who fall under the Ashtar name/title are for the most part in service to the Earth and of ET origin. They are bound by contract and dedication. Their commitment is similar to what you would call a tour of duty. A commitment is considered binding and absolute, but it is based upon absolute choice. The name/title Ashtar is considered a blessed one throughout the universe. By Earth standards, it would be fair to say that the name carries a vibration similar to that of Christ. Implied within the name are dedication, service, oneness, guardianship, honesty, protection, integrity and loyalty. It is not difficult to see how humanity would wish to assign these traits to one being.

Those who are under the Ashtar Command are bound to certain promises and commitments from which they cannot deviate. These are lengthy and comprehensive and leave little room for personal interpretation; in other words, they are not instructions that could easily be misconstrued. Among these are strict policies of noninterference, except where prior or current consent is a certainty.

Those who are in communication with the Ashtar vibration are not so by chance. As frequencies go, it is a very narrow band with a very broad reach. Those who feel an affinity to this vibration are most likely aligned with it, at least within a certain dimensional framework. Emissaries, ambassadors and representatives from places and dimensions beyond this one easily attune to the various communiqués that become available from time to time. For those who are on Earth assignment, the Ashtar Command is like a galactic consulate, a place to learn news from home and share like-minded understandings.

The Ashtar Command does fall under the supervisory guidelines of the Galactic Federation, but not in terms of a governmental edict or a hierarchical structure. It is an affiliation, a branch of service dedicated to the protection of principles rather than the enforcement of regulations. Basically, the Ashtar Command is in service to you via the planet's protection. The Earth is considered by some to be in a state of incubation (this term is more appropriate than quarantine, which has often been substituted). The Earth's environment is monitored during this incubation period so that temperature, humidity, oxygen and other factors continue to support the planet as well as the life upon and within her. Proper maintenance within the guidelines of evolving planets supports the continued growth of as many species as possible. There is as much interest in microorganisms as there is in marine mammal life; those who are attuned to the Earth are diverse in culture and interest. The development of the Earth into a fifth-dimensional world is the top priority. It might seem to you, given certain current world circumstances, that this is not possible, but that is not the case.

The Ashtar Command is not a part of any other brotherhood or organization. It is a directive, an organized fleet of intelligence and protection, science and study. Given that protection is strictly enforced, you might well wonder how or why abductions and other unfamiliar phenomena seem uncontrolled. The answer is simple. You are under your own dominion as much and in as many areas of your life as you claim. There is no ruling power, authority or control other than your own, but if you have surrendered your authority to another being or a greater influence, then you must address or change this authority before another can take precedence. Currently, you receive support and assistance in the form of enhancement within the Earth's vibrational field. In other words, much of the static energy that is used to influence you is deflected at a level that exists before (or beyond) it is inculcated within your fields of expression. This allows you to be in a state of choice more often than you believe yourselves to be.

In order for the Earth to remain in a stasis of free will, it must remain open and creative. In essence, the Ashtar Command is an energetic response to an overmodulation of power. It makes certain that opposing forces do not simply cancel one another out. It keeps the playing field open and level, so to speak, so that your evolution and ascension remain your choice alone and within your grasp as appropriate. The Ashtar Command is not a military fleet. It is an organized system of spiritual intelligence and is quite advanced by current Earth standards. Within the fleet are many vessels that may be of interest to you; some reflect scientific advancements and achievements, whereas others specialize in fields of organic health (not medicine). There are specific enhancements and attunements that are offered, when appropriate, by those who are well trained as personal and planetary liaisons. It is not within my capacity to offer these to you, but I suggest that you seek out such treatment if you believe it is in your best interest.

RESPONDING TO THE ASHTAR VIBRATION

Much has been said over the past many years concerning the celebrated influence of those who respond to the vibration of Ashtar. Much that was said and written long ago was misinterpreted and therefore miscommunicated. Many miscommunications have perpetuated thoughts and beliefs that do not serve you or the Ashtar principle. For instance, it would not be possible for humanity to be lifted from the planet's surface and carried elsewhere. This would be a misappropriation of authority and directive. Plans for world evacuation were considered at an energetic, not an organic, level.

Over time, many Earth and ET delegates have come together in councils and other cooperative efforts. Methods of more efficient communication as well as better language tools have been introduced so that evacuation, for instance, now means the same in many galactic languages. It was thought at one time that the Ashtar frequency could or would be made available to many upon the Earth; this would allow you to visit and experience directional dimensions beyond this one. A directional dimension is a fancy way to explain that which lies beyond the third dimension but still exists in linear time. After a brief experimental season, it was seen that humans were still much in favor of surrendering their power to a higher authority rather than retaining it for themselves. The experiment was halted and later substituted with empowerment teachings that would lead to self-directed purpose and discovery.

For a time, it seemed that the Ashtar frequency was no longer discernible from Earth. It even appeared that the vibration had withdrawn its support from all Earth relativity, but this was not the case. For humanity's sake, it became important that it take a giant step backward in space but not in time. This has allowed the layers of fear that still permeate humanity to make their way more gently to the surface, where they can be assuaged, dissipated and finally dismissed. The Ashtar frequency is just as available to you now as always, but you must approach it from a level perspective in order to fully appreciate and understand it. If you subjugate yourself to it, you will learn little about Ashtar or about yourself.

As humanity quickly approaches its future self, paradigms and dimensions of experience will begin to shift your awareness. At first, experiences will seem similar and parallel to your current understandings. There will come a point, however—a turning point—where unfamiliar ground will greet you and distant stars will seem much closer than they do today. There is a point where light and dark lovingly touch each other, softly caressing the complementary beauty that each carries. I look forward to that moment as much as you surely do, for only then will there be no separation from what you hear told and what you experience for yourselves. Until then, may seamless experience be your guide.

The First Five Dimensions

April 2003

Can you offer an expanded description of the different dimensions that are available to us? I have heard and read a lot but can only recall brief experiences that I would describe as beyond 3D. I would appreciate as much detail and depth as you would be willing to share.

Dimensions are energetic environments, and although each is unique, the similarities far outweigh the differences. Each dimension has its own quality and each vibrates to its own frequency. Some frequencies are lighter, whereas others are more dense; some are imbued with physical attributes, whereas others resonate better with nonphysical experience. Dimensions are like cooperative understandings among friends; there is no competition, only mutual admiration, support and encouragement for the beauty and purpose each provides. It is important to understand at the outset of this discussion that one dimension is not better than another; a larger or higher number does not indicate a more desirable experience.

MORE IS NOT ALWAYS BETTER

In linear experience, more is often considered to be better. For instance, if ten dollars were good, one hundred dollars would be better. A larger home is indicative of more wealth, and a penthouse apartment would be considered more valuable than one located on a lower floor. The "more is better" rule, however, does not extend to all areas. Linear experience must, of necessity, include its opposite, because it is subject to the laws of polarity. More debt, more pollution, higher taxes and higher insurance deductibles are fine examples we can cite.

When your spirit, along with your desire to embody, first descended into third-dimensional experience, you were exuberant and could hardly contain your joy. You celebrated experience after experience and called upon your friends from distant places to come and join you. You found physical experience delightful, and you reveled in sensory perceptions such as smell, taste and touch. You were so enthralled with your Earth experience that you hardly even noticed the stars that greeted you each evening.

THE BIRTH OF THE "BIGGER IS BETTER" ILLUSION

Eventually, new visitors came here from far away. They also descended to Earth as you once did, but in ships that were unfamiliar to you and in bodies that were unlike your own. They had tools that were far more advanced than your own, and you thought them magic. The visitors understood how to harness light and sound for many purposes, and you marveled at this as well.

It was not long before you came to think that they were superior to you, although this was not the case. They told you about their world, which was far away and much larger than the Earth, and in that moment, you forgot that the unlimited rather than the limited was your home. When you called them gods, they did not stop you; and when you forgot that the infinite rather than the finite was your true Source and Creator, they did not remind you. When these beings returned to their ships and to the skies from which they had come, you watched in wonder and amazement. You envied them and wished to be as they were. You began to value what they had valued, even though it had meant little to you prior to their arrival. You cultivated and consumed the foods they had eaten, believing your body would become as theirs. Celebrating the many faces of nature was replaced with watching the night sky and the morning star for signs of their return. You built altars and idols to gods who never were and wrote histories based upon stories that were not your own.

Taller became better, because the visitors from far away were taller than you were; lighter-color eyes were more desirable, because they were also reminiscent of the visitors and of the sky. That which was smaller and less powerful than you was of little value and even less consequence; this was the example that had been set for you. This included children and women as well, because there had been fewer female visitors than male visitors. "Bigger, better, more" was born of illusion, a reality that belonged to others and unconsciously became your own. What you truly seek does not exist beyond the third dimension but through it, not in escape but in experience.

Dimensions offer different ways to experience yourself and the reality that you choose to create. As environments of experience, they each provide a different atmosphere or quality. In simplest terms, you can experience a different dimension by moving from a solitary, arid desert to an ocean community. The ocean is not better than the desert, but its environment provides a different experience. Depending upon your purpose, one may be more suitable than another. With our foundation now properly laid, we can expand the scope of this discussion to include much more.

FIRST DIMENSION: INFINITE CREATION

The first dimension is as the last. It is first cause and original thought. Nothing exists before it or after it, although all thought and all experience move beyond it. The first dimension is the will of the Creator, and as a creator your will is your first cause and original thought. As pure spirit you aligned with first cause and experienced yourself as the All and as the freedom to experience all. Choice is born of freedom, and so you were presented with many choices. You eventually settled upon a path that has brought you to this moment and will continue to expand beyond it. As the All, the first dimension is always expanding. It is infinite, as is its ability to create. As an extension of infinite creation you also have infinite ability to create and to be creative. Of necessity, creativity includes the ability to destroy.

SECOND DIMENSION: REALM OF PURE CONSCIOUSNESS

The second dimension is the beginning of separation and individualization. It is also the beginning of the return to oneness. It is where the formless first considers form and where creativity ponders manifestation. In simplest terms, it is where consciousness considers an idea for relative merit. Individualization recognizes the self as the whole and as an aspect of the whole. In order to understand itself as the whole and return to wholeness, the individual must seek direction and movement; it must recognize its creative self as awareness and purpose.

The first dimension as pure consciousness is the first point of light—Source or First Cause. The second dimension as individualization is the second point of light, or self-awareness. The distance between the first point of light and the second point of light defines the second dimension. It is the birth of space and time, movement and desire. It is the starting point from which one seeks knowledge and in so doing gains wisdom. The second dimension is the closest to Source in that it is only one point of light away from It, and yet it is also the farthest in that the distance between the first point and the second can only be determined by the desire of the individual to return to Source by understanding itself as Source.

Herein we find one of the great difficulties in describing the dimensions, as the unique quality of each can only be defined by individual experience. The experience of separation and individuality varies greatly within each being. Some will go to great lengths to have more individual experiences (lifetimes), whereas others will rue and lament any experience that seems to be outside of Source.

Nothing is beyond the scope of Source, for nothing could exist outside of It, but herein is the first paradox of individual existence. The second dimension is the realm of pure consciousness. Here we find the architectural plan for all creative thought and all creative movement. Birth and death take place here—not in the third dimension as many believe—because all movement and experience begins and ends with thought. Your decision to return to a place of oneness within Source takes place here in the second dimension, confirming that higher is not always better, because awareness is not linear but dimensional.

THIRD DIMENSION: PROGRESSIVE EVOLUTION

The third dimension is the direct experience of cause and effect as a result of free will and choice. All of the awareness gained by the individual in second-dimensional experience serves as the foundation for the third dimension. If the second dimension is the blueprint, the third dimension is the architecture. It is the building process of structure and form from both thought and thoughtlessness, as creativity makes no distinction between the two. From one perspective, it can be said that the farther the second point of light (individual) is from the first point of light (Source), the greater is the distance from the second point of light to the third point of light or dimension—but this can only be said from one perspective, and there are many.

The third dimension is that of creatorship and authorship. It is the realm of dominion and responsibility. In the third dimension, evolution is progressive, as advancement in consciousness becomes awareness, then *self* awareness and finally *Source* awareness. Evolution is not linear; it is only the experience of time that makes it seem so. As a sequence of measure, time is circular or spiral in nature, and time seems to quicken as the dimensions increase or spiral.

That is why time seems to be passing so much faster now than it did a few years ago. The Earth and humanity are undergoing a leap in consciousness. They are currently in between the third and fifth dimensions via a consciousness bridge or grid called the fourth dimension. If you think of a bridge as that which links two great expanses (of thought) or territories (mass), you will begin to see why this would be an unstable time in your history or evolution. A bridge is only as stable as it has been engineered to be; some will stand for a long time, whereas others will fall prey to the tides of time. The current bridge is an unstable one—or so it would seem—and it will take a great deal of stamina, will and desire to raise the consciousness of humanity to a level of awareness sufficient to steady it.

Individual consciousness is as paramount as mass consciousness, because all are standing on the same bridge. Individually, it would seem that it does not matter what your colleague, neighbor or family member is doing or thinking, but First

Cause does not discriminate between any of Its creations. It sees everything and everyone that It (or you) has created as unique and deserving of consideration. This final phase of the third dimension offers an opportunity for all to do the same.

The third dimension is first cause within First Cause. It is the experience of beingness within being. It is unconsciousness becoming consciousness; it is a process of distillation of Spirit from form. It is measured in seasons: periods of dormancy, or winter (unconsciousness); awakening, or spring (birth); growth, or summer (self-awareness); cultivation, or autumn (surrender); and regeneration, rebirth, renewal and ascent of the spiral of being or becoming. How long, far, wide or large is the third dimension? It is as large as the number of angels who can dance on the head of a pin, as the saying goes.

FOURTH DIMENSION: PROVING GROUND

The fourth dimension is to the fifth dimension what the second dimension is to the third—it is that which makes it possible. It is the thought, blueprint and dimensional infrastructure of the creative mind that will assist in physical-izing the fifth dimension. The fourth dimension is perfected in the third—tempered, so to speak.

The fourth dimension is as a manual for the fifth dimension. It is a teacher, which is why there are currently so many spiritual teachers who present theories for you to consider from this perspective. The theories presented are designed to allow you to stay the course or course-correct, if need be. The fourth dimension exists as possibility and probability; it is a resource within which to play out many scenarios without the need to experience them in the physical. The fourth dimension allows you to practice and pretend, so that your plan will be worthy of the creative beingness you are. It allows you to experience nonlinear dimensional thought from a third-dimensional perspective. That is one of the reasons it is called a bridge between worlds or schools of thought.

The fourth dimension is the gateway to the fifth. It is where many of the veils that seem to separate or stop you exist. The veils simply prevent you from carrying incomplete experiences into the fifth dimension. It is like a proving ground for thoughts and ideas, and only those with expansive and creative frequencies are truly able to transit the dimensions. Each time an individual or collective-consciousness creative thought transits third-, fourth- and fifth-dimensional thought, it becomes multidimensional, and humanity moves one step further on its evolutionary path to greater awareness. The fourth dimension, while inconsequential to some because it is both nonlinear and nonphysical, is that which stands ready to propel humanity to great heights.

FIFTH DIMENSION: LIVING IN CIRCULAR TIME

The fifth dimension is your near future. Instinctively, you are moving toward it with precision and grace, even when it does not seem like it. The fifth dimension is not better than the third dimension, but it is clearer. The haze and veils that clutter your present and prevent you from seeing the future will be greatly diminished in the fifth dimension.

Fifth-dimensional experience is not the miracle that many are hoping for; it is a natural extension of that which you are becoming. It will allow you to think dimensionally as well as linearly, which will seem almost instantaneous to you. For instance, imagine for a moment that you are considering relocating to another city. Using your current, third-dimensional linear thought, you might make a list of possible destinations, placing a plus or minus sign next to each potential city or town as you study the relative merit of each. You might consult a variety of resources while you wonder or fret about how you will earn a living or make new friends.

Multi(fifth)dimensional awareness will allow you to expand beyond the gaps and limitations of linear mind/time awareness. Presented with a creative thought, you will experience all possibilities as creative probabilities and choose the one that best exemplifies your desired state of being. Creative probability will take into consideration all facets of beingness, including health; vitality; mental, emotional, spiritual well-being; and so forth. The fifth dimension will allow you to experience life more fully, because there will not be as great a need for trial and error.

The fifth dimension will allow you to have linear experiences while living in circular or spiral time. Although this might seem confusing or disconcerting to you now, it will be much easier than the life of distraction you now lead. Currently you are having experiences in the third, fourth and fifth dimensions. Sometimes life seems so accelerated that you wonder how you will complete what used to be one week's tasks in one day. At other times, you wonder why life seems to have come to a screeching halt. The effects of this dimensional shift will ease with time and awareness.

Fifth-dimensional experience does not require the mind to spend as much time processing thoughts and fears, which will free both the mind and the heart to pursue more creative endeavors. Dimensional time is different, because it takes place in full conscious awareness. Consciousness is not the mind, and the mind is not consciousness. The mind makes consciousness possible, and consciousness assists the mind to expand. Without consciousness, the mind would find itself in an interminable loop, unable to escape the confines and boundaries of past traumas or future fears. Full consciousness assumes that the right and left hemispheres of the brain are equal and creative partners. Theories that suggest left- or right-brain thinking will be obsolete other than in reference to linear thought.

THE PROMISE AND OPPORTUNITY OF THE FIFTH DIMENSION

Future generations will find that evolutionary genetic mutations of the brain will make adjustments less necessary and more natural. History will eventually reflect that the present Earth generations, including the Indigo and the violet races, have borne the brunt of the burdensome evolutionary changes that were required of the human race. Although fifth-dimensional experience will be a natural experience for future generations, present Earth generations will find that it will become easier with time and with attunements of body, mind and spirit. Just as today's generations have greater longevity than those of the previous century, future generations will also have access to awareness and privileges unknown to most today.

Greater clarity and understanding deepen compassion. Those who embrace fifth-dimensional experience will have tired of war. The struggles of those who still hunger for power will go unheeded, for they will be unwarranted and unsupported by those who have opened their hearts and minds to more peaceful opportunities. Again I will say that the fifth dimension is not the purported miracle that has been paraded before you as the carrot that dangles enticingly before the eyes of the donkey. Thoughts of war and warring will still exist, and envy and jealousy will still be your neighbors. Disagreement and discontent will still loom on the horizon, but so will the thought that the Sun shines equally in all directions and the Moon has as many faces as there are opportunities for peace. You will not forget these words then, even if you do so now.

The third dimension shouts, "Me first!" and it demands it "Now!" It boasts of "I" and insists on its "needs and wants." The third dimension wants what it does not have and seeks what it cannot find, because both "I" and "me" are found in "we," and need and want both quietly rest in a cradle called "have." Science, religion, politics and art have been pulling on the strings of polarity for so long that they have become out of tune and out of sorts. Arms that were once outstretched are now stretched out and stressed out.

Where the third dimension shouts, the fifth dimension will whisper, and where the third dimension has made war, the fifth dimension will make peace. Why? Because the long-standing battle between the mind and the heart will finally be put to rest.

LIVING IN MULTIDIMENSIONAL REALITY, PART 2:

The Sixth through the Twelfth Dimensions

May 2003

SIXTH DIMENSION: A COSMIC BRIDGE

*T*he sixth dimension is often bypassed in favor of others. It is less understood than dimensions that offer instant change, access to information or portals to expanded experience. The sixth dimension can be thought of as a country back road rather than a well-traveled highway. Its etheric terrain is different—rough and bumpy, energetically speaking.

It is the dimension of the seeker. It welcomes those who are willing to see beyond the obvious. Whereas other dimensions might test your courage, commitment or intent, the sixth dimension will assist you in examining your depth. The sixth dimension requires fortitude, because it asks you to be your own teacher. Here, there is no one to follow and no one to lead. This dimension invites the seeker to understand All That Is by understanding solitude. It exists just beyond the plane of the fifth dimension, but many who attain fifth-dimensional enlightenment will seek no further. Content with their experience of All That Is, there is little motivation to challenge the soul.

The sixth dimension is the realm of the teacher/master. It ensures that the seeker will discover what lies beyond and underneath purpose and destiny. Those who are interested in visiting other worlds as ambassadors and representatives often delve into the sixth dimension first, because it is like a cosmic bridge. It weaves understandings and wisdoms from a variety of dimensions and perspectives, presenting them as an infusion of light from the One Source. It tempers and fine-tunes, asking much of the seeker but returning tenfold what it asks. One need not ever experience the sixth dimension, if that is the choice. It is not a spiritual requirement, but an unfoldment. Those who assist you at this time as teachers and masters are well qualified to do so, having submitted themselves to the intrinsic properties and vibrational effects of the sixth dimension.

Seventh Dimension: Good Fortune

Many beings find seventh-dimensional experience most delightful. It is a creative dimension and somewhat magical at that. It is considered the dimension of good fortune, because it is here that one truly learns the art of creative manifestation. The seventh dimension invites what can be called perfection— or better put, the art of seeing the perfection in and of all things. It is also called the dimension of the alchemist, because it is the dimension where true transformation takes place. Here, all elements are equal, even as the profundity and individual quality of each element are ranked as unique.

The seventh dimension is somewhat like the fifth, but it is less physical, its substance finer and more gossamer-like. There is less density in the seventh dimension; it can be experienced physically, or not. Again I will say that light and density are one and the same. Truly it is a matter of choice, just as some of you might find certain foods more appealing than others.

The seventh dimension unites students with teachers and teachers with masters. It links musicians, artists and mathematicians. This dimension is often thought to be the patron of healers and the healing arts, because healing acknowledges beauty, perfection and magic. The seventh dimension erases barriers of separation and brings worlds of knowledge together. The phrase, "When the student is ready, the teacher will appear," could have been coined here, because that is what happens quite literally. This dimension is considered the favorite of many, and it is easy to see why.

The seventh and the second dimensions have a special relationship, just as the seventh and the second chakras are in relation to each other. Five separates the two dimensions, but in sacred (spiritual) geometry, five unites the two. The unique energy that both separates and unites is like the cosmic inbreath and outbreath of All That Is. In a different understanding, the second dimension (architecture of physical life and expression) finds its own perfection within and expresses it in the seventh dimension (building of spiritual and divine presence). The seventh dimension is the first portal to other dimensions within other universes of expression. In order to experience other aspects of awareness, it is important to be familiar with the corridors of space and time and how to best experience them. They are like platforms or pavilions where energies are exchanged and reinterpreted. This is an accelerated concept and not for those who are only vaguely interested in the process.

EIGHTH DIMENSION: THE UNIVERSAL TRAVELER

The eighth dimension is the dimension of the universal traveler. It is here that many choices, exchanges and decisions are made. For instance, if perchance you express an interest in withdrawing from your physical body, an eighth-dimensional being would assist you with that decision. This being might show you possibilities you have not considered, given the limited experience offered by the other dimensions. You might be shown the greater alignment understood by your soul elsewhere, so that your physical undertaking will seem more purposeful.

The eighth dimension is well traveled. It is a balanced corridor of energy, meaning that one form of energy can be exchanged, balanced or neutralized harmlessly by another. Many ETs are familiar with this dimensional portal. It is here that they can don a physical human body when needed or receive an infusion of compatible energy that will sustain their own bodies within an Earth matrix. It is the realm of science and chemistry. Many future discoveries that will be of benefit to the Earth are already held here for you, in what can be described as an escrow account. In due time, when certain criteria are met, they will belong to humanity.

The eighth dimension allows that which is possible on other worlds to find compatibility on Earth. In other words, essences or elements that may be beneficial elsewhere but are toxic to the Earth can be introduced with care here. Eighth-dimensional energies support and sustain many different dynamics, balancing and integrating them with frequencies and vibrations that are Earth-compatible. Not all energies become stable enough to be introduced upon the Earth plane, and some creative endeavors must be put off until another time or abandoned altogether. Those that are found to be compatible and beneficial are introduced at specific intervals of time, aligned with the planet's evolutionary growth.

Many physical varieties of plants and animals have arrived upon the Earth in this way; the process of integrating nonphysical properties is almost the same. When a member of the human kingdom eventually stumbles on a new discovery, it is often because a greater wisdom has seen to its perfection first. Energies, species and beings who choose to depart the Earth plane energetically will often select this dimension. The eighth dimension is somewhat soft, energetically speaking; it is less abrupt and subtler than others. It is soothing and inviting, making it a perfect choice for beings who have just emerged from a harsher-dimensional climate or for those who are on their way to one.

NINTH DIMENSION: THE FINAL EXAM

This dimension invites completions, attainments and transformations of a permanent kind. It is the dimension of the final exam, but any perceived barriers or boundaries are only self-imposed. It is the dimension that invites checking and double-checking of all one is or believes. It is the dimension of the will. It is pleasant and accessible to all who present themselves—but few do, unless and until there is purpose in doing so.

The ninth dimension poses no threat and presents no surprises, but it is guaranteed to reveal any perceived fears, illusions, paradoxes or discomforts that exist at a soul level. Some call it the dimension of initiation for this very reason. Consciously or unconsciously, you interact with this dimension every time you encounter a milestone opportunity in your life. The ninth dimension prepares you to meet your life's purpose by encouraging you to overcome your challenges. It is a very helpful dimension in that it will direct you to your greatest obstacles so that you can see them without having to face them. For instance, you might visit the ninth dimension in your sleeptime to see what is coming up. You can evaluate different ways to proceed with a supposed problem. You might choose to test yourself, to see if you are ready to turn the other cheek or walk away if need be. It is a proving ground. How mild or harsh the environment of this dimension becomes is completely up to you. You always move at your own pace here—there are no timed tests, pass-or-fail evaluations or ultimatums to live up to. It is the realm of growth via personal choice and awareness.

It is in the ninth dimension that you ultimately realize how devoted your soul is to what you have perceived yourself to be until that moment. It is expansive and liberating. The ninth dimension offers you the opportunity to discard the need for physical embodiment; it is the door to many nonphysical realities. In an effort to be of greatest assistance to you, the ninth dimension will invite experiences from the past or the future to join you. If you walked away from an experience without completing it, here you will receive an opportunity to complete it. If you long for an event or a future that is not aligned with your greatest purpose, you will be invited to experience that desire holographically rather than by playing out a reality that would not serve you. In the ninth dimension, you can surrender your need to identify with a physical body. Here, the body is seen as a vehicle for the soul's awareness. When the personality aligns with the soul first and the body second, the axiatonal lines of perfection are activated.

This spiritual response is similar to the activation of kundalini energy within the physical realm. The axiatonal lines of perfection are energetic patterns that are specific and individual to each soul. They are like your cosmic link to All That Is. They carry the perfection of all that has ever been or ever will be you. They restore any and all aspects of the self that are perceived as less than whole. They are the true source of all healing. Any time you have been ill or close to death and have chosen to recover, it is because you have visited this dimension and chosen to align or realign with your perfection. It can never be otherwise, and no other being can do this for you. The best healers will remind you of this and show you the way there. They will care for your body and personality while your soul rediscovers its perfection.

Axiatonal lines are similar to the Earth's ley lines in that they cannot be permanently damaged, only altered. You can discover more than one way to see or understand your own perfection, but it cannot be removed or taken from you. You cannot surrender your own perfection, because it belongs to you and to All That Is, who holds you in a state of abiding devotion and deep love. Axiatonal lines are energetically tied to your intent and integrity. They support the purpose of your creativity in this life and in all other lives, especially those in which you have been most conscious, aware and aligned with spiritual tenets. They help you to know that you are more than human, and they are associated with the divinity you participate with in other realms.

The Earth's ley lines help me to hearken to my conscious awareness; they are perfectly placed within an energetic grid whose alignment shifts and changes as my being does. Their placement is based upon a spiral evolution, a cosmic dance that has gone on for eons. The ley lines have little or nothing to do with geographic lines of location such as longitude or latitude, but by agreement, there is relativity between them—a point of reference to assist those who participate with both. The Earth also relates to its own axiatonal lines. They allow a sentient Earth to be aware of and connected to the galaxy, the cosmos and the universe. They are a cosmic link between my sentience as a physical planet and my understanding of the nature of all celestial bodies and their cosmic purpose.

The ninth dimension is also a continual source of assistance to those who have come to the Earth from nonphysical worlds. Here, they are able to receive cosmic attunements that allow them to remain in (or return to) their physical bodies for extended periods of time, without adverse effects to their natural state of being or human health. This dimension is the closest to their cosmic home and the farthest from third-dimensional Earth, which makes it an ideal choice for those who do not wish to surrender their human bodies in order to receive the rest and restoration they require.

TENTH DIMENSION: BEGINNINGS, PARADOXES, QUESTIONS

Little will be said of this dimension and the next. The tenth dimension requires an understanding of the self as more than the self in order to be well understood. You cannot move to the tenth dimension from the ninth, because dimensions are not linear; they are not natural progressions of each other or the next step on a cosmic ladder. They are purposeful, accessible realms of energy; each relates to all others in unique and specific ways that cannot be understood by the logical mind. You will not find a classroom or a teacher on this subject, but you will find many classrooms, teachers and other forms of assistance when you present yourself in any of these energetic areas.

The tenth dimension is a place of energetic beginnings; it answers questions that are never asked and solves paradoxes that have not yet been experienced. As a simple example, imagine that you have already completed all of the experiences you had set out to have in this lifetime. Additionally, imagine that the objectives and purpose of this life have already been met, but curiously, you are certain your time upon the Earth and within your physical body is not yet complete. The wisdom available in the tenth dimension could assist you in redirecting your highest potential by redistributing your energetic makeup and aligning you with a new purpose. Those who need the kind of assistance found within this dimension simply find themselves there; there is no other way. You cannot, for instance, find that your purpose has become too difficult or distasteful and decide to go to the tenth dimension and exchange it for another purpose. That is one of the reasons it is inaccessible to your level of consciousness. (This is not meant as a judgment, simply a statement of fact.) Given the condition of the world and the current juxtaposed alignment of most souls with their unique purpose, the line of beings wishing to exchange, trade or return their purpose would be longer than a comet's tail!

The tenth dimension is the one of the second chance or new beginning. It can realign a being with a new purpose when specific criteria are met. Using another example, let's say that karmic purpose has placed you in prison for many years. During your imprisonment, many things have been changed or altered relative to your original intent, which is more inclusive than the obvious compensatory time in exchange for a crime committed. Imagine, for example, that those to whom you had pledged devotion in this life have already discovered the means within themselves to move forward without your assistance. Perhaps they found the forgiveness within themselves that allows others to be forgiven as well. In that case, there would be no purpose for you to fulfill upon your release, but a persistent and resolute yearning within you is still focused and determined to live a purposeful life. It is likely that your yearning would lead you to the tenth dimension.

Walk-in experiences are often associated with this realm, as are other tragic circumstances in which a soul becomes temporarily separated from its source chord (divine frequency). Very brief lifetimes, such as the ones that bring about a condition currently called crib death, are also associated with this dimension, as are aborted lifetimes—regardless of the reason or the source of choice for the abortion. Suicides and homicides are another matter altogether; they are often quite relative to a purpose even when they do not appear to be so. A being does not receive a new life or a purpose simply because he or she has terminated his or her own or had it terminated by another being.

ELEVENTH DIMENSION: SUPPORTING ANGELIC ENERGIES

The eleventh dimension is the access point or place of intercession invoked by those of angelic origin. It is the dimension where prayers are answered—or better put, it is the dimension that creates the spheres of divine energy that offer angelic guidance and support. It would be improper to direct prayers to the eleventh dimension, because they cannot be received there. The eleventh dimension supports angelic energies that sustain physical and nonphysical realities, including those on the Earth plane.

Angelic energies and beings are directed by specific frequencies that are attuned to perfections within All That Is. Angelic energy emanates from the mind of All That Is. It is created there and mandated to flow and follow within the plan of perfection of All That Is. Angelic frequencies are attracted to that which is perfect and that which is the opposite of perfection, which is why angels are most often experienced by what humanity would call saints and sinners. This does not mean that you must fit into one of these categories in order to receive assistance from the angelic realm; it does mean that you must be willing to receive assistance by placing yourself in an energetic state of receptive propriety and good will. In other words, you must be willing to participate in your own healing or your own miracle as the case may be. That is why it would seem that some prayers are answers while others are not. All prayers are received vibrationally and answered in the same way. How each being responds to what is received is another matter altogether and a subject upon which volumes could be written.

The eleventh dimension is also an access point for Earth angels, angelic beings in physical bodies. The light, etheric nature of their beingness allows for easier transitions to and from other realms of experience, if that is their choice. Most often, it is not. Earth angels are here to have human experiences that are physical in nature. They did not sign on for the easy or tourist adventure of the Earth plane. They are here to be of assistance to humanity by relating to you as no other beings could. They are among you in every facet of experience and life condition—and yes, they can even be found in the military.

The eleventh dimension holds the frequency for the miraculous. It is the field of all possibilities infused with purpose and presence. Although you cannot access or participate within this realm, you can invite what seems impossible in your life to become possible. You can access its energy indirectly by assuming a position of faith, trust and hope in all of your desires and aspirations. Although you cannot invoke or invite the eleventh dimension, you can certainly invite an angel to tea!

TWELFTH DIMENSION: THE UNIVERSAL MIND

The twelfth dimension blends mind, consciousness and awareness with heart, soul and purpose. In the twelfth dimension, the mind no longer exists as an individual aspect of self, but as an expanded awareness of united purpose. This is the dimension of the universal mind, which exists beyond the linear past, present or future. The twelfth dimension allows access to all of your lifetimes as aspects of the grander self rather than the lower awareness of self. In this dimension, you would experience your lifetimes and know that they were yours without feeling attached to them in any way.

The twelfth dimension is an extension of the creative mind of All That Is. It is unlimited and rich in ideas and possibilities that are yours for the asking and taking. The twelfth dimension makes these creative expressions available to all who choose to participate in them. That is why it is possible that you might have entertained an idea for a creative expression for a long time, only to see another manifest it. It is an unlimited, unconditional platform of expression. The twelfth dimension can be accessed at any time and from any other dimension of experience, yet few choose to do so because they do not consider themselves worthy of such preferential treatment. Many, if not most, beings are well accustomed to working for and earning any and all experiences. This dimension offers no lesson, and you need no pretext or secret password to gain admission. It is the dimension of the secret cave of Merlin and the wonders and treasures encountered by Aladdin. It is accessed via the desire to be in a state of creative oneness with Source—there are no other prerequisites.

The twelfth dimension is the last dimension of imperfection or the first dimension of perfection, depending upon your view. There are twelve experiences or layers of density within the twelfth dimension, each inspiring a subtle but specific aspect of creative divinity. When accessing the twelfth dimension, you will automatically find yourself in the creative density most appropriate for you. Within each density there are also 360 degrees of aspects or alignments, and because the twelfth dimension is not linear in scope, there is an infinite amount of space between the alignments of creative energy. You can well begin to imagine the unconditional brilliance of this dimension while you ponder its relative significance in your life and your creative endeavors.

This dimension ensures that no beings and no purposes are ever alike. It guarantees that you are unique among all others and so are your ideas, concerns, desires and perfections. The twelfth dimension is your unconditional connection to All That Is. All kingdoms access this dimension and perfect themselves through it. It is because of this dimension that a wolf knows when it should fear a human and a cow understands that it will one day be eaten; that a tree knows where to place its roots and how high to stretch its limbs; and that a bird knows what song it will sing. Long ago the dinosaurs learned of their imminent transformation, and humanity discovered its cosmic future.

The twelfth dimension is the key to the past and the future via the beauty and perfection of the present. It holds the cosmic code for all that you have been as well as the creative instruction for all that you can become. It is both your undoing and your becoming. The twelfth dimension is associated with the crystalline kingdom; it is the sentience or awareness of all the minerals and gemstones you hold dear. It is the perfection of the twelfth dimension that ensures humanity's transition into a crystallized version of perfection that cannot be shattered by any other reality. It is all that you could want or hope for at this time.

EXPERIENCE THE UNIVERSE INFINITELY

Although this universe is not infinite, the ways in which you can experience it are. This paradox cannot be explained, but it can be experienced because you are an aspect of Source, and Source is infinite. The twelve dimensions that have been described here are offered as an overview or initial understanding. They are not meant to limit or define that which can only be experienced. The unique nature of each being will expand upon the ideas offered here and confer upon you your own original understanding and truth. I offer you a dimensionless love coupled with a fathomless depth of devotion and consideration.

All Roads Lead to Rome, but Seize the Day Anyway

June 2003

The current shifting of paradigms and energies can throw us off center rather easily these days. Our purpose is sometimes difficult to define, and our truth lies somewhere between fact and fiction or illusion and reality. Gaia says we are living in a distortion and that nothing is exactly as it seems. As news broke that the war in Iraq had begun, I found myself riveted to my television, unable to look away or change the channel. I told myself that this was not my reality, not a choice I was willing to make, but the next day found me doing the same. By the third day, I was watching the news from my bed, because I had begun to feel ill. I felt fatigue, stress and various other symptoms brought on by my being captured by the television. In my own way, I had allowed myself to become a prisoner of war.

On the fourth day, Gaia asked me if I was planning to become a casualty of war or a victim of circumstantial evidence. I wasn't sure what she meant, but I said no because it sounded better than yes. She reminded me that while it was all right to participate in many realities and try on many pairs of shoes, I need not claim them as my own. She went on to explain that my health and vitality were linked to my willingness to walk my own path and experience my own purpose. In essence, as I slowly abandoned my truth, my ability to maintain balance and wellness was abandoning me. I asked Gaia if others were feeling as poorly as I was, and she said yes, they were. "What can we do?" I asked. She told me to hold fast to the reins of my vehicle of light as if it were the saddle on a majestic horse and then to ride the wave of light in the direction of the sunrise rather than the sunset that was drawing me down. It sounded a bit poetic and simplistic, but I did as she suggested, and by that afternoon I was up and about again.

A few days later, Gaia asked me to arrange an evening of channeling in order to address the concerns of the war and other relevant topics. Her exact words were, "Please arrange a council of those willing to ask the questions that others cannot or will not. Make certain that the foundation is broad and that opposition and resistance are as well-represented as friendships and allies." I knew that she was demonstrating her willingness to be presented with difficult and challenging questions, and in her own way, she was preparing me to do the same. The following is a transcript of that evening. Additional questions and answers from a later date have been included in an effort to offer the most up-to-date information.

I extend a warm welcome to those gathered here this evening and to those who will join these words later on. I have come prepared to offer the fullness of that which I am, but in return I will ask the same of you. I ask that you be fully present in your hearts and in your bodies, that you represent yourselves well and in wellness. Take the best and the most of what I offer, but give the same in return. Be the same in your daily activities and your evening meditations.

Your presence here affords an opportunity to ask questions that others will not or cannot. Therefore, dare to share the thoughts you have been saving for the kinship of a private moment with those of your own spirit. I have invited you for this very purpose. Refreshments suggestive of a social gathering await you, but there is a greater purpose in coming together this evening, and it must not be overlooked.

The purpose of this gathering is a simple one. It is to actualize a relationship that will create a consciousness called unity. If gatherings such as this were now taking place around the globe and around the clock, little would be done or said that was not in the spirit of friendship and communion. This gathering and others like it will begin to recognize a power called socialized action, a broad and creative expression that blends the self with the selfless. Those whom history recalls as the founding fathers of this country [U.S.] gathered in such a way. They came together in agreement and disagreement, in secret and in public. By candlelight they peered into subjects that would otherwise not have seen the light of day.

The Earth does not belong to you, but it is yours. This room does not belong to you, but it is yours this evening. This community is also yours, and your life is most certainly your own. If so much is under your care and direction, why are so many lives about to be surrendered? What is more precious than life? The purpose of this evening is to discover how to recover life rather than surrender it. Your purpose tomorrow will be to seek fulfillment, understanding and unfoldment. Purpose and reality can and must create purposeful experiential reality. If not, purposeless reality will collapse into the emptiness called uncreated.

WAR AND PEACE ARE EQUAL IN POLARITY

To all who protest the current reality, I offer words that include both praise and caution. Destiny will assist you to design your desires, but not because you protest what you do not abide. In order to experience the light of your desire, you must ignite the passion that will free it from the stronghold where it has been closely guarded. Be a living example of your own light rather than protesting the darkness that still exists within others.

War is one extreme; it can be found at the far end of the spectrum. It might surprise you to know that peace is another extreme; it resides at the opposite end of the spectrum. Both are aspects of the spectrum called polarity, and both are in a state of decay and near collapse.

Peace is not better than war; it is simply its opposite. Peace is the absence of war, conflict or hostility. It is an attitude or understanding based upon a partial or limited vision of truth. Peace is unilateral, not multilateral. One person's definition of peace is often different than another's, and the line between a hero and a villain is often blurred.

In the absence of one mind and one heart, the battle often continues to rage within, even when it does not manifest without. A battlefield will always exist where unrest spans the distance between duality and oneness; where opposites oppose, there can only be the illusion of peace. That which passes for peace today is little more than ignorance temporarily replacing agitation. Resolution lies in unity and balance, in neutrality and in compassion.

If polarity were to be balanced on a scale, war would be on one side and peace would be on the other. They would be equal, do you see? Not better or worse, just equal. Objectivity and unity can be experienced only when both sides are moved into the center, which shifts the entire balance of power, not just one side. Those who fear this shift call it a pole shift or a cataclysm, but is it?

I ask you to think broadly and speak openly, to consider this subject and many others as well. Know that you represent those who cannot or will not say what is within the heart or upon the mind. For a variety of reasons that include fear, doubt, prejudice, religious or political zeal, apathy and cynicism, important questions are not being asked. Collectively, you comprise a forum or council that bears a certain responsibility. This responsibility is not to be borne upon your shoulders as a burden or liability but as a state of authority within a place of accountability. With that being said, I offer the floor and my counsel to all who wish to speak.

THE CLASSIC BATTLE BETWEEN LIGHT AND DARK?

Many people in the world are wondering why the government of the United States is so hell-bent on attacking Iraq. Could you talk about that, please?

Indeed. To put it bluntly, Iraq is attackable. It is the country most willing to be attacked. One country [the U.S.] is, as you say, hell-bent on attacking another. On the polarity/duality scale that was referenced earlier, Iraq is that country. Its dictatorship is the most hated and despised at this time. As far as auditions go, his was the most believable. There is worldwide agreement on this. At first glance, it would seem that the world has found the two players most willing to reenact the roles that exemplify the classic battle between light and dark.

A second look might prove different. Who or what is light? Does light really attack dark? Can dark attack dark or light attack light? These questions cannot be answered now, because they are experiential in context, but perhaps it is appropriate to say that the answers are hiding in plain sight. That which is hidden will be revealed. Those who search the desert for treasure will find it, and those who search the desert for truth will find that as well.

A TREASURE HUNT

Is "treasure" your word for resources such as oil, or is there another form of treasure hidden or buried in Iraq? It whets my curiosity to know what our government is so eager to get hold of.

It is important to begin to think in broader terms than one government or country seeking the spoils of another. This is not about one country or one being; it is not about good guys and bad guys. It is about energies. There are energies that desire one movement or direction and those that would prefer a different understanding. The battle is one of duality, and the spoils of war lie beyond the boundaries of one country or one dictator. The treasure was left here long ago by another race of beings, and so was the truth. Both are being actively sought at this time. Ideally, each energy would like to own and control the treasure and the truth.

Iraq was a garden long ago, a vast and important one, historically speaking. A garden can support a variety of species—some grow and others destroy them. Energetically, the Iraqi desert still remembers that it is a garden. The treasure and the spoils are both the garden and the contents of the garden. In other words, some of the treasure is physical and some is nonphysical; some is accessible and some is not. Fossil fuels are certainly useful to your generation, but they are limited in scope and duration. In order to discover the treasure, you must think as one who seeks it; think as one who will conquer in order to gain, to have, to own and to control.

I tend to think of treasure as buried, especially if it has been there for a long time. I have heard that there are many underground tunnels in Iraq. Is the treasure there?

In a manner of speaking, yes. There are secrets underground that are the keys to the treasure. The difficulty remains in putting all the pieces together, and this is not an easy task. It is obvious that those who seek the treasure are willing to sacrifice a government, a people and a desert in order to attain it.

THE TREASURE IS A TECHNOLOGY

Is the treasure that you refer to a technology of some kind? If so, how does that fit into our history?

The term treasure is a relative or subjective one, just as beauty and art are individual and subjective. In this case, buried treasure implies both truth and power. Power lies in the ability to control, disseminate or hide truth. Truth lies buried but can just as easily be unburied. Yes, technology is a large aspect of the treasure trove, and there are currently at least two interested parties bidding for it. There are off-planet interests as well, but they are choosing to remain on the silent sidelines for the time being.

The technology is not new; by galactic standards, it is quite ancient. It was left here long ago, safely tucked away, or so it was thought. Those who left it behind did not think in terms of padlocks or childproof locks. They did not believe a simple race of beings (humans) would think or act in such a way, but interested parties have been able to decode a schematic that may make the technology operational.

Energetic wave bands of acceleration and evolution expand in all directions and eventually reach all worlds and all beings. Acceleration is neither selective nor destructive; it simply is. Acceleration applies to all areas of thought and experience—spirituality and technology are both quickened, light and dark are activated, the past and future are experienced in the Now.

Acceleration is affecting humanity in a variety of ways; some feel anxious and harried, whereas others feel dispassionate and disenfranchised. Depression, hopelessness, aggression and other states of mind are common as well. It is important to remember that these are states of mind but not states of consciousness; the mind understands itself as separate while consciousness seeks to unite and expand.

HASTY EXPERIMENTS WITH TECHNOLOGY BACKFIRE

The technology/treasure is a substance. When stable, it has many uses, some of them humanitarian and ecological. Currently it is unstable, which makes it dangerous for children who do not understand that they are playing with fire. Those who search for the treasure have a variety of motives for doing so; those who would prevent or preempt the discovery have motives of their own. The race is on to see who will discover it first.

Interestingly, each faction is working from a different set of clues, because there is more than one interpretation or understanding, depending upon the original premise or hypothesis. Neither faction knows how to master the technology, and their knowledge is rudimentary at best. They have each had successes and failures in their attempts thus far and are even now scrambling to read and decode further data.

The data is encoded or embedded within a language that can be interpreted in a variety of different ways. The encoding was designed to be purposeful and multidimensional. It is open to conjecture, interpretation and misinterpretation. Perhaps it is an educational tool as much as it is a technology. Those who seek it received assistance from another race, but there must be honor even among thieves, and that is no more. "What is the harm," they thought, "in a little experiment here and there? What is the harm if we by chance discover another use?"

But a violation is a violation, and a bond, however thin, was broken. It is wise not to bite the hand that feeds, they say. Now there is no more assistance to be had at any price, so they are scrambling about in an attempt to discover what they can remember and rebuild. In all fairness, they have accomplished much, but their job is not complete, and without the missing pieces, they are at a standstill. Can you now guess who has what hidden where and why there is a rush to get from here to there as quickly as possible?

Did the recent Columbia incident have something to do with this technology?

Indeed, yes. It was one of the tests that backfired. They assumed the technology would work, but it did not. They took an unstable element into space, a safe distance, they thought. From space they thought they could use the aspects they already understood to locate and access what they still lacked. But their understanding was not precise or perfect, and the substance became unstable in space. When it was reintroduced into the atmosphere, its properties could not be sustained. This unfortunate event could have been prevented. Radiation was released, and a sequence of unavoidable events led to demise of the shuttlecraft.

About a year ago, you referred to a nuclear explosion that would most likely occur. I remember you said it would not happen in any predictable way. Is this what you were referring to?

Yes. The indication was that all eyes would be focused elsewhere and that stripping this or another country of its weapons or power would be of little consequence in avoiding what would happen in due course.

HOW CAN WE SAVE THE PLANET?

What do you need us to do in order to save the planet and ourselves?

Rephrase your question from a place of power, and I will answer it.

What should we do to reestablish peace, harmony and justice?

Rephrase your question so that it acknowledges your wisdom and mine and I will answer it.

What can we do to further our understanding and continue our evolution as whole beings?

Thank you. Choose to be what you are in the highest and most purposeful expression that is available in each moment. Choose a deeper awareness of self, selflessness and partnership with everything physical and nonphysical. Locate the true source of wisdom within you so that you can express it without as well. Do not follow when you can lead and do not lead if you do not know where you are going. Align with Source/All That Is, and you will discover your own true nature.

ROMAN EMPIRE RISES FROM THE PAST

Gaia, many of us in this country [the U.S.] fear that our government is becoming a lot like Nazi Germany was. I love this country, but I share that concern. Would you be willing to offer some guidance on this subject?

The United States will not embrace the Nazi way. After all, that campaign ultimately failed, and those who currently rule have no intention of failing. Think broadly now and follow your thoughts backward in time. It is the Roman Empire that rises again from the past. The eagle flies again, but this time it will encounter the phoenix, which has recently renewed itself in the ashes. The legions of Rome will be active once again, and the flag of the eagle will uniform the soldiers. The legions will move from one land to another, directed by the one who would crown himself emperor.

But remain confident: Those who would crown themselves are often of small mind and even smaller heart. A fairy tale once described an emperor who went naked before the masses because he thought himself clothed in fine but invisible spun gold. This one will be no different, but one must look beyond the present moment in order to see that. If you look with eyes of fear or disgust, you will miss the humor and satire in the tale and its telling. What the world has not yet done cannot yet be undone. The world has temporarily empowered this one to act as head of state, and so he does. He draws his power from those who offer it, and many do. He seizes power from those who fear it, and many do. When his totem, the eagle, rejects him, others will reject him as well. When the eagle no longer flies by his side, another symbol will represent America and another man as well.

DEMOCRACY WILL ACKNOWLEDGE SOVEREIGNTY

Will the United States still be a democracy?

It will be a democracy of aristocracy that dies in atrocity. A country must honor its soul and follow its path in order to thrive rather than survive. This is the prime directive of all living things. The United States must stand united, but they do not. They pull and tug and struggle to stay aboveboard or above water in all affairs. Without spirit or soul, it cannot see its poor reflection in the mirror.

What will eventually replace democracy?

In the throes of death, democracy will finally call upon and acknowledge sovereignty. In sovereignty there is little need for democracy. One is sovereign unto oneself and within oneself. Allegiance is offered to that which is, to all who are and to All That Is.

Do we have to transcend the ego in order to become sovereign?

The ego is simply that which currently assists the mind. Sovereignty already exists within beingness, because it exists at the soul level rather than the personality level. Soul-directed sovereignty will empower the being when the mind is no longer required to assume the burdens it now carries. Sovereignty already exists within humanity, but there is no source of power aligned with it. It is like a very bright light, but the switch is currently in the Off position.

DEMONSTRATING PEACE REPLACES DEMONSTRATION FOR PEACE

Many peace demonstrations are taking place all over the world right now. Are they helping to move us in the direction of harmony and balance?

Many of those who demonstrate for peace demonstrate very little peace in their own life. Today they wear an appropriate banner, and the purpose for which they parade is grand. But what about yesterday and tomorrow? Was there not purpose in family and will there not be structure in community? One must hold up one's personal banner of peace alongside one's contempt of war. Those who hold a banner in higher esteem than their neighbor do not yet see all life as sacred. Demonstrate peace, and you will have no need to demonstrate for peace.

Unite rather than separate; rally together rather than rail against one another. I do not offer these words to disenchant or disenfranchise those who have chosen to offer themselves in this way, for their purpose is well suited to their needs. Those who parade today do so to complete an incomplete past—even where the children are concerned, this is true. Eventually, demonstrations of peace will come from a deeper source. Other ways to express displeasure will become obvious and more useful than those that present themselves today. When demanding that others choose peace, it is wise to ask the same of oneself, privately and publicly.

RESTORE YOUR FULLNESS AND INCREASE YOUR WELL-BEING

I feel danger and sense fear regarding our government and the subject of democracy. Can you elaborate on that?

Fear will not help you navigate this form of turbulence, but acknowledging that there is fear surrounding it might. The government is simply the long arm of the law. The law is still the law of attraction, regardless of how it manifests. Before you react to the energetic choices that are put to you, remember that you have a choice. The government is the manifestation of humanity's belief in abundance of authority and lack of power. It directs energy that is equal but opposite to personal empowerment and sovereignty.

If alignment were empowering, then the energy of government would seek to misalign you. If balance is power, then imbalance would keep you in lack of power, do you see? Opposition to what is natural is the current weapon of choice, which is why there is so much disrespect and obliteration of natural recourses and natural laws at this time. Stress, economic hardship, war and other burdens also oppose that which is natural. As long as you are off center or out of balance, your fullness cannot be restored. Once you choose the restoration and expression of your natural fullness, your health and well-being will increase and you will feel more creative.

SING AND HUM TO FREE YOUR MIND

Would it help our ability to become sovereign if we removed ourselves from participating in the illusion of democracy? Would it help to balance or rebalance the planet? Is there anything we can or should do to resist the one who would name himself emperor?

It is best to release the resistance you hold within you to the degree that you can. Resistance is resistance, to whom or what does not matter. In one sense, when you resist what is, you also resist the means to change it. The energy of resistance pushes and pulls; it does not flow in any direction. Many believe that lack of resistance equals agreement, but that is not so.

Resistance equals struggle, and lack of resistance equals allowance, which makes all forces and possibilities equal and creative. Resistance calls upon all your resources to be in reaction instead of in action or creativity. A reactive mind cannot be actively creative or in balance. Wherever and whenever you hold a resistant stance, the Earth does so as well, because it is your complement. Likewise, whenever you release the need to control or resist, the planet and its resources benefit as well. Your body benefits, because resistance and density are closely related. As you release your obligations to be in resistance, denial, obligation and doubt, others will be obvious beneficiaries. The lighter the thought, the lighter the body—substance always follows thought. A lighter thought equals a more enlightened path for you and for others.

If you would resist the emperor, do so with laughter rather than anger. He is not funny, but he is humorous—at least, your comedians seem to think so. If you cannot laugh, then perhaps you can sing. Sing songs of peace, by yourself or with others. Sing to your body and to your soul; both will reap immense and immediate benefits. Singing sparks creativity and relieves stress. It frees the child within to play and instills within the mind a sweet surrender to the soul, one that aligns but does not capitulate. Singing and humming restore balance and release impurities, because they are whole activities; they create and complete a circuit for both the body and the mind. When you hum, for instance, the mind creates it, the heart delights in it, the body participates in it and the auric field receives it and transmits it. This simple act creates a vibrational correspondence with wholeness, which makes what is less than whole less attractive and disruptive to your energetic field.

Television, talk radio and most music are not whole or purposeful; they are a distraction and a disruption that allow imbalanced frequencies and thoughts to easily penetrate your auric field. Think back to those who were enslaved and inden-tured; think upon your own lifetimes if you can. Remember the healing benefits of singing, humming and meditating to vibrations and wordless sounds. These whole movements and moments can free a mind from a captive body. These meth-ods are both timely and timeless. Following a dream or a purpose from beginning to end has a similar restorative quality. In terms of the emperor, his platform is not as firm as it would seem and his wardrobe not as grand as he believes.

EMPOWERED CHOICES ARE CHOICES WITHOUT FEAR

I feel a great sense of frustration in how our personal resources are being used. For instance, I do not like the fact that I am helping to fund this war. Is there a way we can choose not to participate in this activity, such as removing ourselves from the tax rolls?

This is certainly a choice, but from a viable standpoint, it would be best to wait until there is more agreement and structure in place. If you make this choice now, it will more than likely be accompanied by a fear of discovery or persecution. It would not be an empowered choice, do you see? There will be a time in the near future that will empower and instill confidence within those who make this choice. They will inspire others in similar ways, and fear will no longer hold them in reserve. When you no longer fear the effect of your decision, you will know that it is appropriate to pay the emperor his due and no more.

Other methods of redistributing wealth and resources will also be presented, and some will have merit. It is best to participate in these rather than to with-draw from the process entirely. Changes are forthcoming in this area and in many others. There will be different ways to direct how your money is spent within the economic structure you choose to participate in. There will also be changes made within investment structures and monetary policies. Individually and collectively, the population will discover that it has more power than it yielded or wielded before.

IF YOU DON'T CHOOSE THE HIGH ROAD, THE LOW ROAD WILL BE CHOSEN FOR YOU

We've touched upon so many topics this evening . . . choices, new scientific technologies, wars, sovereignty and emperors. So many of these subjects seem to involve self-imposed barriers that we've placed upon ourselves. This pattern seems to have played out cen-tury upon century. Why would we have done this to begin with?

It is one way to grow and to evolve. Many choices were and are considered moment by moment; from a certain perspective, the least interesting of all choices receives the most votes. Your last presidential election is a perfect exam-ple of this phenomenon. He [the winning candidate] was also described as the least pleasing of all choices, but by hook or by crook, he garnered the most votes. Experience is like that; it is what becomes reality when another reality is not chosen. If the higher road is not chosen, the lower road inevitably is.

This choice did not originate here on Earth; it was a decision made elsewhere but experienced here. It was brought here and allowed here because this is an environment that invites free will. The experience or experiment continued here for the same reason. Humans did not choose this path, but they chose to continue to participate in it. They did not remove themselves from the experience so they became somewhat blinded by it—unwilling or unwitting participants.

What was happening at the time other choices were being considered?

It was seen as an opportunity, but it was only outlined. In other words, it was painted with very broad brush strokes that left much room for interpretation and experience. It was not envisioned that it would go on for as long as it has. It was not envisioned that it would be a battle between forces of light and dark as it is described and experienced by some—that was added later. It was simply a choice, an experience. Every day you make decisions that will result in beginnings and endings, and this was no different. It is important to remember that only one aspect of you understands this choice as having been imposed upon you; other aspects of you remember it differently. Divine grace and order ensure that eventually you will see, know and understand all that you are, even the parts that you would deny today.

UNITED NATIONS: EVOLVE OR DISSOLVE

Will the United Nations be in wreck and ruin by what the Bush administration is about to do?

The United Nations has placed itself on a collision course with an explosive reality that will not offer it a choice platform on which to stand. If, as a body, it cannot find the means to correct course, it will falter and then wreck.

The members of the United Nations have put a stamp of disapproval upon themselves by not acting in the spirit and charter of their authority. It is important to note that they did not come together as one body, representative of peace, but as many individual agendas that happened to include one or more versions of peace. Fear, political allegiance, contraband, financial necessity and a series of tragic compromises have pitted a council of representatives against itself.

The United Nations envisioned and prepared for many moments but not this one. It knew that it would at times bully others into submission or surrender, but it did not know that a bigger bully would bring it to its knees, and so easily too. Safety and power are in rank and sheer number they thought, but the balance of power had already shifted to one of volume and financial blackmail.

The United Nations' ability to survive rests in its ability to act as one body and to resuscitate its purpose by envisioning a different future than the one that has been proposed by those who wield the most power. Currently, it is outmanned and outgunned in almost every way. Those who call themselves representatives can barely represent their own nations, much less a body called the United

Nations. As an entity it must decide whether it will live or die and in what way or by what hand. Is it a body of knowledge? Is it a body of government? Is it the puppet front of individual nations or the representative body of many nations? The United Nations must evolve or it will dissolve.

Some already believe that it might have outlived its usefulness. If another body readies itself as a replacement, then it might very well assume that position. The ability of the United Nations to survive is dependent upon the ability of its member nations to thrive. It will become united when and if the world's nations become united. Its purpose can unfold and rebound in a new season of purpose and growth if it becomes a body of wisdom rather than the strong arm of one country or one being.

Unrest in the Middle East Continues

What effect will the invasion of Iraq by the U.S. have on the Middle East? Will Syria and Iran be next?

The invasion of Iraq will be smooth and easy. Possession will pass from one owner (ruler) to the next as quickly as escrow is closed upon the sale of any other property. Iraq will be assimilated into the mainstream consciousness of the world. It will be rebuilt, modernized and industrialized. In the future, a great university will be built there and many will choose to study there. It will continue to be the land of secrets, as many will lie buried there for some time. Iraq will be rebuilt as no country in history has ever been. It will be chosen as the seat of power one day, but that seat will not be filled.

The Middle East will continue to know unrest; it is ungovernable, at least for the time being. Many plans will be proposed, but none will be well thought out or balanced. The seat of power is corrupt there, and it cannot be recovered. The Middle East will be opposed and defended on all sides; blood and tears will continue to be shed. Syria and Iran will be licking their wounds for a time. They quite enjoyed sitting on the sidelines while their neighbor took the world stage. They hated him and envied him and supported him because who else would? Now they will be called up as well; they will be interrogated, ridiculed, threatened and courted. Their response will determine what happens next.

Where Is Saddam Hussein?

What happened to Saddam Hussein?

He is vacationing underground. His contract is complete. He has played his part well and will now receive the reward he was promised. The curtain has closed on him for the time being. The world stage has little patience for players who tire of playing. Just as in comic books and cartoons, a hero is only a hero as long as there is a bad guy to oppose. Superman created a need for himself in Metropolis, otherwise he would have been standing in the unemployment line along with the other heroes who had outlived their usefulness.

NUCLEAR TECHNOLOGY WILL BE OBSOLETE

What will happen with North Korea's nuclear program?

It is proceeding as planned with the blessing of those who support it. By the time it is operational, it will be obsolete, because the treasure will have been fully discovered and translated by then. New technology will make nuclear technology obsolete. All the monies and agendas that were funneled in that direction made for an interesting sidebar but little else. Technology will soon be weaponized, but it is wise not to underestimate the power of a disgruntled despot.

ENEMY OF THE STATE IS FEAR

Will there be a multilateral, international effort to attack the United States in years to come?

Yes, but not as you now imagine it. The United States will be safeguarded and protected on all sides. Its military will be prepared and advanced. It will continue to make alliances and partnerships. Eventually, it will be infiltrated, but it will not know how or where. It will fear even its own shadow and the shadow of its shadow. The game will be turned inside out and from front to back. The branches of government will not trust one another or themselves. Yesterday's secrets will become today's headlines, and today's headlines will become tomorrow's obituaries. Today power corrupts, tomorrow power will be fatal. The enemy of the state is not the Middle East or the Far East; it is fear. Eventually, false power will succumb to fear, and eventually, true power will overcome fear.

WHAT ABOUT GEORGE BUSH?

How much of the Earth will George Bush destroy before he is stopped?

He will destroy as much as you allow him to. He is an aspect of you and of everyone else. He embodies and represents all the aspects you do not wish to embody or represent. All that he is you have also been or have contemplated becoming or have enabled, empowered or assisted others in becoming. He is a mirror that you must look at, and—like it or not—there are aspects of you represented there. His path and yours are entwined, at least for the current moment.

Will George Bush be reelected?

Possibly. It will depend upon whether humanity hungers for war or tires of it, because this president will not tire of it. It will depend upon the true definition of a patriot and a citizen. It will depend upon the rest of the world, because this election, more than any other, will be influenced by the citizens of the world, even if it is only the citizens of the United States who are eligible to vote. There will most likely be the largest voter turnout on record. The 2004 election will be pivotal for the years that lead into the transition of 2012.

The Last of His Line

Will Pope John's peace plan get anywhere?

No, not at this time. His voice will not be heard above the cacophony of other voices and agendas. The scandals that have ravaged the Vatican's court have silenced voices that would otherwise rise in power. This was foreseen and engineered accordingly by those who whisper in the halls of injustice. The current pope has not passed the scepter to another because he is the last of his line and the last of his kind. There will not be another, not in the same way.

The Christian Church will replace the Catholic Church in position and power. Another, newer or younger pope is not a viable solution, and the current pope knows this.

Making Sense of Terrorism

I can't make sense of terrorism, can you? What is it about? Why is it here at this time? What lesson are we supposed to learn from it?

A terrorist is someone who is afraid of the (their) future and would rather not experience it or have you experience it. The terrorists' fear and apprehension cannot put an end to their pain, but their pain can put an end to their decision. Terror is that which is afraid to see beyond the present moment. It sees the past as without hope and the future as hopeless. Where can that leave the present? A terrorist believes no promise and has no faith. A future that cannot be envisioned cannot be lived. The lesson regarding terror and terrorists is to live with it or live without it, but to live fully and completely.

Whenever possible, acknowledge, respect and appreciate who or what you fear most, even if it is a terrorist. Find pity within your heart for those who value life so little as to take it for granted in such a way. How sad it is that a being can be talked out of his or her future or tricked off his or her path because another has given that being a vision that does not include tomorrow!

Trust in the Unlimited

Is there an alternative source of energy or fuel that we can look forward to using instead of oil?

Yes. There is a variety of alternatives, but most of them are not available to you yet. Some of them have been purchased from those whose brilliant minds found the source within the mind of Source. On the one hand, it would seem that you are being denied what is natural and free, but would you want what is natural and free if you had to pay for it?

This is but one of the many paradoxes that seem to reign at this time. It is a puzzle that will be solved in due time. In order for you to participate in free energy, you must participate in freedom rather than the illusion of freedom; otherwise, how will you truly know that it is free? In the meantime, it is important to adapt and adopt. Adapt to every moment so that you are a part of it rather than apart from it. Adopt an open mind so that its resources are available to you even when others are not.

The planet's current resources will continue to diminish, because it is time for them to do so, not because humanity is good or bad, intelligent or foolish. Everything has its time and its season. Do not hoard what you have or who you are, even if it is scarce. Even if your resources seem limited, the source from which they are offered is not. Trust in the unlimited even while you participate in the limited. Share what is limited, and you will continue to receive from the unlimited.

THE NEW SUBLIMINAL LANGUAGE

We've spoken very little about the media and its influence upon us. It seems that television, film and the print media are more distorted and manipulated than ever. Will there be an avenue of expression for light in these areas? Will projects and promotions that offer other perspectives present themselves?

The media is subject to the same choices as all other forums of expression, but of all forums, it is the most captivating at this time, because it is the finest example of the technological age available. Film and television and even radio are learning and practicing a new language now, a form of autosuggestion; a subliminal language. It is a language that the mind responds to particularly well. It is a new realm that is being explored, and it is available to all creative sources, meaning that it is not simply a tool of the covert or those who would control. It is a form of light that the mind reads or interprets much faster than even the eyes can see.

From one standpoint, it would seem that you could be unconsciously bombarded with messages and suggestions to act or participate in a certain way. On the other hand, once the mind perfects this language, it will take it to greater heights than are currently imagined by those who test-market it even now.

Expressions of light, as you put it, will have just as much access to this language as other expressions of polarity. When humanity can choose no more, receive no more, follow no more and so on, it will dissolve all that stands in the way of full-spectrum light or expression. Look for an experience that captivates rather than one that holds you captive. It is self-serving rather than all-encompassing to choose only what you call light, because when you do so, gravity will inevitably pull you from one polarity to another or from one extreme to another, as the case may be.

Absenting yourself from what you call the dark or the shallow is another aspect of the same duality scale. Whenever possible, stand poised, balanced and neutral to all languages and eventualities. Evaluate all truths and teachings with the same scale; do not place more emphasis on one perspective than you would give to another. Be not right-handed or left-handed, right-brained or left-brained. The right side might be stronger, but the left is more adept; they are both equal.

Will we be aware of the new subliminal language?

Not at first, no. You are being bombarded by microwave energy and other energies at this very moment. Are you aware of it? It will be like that. You will not be aware of it in the moment—until you will become aware of it. Are you aware of all that you experience during a meditation? No. Can you recall or recite all that you experienced today or yesterday?

Energy draws energy to it and communication draws communication. Language draws light and its absence. Do not be too concerned with what is said in language; be more concerned with what is conveyed and what energy conveys it. Be aligned and attuned to all that you are, and you will see that this is as much a vehicle for your evolution and growth as any other you currently consider.

ON THE DEVELOPMENT OF HUMAN GENETICS

It is my understanding that there are a certain number of human families who are in full control of the planet and that it is their will that is being acted out at this time. Can you comment on this?

There are families and there are interests that are grouped together. They are not tight-knit or well organized. Their lineage is as pure as their intention, and their royalty is little more than a rhyme for their loyalty. They have an interest and a purpose in being here, but so do you. They battle within themselves, between themselves and against themselves. They battle what you call the light as much as they battle the dark; it is simply how their energy is aligned. They can be boastful and aggressive, unstable and insatiable in their pursuits. They find equal attraction in the strong and the meek, and they take great pride in affecting or controlling both. They are not in full control of the planet, although they would like you to believe that they are. Another cannot really control you, but you can allow yourself to participate in an illusion that would make it seem so.

Can you speak about the origin of those who are said to have "seeded" this planet and how they relate to present-day humanity?

So many stories surround you at this time. Some are factual and some are simply contextual, which means that the embedded symbolism is more relevant than the information itself. As you attempt to rediscover your history, do not discount that which seems too outlandish or farfetched. A common adage purports that truth is often more strange than fiction, and where this subject is concerned, that is so.

This planet (Earth) has been seeded at various times and by a variety of beings. It would be unproductive and inconclusive to stress the importance of one time or one being over another, because each has played an important role in humanity's evolution. Each time the Earth received a "seed," a different species resulted because the seeding process itself involves genetic mutation and/or splicing of genetic material. Planetary acceleration and axial tilt also contributed to the many changes in genetic disposition. Each seeding can be thought of as experimental, because the outcome was not known. This form of experimentation should not be confused with manipulation of a species, which is altogether different.

Seven different seeds and experiments were successful; other attempts were not. Seven other worlds and species contributed genetic material to what would become the Earth human. It has been said that beings from other worlds resemble you; perhaps it is more appropriate to say that you resemble them. Are you descendants of monkeys or apes? No, but there is primate energy within you. Are you reptilian in brain and creation? No, but you have received a genetic adaptation that has allowed you to blend with many environments and many circumstances. Human genetics have been adapted, spliced, enhanced, turned on, turned off, altered and manipulated.

Some of the changes have been environmental, some have been generational and others have been purposeful manipulations. In many ways, humanity benefited by the genetic intrusion, and in some ways, it did not. Magnetic manipulation of the genes created polarity, which was not present before then. As human genes became polarized, humanity had little choice other than to explore polarity. This single act above and beyond all others changed your destiny, because it removed your free will. You have searched to understand it, recover it and reclaim it for a very long time.

Without free will, humanity became a race of followers rather than leaders, and it has followed many leaders for a very long time. Off-planet races visit humanity at specific intersections where time and evolution come together in unique combination. This is one of those times, so there is a great deal of galactic interest in humanity now. This time period can best be described as a galactic window of opportunity. Past moments such as this one have led to more separation rather than less. In other words, humanity found less in common with itself instead of more. If it cannot find common ground and acceptance for itself, it will not find it for humans upon other worlds either. Separation causes fear, and fear causes stress and anxiety. This must be overcome during this window of opportunity so that you will rediscover your free will.

Free will is that which allows you to choose rather than to be chosen, to lead rather than to follow. Your galactic family currently awaits your decision. It is true that other worlds seeded the Earth; but in many ways, it is also true that the Earth has seeded other worlds—this is one aspect of the story that one hears very little of. Your galactic family is quite grand and diverse. You are all much more related than you presently imagine, certainly much more than you are prepared to agree upon.

INTERACTION WITH SPECIES FROM OTHER WORLDS WILL INCREASE

Within our lifetime and in the near future, will there be agreement for interaction with species from other worlds?

Agreement for local gatherings of this nature already exists. They take place here and there with those of like mind or body just as you have gathered here this evening. Meetings and gatherings include those of other races, cultures, beliefs and worlds. Some gatherings involve exchanges of energies that you would call channeling, and others are quite physical. Some of the physical gatherings allow for a temporary occupation of physical human bodies, an exchange of sorts.

Other species from other worlds are not yet truly welcome upon the Earth, and they know this. There is a curiosity that would summon them, but that is not the same as true interest. That is why they share their thoughts and wisdom with you for now so that humanity will come to see what is in common rather than what is not. When humans can welcome their own neighbors, they will also be able to welcome those from other worlds. When there is acceptance and companionship instead of censorship, a true program of exchange will begin. Many who understand and are attuned to frequencies that exist beyond the third dimension already participate in these cultural exchange programs, in one form or another. There is much to be gained from physical and nonphysical communication alike, but it must be welcome rather than imposed.

Humans must also be willing to acknowledge themselves as equal to other beings and other kingdoms before other races will fully demonstrate themselves to you. Another race cannot and will not save you or your planet from yourselves or from your emperor. As agreement for communion and companionship in this area expands, there will be more contact, and yes, it will be in your time and in what you call the near future.

TRANSCEND LINEAR TIME TO TRANSFORM IT

There seems to be so much conflicting information about transformation right now. For instance, I find the Mayan calendar interesting but do not understand it. I also don't think I understand the difference between the third, fourth and fifth dimension that we are about to embark on. Can you add any clarity to this subject?

Linear time cannot access transformation, so it cannot understand it either. One must transcend linear time in order to transform it. As long as you are transfixed by it, you will not move beyond it. None of the definitions that have been offered thus far are completely accurate, because they are all based upon systems of belief that are in decay and near collapse. Even the system by which the hours, days and years are measured is no longer valid.

Mayan calendars are based upon galactic time rather than linear time. Galactic time is dimensional; it is stacked like one of your skyscrapers, and the dimensions intersect and overlap. When humanity's collective awareness shifts beyond the linear third dimension, it will begin to make a little more sense.

For now it will be helpful if you do not struggle to understand a nonlinear concept with a linear mind. If a child cannot yet add or subtract, it would not matter how much he struggled to memorize a multiplication table, because the information would be useless in the present. In the future, however, it would make a lot of sense. Do not dismiss the subject altogether, but think upon it with both hemispheres of the brain whenever possible. Release time from its current obligation, and space will follow. When this becomes a reality rather than a conjecture that requires confirmation, the conflict within you will ease.

BE MORE THAN HUMAN, NOT LESS THAN DIVINE

How can we be aware of ourselves in the present moment and in present multidimensional moments as well?

By acknowledging that there are aspects of you that are human and aspects that are divine. Earth days last approximately twenty-four hours, but cosmic days are measured differently—and so are galactic days, universal days and solar days. Each day understands itself as independent and interdependent upon all others. The Sun shines upon all planets in this solar system, but it does so differently in each case. It relates to each world in unique and specific ways, but it is simultaneously a part of each world at all times—and so are you. Adopting an awareness and a posture of being more than human and not less than divine will assist you in this process.

Whenever possible, take the time to acknowledge that you are more than the human awareness that reveals itself to you in the moment: "I am more than this linear moment. I move from simplicity to complexity and back easily and effortlessly. I attune and acknowledge all realities, even those that exist beyond my current awareness. I receive more and retrieve more in every moment. I regain and retain more every day." Do not attempt to define "more," because you could only do so with the linear mind. It is in the allowing, the calling forth and the acknowledgment that you become more—be-come; come to be more.

EXPERIENCE SIMULTANEOUS TIME AND CHOOSE YOUR REALITY

I have heard that Europe is already moving into the fifth dimension and that the rest of the world will be making the same transition by 2011 or 2012. Can you speak about that?

Your hearing is accurate, but what you have heard is not. It has been passed from one person to another, first in the spoken word, then in the written word. By the time it was published and sent around the world by electronic means, it had become inaccurate. Your history books are published in similar fashion, so it is not surprising that other material would follow similar suit.

Certain aspects of the Earth, of my sentience, already experience the fifth dimension and beyond. Time, space and dimension are relative. The third dimension relates to them in one way, while other dimensions relate to them quite differently. Linear time is only an aspect of dimensional time, just as a line or an angle is only an aspect of a triangle or another geometric figure. All aspects must be considered in order to express accurate information. When information is diluted, skewed, altered or embellished, there is less room for truth to take up residence.

The year 2012 is a point in time based upon linear or third-dimensional understanding. Collective agreement has placed a great deal of emphasis and excitement upon this window or corridor of time. An opportunity currently exists to experience more than one dimension of experience at a time; perhaps "simultaneous" time is a better description than "dimensional" time.

The principle of simultaneous time allows experience to take place in the third and fifth dimensions simultaneously, do you see? By this understanding, the Earth is already in the fifth dimension and has no need of arriving at an arbitrary point in time called 2012 before it can experience the fifth dimension. The difficulty does not lie with 3D, but with the belief and perceptions that accompany 3D.

Beliefs have form, structure and rules; they are not fluid. Currently, the rules say that humanity has many expectations surrounding the 2012 date. If the rules were changed, the date might be changed as well. Those who initially put forth that aspects of Europe had already moved into the fifth dimension shifted any and all beliefs relative to linear time. They invited the 2012 window into the Now moment, envisioned the possibility and then chose the reality. Is all of Europe in 5D because they did that? No, it is the reality of those who chose that experience, just as your reality is based upon the experience you choose.

Can you do the same? Yes! Begin by acknowledging that the Earth is already a fifth-dimensional entity, because it is and so are you. It is not difficult to imagine if you place your awareness in an expanded state that invites many possibilities, such as your dream consciousness. Allow simultaneous time and dimensional time to be the companions of linear time. This will make the experience gradual and graceful rather than abrupt.

The year 2012 is the end of a system of measuring time; it is not the end of time itself. There is no fear when the date on the calendar says that one season will end and another will begin, but there is a great deal of fear surrounding this date. Fear invites prophecy, and there is a prophecy that states that the world will end in 2012. It says that a cataclysm will destroy the Earth and all upon it. Fear/prophecy says that time will run out in 201, or that it will come to a standstill.

That would certainly invite cataclysmic results, but what if prophecy simply invited you to think differently or choose differently? What if it invited you to evolve from one dimension into another by choosing a different path? Be a part of all that is presented to you; imagine and envision many possibilities, but be certain to include the best possibilities while considering the worst.

THE CHANGING HUMAN BODY

I understand that sound and light frequencies have shifted—or are about to shift—how we relate to healing mind, body and spirit. Would you be willing to speak about that?

Frequencies shift and change all the time. Any beneficial changes, including the smallest fluctuations, are immediately available to any being who vibrates in resonance with the Earth. That which you speak of is accessible to humanity, but a conscious acknowledgment of its benefit is still positioned in the future. Humanity's consciousness cannot acknowledge it until the mind and the body can acknowledge it.

The human body still understands itself as solid and dense; it does not yet have an understanding of itself as light. Its movement is not yet fluid, and the body has not yet rid itself of small plagues and inconsequential malaise. The mind still processes unwanted and unconscious thoughts and is only sometimes aware of this. Even Spirit is dependent upon belief systems that prevent It from expressing Itself naturally and completely. Humanity is moving in sync with those energy fluctuations that are already aligned with it. Others await a more opportune moment.

As body, mind and spirit become lighter in frequency and density, the organs of the body will release their toxins, and it will seem that many of the population are ill and can no longer process the same foods they have consumed before. Food poisoning will be rampant, and there will be a strong desire to return to the natural foods that can restore health. The body still holds toxicity within the density; one complements the other even if it does not seem so. Attunements of crystalline light and other acknowledged methods of healing are available now, but their full benefit will not be felt or understood for a few years yet.

THE TRUE SOURCE OF WEALTH

If the universe is a representation of total and complete abundance, why are we still dealing with money? Are we waiting for everyone to get a piece of the pie before it is gone?

Money is a system of energy exchange. It is well understood by this time that very little energy is being exchanged. When energy is not exchanged, it dwindles. All resources respond accordingly, and world economies are no different. Lack of energy exchange will continue to cause a reduction of resources, and some banks will be forced to close their doors. There is not enough money in the system because humanity no longer believes in the system. All systems must have public support in order to be viable. A firm foundation no longer represents this system, so it will topple and fail.

It must also be said that the monetary system is not what is keeping humans from realizing themselves as abundant. Replacing this system with another will not automatically restore an abundant nature. Humans must first discover that their wealth does not come from their monies or their gold. When they realize that their resources are within their collective heart, spirit and soul, they will find that they are resplendent and abundant on all fronts.

THE TRUE SISTERHOOD

As women, we have been gathering, becoming more empowered and discovering a united sisterhood. It feels as though we are finding our voices and our strength more than ever. I am wondering what our next role is. Where are we going?

Perhaps it is more appropriate to say "coming" rather than "going." You are becoming more than individual women; you are becoming a oneness of women. Womanhood will become womankind when she acknowledges the sensuality of the divine feminine rather than the sexuality of the human feminine. The divine feminine is found in partnership with the divine masculine. This should not be mistaken for the current male and female gender roles that are deemed culturally acceptable at this time. A divine partnership also exists between the child, the youth, the aged and the wise. Womankind will blossom when she acknowledges all aspects of humanity as herself. Mankind will come into his fullness in the same way, and humankind must also experience itself as one.

Women are not yet in true sisterhood, because in order to do so, they must find strength and equality in the mother, the daughter, the wife, the grandmother, the mother-in-law and the whore. When the wisdom in all beingness is acknowledged—including the animal kingdom, the plant kingdom and the mineral kingdom—the true meaning of sisterhood and brotherhood will be understood and will expand. Any form of separation, however exalted and purposeful, is still separation; it divides but does not unite.

EXPRESSING NONPHYSICAL ENERGY PHYSICALLY

Can form and formlessness come together in ecstasy? Is sexuality the bridge to this experience? Will we find ecstasy in the unified field and unity within our physical vehicles? Is all of humanity capable of experiencing and merging with God in form, awareness and consciousness?

God/All That Is carries form and formlessness within It and distributes and demonstrates it in ways that you would marvel at. Ecstasy describes the experience of momentary union with God/All That Is, but it is only a word, an understanding between one or more individuals. God/All That Is can only be experienced; It cannot be described, for no words could suffice. Form and formlessness are both experiences of God/All That Is, because they both emanate from the same Source.

The perception that ecstasy is best experienced out of body or beyond body is a human one. Form is not less ecstatic than formlessness, but it is denser. Density is an illusion just as separation is an illusion; both are designed to keep you from feeling or experiencing All That Is.

Look beyond the form and the formless and beyond your definition of ecstasy too. There you will find an experience of All That Is both within and without. It does not differentiate or separate Itself. Intimacy and sexual expression are vehicles for expressing nonphysical energy in physical ways. Sexuality is an expression of physicalized union with Spirit when it is experienced as more than a physical act for the sole purpose of sexual gratification. Sexuality is a forum that can express two as one, but it can also express one as One. Humanity is God in form; it is simply not consciously aware of it at this time.

ALL CHILDREN ARE PSYCHIC

There is a lot being said these days about psychic children. Is it true that these special children are carriers of unique frequencies that will assist and unite the planet?

There are many special and unique children upon the planet at this time, but tell me: When your children were born, did you not look upon them in the same way? Did you not believe their presence would make a difference upon the Earth? Did you not think their generation was more capable and advanced than your own? Your parents believed the same about you.

All children are psychic; this generation is simply the first to be acknowledged as such. If you acknowledge their brilliance, you must also acknowledge your own, otherwise the flow will be cut off between the generations. Every generation can heal itself, its past and its future if it is allowed to. All beings receive this gift from Source/All That Is. Each being and every collective essence is a gifted carrier of special purpose and unique alignment.

Will the children be a blessing to the planet? Yes, but perhaps it is not appropriate to assign them too great a task before they even come of age. They need not take on the burdens of past and present generations in order to be effective, and they should not be asked to complete what others do not wish to do for themselves. They are gifted, but their childhood is also their gift. Make certain they are not robbed of it.

GATHER IN GROUPS AND COUNCILS

I am actively remembering that I chose to be here at this time. I feel a calling that reminds me that my soul volunteered for this long ago. It feels somewhat revolutionary and militant, as if I'm on the front lines of something I cannot define. I understand the necessity of being in personal balance, peace and harmony, and at the same time, I am longing for a coming together of groups and councils so that a new structure for living can be created. Am I on the right track with this?

Yes, you are. On this night, there are many people and councils who have come together; this is not the only one. This gathering is representative of others; there are physical and nonphysical councils and gatherings. All who are here are part of other councils and conferences—as long as you are multidimensional beings, it cannot be otherwise. A pebble tossed into a pond creates ripples that move from the center outward, and your energy is not different. The guidance and essence that is you has quite an entourage assigned to its detail, one that is actively aware even when you are not.

Do you believe that only humans gather themselves to discuss peace? Other kingdoms and other beings also gather. The animal kingdom gathers in expression of its willingness and desire, as do the plant and mineral kingdoms. The forces of nature are not idle or at the whim and fancy of others. More councils will soon gather as well, some upon the planet and others within and beyond it.

Be in knowingness and awareness regarding the subject of council so that messages and invitations will come your way. Remind yourself that you are purposeful and that your life continually creates purpose for both active (doing) and passive (being) participation. Your life is an emergence of expression that acknowledges access, evolution, growth and discovery in all areas.

I am very interested in the subject of council gatherings. It stirs something deep within me, and I would like to continue council gatherings even beyond this evening. Tonight we have the benefit of your presence and the gift of asking questions and receiving answers, but what else can we know about coming together in this way?

Indeed, a fine question. You always have the benefit of my presence. I do not exist within the channel, and she does not exist within me. You might not always hear words expressed as they are here, but that need not be a limitation of expression. Too often humans surrender their power to another, regardless of whether it is another authority or another channel.

Each being is aligned with an original codex, an original understanding of self. Original means that which originates within Source; it means that which is a perfect expression of self within the mind of God/All That Is. A codex is the part of all awareness that has never known nonperfection. At the time of physical birth, each incarnation is aligned with his or her codex or perfection. The unique position of the sky at the time each being draws his or her first breath ensures this. Your codex also aligns you with your multidimensional awareness, drawing support and wellness from other aspects of you.

Even when you are first born, you already participate in councils of awareness, because only one aspect of you is a newborn. You already know a great deal about the subject of council gatherings, and you are about to bring forward much more of this knowledge so that it will be available to others as well. Council gatherings are of energetic benefit to humanity and to the Earth, because they acknowledge perfection upon perfection upon perfection. They acknowledge a sacred geometry based upon perfection, do you see? They are amplifiers of an unparalleled source of perfect energy.

Would you recommend that we continue to gather in groups and councils? If so, is there a particular focus or purpose that would generate the most interest and benefit?

It is appropriate to gather for the purpose of discovery and empowerment. It is important to gather to see what is of interest or boredom to those who attend, but there must be an agreed-upon purpose so that there will be a firm foundation rather than a flimsy one. Many are gathering, but they are gathering to discuss and agree upon the drama. This is a limited rather than an expansive use of resources.

Would it be of benefit to gather at places that are of higher vibration than others? Are there certain activities that should take place when we gather?

A place is only as sacred as that which is upon and within it. As long as you bring your creativity, interest and purpose with you, it does not matter where you gather—although you will certainly have your preferences. Intent builds interest and desire. All other matters, including agenda, are secondary or tertiary to intent. Desire draws and expands energies. Expansive energies could not remain in only one location. That would be true even if you gathered at that one location every time, do you see? Make your intent to commune with the Earth and partner with it to amplify and diversify energy.

TAKE THE NEXT STEP

Is there any last thing that you'd like to share with us, Gaia, before we call it an evening?

I will perhaps only reiterate the importance of thinking and feeling expansive, of moving in the direction of awareness, knowingness and supported guidance. Choose unlimited and unbridled thought and purpose. Remove blinders, and you remove boundaries; remove limitation, and you remove prejudice. Open your outer eyes wider, and your inner eyes will see better as well. Learn to see in the dark, and the light will not blind you. Walk side by side and hand in hand with all aspects of your beingness. Assign sovereignty and free will to all kingdoms, species, elements and beings. Envision the best of all worlds that you may live in it. Take the next step and then the next.

The Key to Dealing with an Epidemic of Global Fear

July 2003

My job takes me to cities and countries that many do not have the opportunity to visit. I consider myself fortunate and have counted my blessings many times over. Recently, however, I have begun to experience the same discontent and malaise that many of my friends have already succumbed to. Everywhere I go, I see depressed and unhappy faces, ill health, fear and even death. The fact that I carry a U.S. passport now seems to add an additional blight to an already gloomy circumstance. I have experienced firsthand the impact that SARS (severe acute respiratory syndrome) is having upon an entire population. I must confess that I have been deeply affected by this, as never before, and would sincerely appreciate some perspective on this unpleasant subject.

SARS is a bioengineered pathogen. It is being test marketed in both the Eastern and the Western Hemispheres of the planet. It is mutational, meaning that it can reinvent itself and even change its symptoms. Different strains are already being discovered, and it will soon be seen that the virus can be dormant or active. Those who are fortunate enough to survive its devastating effects will still carry it within their bloodstream for a long time. It is inadvisable to give or receive blood that has been exposed to this biogerm.

SARS is not new. It was created long ago as a byproduct of a well-funded study that sought to merge the science of species' survival with an in-depth understanding of populational fortitude. It is one of many "inventions" of the late twentieth century based upon the translation of an ancient manuscript that described in great detail the decimation of a species that had proliferated elsewhere.

The world cannot sustain its current population, given that resources are being underappreciated, overextended and taken for granted. Those who govern from behind walls, masks and screens know this. They have studied the statistical outcome of many eventualities, including nuclear war and other unfathomable realities. Computer programs have been assigned full-time tasks that include computations of every imaginable "what if" scenario. Country, religious sect, longitudinal and latitudinal coordinates, seasonal and climatic variances, ozone layer viability, campaigns of aggression, cultural and genetic genocide and other statistical demographics are evaluated and updated day by day and sometimes hour by hour.

DISEASES ARE CREATED LIKE A NEW PRODUCT

Given an ongoing desire to reduce the surface population of the Earth, do you believe that a cure for cancer will be announced any time soon?

Several cures for cancer already exist, as do vaccines for the prevention of AIDS and other twentieth-century inventions. These have been temporarily silenced, but not for long. The research was purchased with grants and contributions from endowments that have strong connections to those who influence leadership and policymaking.

Charitable organizations have solicited and received dollars in your name and the names of others with sincere and altruistic hearts, but this has been the result. It is not difficult to find a cure for a disease that has been created—unless one is prevented from doing so. Most often, the disease and the cure are both created at the same time.

A disease is created in much the same way as a new fragrance or product might be developed. It is first designed with great care and then created. Is it not obvious that most of the current diseases seem to afflict the elderly and the otherwise vulnerable? Would these individuals not be considered expendable to those who think but do not feel? Are not the old and the weak more costly and burdensome upon both government and society? These words carry a disheartening tone, but think carefully. Have they not already been whispered to you before now?

Those who purchased the rights to the cure for cancer are the same as those who paid for the well-funded, all-inclusive studies. Knowledge and intelligence are both commodities that are bought and sold, and they are not as expensive as many would believe. Are those who sold this intelligence bad, wrong or evil? No, they are not. Just like you, they are interested in leading productive lives, raising consciousness and making a physical and spiritual contribution in their lifetime. Their reality has been distorted as sometimes yours is too. Fact and fiction are no longer opposites but partners who share the same page in history.

The cure for several kinds of cancer will soon be announced. The cure for AIDS will come shortly after, perhaps within the next year or two. Why? Because the path the disease takes has been discovered by more than one source. Its origin and energetic signature have been compromised. If a secret is no longer a secret, then it might as well be a well-publicized event, do you see?

The announcement will be well timed and managed with the political campaign of the chosen victor. There will be much ado and fanfare that will include the promise of more dollars spent in the name of medical research. The pharmaceutical industry is a powerful cabal, perhaps even more so than the tobacco industry that has recently fallen so far from favor.

SARS is not a disease, but a political commodity; it is a tool with which to govern. What is the fastest way to turn the tide of political and economic unrest? Fear. What is the fastest way to ensure that a population needs its government? Fear. What is the fastest way to control a population's movement and freedom? Fear. Again I say that there is a product being test marketed worldwide, but it is not what most believe. It is called fear.

LACK AND FEAR LEAD TO DEPRESSION

The malaise you describe in your communication is currently afflicting more than 50 percent of the world's population. Minds and bodies are becoming depressed at alarming rates. Antidepressant drugs are currently being prescribed in greater numbers than any plague-eradicating solution throughout the course of human history. As the natural nutritional content of consumable food continues to decrease, the artificial content continues to rise. The body makes do with vitamin and mineral supplements when they are available and introduced in healthful quantities, but otherwise it suffers. The body speaks to the brain and makes its needs known in ways that are small or large, easy or difficult—as the case may be. Unmet needs become demands, and unmet demands become unhappy, unfortunate and distressed individuals.

Is it wrong to depend upon narcotics such as antidepressants? No, as long as it is understood that they are a temporary remedy for a situation or circumstance that has a permanent answer elsewhere. Antidepressants and other drugs do not repair the body; they help sustain it so that a more appropriate choice can be made, from a more balanced and integrated perspective. They help merge the hemispheres of the brain that have drifted so far apart that reality and illusion exist side by side. If the brain cannot differentiate between reality and illusion, it shuts down or rebels, depending upon the chemical makeup of the individual.

Depression is the result when fear is not addressed or is dismissed. The greatest fear among conscious humanity at this time is that it will not realize its purpose, or that a purpose that includes a creative life beyond basic survival is only a fiendish interpretation of the imagination. The greatest fear among unconscious humanity at this time is that it will not become conscious enough to experience its imagination or that its purpose may be basic survival after all. Can you see how thin the divide between consciousness and unconsciousness really is? The veils that separate you from your self are just as thin; certainly thin enough to begin to see how to erase the illusion of separation.

HERE'S THE KEY

Weakness did not create SARS, but it allowed it to become a part of its reality. Fear did not create cancer, but it allowed it to share an otherwise healthy body. Depression did not create Prozac, but it gave access to the brain's hemispherical references. Cynicism and apathy are not diseases, but they invite malaise into the spirit. An unlived life does not suggest pain as an alternative, but it does not celebrate creativity.

Your life on Earth is a commemorative event. It is not meant to be taken with a sedative or lived like a flag at half-mast. Those who search the past do so for clues that greatness existed, and those who look to the future do so with the same expectancy. Humanity is Earth's treasure and its treasury. It is a pity that unconsciously humanity continues to search out debts to pay that were never incurred.

Opportunities to choose the pitiful or the plentiful will continue to present themselves. SARS is one example; there will be many others. Each opportunity will offer itself differently, but they all will have many similarities. Fear versus power will continue to be a common theme, as will truth versus the clandestine, wealth versus poverty, illusion versus reality, illness versus well-being, consciousness versus unconsciousness and awareness versus ignorance. When separation is discarded in favor of unity, SARS will be discarded as well.

SARS is a debilitating assault on the immune system. It makes the body stand as a lone soldier on the battlefield, attempting to hold off an invasion on its own. The soldier cowers in fear at the immensity of the opposition that stands against it, watching helplessly as the invading army prepares to occupy a body that once knew desire, free will, well-being and choice. The solution and the antidote are well within reach. It is not a newfangled pill that just arrived on the scene at substantial cost, although this will more than likely be introduced as well.

The key is in choosing wellness, vitality, vigor and a creative use of every cell, molecule and atom in one's keeping. The door to the dormant is in awakening the creative life and in fulfilling one's purpose. A purpose is a creative expression of a self-aware soul. The purpose is to live the imagination, not to imagine a purpose. You will travel many miles in your purpose and even more in the journey that spans the inner self. In accumulating your "frequent flyer vouchers," make certain that you do not miss the opportunities to see that courage and fear are both dressed elegantly.

To the Moon and Beyond

Gaia and the Moon
August 2003

Did we really land on the Moon? I want to believe that we did, but I have heard and seen enough plausible evidence to suggest that the entire event was staged. I'm not sure that it even matters, but I'd still like to know.

A few humans did land on the Moon in your recent past, just as others landed there long ago. As far as space travel goes, a roundtrip to the Moon was not a very grand accomplishment, but in terms of its effect upon humanity's awareness, it was—and still is—a huge leap.

As you can see, the controversy regarding this event has not diminished and, in fact, continues to this day. And why wouldn't it when there are still those among you who believe that the Earth is flat? Would it not stand to reason that humans' ability to walk upon the Moon would remain in doubt? As long as polarity and duality exist, doubt will be their companion, because one direction or extreme cannot be less or better than another. Truth is as relative as experience and, as they say, there are always at least two sides to every story.

Those who supported and financed space travel in the past are the same as those who support it today. Their faces have changed a little; some have aged, whereas others have not. Names, titles and positions have shifted a bit, as have alliances and contracts, but the players are still basically the same. The original agenda had little to do with the Moon, but it was as good a place as any to begin. It was and is, as always, about power and control.

On the surface, it appears that the seat of power is within the government and upon the Earth, but for those who make it their business, it is obvious that the Earth is only a small cog in a very big wheel. Archaeological discoveries that suggest humanity's lineage is hidden within the stars are only now being given due consideration, but those who financed the early space missions already knew otherwise.

FACT AND FICTION ABOUT THE LANDING ON THE MOON

If the financiers had been honest and forthright with you, Earth's population would have become equal partners in an unfolding understanding of itself, but that was never the intention. In all fairness it must be said that humanity was not ready to abandon its beliefs or religions. Even now it teeters on the subject, but truth has a way of decimating everything in its path. Truth is both a creator of possibility and a destroyer of falsehood.

Upon studying several different scenarios, the elite among you made a series of plans and then layered them with additional contingency plans. They knew what they hoped to find on the Moon, but they did not know if the discovery could be made on the first attempt. In order to ensure loyalty and continued support on the part of the population of Earth, a well thought-out and well executed plan was a must. The result had to be an unequivocal success; the possibility of failure or delay was not given more than a moment's consideration. The lives of the astronauts were expendable, but the success of the mission was not.

Still, a shadow seemed to be suspended above all who had cleverly rehearsed every nuance of every decision. Although failure was not an option, it was a possibility. The sane among the planners approached the logical among the thinkers, and in secret, a worst-case scenario was broached. Together, they went to the next echelon, which guarded the doors of the inner sanctum of power. In hushed whispers, they developed a secret contingency plan; with muffled voices and directions, they carried it out.

"What does the average world citizen know about the Moon that we do not?" they asked themselves and one another. "They are not as interested in what we will find so much as whether we can get there and back," they all readily agreed. "If we can guarantee what the world will see, we can also guarantee what they will think." So they did.

The plan was not nearly as elaborate as it could have been, and it was relatively inexpensive to procure. The costliest aspect of the plot (as with any other) was the cost of silence. A desolate desert provided an excellent canvas and backdrop. Skilled artists, under the direction of less-than-skilled scientists, attended to details that Hollywood would surely have overlooked. The project came in well under budget, even including script and director. Under the auspices of a training and recruitment film designed to elicit contributions, funding and potential candidates for an upcoming aeronautical academy, the task was completed in a matter of weeks.

While professional astronauts underwent rigorous training elsewhere, amateur astronauts (actors) rehearsed their roles earnestly and intently in the quiet desert, believing all the while that they were serving their country as best they could. They believed they were performing what today you would call a Public Service Announcement, or PSA. They emulated the real astronauts they were shown on the training films, where gravity was altered and simulated in great cylinders. They took great pride in their rehearsals and worked hard to perfect mannerisms and maneuvers alike. When their job was done, they were thanked profusely and paid handsomely. They were also asked to swear an oath of silence that implied national security was at stake. They were even told that Russian spies or intelligence officers from other governmental agencies who would make inquiries about covert plots to discredit the space program might contact them.

The real astronauts did eventually travel to the Moon and back, and the images relayed around the world were a fine depiction of actual events . . . but not all of them, because an important aspect of the mission took place away from public cameras and commercial eyes. Substantial proof of past, current and future contact was evident and abundant. There were barriers and boundaries, however, which inexplicably could not be breached, because a magnetic field that used the Moon's gravity against it kept the visitors at bay. Their arrival had been anticipated for some time, as the technological divide between Earth and other "space" cultures was great. It was the opening act of a wonderful performance, and the stage was well set. The astronauts saw and recorded exactly what they had been meant to see.

Back on Earth, all was celebration, handshakes and complimentary backslaps. The mission was a success, and in many different ways a multilayered human society awoke from a deep slumber the next day. Were humans duped? No more than they expected to be. Those who still believed that the Earth was flat went to bed that night believing that was the case, and those who believed a Moon landing was impossible awoke the next morning believing the same thing. The vast majority of the population witnessed a great moment in human history delivered right to its doorstep (or television screen). All things considered, the addition of a Hollywood ending simply set the tone for future events to unfold.

Looking back upon that time, it is easy to see how much of the film footage was classified and then declassified, hidden from view and then offered to the public, taken apart frame by frame and then spliced together again. Fact and fiction will remain fused on this subject, at least for the time being.

Soon other, more exciting revelations will make this question much less interesting than it seems today, because the present present, the past present and the future present hold many more clues than the near past present. Careful investigation will reveal what science cannot, and the celestial bodies will reveal more than you could hope for. As you gaze at the Moon in the night sky, do not forget to turn your attention toward my brother, Mars, who has his own interesting stories to tell. He will not disappoint you.

The unfoldment of my companion and medium [Pepper Lewis] has at times been slow and deliberate or, as she would say, tedious. Nonetheless, it has been my pleasure and my duty to introduce her to a variety of beings, energies and sentiences. As our relationship progressed, other celestial bodies presented opportunities for an exchange of thoughts and ideas. Five years ago, as linear time goes, the Moon brought such an opportunity forward and the channel [Pepper] agreed. That transcript is made available to you here, as it is just as relevant now as it was then.

A Conversation with the Sentient Moon

Greetings, blessings and many words of welcome! I am the sentient being who embodies and enlivens that which is your Moon. How wonderful to establish this communication link between us, for I have much to say and share with you. In turn, there is much that I would like to learn about you. I see this as a mutual and beneficial exchange, then, and it is my sincere desire that you will see it as such as well.

Over these past years, as humanity has rediscovered communication with beings from different levels of time and space, it has been my hope that you would once again remember the intricate and deep relationship that we have shared with one another. My desire for this communication has intensified as I have seen bonds rekindled that were established long ago with master beings whose love and devotion to you and to planet Earth are so strong. My relationship and respect for her whom you call Gaia has allowed me to participate here and there in some of her interaction with you.

It has been both wonderful and exciting to share firsthand in the experience of the light that continues to expand and grow upon and within the planet. I have become accustomed to the turmoil and rush of activity that permeates so much of the planet's surface, but there is also an undercurrent of peace and a seeking for truth that are easily discernible to those who would look. This has brought a measure of excitement to my soul.

These words of introduction will assist you in acclimating to my frequency and energy, for they are uniquely different than those of the Earth, as you can already sense. I offer you this time to modulate your own frequency so that a smooth and firm communication link might be established. This is also a good exercise for you to practice from time to time, as it will make future visits and exchanges of many kinds easier. Of course, I am jumping ahead in assuming that this would be of interest to you and to others. Please accept the over-zealousness and enthusiasm, which I now feel as just that. As always, I honor each decision you make with respect to the continuance of any communication we might have.

I am aware of the many questions within your being, and I will do my best to answer most of them and to put you at ease during this first communication. Perhaps at some point we will do some energetic work together, for I would be remiss and unclear if I did not say that it is my intention to ask your assistance—as well as that of others—with certain matters that affect not only my livelihood, but dear Gaia's and yours as well. That having been said, please begin your questioning.

COMMUNICATION WITH THE MOON IS ONLY NOW POSSIBLE

Thank you. Can you tell me why I (and many others) have been able to communicate with the Earth for many years and yet communication with you seems new?

Yes. Simply put, you were not ready to accept this communication as a viable avenue of expression until now. Not only was your frequency not yet within the same band of compatibility, but it could also be said that you had your hands full, so to speak. Also, while you and many others have readily accepted the sentience of the Earth as a life-giving, life-sustaining organism, you were not yet ready to accept the same truth about your Moon. The myth regarding the Moon being a lifeless rock caught in the Earth's gravity field was too ingrained in your psyche.

You were actually more apt to accept this communication as real prior to your earlier lunar landings of the 1960s, because before that, you stood and looked up in wonderment. After those early Moon missions, most of the population came to accept the stated fact that there was indeed no life upon the surface of the Moon.

Did that disappoint you?

No. You must understand that I do not emote in the way you do or your dear Earth does. Please do not take this fact as a lack of interest on my part. It is simply that I am a being who is made of a different substance and energy than you are presently accustomed to. Perhaps it would be easier for you if you could relate to me as a visiting relative from far away who is not aware of and does not participate in your customs, for in truth, that is exactly what I am.

As you become accustomed to these communications, you will pave the way for yourself and others to experience various other forms of communications that are quite different from what you now experience. Many sentient beings desire to relate to humans in new and interesting ways. There is little holding back these communications at this time save for preconceived perceptions of what kind of communication is to come and how it will take place. Simplicity of spirit and an open heart are the only requirements.

To return to your original question, the majority of the population of Earth was not ready to have reciprocal communication before now, and the severe discrepancy in frequency would have made any communication sound like useless gibberish anyway.

ABOUT BASES AND UNINVITED GUESTS ON THE MOON

I've heard that there is some kind of a base on the Moon or even an intergalactic substation. I've also heard that you are or are near a star gate of some kind. Is this true?

Partly. There are a few beings who are currently using a certain segment of the surface as a base of operations for a specific purpose and for an agreed-upon length of time. There are others here who might be termed uninvited guests, and though their presence here does not affect me adversely, I would still not seek out their company.

Can you say who these beings are?

Yes, certainly. Some of them are humans from Earth; others are of human origin but not Earth origin. Neither is particularly welcome here, though I will say once again that their presence here is not considered an intrusion.

Why are they not welcome and what are they doing there?

They have their own agendas, and although they do not conflict with mine, they are nonetheless not aligned with the highest vibration available in this sector of the galaxy. Their vibration does not support the universal love vibration of what you term God, though it is not in conflict with it either. Simply put, their priorities lie elsewhere.

Does their presence on the Moon affect us here on Earth?

Only in that they are not concerned with your growth as a species or in your personal or planetary ascension. It is not in their best interest for you to become self-realized human beings. They are, however, prepared to deal with this eventuality if and when it becomes a reality. I will not comment further on this question, as this introductory meeting was not meant to become a political or philosophical conversation on the purpose and movement of this universe. I hope that is all right with you.

I have also heard that there is a race of beings living within the planet. Is this true?

There is a unique race who has carved out a niche within the surface. These beings do not make their home there all the time. Even when they are present, their full essence is not in attendance, only an aspect of it. Their presence here is not considered an intrusion.

THE MOON RE-CREATED ITSELF IN ITS CURRENT LOCATION

I'm sorry to go on like this, but I have also heard a theory that our Moon (you) was not here originally, not pulled in by gravity as is commonly believed. This theory supposes that you were "made" elsewhere and later driven or brought here. Is there any truth to this?

There is no unnatural way to create something unless it is somehow forced into existence, which is rare. It is true that I was not created or birthed in this vicinity. It could be said that I am older than the Earth, but this is only in a manner of speaking. Long ago there was a sequence or coordination of events that made my being here an important event in the development of an aspect of the human spirit. I was brought here to have an influence upon the Earth and upon humanity. Through a kind of bioengineering process, I was assisted in re-creating myself here, in this current place. It is quite far from my previous installation, which was also not my original location. This is an expression of home for my sentience, just as your physical vehicle is a temporary expression of home for your soul.

Moons in and of themselves serve a specific purpose within their defining sphere of influence. The kind of moon, the rotation, the angle of presentation as it relates to the planet whose field it is in and its relation to the Sun—all are important and all affect and influence the race of beings inhabiting the planet in question, if indeed there is a race of beings present.

CELESTIAL BODIES HAVE NO GENDER

It is said that the Sun reflects masculine attributes and the Moon reflects feminine attributes. I don't feel any such gender representation in this discussion or in your vibration. Would you comment on that?

Neither the Sun nor the Earth nor I has any apparent gender that you or anyone else would detect. This having been said, it is important to note that celestial bodies influence your emotions and your psyches. Therefore, your own male/female, passive/aggressive structures are influenced.

This, in turn, causes you to assign certain attributes to an otherwise androgynous being. You will soon be meeting many other species of an androgynous nature, and these experiences will begin to dissolve old belief structures and perhaps introduce you to new possibilities, which in turn will spur your growth beyond any boundaries you might perceive today.

ANXIETY ABOUT THE FUTURE OF THE HUMAN RACE

Were you aware of the lunar landings in the late sixties and early seventies? If so, how did you feel about them?

I felt sorry for the tiny beings who came here, and I had much admiration for their bravery. They were quite frightened and had resigned themselves to the possibility that they might never be able to get home again.

If you've ever marveled at how your ancestors called the Pilgrims voyaged to your shores in those tiny, rickety ships, you can certainly imagine how your rudimentary vehicles would appear to others who have made more progress in this area. I marveled at human ingenuity and felt content to observe your race and see how it would lift itself up by its breeches, so to speak. I felt anxious about your future as a race, if indeed there was to be one, and looked forward to the possibility of a discourse like the one we are currently having. Does this answer suffice?

THE SONG OF THE UNIVERSE CONNECTS ALL

Do you communicate with the Earth and with other planets or celestial bodies?

There is a network that allows for an interconnection between us. It is like an invisible web that lets us be separate and yet behave as one at times. There is a song of the universe that likens itself to the weave of a very soft and beautiful garment. In this way, we are all part of the One much as you are.

Does the song of the universe sound anything like the space sounds I have heard?

No. Please do not be insulted when I say that you cannot yet begin to perceive the beautiful intricacies of the sacred-geometry instruments that originate this music. You will, however, experience this and much more in your current lifetime. Again, be not offended by an honesty that does not judge.

COMMUNICATION WITH THE MOON ALWAYS TAKES PLACE

Will I have much more communication with you, as I now do with Mother Earth? Will others?

Communication is a relative term. We can interact to a greater extent, if you wish, as long as you do not forget that we are constantly influencing one another and that in this way, communication is always taking place. It does not stop when these words stop. You must also know that you may not call upon me at all moments in time as you currently do with other beings who are in place to assist you. Although I grandly support your efforts and those of others like you upon the Earth, there are other ways in which I choose to serve. This meeting, however, is not one of pure chance, and there will be more opportunities for us to interact in the future.

Would you like to communicate a message to others who might want to know about this exchange we have had?

Yes. Please pay attention to the details within your life's experience to an even greater extent than you already have. The future you have looked for and long awaited is here now. It is in the offing. Choose wisely how and with whom to interact. Lift your vibrations simply by being even more open to new possibilities than you have yet embraced. Do not judge your experiences or that of others or the choices you do make and will make.

Choose to be fully present upon the Earth's surface and not elsewhere, so that you do not miss what you have longed to experience because you have placed your attention elsewhere. Follow the example of your dearest friend and fondest supporter, the Earth, and cleanse and purge what no longer serves a purpose in your life. Seek out others like yourselves who are prepared to take the next step and then do so together, for there is more power in togetherness than in separateness. Do not take for granted who and what you are today, yet at the same time look beyond that to confirm for yourself that there is indeed a brighter horizon and a grander purpose.

I appreciate this exchange we have shared and look forward to another in the near future. Blessings to you and to all who would find themselves within these words.

One Tenth of Infinity:
The Story of Tithing

September 2003

I have begun to recognize the agency of tithing in my life as a source of abundance, nourishment and wisdom. Tithing has taught me to believe in trust, faith and magic. It has allowed me to experience an inner shift from fear to joy and has shown me that I am supported by dimensions and realms beyond my knowing. Could you describe the energy of tithing, Gaia? What role does it play in assisting humanity at this time? Is there a story you could share with us about people who lived in accord with tithing? Do you have any contemporary suggestions as to how to bring the subject into greater balance and awareness for everyone?

Your question is thoughtfully formulated, well crafted and humble in foundation. It is a question that has been asked before throughout history upon this world and others. Its true origin lies far away and long ago; its roots run deeper than you now remember.

Let's begin with a statement of premise, which says that the universe is as infinite as its supply is ceaseless. And for the sake of clarity, let's include the textbook definition of a tithe, which is quite literally an offering of one tenth of one's goods or earnings during a given period of time. The origin of the word is Hebrew and it is quite old, as you might imagine, but long before a word existed to define the experience, the experience still existed. Those who named the experience also gave it form, and form gave it density.

In its purest sense, tithing exists in a state of perpetual grace. It is elegant by nature, beautiful to behold and dignified in movement. Its expansive capacity tolerates, liberates, accommodates and forgives. It is infinite love in action and exemplifies the law of goodwill. By contrast, it also has a dense counterpart that includes hypocrisy, obligation, judgment, guilt, taxation and levy. The wide spectrum that separates these seeming opposites exists only in the mind, because our premise guarantees that the universe is as infinite as its supply.

What mathematical formula expresses one tenth of infinity? The question itself gives rise to a paradox within a paradox, one from which there is no escape. Given what we have discovered so far, is tithing necessary in a limitless universe? No. Does an active belief in tithing automatically enroll you in the school of limitation? No. Paradoxes often give birth to more paradoxes, and this one is no exception.

The universe is an ordered extension of All That Is. It exists in a condition of free will, which is absent of sin. A sin is not a moral or ethical offense. A sin is an act, thought or behavior that exists outside of All That Is. As no thought or act can exist outside of All That Is, we can now safely assume that the universe is sinless, blameless and limitless.

When space and time were fashioned into an illusion called form and density, tithing was born. Tithing was the Creator's response to infinite sustenance expressed within a context of finite structure. Originally, it was understood as the "law of infinite blessings." Later on, it was reduced to the lesser sounding "law of plenty." By the time tithing became socially and culturally accepted, it was little more than a voluntary taxation, a moral code of conduct or ethics to live by.

ASYNCHRONOUS TIME IS INFINITE AND PORTABLE

In its purest sense, tithing suggests that because some have, all may have. It acknowledges that infinite formlessness can be expressed within finite form but without limitation. It is the answer to the paradox, but that is only the beginning of the story. Long ago a very specific alchemical formula was written within the halls and corridors of time. It was left for those who were adept to interpret that time was not only infinite, but portable as well. In other words, it could be carried here and there if one understood its properties. Portable time was not limited to a specific time period, because it was undefined; it was contextual but not sequential. Contextual or portable time could be expanded or contracted as need or desire dictated, which is exactly how certain civilizations came and went at will, unfolding time within a certain context or understanding and then folding it back up again when the experience was complete.

Portable time was also abundant. There was no shortage of time then as there seems to be today. Time was not an infinite abstract, but it was asynchronous. Its measure worked with humanity rather than against it. Humans did not age then as they do today, because they related differently to time. Early artwork and manuscripts depict abundant harvests and seasons of plenty. More can be gleaned from the remnants of the past than what is currently interpreted. The ancients understood the twofold, or dual, nature of time and they made good use of it. Later on, time became synchronous and aging began. Synchronous time was sometimes depicted as an old man with a white beard. The indication was that one could no longer find wisdom while lost in the beauty and timelessness of youth.

When synchronous time was born, the world became finite. Youth could not be wasted, and ill-accomplished moments could no longer be spared. Harvests were limited to specific seasons and locations, and workers could little afford to be idle. The law of plenty was in effect then as it is today, but few paid it any mind and even fewer aligned with it. Synchronous time brought with it shorter life spans. Good health and good fortune were no longer the norm. They became something one strived for and hoped and prayed for.

A DISCREPANCY OF TIME:
ASYNCHRONOUS VERSUS SYNCHRONOUS

Synchronous time did not begin the moment asynchronous time ended, and there was a period of overlap that lasted many centuries. There is much discrepancy in your history regarding this time period, because as many perished from old age others who were born within weeks of one another continued to live in seeming perpetuity. All were aging, but at varying rates, which for the most part depended upon their ancestral cellular structure as well as the beliefs they adhered to. Those who aged fastest began to believe that they were inferior, and this belief only caused them to age even faster. Those who aged more slowly came to believe a common myth, that they must be godlike or at least the sons and daughters of gods. Those who aged more quickly came to be called lesser or lowborn, and those who seemed never to age were called highborn, perpetuating the myth that they were gods whose eternal home was in heaven. Most of the highborn had blue eyes, whereas brown was the predominant eye color of the lowborn, so blue eyes became good omens of longevity and reminders of the sky. Brown eyes were as the Earth and so they held little promise of good fortune.

The godlike human beings knew that they did not have the power to grant long life to the lesser born. More was the pity, because many a great love was separated by time rather than circumstance. With sympathy and compassion for the irreversible changes that were taking place, those who lived long upon the Earth devised a system by which they could enrich, albeit temporarily, the lives of the lesser born. The system allotted one tenth of both time and sacrifice to be tithed on behalf of each of the lesser born. A sacrifice could be a labor or the reduction of a labor. Riches were still earned, but they could also be bestowed. Time could not be purchased, but it could be given. No one was compelled to tithe; those who volunteered did so from the heart. Long after the custom was adopted the tradition continued, but as with all things temporary and temporal, corruption and malice found a foothold.

TIME BECAME A COMMODITY

Synchronous time was now well anchored upon the Earth, and the godlike beings had long ago departed. Those who incarnated upon the Earth did so in sequential rather than contextual time. In other words, the karmic wheel of birth and rebirth was now the guardian of time. Asynchronous time was expansive, but synchronous time was not. Consciousness gave way to unconsciousness, and time became a measure whose worth could be calculated; a commodity that could be owned, controlled, bought and sold.

Priesthoods and kingdoms now stood where the highborn had once sacrificed time and tithe to the lowborn. They saw little and no reason to bestow sacrifice when it could be received instead. They saw even less reason to tithe when they could tax. Ten percent of infinity now became ten percent of one's household, a sum that even the simplest mind could calculate. Most priesthoods did not have the authority to impose or collect a tax on the communities they served, so instead, they devised a legal means by which they conferred and intervened with deities and past gods on behalf of those who were not considered qualified to do so. In return they received a god tithe, later called a good tithe, and the greedy law of spiritual compensation ran rampant across all lands and most religions.

TITHING TODAY: UNSUBSTANTIATED TAXATION

The sands of time have shifted often since then. Civilizations have come and gone, and magnificent continents have disappeared under the waves. Kingdoms and cultures have fallen from glorious heights, leaving great councils and benevolent leaders to be replaced by governments, corporations, monarchies and tyrants. Taxation and levies have taught citizens to subtract before they have even learned to add, and the law of plenty lies buried in the ruins of asynchronous time. Governments now tax by decree as well as by force. Intricate systems have been devised whereby taxes are levied upon most types of income, earnings and even purchases. Authority to impose and collect taxes has been placed with the few and the many, the scrupulous and the unscrupulous. Power is now hungry for more power. It has become a volatile machine that assumes, abuses and usurps.

As long as humanity allows another entity, faculty, government or belief system to control its power, it will subject itself and its children to taxation. That which today is called tithing is little more than unsubstantiated taxation; it is an imposition of the *will-ful* upon the *will-less*. It is an ill-conceived system, encouraged by those who benefit by it and supported by those who fear changing it. Hidden within history are truths that support these words, which, when uncovered, will return the wealth of the greedy governments, corporations and churches to the people.

TITHING IS A CHARITABLE DEED

Is tithing considered a charitable deed? Yes, as long as it is conceived in the innocence and simplicity of the heart and offered cheerfully. It need not follow any custom, tradition, law or percentage. Is charity or a charitable donation also considered a tithe? It depends upon the awareness that is present within the moment in which it is considered. For instance, if the charitable deed is a box of superfluous items extracted from a crowded attic and dropped off at the nearest collection bin, then it is a charitable contribution but not a tithe. Why? Because the original intent was to make one's attic more habitable, do you see? Charity is best defined as a voluntary provision of money, materials or help offered to those who may benefit from it. True charity includes an impartial acceptance of others; it is tolerance expressed in greatest measure. Charity observes without judgment. It does not ask you to determine who is needy versus who is not.

Is a donation a tithe? Yes, if it is given voluntarily and without obligation or expectation of return. To donate is to give, present or contribute something when a good (god) cause presents itself. Science has its own definition for "donate," which is to transfer electrons to another atom or molecule in a chemical reaction, and that is exactly what happens when a true tithe is made! A physical and nonphysical reaction is experienced within one's entire being, one that promotes alchemy and magic within one's sphere (of influence).

TITHING INSPIRES GREATNESS

To tithe is to inspire others to greatness by conscious thought, act, deed or prayer. True tithing exists in a state of grace. It is elegant, smooth in form and movement, dignified and polite, decent in behavior and beautiful to behold. True tithing includes a capacity to tolerate, accommodate and forgive. In other words, it does not judge itself worthy for initiating the tithe or another unworthy for receiving it or using it unwisely. Tithing is a demonstration of infinite love, mercy, favor and goodwill. It begins with a condition of being free (of sin) and then offering the same to others.

Tithing does not purchase or promise eternal life or anything else, and it does not erase other obligations you might have incurred elsewhere. It does bring about a quickening, a life-giving spirit. As a creative act, it is complete within itself. It requires nothing and it asks nothing, but it offers all to all. Tithe because your heart compels it, but do not mortgage your home or your soul to build a church or altar to All That Is. Is there something to be gained by tithing? Yes, but you will not be able to put your finger upon what it might be. What is there to be gained by living fully and completely each day, do you see? Over a lifetime, the answer is expressed exponentially. The origins of tithing are still present and its cosmic formula is intact. The universal law of infinite return and the earthly law of plenty still guide the process. Everything you give to another you also give to yourself; it can be no other way.

What will you tithe? What if you have nothing to give or so much that it is difficult to know when not to tithe? Charity begins at home, as they say. Begin by being generous with yourself and then see where else generosity exists within you. Escorting a moth safely to the door rather than seeing its life force extinguished by the heat of a lamp is an act of generosity, do you see? Do not measure yourself by what you offer, and do not measure others by what they accept or receive. Do not compare yourself to your neighbor, because you are unique. Your path is that of the demonstrating master, not the course of the follower or the disciple. Allow your creative nature to guide your heart, your hands and your purse strings in all endeavors, and remember well that the law of plenty is well endorsed by Spirit. Be willing to receive as well as to give, even when it is only support or a kind word that is offered. Simple words and warm hugs have been known to save many a life.

Portals to Perfection

October 2003

I greet you from that place of oneness that is your own. It is not separate or apart from you, because it is you. It is more within than without, because there is a greater or more substantive truth carried within you than that which is expressed without.

Namasté: I Greet You

Long ago it was customary, when encountering other beings, to greet them by honoring their inward momentum as much as their outward motion, as both were considered equal. "Namasté," accompanied by a gesture such as a warm embrace or a respectful bow, is recognition of the depth and the oneness of the spirit that enfolds all. Namasté is not good morning, good afternoon or good evening. It is not hello or good bye. It is much more than that. It is a total and complete acknowledgment of the indwelling spirit that expresses itself within and without form.

Namasté is as profound as the deepest well and as golden as sunshine, but many consider it out of date. As a consequence, it has fallen from favor. Reduced in rank, it has been replaced by more common and superficial greetings, such as those that acknowledge what one has been doing with oneself of late rather than simply being the living word of All That Is.

So let us greet one another in the ways and words of another time and another place. Namasté, dear ones! I salute the being who resides within and demonstrates without. I bow deeply before you, as you are among the mighty who speak truth and stand before it, even as others would hide behind it. You are the ones who effect and affect change while others stand idle and wait to see if and when the world will change. Those who read these words now know that they are agents of change and to that I say, namasté, dear ones.

WE GATHER AT A PORTAL

We gather here as if in timelessness, a placeless place where we meet and greet one another. It is nothing more than a portal used to access a state of conscious awareness. It is both a circle and a spiral within your own matrix, and even if the experience seems quite physical to you, I would argue that it is not. It is a grounding of energy, a formalizing of energy, in which energy takes the form of words with the intent to insist that you are more than your physical form. I have used form to show you that you are not form but formlessness, which is why I call this a spiral within your own matrix, do you see?

An acknowledgment of your existence as form within formlessness is a very potent thing, because it immediately opens a portal, or at least the possibility of a portal, but of what nature? Is it a portal into what or where? Is a portal a simple doorway? For some it is nothing more than an entrance to or an exit from, but it can also be much more.

A true portal is a way to something greater than the self or at least greater than the self's consistent reality. A portal is the manifestation or doorway that confirms the desire to experience something beyond (not outside) the self; it is an energetic door of intent. When one desires to move beyond a certain threshold, a creative act called desire (or need) invites energy to participate and interact in new and different ways.

An invitation does not always result in an experience—it is an invitation after all, not a commitment. Sometimes a glimpse into, through or beyond a portal can be very satisfying, even if only temporarily so. Contemplation upon the threshold of experience can also be quite fulfilling. For some it is enough to say that they have stood upon the precipice—they need not leap from it to make the experience more real. For others it is enough to say, "I will return tomorrow or the next day, because today I am not ready."

ENTERING A PORTAL IS LIKE ACCEPTING AN INVITATION

Another example of a portal is that which is created when a being chooses to transition from this world into the next without his or her physical body. Many call this experience death, and that is sometimes the result, but such a profound transformation deserves richer words, if nothing else. Opening this portal or lifting its veil reveals more realities and possibilities; crossing its threshold implies accepting an invitation to witness and participate in experiences beyond the ones offered in this world.

The proverbial tunnel of light that has been described so often is but one manifestation or confirmation that reality as one has known it (or memorized it) has shifted. Experiences that include one's angels, guides, teachers or other emanations of Source are similar examples of conditional transition. All explorations, experiments and experiential forays into or through portals are through individual choice. One cannot be forced or coerced. A creative act such as desire is the energetic key for attaining success in this model. Without this key, energy can become dense and sluggish; true creative energy is fluid, mobile and light.

A Portal Offers a Glimpse of Something Different

What is the purpose of exploring the energy of a portal? It is to experience a moment, a purpose or a lifetime that is greater than what is available in the current reality or experience. It is to be in choice regarding one's reality and experience. Near-death experiences (NDEs) are just that, opportunities to experience the self in a reality that seems greater than the present reality or the present self. If the perspective within a given reality shifts as a result of the portal experience, does the self shift too? Interestingly enough, no, it does not. Why? Because the self is eternal, whereas a reality is only ephemeral; it lives only as long as the perspective to which it relates. True growth is accomplished when the self relates to the Self in all perspectives and all realities in the same way. In other words, when this ceases to be better than that, which is still worse than the one before but not as bad as the next, the self can relate to the Self, which recognizes itself as All That Is in all realities.

A near-death experience is a severe example, but it is one that everyone can relate to. In terms of ready examples, it is but one of many, and the universe is adept at supplying as many examples as need be. A portal is a crossroads of energy that enables a creative sequence or string of opportunities, which in turn manifests different realities and experiences. Portals are one of the ways in which the universe invites you to participate with your Self. When you chose your present life, you accepted an invitation to express yourself in certain ways, but that was only the beginning.

A creative moment does not become less creative if it is temporarily set aside in favor of a noncreative moment; it continues to be what it is. Likewise, you do not become more of what you already are when you cross a threshold or pass through a portal, because you already are All That Is. Why bother, then? Because for the soul, the joy is in the experience of understanding itself as Itself and in the expression of Itself as itself. The parent sees itself in the child, and the child expresses itself through the parent. They mirror to each other the relevance of the creative act of self-expression; they reflect the joy and the sorrow, the excess and the lack.

How Does Purpose Enter In?

Can one create a portal to self-expression at any time and in any moment? Yes, but in order to activate the portal, which is to say to have something on the other side of its threshold, one must also have purpose. So purpose plus creativity equals experience. Those who stand upon a creative threshold but find themselves unable or unwilling to cross it must first find purpose within themselves and then make it their companion. What is purpose? Purpose is active intelligence, and it is a byproduct of creative desire. It is the yeast that makes the bread rise, the coming together of form and formlessness and the ideal that becomes the idyll.

What if purpose or active intelligence is not present? Is all for naught? Certainly one might think so. But just as a fine wine cannot be rushed, divine timing responds only to the soul's call. The soul will sometimes offer a glimpse of a new reality, a new paradigm or what lies beyond a threshold in lieu of a full experience if the timing is not divine (perfect). A glimpse can encourage creativity or engage active intelligence; it can also increase desire in physical and nonphysical ways. Your soul will not tease you, but neither will it simply appease you.

Purposeful, creative desire is not need. Need is based upon survival, whereas the soul understands that it is eternal. A soul upon the threshold of a portal has surpassed the need to define itself by doing or undoing. By contrast, it acts upon influence rather than reacting to stimuli. To be is to choose; to do is to act or react to a choice that has already been made. To a certain extent, all doing is the past tense of being, but if that is the case, are you simply going through the motions? Is everything predetermined? Where is free will in this unkind equation? Free will exists within, and as your consciousness, it is what you are—not what you have, do you see?

A Portal Is an Opportunity, Not a Requirement

A portal can take you to the past, to the future or even to another day within your present. It can take you to another paradigm within your current reality so that you can experience it differently. If you are uncertain as to a given direction or decision and wish to experience it from a different perspective, a portal—or in this case, a window—can help you do just that. A portal can also be experienced as energy without expression, because experience does not require form, only context. A contextual portal has the advantage of allowing you to experience, whether it is the thought of having or doing something or the experience itself that you really desire.

There are many realities from which to choose, many dimensions to explore. Densities within dimensions offer even more variety and infinite ways in which to explore and experience life. Portals are opportunities to experience yourself as beyond your everyday self. They activate expansion within and without and allow you to choose a reality rather than have one chosen for you. Experiences beyond the third dimension are best accomplished when desire, creativity, active intelligence and participation are all present. These conscious, transformational experiences are available and accessible, but remember, they are possibilities rather than requirements. They are not prerequisites that you must accomplish on your way to here or there. They cannot gain you entry or reentry to that which has always resided within.

Stepping Outside the Circle

November 2003

I am lost in a sea of despair and need your help. I have spent what feels like many lifetimes devoted to a belief in love and compassion for all beings above all else. Until now, I have always believed that the depth of our soul cannot be measured (or judged) by what our surface personality says and does, and yet I have allowed myself to become the victim of a painful emotional wound inflicted by the words and actions of someone I deeply loved and admired. I suffer from what feels like an irrevocable injury, and I see no apparent relief in sight. All attempts on my part to take responsibility for what has happened have only led to my heaping blame upon others and myself. My heart is broken, my mind is fragmented and what is left of my faith lies in tatters of self-pity. Breathing is difficult, and living is worse. Where have love and compassion gone? Without them I have no purpose, and without purpose my life is in decay. Please look beyond the drama of these words long enough to share some words of wisdom in this most desperate hour of need.

*D*earest heart, seed of my beingness, star of the bright heavens, love and compassion are your middle names, even if you will not claim them today. You might leave them by the wayside for a time, but you cannot truly abandon that which you are. Love is a universal force of nature; it is an indestructible fabric that stretches across all time and awareness. True love is not simple or deep affection, nor is it symbolic worship or adoration; and it is not courtship, sexual desire, romantic pleasure or intense longing. Love is a gift that cannot be returned or exchanged. One can exchange feelings of love, but not love itself. Love is a gift from All That Is to all that is, and for that reason, it cannot be removed or separated from that which you are. Love is what you are. Love does not need to be experienced or appreciated in order to be present. It can be shared as long as all concerned understand that they own it in equal measure—to the extent that it can be owned. Love is a universal law, and as such, it is indestructible.

Now that we have an understanding of what true love is and what it is not, we can begin to consider what it does. The law of true love and compassion is that which heals and completes all things. Love and compassion make that which is fragmented and separate from it whole. All healing modalities, world religions, spiritual movements and personal beliefs incorporate this law to the extent that they understand it. When this law is misunderstood or less understood, gaps are created within its fabric, and these gaps are the black holes within which good intentions and misinterpretations fall, day after day and century upon eon.

DISCOVER TRUE LOVE AND COMPASSION

As you have managed to remain with the subject at hand without turning away, shutting down or becoming absent from this moment, I will continue with the more difficult aspects of this communiqué that are yet to be discovered. Before you (or anyone else) chose this (or any other) lifetime(s), you gave careful, wise and deliberate counsel to every thought and experience that you might perceive within and throughout it. Your mind might feel clouded today, but your soul's perspective is very aware of the experiences and choices you are making.

Humankind chooses lifetimes upon Earth in order to discover the true meaning of love. The only way to discover true love is through its experience. True love's greatest teacher is its very own opposite, which is not hate. Hate is an aspect of passion; in its most refined derivation, it cannot be considered a true emotion. Hate evokes feelings and elicits reactions of intense anger, hostility or animosity, but it is not those feelings. The opposite of love is differentiation and separation. That which sees, believes and understands itself as outside or separate from itself cannot experience itself as itself or love as true love. At best, it sees a mirrorlike reflection, which is tantamount to what it is not. Experiences upon Earth reveal what you are not so that you can discover what you are. The difficult part is remembering that human experience is an inverted reality, designed to represent an illusion, not a reality.

Your sorrow and sadness have led you to believe that an unjust cosmic joke has been played upon you, but that is not so. Creator's sense of humor is compassionate, not vindictive. Hidden within the trauma of this experience is the gift of discovering an aspect of your purpose, which is to realize that trauma is unnecessary and irrelevant. Trauma does not bring growth, but lack of growth can bring trauma. I do not expect you to see the gift in this experience now, but when the salt has washed away all of the tears that stand in its way, you will welcome the gift as it was intended, because no distortion will prevent it. You are disillusioned by life, which is an uncomfortable place to be, but within the discomfort is a place that knows that you stand upon a threshold that leads to your true self and your true purpose, which is to be the radiant expression of the law of true love and compassion as it was meant to be.

An illusion is a mistaken belief, identity or ideal that is tightly held. Illusions deceive the senses, especially the visual ones wherein the stimuli seem to be objectively present, thereby representing a physical rather than a spiritual cause. Illusions are powerful because they are taken at face value by the mind, which believes that they exist when in truth they do not. They appear as one thing, when in fact they are another. The mind is capable of being deceived by illusions, but the heart is not. That is why you cannot always trust your thoughts, but you can always depend upon your feelings. Disillusionment is the undermining and destruction of beliefs that no longer support or uphold you. To be disillusioned is to be beyond the influence of illusion. Taken from this perspective, it is not a bad place to find oneself.

A belief is an acceptance by the mind that something is true or real, often underpinned by an emotional or spiritual sense of certainty. But are you certain of anything today? A belief is a confidence that someone or something is good and will therefore be good to you. But are you confident today? A belief is a statement, principle or doctrine that is accepted or adopted as true. But based upon what you know, are you prepared to do so today? A belief is a firm and considered opinion, especially one that involves faith. But how solid is your faith this day? Humans have bound their beliefs into a unified system, an organized collection or set of beliefs that has become commonly associated with community and society, but this characterization is not authentic and is no longer valid.

You are being asked to stand beyond (not apart from) the false ideas, premises, conceptions and beliefs concerning yourself and humanity. You are being asked to be love and compassion rather than a mere reflection of it or a belief in it. Would it be unkind to say that you could not have invited this experience without first suffering its lack?

KARMA AND DHARMA EXPLAINED

Universal laws are easily understood, but experiencing them is another matter altogether. Universal laws are called such because they apply to everyone and everything in the universe. They do apply here, but not there; to this one, but not that one; in this case, but not the other; this time, but not next time. They exist beyond humanity's good or bad opinion of them; they are, just as you are. You cannot disobey universal laws, and they do not seek your obeisance. On the other hand, attempting to live outside universal law has certain consequences, which include misplaced devotion, listlessness, distraction by common or uncommon stimuli and excessive sentimentality. Humanity calls this karma.

The general definition of karma includes a philosophy in which the quality of current and future lives is determined by the behavior in this and previous lives. In other words, fate and destiny influence and contribute to experience. But if that is the case, where is the ability to transcend one's past, present or future? Such a narrow interpretation demands that, having learned the lesson or gained the experience, one will still be forced to live a fate that is no longer appropriate. Would Infinite Spirit be so vague and merciless?

Perhaps dharma—which, simply put, is the truth about why things are the way they are in the universe—can best answer this question. Dharma explains the perfection of nonperfection or, better put, the righteousness of discovering reality through the path of illusion. Dharma stimulates goodwill by activating mercy, grace and compassion. Dharma releases karma's hold upon you once you rescind your vested interest in walking the karmic path. Mercy and charity are the kindness that your soul shows to you when you have forgiven yourself for perceived transgressions whose premise was false to begin with. It is a welcome event and cause for celebration. Mercy is said to be the throne of God in heaven; can it not be your throne as well? Charity is the willingness on the part of your soul to be impartial, tolerant and nonjudgmental of all thought, deed and action. Can you ask the same of yourself by acknowledging that there is no separation between you and your soul other than the perception you hold?

By way of divine choice, you could not have chosen another path that was not this one, because this is the path you have followed lifetime upon lifetime by your own admission. It is the path that understands pain by suffering, experiences reality by submerging into illusion, defines abundance by seeking prosperity and searches for love where calcified hearts dream of wakefulness. All (not some) of your experiences have brought you to this threshold of awareness. Whether or not you will cross it still remains to be discovered.

THE CURE FOR SELF-INFLICTED WOUNDS

Self-inflicted wounds are often the most difficult to bear, and such is the case with this one. Before you twist the knife any more, ask yourself this question: "Who am I?" and if the answer is anything less than, "The light of All That Is manifest as a human being," continue to ask the same question until you receive that answer or until all time and awareness cease, for only then will you understand that you are equal to the question and the answer. The cure for the wound is in the question and the answer both. There is no other remedy for an affliction of this magnitude. With love and compassion, I therefore offer you a near-lethal dose by placing a cosmic mirror before you in the form of these words. Look in the mirror, dearest, and avert not your eyes. Is it despair that you still see reflected in the mirror or has it transformed into truth? Do you see the dagger of death or the cup of life?

The only antidote for this type of poison is life itself. Combined with love, it is the only substance that can counteract the effects of such a toxin. Poisons are severe and harmful substances that cause illness, injury or death if they are accepted at face value. They are a powerful, destructive and corrupting force— and an insidious one at that. Poisons have been known to diminish or delay the activity of a catalyst; therefore, know that any attempts to Band-Aid or cordon off your pain will be to no avail. Likewise, anger, hostility and guilt are no match for this form of spiritual poison that incapacitates your heart, brings distrust to your soul and threatens your very existence.

You have no weapon with which to fight, and yet you have no other choice than to combat the unpleasant and abusive place you find yourself in. I offer you no solace, for it is wisdom that you have requested instead and that you will find here in great measure. "Who am I? Who am I?" You are a boddhisattva upon both Earth and heaven. You are enlightenment worthy of nirvana, were it not that love and compassion for the Earth and for humanity currently prevent it. In your body and in this world, you will remain until you choose to transcend suffering and see it for the illusion that it is. You will walk a path that is free of ignorance and prejudice, and you will share that path with many others. You are not attached to this world, but you are bound to it by promise. You have inflicted a grave and life-threatening wound upon yoursel;, now let us see to its healing and repair. Rest in the comfort of angels, dear. Your path is a long one, but you are in good company and time passes quickly. Peace, harmony and joy all await you when you are ready.

❋   ❋   ❋

Dear readers, Gaia asked me to reveal the name of the questioner in this case, because it served a greater purpose. I thought long and hard on this, because our right to personal privacy is very important to me. After careful consideration and emotional anguish, I agreed.

I was the one who posed this perplexing question, as a chapter of my life was closing behind me in one of the most difficult ways we can choose. "Why does it have to be this way?" I asked myself time and time again, but no answer was forthcoming. As my sorrow intensified, my flood of tears soon became a downpour of despair. With no letup in sight, the torrent continued until I began to hyperventilate. Alone on the floor, curled up in a fetal position, my breath was shallow and much too rapid. In a condition of organic anxiety, my body attempted to dump all the toxic feelings it was holding. On an emotional level, this hurrying to release is extremely unhealthy and inju-

rious, because it creates an imbalance in the body's ability to respond to excess. On a physical level, it can be quite dangerous, because hyperventilating causes the body to lose too much carbon dioxide. This, in turn, promotes faintness, which is what was about to happen to me.

As I entered this semiconscious condition, I found that I was willing to remain there rather than gasping for the air that would return me to full consciousness. In an altered state of awareness, I became both a participant and a witness to the experience. Somewhere within me, I realized that if I was not careful, I would inadvertently push myself beyond my body's ability to retain its physical integrity; in other words, I knew that I might die. Still, there was a part of me that wanted to do just that. Haven't we all wished it at some time or another? Here was my opportunity to do so easily and righteously, I thought. I can't begin to tell you how tempting an experience it was.

While I was not so carefully considering my options, I traced the circuitous route of my body's meridians and explored all of its energetic entry and exit points. I located the most and least aware places within me with detached amusement, as the observer within made mental notes of a probable exit point. From what seemed like opposite directions, I could hear two distinct voices. One was the voice or impulse of my guardian angel gently explaining to me that I had clearly not chosen to abandon my body via this experience. "The world does not need another martyr," she said, "but it does need you." I smiled at her, but found her words somewhat nebulous and almost silly. To me, the choice seemed a simple one. On the one hand were sorrow, pain and suffering, whereas on the other hand were what seemed to be ecstasy at best and release from density at the very least. The other voice I heard was that of my dear friend telling me that I had to breathe and that I was scaring her no end. When I refused to listen to her, she spoke to my heart, to my soul and even to Gaia on my behalf.

It's hard to describe what happened next, but I'll try. At some point, my present life seemed to merge with many of my other lives, especially the ones that in any way resembled or identified with this experience. I saw the irrelevance of my immediate decision in the scheme of things, but I also saw the relevance and purpose of my life. I knew there was only one choice I could make that supported my truth. I willed myself back into my body and heard my friend as if for the first time. She was gently instructing me on how to breathe, offering herself as my spiritual midwife; strange how quickly and easily I had already forgotten how. Our beingness naturally exists within the cosmic breath, but our body remains one dense step behind this ability, at least for now.

Relating to you how much my body ached when I returned to it is not easy. Although I have never boxed, I imagined that I felt like a boxer who had gone too many rounds when the fight should have been stopped long ago. Every cell in my body admonished me for my insolent behavior concerning my physical and emotional well-being. It was certainly not the "Welcome Wagon" I would have hoped for! I was surprised that my teeth, gums and jaw hurt most of all, but I have since discovered that we store our most deep-seated emotions there. Our teeth have roots, after all, and our wisdom teeth (which we mostly remove today) have some of the deepest roots of all.

Bed rest and sleep do not come easy to me, but my body demanded it and I succumbed. The next day, I entered another semiconscious state, but this one was more like a meditation. In my altered state and transfigured body, I seemed to be transported to the Himalayas, where I was set down upon a soft rug. I found myself in the company of five very gentle beings, whom I assumed were simple yogis or humble monks. They inquired as to my health, and I found myself sheepishly telling them what I had done. I tried not to defend my actions, but the temptation to do so was there.

They listened patiently and with what seemed like a great deal of reverential devotion and loving compassion. They did not reprimand me as I thought they would. Instead, they reminded me how wise I was to have made the decision to return to my body in order to live out its purpose. They also told me that I was never to attempt such a feat again. They reminded me that our bodies are very resilient but should not be treated with such blatant disregard. In my stupor, I had come to believe that I was doing my body a favor by releasing it from its burdensome obligation. They told me that time would heal my sorrow, and devotion would heal my despair. I didn't believe them, but I liked the soft tone of their words just the same. I heard myself promise that I would never again place my body in such a place of low standing, and before long I found myself back in my own bed, awake and hungry.

A few days after my partial recovery, I found myself relapsing again. My mind would not release me from my painful ordeal, and nothing seemed to satisfy it. My mind forced me to replay the hurt and the pain over and over again. It owned me, and try as I might, I could not release myself from the drama that demanded I remain an unwilling participant. In anguish I said to my dear friend, "I can't go on like this much longer; it's not like I'm Mother Teresa, after all."

Well, interestingly enough, Mother Teresa paid me a visit that same afternoon. I have communed with her from time to time when my spirits have been on the low side, so I was not altogether surprised. She looked upon me with compassion when I would have preferred pity and said, "You are me because I am you. You are every Mother and every Teresa and every saint and every Saint Teresa there has ever been. Without you I am purposeless, not the other way around. Think on these words and on the next ones I offer to you as well. You have two sons whom you deeply love, and in them a great future lies in wait. Would you see them forgiven or punished? Would you offer them compassion or judgment, insight or defeat? Think well upon your answer, and say it not to me but to them, for the depth of your ability to love and offer compassion lies not in this moment but in their future. Offer to others, then, what you would see the world offer to them."

I felt unfairly cornered, but I knew that she had spoken the truth I was not yet bold enough to call my own. My sons are my passion, and in them I see Gaia's future securely nestled and safe. They and their generation of brave and creative companions will champion Gaia without the need to fight. Their light is like a golden torch and their hearts are already wise. I breathed deeply, fully and compassionately for the first time in days. I slept again, and I dreamed that I had traded in my damaged heart for a healed one. I would like to be able to tell you that I am fine now, but it's still a little too soon for that.

I am sure that you can understand my hesitation in sharing this experience with anyone outside a small and intimate circle of friends; it is not a moment that I take great pride in. Several times a month, however, clients and friends remark upon how fortunate and charmed my life seems to them. I do not deny this, and I am grateful for the gifts that have been entrusted to me, but I am also just like you. My path has been one of joy and sorrow, learning and teaching, laughing and crying. My life has been as carefully laid out by my soul as yours has been by your own soul. If I choose to believe that I am special, then I must first acknowledge that you are as well, and if you will acknowledge my gifts, then you must also acknowledge your own. The only way to mastership is through stewardship. Hand in hand, the kingdoms of Earth will lead us to the kingdoms of heaven. May I see myself reflected in your eyes daily and behold the beauty of All That Is that is also you.

—Pepper Lewis

Making It Real

December 2003

*H*ow can you tell the difference between reality and illusion? Do you know the difference between experiential reality, multidimensional reality and third-dimensional reality? Can you tell the difference between light, dark and shadow? Are you sure?

Encoded within this text are the answers to those questions and more. Encoded does not mean hidden—please remember that as you read, acknowledge and receive. There is no puzzle to solve; the correct answers have not been placed upside down or backward at the bottom of the page. To encode means to translate or, as in this case, to convert mundane text into a sequence of signals, characters and symbols that are immediately recognizable to the essential or eternal self.

Even as my sentience is busy guiding the encoding process, your beingness (that which you are) is busy decoding it into conscious information modules. These evolution-based modules carry new genetic information directly to your RNA molecules and to other constituent cell groups where genes and codons are produced. What does this mean? It means that even though your mind might not yet be able to tell the difference between fact and fiction or reality and illusion, your body can, because it has been undergoing a chemical metamorphosis, a spiritual puberty. The bad news is that it is catching; and the good news is that it is catching!

Boring Illusion

Humanity can evolve only to the degree to which the most eager segment of the population is motivated to awaken the other segments. There can be disagreement on this only as much as there is agreement in other areas, because a state of balance must exist. Chaos is balance reorganizing and redefining itself; it is chaos amidst new order. The world around you currently finds itself in similar straits, an often chaotic and semidestructive force in which we find the death of some ideas and the birth of others.

THE WHEEL MUST BE REINVENTED

"Push me, pull you" has been the name of the game for a long time, but it is old and tired and no longer fun to play. Humanity cannot reinvent the game without reinventing itself, and that is exactly what is happening. I hear the cries of those who say, "Why reinvent the wheel?" The answer has two parts:

The first part is that the wheel no longer is round; it does not turn, spin, rotate or even look good by itself. It requires tune-ups and tone-downs, and even with these in place, it can barely make the grade. As soon as the terrain changes or becomes a bit bumpy, it gives up and waits for the tow truck to arrive.

The second reason the wheel must be reinvented is that it has become obsolete. The wheel has been around since the Stone Age and before. It has served humanity well, but as far as inventions go, isn't it simply time to move into a new paradigm? How will you evolve into a generation of space enthusiasts if your inventions do not evolve with you? Combustible-engine automobiles and fossil fuels are relics of the past as are natural-gas-fed and coal-fed electricity, whose hunger is never quite satisfied.

REALITY IS PERMEANCE

A carbon-based, meat-fed, drugged, overstuffed and unconscious humanity will also become obsolete if it does not reinvent itself soon. You cannot make your illusions real, because they are not. They were never meant to be real. What is real, then? How will you know what is real when you have draped yourselves in illusion? The answer is easy; it is revealing itself to you even as you read these words. Illusion cannot stand on its own merit. It can be created and experienced, but it cannot create itself or experience itself—only that which is real can do that.

Reality is another word for permeance or presence, which is not the same as permanence. Only two things are permanent: the absolute and the nothing, and even these two are debatable. The universe is not permanent; it only seems so. The solar Sun is also not permanent and will one day implode, and on that distant day when the galactic Sun acknowledges the completion of its journey, it will do the same.

Permeance, on the other hand, is a saturation of every part and every path within self. As understood by science, permeance is the property by which a material can alter the magnetic field in which it is placed. It is the rate at which a substance, such as a liquid or a magnetic field, passes through a membrane or other medium. Permeance is the act of passing through a porous substance or membrane. Essentially, that is what you do every time you choose the path called human incarnation. Your precious magnetic field passes through a porous substance called illusion, and the membrane that holds it thinks that it is real, but it is not real—you are.

REALITY IS PRESENCE

Reality lies in discerning the difference between presence and the present. Presence is eternal, but "the present" lasts but a moment—only as long as your awareness rests upon it. It is temporary, or illusional. A moment can last an eternity, as you well know, but that does not make it eternal. If a moment can last an eternity, how long can an illusion last? An illusion can last as long as time, space and creativity find it interesting and amusing to make it last. How long can the juggler juggle? He can keep juggling as long as there is an audience, do you see? When the tricks are no longer fresh and exciting, the audience becomes bored, tired and wants to go home.

And that is exactly what is happening today. By 2004 the audience (you) will have grown tired of watching the same juggling acts over and over. They will seem less amusing than ever and even a bit tiresome. Many will want to go home, and some will do so. Is that the end of the story? No, it is only the beginning.

Masters' Paths

A forgotten master is one who cannot remember that he or she is a master, or one who suffers from the same form of amnesia that most within the spectrum called mass consciousness have succumbed to. Forgotten masters are everywhere and appear in many guises. There are disgruntled masters, misplaced masters, deluded masters, shy masters, messiah masters, intellectual masters, mystical masters—just to name a few.

THE PATH OF THE FORGOTTEN MASTER IS WELL WORN

The path of the forgotten master is well worn, because it has been walked upon many times. It is an inviting and appealing path, one that seems to say, "Enter me and you will discover you." What could be better? But it also says, "Discover you and you will enter me," which is one of the most forgotten, overlooked and misquoted spiritual truths of all time. Masters forget because they must forget in order to continue learning. They do not forget because they did not get it right or because they need more practice. Masters forget in order to re-create themselves within new contexts, paradigms and environments.

If you remembered all that you are, you would immediately have an experience within the context of All That Is. That experience would expand your consciousness to such a degree that you would no longer fit into your physical body. There is a physical limitation upon how much light a human body can sustain. Interestingly, there is no limit on how much light a human vessel can generate. In other words, when fully charged (enlightened), you must share (instill) your light in order to maintain its integrity (wisdom).

Gathering and sharing light in the many varieties in which it arrays itself is one of your soul's favorite activities. It is second only to hide-and-seek, which is almost every soul's favorite game. Hide-and-seek allows a soul to invent itself as new. It allows you to be a mother this time and a father next; it allows each sorrow and every fragrance to be new and unique. It is rediscovered desire and resurrected passion, and without forgetfulness you would not have remembrance.

YOU CAN'T MISS THE PATH OF THE REAWAKENED MASTER

The path of the forgotten master serves many purposes, and it has been in place for a very long time. Even so, it has its limitations, and most souls eventually outgrow its usefulness. The path of the forgotten master leads to the path of the remembered (or self-realized) master, but its elusive nature must first be recognized so that its footlights can illumine one's path. You cannot miss the path altogether, but it has been known to suggest detours, alternate paths and delays that can seem very attractive to an exhausted, semiconscious soul looking for a respite from the maelstrom that is awakening within.

In 2004 those who are willing but have not yet gained a foothold on the path of the awakened master will find it and/or secure it. The paths of the awakened, reawakened or remembered master are one and the same. Do not be misguided by semantics, because a path is much like a vibration or a frequency: It is something you sense your way into. It is always best to establish a relationship before becoming intimate within it, and this is no different. Your path is already set to intersect with mastership, so you need not steer a different course. But whether you sail into its cozy harbor or collide with its iron gate is up to you, do you see?

Why 2004? After all, you have already been around a long time. You (your soul) are almost as old as All That Is, but who's counting? You are, or at least your soul is. Collectively, 2004 can best be described as a fail-safe year. There is an energetic bubble resting at a location on the galactic calendar that corresponds to the year 2004 as it is measured on Earth, and it is sequenced to burst into light this year. In all likelihood, you either helped place the bubble there or you were shown its exact cosmologic location in relation to your own prior to this lifetime, in hopes that there would not be too many surprises.

The year will pass very quickly and will carry you into 2005, a full and eventful year that will inspire excitement and activity. It is therefore wise to plan and prepare accordingly before embarking upon the next segment of your journey. Although 2004 might evoke feelings of needing to choose sides, teams or allegiances for reasons of caution and creativity, I now invite you to consider doing otherwise.

WHAT IS REAWAKENED MASTERY?

Reawakened mastery sounds grand, but what is it? Is it for real? Yes, it is. Let's begin with what it is not. It is not power over others; you will not be able to feel superior, that you know something they do not. It is not knowledge, at least not the kind you can commit to memory and claim ownership of. It is not a new (or old) healing modality; there are no certificates to hand out or practitioner licenses to apply for. The path of the reawakened master is a path of mindful restoration. It is a conscious knowing and acknowledgment that you know who and what you are. Some of you will also have certainty as to why you are here; others will not discover this until 2005 or 2007 at the latest.

To embark upon mastery is to embark upon the path of service. Although mastery and service are unique and distinct from each other, they are never separate. The first hatchling in the nest often steps all over itself, but in so doing, it helps to crack open the shells of the other hatchlings who might be having a harder time, perhaps because the shell is thicker or the egg was placed at a more difficult angle. In any case, purposefully or inadvertently, the first are here to assist the rest.

It might surprise you to discover that in 2004, guides, angels and other teachers from long ago will return. They will surround and support you with their guidance and companionship; they will remind you of forgotten dreams and promises. They will inspire you to attain greater insights and prepare you to respond to challenges as minor obstacles on your path. In turn, you will find yourself doing the same for others. Ill-fought battles that return little gain will be set aside in favor of more creative endeavors that are more rewarding. Mastery is both knowing and not knowing, doing and not doing. It is the balance between the two that brings peace and wisdom to the seeker.

Dreamspell of the Maya

The Maya were a race of superbeings. By current measure, they would be considered an advanced civilization. Academics within the science and archaeology fields are quick to acknowledge Mayan engineering feats as well as their highly developed skill in mathematics, religion, astronomy and culture. But for the most part, the Maya are remembered as a primitive and bloodthirsty race. As I was there, I simply and humbly ask that you make your mind an open forum, allowing many possibilities to reveal themselves for your consideration.

The Maya imagined themselves here and arrived shortly thereafter. They envisioned their culture and then created it. They called upon the cooperation of the natural resources and then availed themselves of them. They invoked the anima and animus of the elements and made good use of their balance.

The Maya did not believe in time, so they were never caught in its net. They invented the dreamspell so they could live within time without being compelled by it. The dreamspell is a cosmic understanding of how time works, but it is not time. The Maya were master time-benders, which is to say that they traveled it much as you travel your highways. Just as you travel from here to there, the Maya traveled from here to then and back again. They understood the mechanics of time; they did not attempt to manipulate time as some do today but simply understood how to operate within its cosmic properties and laws.

THEY CAME TO EXPERIENCE ILLUSION

Why did the Maya come here, and why did they leave? The Maya came because they were directed to do so by an intelligent energy within a specific wave band—an expansive form of light that inspires evolution of worlds and the species who reside within and upon them. The wave band, a conscious and intelligent nexus, offered the dreamspell to the Maya as well as the means to experience themselves in it.

The Maya entered the dreamspell consciously; they did not cloak themselves or forget their true identity. They understood the dual nature of both physical and nonphysical reality. They created a myth as well as the means to live in it. They did not pretend to be what they were not, so they did not become lost or mired in time as other races did. When the experience was complete, the Maya departed just as they had arrived: through the dreamspell.

Would it be more accurate to say that the Maya lived in illusion or in reality? Physical evidence suggests that they were real, and archaeological findings confirm this. But if you asked them, they would say that they came here to experience illusion and that they left reality back home.

The name by which they called themselves here is a testament to their belief in manifested illusion. Maya is an ancient Hindu word meaning the material world, or a world in which illusion is considered reality. It further suggests the ability to create illusion through supernatural, magical or sacred power. The Maya knew that most of what they left behind would crumble into dust; in fact, they made certain of it from the outset. But they also knew that humanity would discover its future in their past, and the clues that they have left you are astounding in both simplicity and genius.

The Maya revealed a game board within a context of space and time that allowed them to participate upon the Earth as if it were the only reality. Some of the Maya chose to be completely unconscious or asleep to their eternal truth, whereas others elected to be conscious and aware throughout the entire experience. Their culture flourished and their society expanded as a result of this semiartificial balance. Can you see some of the obvious similarities between their culture and your own?

Eventually, the Maya tired of illusion. Those who were most aware invested themselves in dissolving the veils of separation that had served them so well. They studied the cyclic energies of the middle heavens to discover the most opportune time to rejoin the nexus within the wave band, as this was their ticket home. The least aware among the Maya were told ancient stories and mythologies designed to inspire their creative awareness to look beyond their present environment and reawaken the magical realm that lay sleeping within. They were taught how the conscious imagination could realize its potential by witnessing the relevance of experience rather than participating in all moments. In other words, they were taught how to choose which experience would be most helpful, beautiful, creative or important by superimposing their own vibration upon that of the potential experience. This multilayered inculcating of creativity was the method chosen most often by Mayan elders, scholars and artists.

THE MAYAN LEGACY IS YOUR TREASURE

To the Maya, all was experience, and what could not be learned experientially was not worth learning. They did not study; they learned. They did not memorize; they created or repeated a creation until it was recorded with exactitude within their cellular structure. They believed in transformation, magic and alchemy. Time was a tool within which they poured themselves for a time, resulting in grand creativity and evolution. Coded within the archaeological archives of their art are the keys to their transformation from a physical civilization of human beings to a nonphysical race of superconscious beings. Those who study the Maya call this form of art Mayan transformers, an accurate but little understood description.

The Mayan system of layering or coding knowledge bridges art and science, weaves mythology with learning and blurs illusion and reality into one. Their legacy is your treasure and should not be relegated to the archives of the few who suppose they understand or own its principles. The Maya have left you clues that will assist you in finding them by following their steps and opening the doors with the keys they have left you. This is destined to be an interesting year within the halls of study. Those who seek truth and offer themselves diligently to the task can expect to receive rewards beyond the scope of their current imagination. Mayan past might well reveal the future of the human race upon the Earth and beyond its boundaries as well.

A NEW RESOURCE BECOMES AVAILABLE: TIME

This will be a revealing year in which science, art, religion, technology, astrology and mathematics discover that they have more in common than not.

A transformation within academia-based minds will make a new resource available. This resource is called time. By current definition, time is a system for measuring limited intervals or periods during which actions, processes and conditions exist or take place. But time also exists as a concept, and as such, it is an unlimited resource. The Maya understood this and used it to their advantage so that they would not become trapped within linear time.

A spaceship or other vehicle must employ a certain amount of thrust with which to escape the gravitational pull of a force field. A vehicle of light (a human being) must also employ a certain amount of force or energy in order to escape the confines of linear time. The exact momentum needed is measurable and can be expressed in units of consciousness. The Maya gave the formula to you long ago. It was coded within their art and inscribed in their language. It was the foundation stone of their engineering feats and a marvelous wonder to those whose consciousness saw only magic.

Time is a concept that enables a dimension to express or manifest itself. Time is not static; it is fluid, poetry in motion if one could behold its perfection. Time allows two or more events occurring at the same point in space to be distinguished or measured by the intervals that occur between events. But what if there were no intervals? What if one could experience simultaneous time rather than extraneous time? This year, 2004, will mark the beginning of simultaneous consciousness. The thinker, the thought, the creator and the experience will be discovered to be one and the same. Furthermore, it is art that will reveal this truth, not science. And if that were not enough, religion will be called upon to confirm it.

The Maya encoded all that humans need to discover about themselves within the remnants of their civilizations. They watch now, as do others who have come and gone and will come again during another great twilight. They watch to see what you will do with knowledge, how you will use it. They watch to see what will be revealed and what will remain hidden. They watch in order to understand, for there is no greater teacher than experience.

Path of Oneness

Loosely defined, the universal law of one states that in oneness there is no separation, only unity. Long ago humans understood this law, but today they are at odds with it. Nonetheless, it is a law within this universe. Must universal laws be obeyed? No, but they must be understood. Universal laws are designed within a vibration of associated love. Their very frequency emits peace and restores balance to all things in all places.

A fine example of this is the vibration of the sacred syllable Om or Aum. All that is associated with, in or around this sound receives the perfection of All

That Is through the vehicle of expanding love via association with sacred sound coupled with desire. Aum is a mantra, a sacred word, chant or sound that is repeated in order to facilitate a spiritual transformation of consciousness, but it is also much more.

Is all that is considered sacred also considered a spiritual law? No, not necessarily. That which is sacred is worthy of respect, but respect for self and selflessness must be acknowledged before one can dedicate oneself to any deity or religious purpose; otherwise, a state of imbalance would exist in which one thing or being becomes greater than another. Such is the imbalance that exists today, where one belief or religion is thought to be more perfect or more original or more sacred than another. The universal law of one upholds the law of spiritual perfection, which upholds the law of alpha and omega. Universal laws do not contradict one another; in and of themselves they do not create conflict.

Humanity, on the other hand, sometimes chooses to learn through conflict. That is why there is pain, suffering and conflict in the world: because humanity has chosen this experience above all other possibilities, time and time again. When humans no longer chose to express themselves through the law of one, it acknowledged separation. In separation they saw themselves as outside the circle of perfection. In other words, they saw themselves as less than perfect, less than whole. Mass consciousness was born when a majority of humans began to believe that they were less whole. That which believes it is not whole is destined to seek wholeness, and so it was with humanity. Mass consciousness still believed in perfection and wholeness, but it did not recognize it within itself. Instead, it set out to find it.

THE WAY OF THE ONE AND THE WAY OF THE MANY

Creator so desired Its creation to understand itself as whole again that It set humanity on a path of discovery and remembrance. Along that same path, Creator sent many messengers and teachers to remind humans of their divinity and perfection. For a time, it seemed that humans would do so; they became more vibrant, effulgent and self-reflective. Yet, for a reason that was not immediately evident, self-reflection became self-defeat, for it seemed that every time humans were given the opportunity to choose the teacher or the teaching, they would choose the teacher. Thus the messenger became more important than the message and the mystery more interesting than what it revealed. As humans became less enthralled with the way, they became more dependent upon the way-shower. Almost seamlessly the way of the one had arrived, and the way of the many slipped silently into history's oblivion.

The way of the one satisfied the humans' yearning to be led back home, because they had long forgotten where home was and what it was like. Vaguely, they saw their own reflection in the many teachers and teachings sent by

Creator, but humans followed these teachings blindly and in darkness rather than receiving the radiance that was offered to bring illumination to their own path. Humans longed for a leader to follow because they did not wish to lead. Their prayers were answered, but not in the way they had imagined, because Creator's longing was that humans lead themselves into oneness. Creator's infinite wisdom guided It to lead humans to the path of oneness by immersing them in the journey of the many.

The year 2004 will bring you near the end of the journey of the many, and the path of oneness will once again come back into view. In some ways, it will seem that you have so many choices of whom to follow and where to go that you will be uncertain as to what to do—which is exactly the point!

LEADERS AND FOLLOWERS, MASTERS AND DISCIPLES

What is a leader? What is the difference between a leader and a follower, between a student and a disciple? Leadership is not an office or a position. True leadership guides and directs by example. Leaders are first in line when there is danger and last in line when there is safety. True leaders are not martyrs; they are way-showers who influence by their light, not because of it. A disciple is someone who believes in the teachings of a leader and acts according to them. A follower, by contrast, is someone who is led and influenced by another. Followers are typically attendants, servants and subordinates of those whom they follow; they are usually one of a number of people accompanying a person who is thought to be important.

The year 2004 might yet be called the year of the spiritual master, but who and what is a master? A master is someone whose skill has reached a certain level of excellence. Masters are qualified to teach because they have acquired an understanding of that which they propose to teach. Masters do not seek followers, although they are adept at discovering disciples. This year will offer you many choices and many beings who wish to be followed, but perhaps you will be better served by discovering who among you is fit to lead and to teach by example.

There are those among you who would break the will of man and nature alike, and you will encounter them this year. Likewise, you will meet those who would control their behavior and yours, their feelings and your own. Look carefully upon those who would defeat or reduce another's teaching and ask yourself if a true leader would do so.

In order to return to the path of the one, you will need to move beyond the journey of the many. Who are the many? Are they indeed qualified to lead? Will you be compelled to follow, and if so, to what end? This will be a year of many endings and few beginnings, because the journey of the many who believe they are separate will be curtailed and derailed. Decide now if you are a leader or a follower, a teacher or a student, a master or a disciple. Define yourself by broadening your reality rather than narrowing your choices.

Lemuria and Atlantis

The history of Lemuria and Atlantis is now buried beneath the waves and what remains are the stories and the myths. These still hold great power, mystery and allure because they tell your story. Just as children enjoy being reminded of their childhood days and their antics, so does humanity find value in stirring up the remnants of the past to see what aspects are still relevant today.

Lemuria and Atlantis were more than just civilizations reduced to dust— they were continents! They were not invaded by the armies of another country, culture or monarch; they succumbed to their own vices. In their own way, each believed that they were righteous and invincible, and to a certain degree this is true, because their legacy is still alive within you.

The popular myths and stories about these cultures are not altogether true. For the most part, it seems that Lemuria has been assigned the role of the "good guy," whereas Atlantis reflects a civilization that did not anticipate its own demise in spite of its technological advancements—or perhaps because of them.

WHAT WAS LEMURIA LIKE?

Lemuria was a peaceful place, and that memory still calls to you, especially now when the world panorama does not seem to reflect this quality. Lemurians were hedonistic by nature, which is to say that their philosophy upheld pleasure as the highest good. Although their lifestyle was not self-indulgent, Lemurians believed that happiness was the very source of moral value, and they made certain that it was well represented in their way of life.

Personal or self-happiness was just as valuable and important as selfless happiness; therefore, what today might be called an act of public service was simply an aspect of happiness to the Lemurians. It gave them as much pleasure to plant another's garden as their own, and the sheer joy of raising one another's children was boundless. The Lemurian society was less structured than one might imagine: There were no laws to govern, and only a handful of understated rules carried any weight. Even so, their culture thrived and expanded for a very long time.

The Lemurians were not a technologically advanced people, but they were socially motivated. They did not believe in fences, for instance. Who would they fence out and for what reason, and why would they ever choose to fence themselves in? They did not believe that they owned the property they lived on, for if they did, they would be able to move it elsewhere, and this they could not do. They did believe they had a right to be on it, and for them this was enough. They were respectful of their neighbors and devoted to their elders, many of whom were four hundred and seven hundred years old!

They had a great respect for nature, and their knowledge of pharmacology is yet unparalleled. They understood the sources and the chemistry of plants, flowers and trees. When they treated the physical body, they also treated the emotional body, the more subtle lightbodies and the spirit. The most adept among them also understood the properties of pharmacokinetics, which is the way the body reacts to drugs and medicinals, including their absorption, metabolism and elimination. The Lemurian body did not scar as yours does today, and although it did age, it would be almost imperceptible to you.

THE ATLANTEANS CELEBRATED YOUTH

The Atlanteans, by contrast, were very interested in their appearance. They celebrated youth and youthful looks as no other culture has done since. But the Atlanteans were not as adept as the Lemurians at maintaining their youth. What the Lemurians did naturally, the Atlanteans had to create or manufacture. Still, the Atlantean mind was skilled, intelligent and well developed. What they did not know they immediately set out to discover, and to their credit, their civilization advanced by leaps and bounds compared to others. The scraps of pieced-together history that remain today do little justice to this great race of beings. But if their knowledge and technology was so advanced, why did they age so much more rapidly than the Lemurians?

The Atlanteans would do almost anything in order to achieve a young appearance or to recapture one if necessary. Cosmetic laser surgery was in vogue for a time, as were other rather strange and somewhat vulgar techniques. These would certainly raise an eyebrow today, but are your current practices any less vulgar to those who would look upon them from beyond this corridor of time?

The Atlanteans were not as obsessed with beauty as they were with youth. Young minds and youthful bodies were worth a ransom in dispensations, favors or wealth from those who were in a position to grant them. Just as there are beings among you today who would sell a liver, a lung or a kidney, there were Atlantean citizens who were willing to sell their youth, strange as that might seem. Suffice it to say that the technology that could accomplish this did exist then.

Unfortunately, the Atlanteans believed that only a youthful culture could sustain itself or reinvent itself. The ruling class believed that Atlantis had been blessed by forces and beings of great power and wisdom; their legacy included youth, technology and power, but it did not include longevity. Above all else, the Atlanteans wanted their culture to survive in perpetuity. When conventional means did not yield the desired results, they turned to unconventional means; and when these were found lacking, they became desperate. They began to genetically modify their food and medicines in order to alter their appearance and their health. They went against the better opinions of the wise and the counsel of the ancients. Eventually, they even went against all that was natural, but fate inter-vened. And when she did, destiny spoke harshly and shook fiercely.

DEALING WITH DIFFICULT QUESTIONS

Lemuria and Atlantis were realities apart from each other in many ways. Chronological history is not an accurate record of events, and timelines criss-cross more often than not. Linear time is sometimes parallel time, and calen-dars are subjective measures of spatial units of evolution. Lemuria and Atlantis did not exist side by side, but they were aware of each other's presence the way you are aware of a distant culture you know little about. Another race of beings who made their home within the planet related to both the Lemurians and the Atlanteans from time to time, and when things began to deteriorate, news traveled swiftly.

Can a civilization predict its own downfall? How does a culture know when it is too late to save itself from extinction? When does a generation stop plac-ing hope in the next generation? What can the dying offer to the living? What advice would you give to the Lemurians or the Atlanteans in hindsight? What do you believe they would offer to humanity at this time? Does having hind-sight or foresight offer any advantages, or is each civilization and culture assigned its own date with destiny and demise? These are appropriate questions and, albeit difficult to answer, not impossible.

The Lemurians and the Atlanteans are among you today. Can you recognize them in your friends, family and neighbors? They are living proof of what is worth living for, but is anything really worth dying for? Ask yourself this ques-tion today and be willing to answer it by the time the Sun is in the midheaven in 2004, because difficult questions such as this one will soon reveal themselves in several different scenarios. They will present themselves for your considera-tion, and a reply on your part will be necessary.

If your water is over-fluoridated, will it stir you to action? Does consuming genetically modified food frighten you? Will you fight for the right to vote if it is taken from you? What is your freedom worth? Is your privacy subject to piracy? Do your sons and daughters have a future? If you will not put a price on their heads, will you allow others to do so? What would you surrender in order to save your culture? What will your civilization surrender in order to save itself?

Time shortens now and the past whispers to you, but will you listen? The Lemurians and the Atlanteans both share center stage with you now. They are counting upon you to take up the causes that they unconsciously laid down. Lemuria and Atlantis both rise in 2004. Lemuria will be rising within you and Atlantis will be rising without. Both will be accompanied by undeniable celes-tial events that herald unprecedented change.

Seek counsel within and it will manifest without, but ignore sage words at your own peril. Light and shadow both offer themselves as trusted guides: In which will you invest your faith? Lemuria offers ancient wisdom and natural law, whereas Atlantis offers alternatives to discontent and possible demise. Relate to them as partners and companions rather than competitors or adversaries from the past. Look not upon the admonishment but upon the advice.

Angels

You will hear it said that 2004 is a good year for angels, but what does that mean? Do angels have good years and bad years? No, not necessarily. Nonetheless, 2004 is a grand year for angels because they will be more understood and better appreciated than they have been in the past.

Angels are aspected light. In other words, they are lightness of being on which shadows dance. Shadows are created when darkened light falls within reach of someone or something that is blocking the light. Shadows create relative darkness, but they are not darkness itself; they are screens. Someone who follows another person around wanting to be with that person is also called a shadow, and such is the case with angels. They follow humanity (you) closely, because they want to be with you.

Angels are a reflection of you, and they are an imitation of what you are when you are not immersed in your shadow. When you place great importance upon your shadow, you cannot see your angels because they deflect shadow and attract light. Angels learn about you by observing you regularly. They see you clearly even if you are only vaguely aware of their presence. Humanity believes that angels move about mysteriously or obscurely, but many angels believe the same about you.

What is an archetypal angel? Is it a divine being acting as a messenger on behalf of God? Are angels kind and beautiful? Do they look like humans with wings? Is their divine purpose to protect you and offer guidance? What about celestial hierarchy? Are angels lower in rank than archangels?

Angels are aspects of you. They are the divine aspects of you that you are not yet willing to acknowledge as that which you are. That is why they are most often portrayed as humans with wings. Angels are the divine aspects of you that feel more resonant with heaven than with Earth. Aspects of you are selfless, just like angels. Aspects of you wish only to be of service to God, just like angels. Aspects of you are pure and innocent, just like angels.

Are all humans also angels? No, not necessarily, but many are. Angels are aspects of your beingness, not your humanness. They are not separate from you, which is why they brush by you as often as possible. They are unique, individuated aspects of God. Some angels have merged with you sufficiently to consider themselves human or, at the very least, Earth angels. And some humans have merged with their angels so as to consider themselves angelic in origin.

ALL HUMANS HAVE ANGELS

Do all humans have angels? Yes, they do. Angels are a daily occurrence for some and an unexpected miracle for others. Angels are manifested light and a testament to your undying faith in yourselves. As long as you continue to believe in angels, you will never doubt your ability to return to the unity that is All That Is. Do angels grant wishes and answer prayers? No, but they do assist you in creating and manifesting your desires. How do they do it? By placing an ideal of you as God and God as you in undeniable places. It is not so much that they help you to create miracles; it is more accurate to say that they show you how to stop preventing miracles from happening. Angels teach you to pray for what you really want rather than for what you think you want or need. They show you how to relate to your God aspects by reminding you of your own divinity.

Angels do not set themselves above you, and archangels are not greater than angels. They are simply more divine, which is to say that they carry a lighter celestial essence. Angels do not rank themselves or you. They belong to unique orders of purposeful expression. Their journey is much like your life purpose, but to you it would seem much longer. If you could see your essence as a spiral, you would see that the inner aspects of the spiral seem to travel much faster than the outer ones. In the same way, angelic beings guide you, surround you, insulate and protect you. They allow you to expand within the spiral at your own pace, moving closer to divinity all the while. Expansion sometimes looks like moving away from something or somewhere rather than into someplace, which is why many of you believe that your being human makes you less than angelic or godlike.

ANGELIC ASPECTS IN THE NEW YEAR

In late 2003 and early 2004, there will be a merging of the conscious aspects within humanity. This merging will allow left-brain and right-brain activities to become a little less separate. The unconscious aspects of humanity will continue to be unconscious, but this fact is not to be taken at face value. An average human being is 17 percent conscious, 73 percent unconscious and 10 percent angelic reservoir. These percentages are average and vary somewhat on an individual level. Superconscious humans are still in short supply, but this could change significantly in 2004, because it is the year in which aspected light will filter into and through the more permanent and semipermanent dimensions and densities within which humanity expresses itself.

Aspected light has two polarities: ascendant light and descendant light. The ascendant polarity is that which assists humanity in recognizing the more angelic, heavenly or celestial aspects of life; the descendant polarity assists the angelic reservoir to recognize the divinity within the conscious/unconscious human. This measure has very little, if anything, to do with the fallible intelligence quotient that humanity is so fascinated with. The mind and the brain are related to each other, but they are by no means the same. Humans use very little of their brains at this time and are only capable of increasing that usage by a small amount. The mind, on the other hand, is quite capable of expanding its awareness above and beyond its current understanding.

The various angelic orders will be reviving and reconnecting specific areas within human consciousness in 2004. By way of experience, this will be felt as a resurrection of spirit, spiritual understanding and religion. As consciousness expands, the dams that have controlled the flow of awareness will give way. Human awareness will be flooded with feelings and emotions that have been blocked for eons of time. It is difficult to predict the many expressions of self that this will evoke, but it is appropriate to expect new teachers and teachings as well as a considerable resurgence in religious fervor to appear.

Aspected light in the form of angelic support will be present within and without in 2004. Angels are lightbeings, and their light is also expressed as divine angles within sacred geometry. The year of 2004 can also be described as a year in which the acute angle within sacred geometry becomes spiritually responsible, which is to say that the more keenly perceptive and sensitive among humanity will find angelic presence among them the norm. An acute angle is one that is less than 90 degrees, and an acute triangle has 3 internal angles of less than 90 degrees. Angles also relate to probability, but conversely so; therefore, there is a greater than 90-percent probability that angels will divinely intervene on humanity's behalf in 2004—in what way and for what purpose is still to be revealed. I do not withhold this information from you, but inherent within the energy described as acute is a brief, severe movement that quickly becomes a crisis or a conflict that demands a resolution of equal measure. Were I to offer a variety of scenarios requiring such a response, I would only feed the probability scale, which would not be in your best interests.

An angelic encounter usually lasts only a moment or so, and no two experiences are ever alike. Light dances and moves in purposeful but nonspecific ways. Angels are employed by the most aware aspects of Source to be of service to the least aware aspects of self; therefore, 2004 will bring great light to dark moments.

Agriculture

The expression "betting the farm" is an old one. Today it seems outdated and far-fetched, but the truth is never far from the yardstick, which means that its relevance is measurable.

When someone places a wager, one is relatively certain that he or she understands the measure or the extent of the wager that is being placed. After all, there are odds and oddsmakers, officials and professionals. A bet is an agreement based upon risk that pledges compensation, restitution or forfeit of something of value when or if the outcome of a game, event or uncertain situation does not result in a win for the bettor. A bettor is therefore confident in the wager and certain that something will happen, has happened or is true. Odds are the likelihood or probability that something will occur and are often expressed as ratios. Odds sometimes offer handicaps, or advantages, in order to equalize the odds or to stimulate bettor certainties.

The purpose of this discussion is not to make you good bettors but to prepare you to recognize that the odds are not in your favor regarding farms, organic produce, dairy products or food and vitamin supplements.

NATURAL RESOURCES CHURN OUT SYNTHETICS

Human bodies are organic; they are derived from and relate to living things. They are designed to develop gradually and naturally, without being forced or contrived. Organic elements have a natural and efficient relationship to one another, as opposed to synthetic elements, which depend upon chemical relationships to bridge potential gaps. The human body is a functioning system of interdependent parts and must be cared for and properly alimented if it is to survive in the long run. Synthetic organisms are artificially made to resemble organic ones, by a process called synthesis. Synthesis is the process of forming a complex compound through a series of one or more chemical reactions involving simpler substances. Synthesis can also apply to ideas, influences and objects.

A chemical process instead of a natural one produces synthetic material, which tends to last longer than natural material does. By its very nature, that which is natural lasts only as long as it is useful. Which one is better? Which one would you bet on? Would you bet the farm on being right? Those who control the agricultural processes in this country and seek to do the same elsewhere have done just that. They have bet their farm and your farm on it, as well as that of your sons and daughters and grandchildren for many generations to come. Why? Because they went with the odds in a subject they knew little about. Fertilizers, pesticides and chemicals seemed like the odds-on favorites to win the battle against diminishing crop returns and the increasing needs of a growing population. But land is a living organism that is interdependent with all that it touches and relates to—not a vast laboratory whose failed experiments can be fed to an already suffering population.

Agriculture is the science of cultivating land and producing crops in order to nourish hungry children, but it has deteriorated, and in its place stand even hungrier biotechnology giants whose scientists would own and control the very seeds of nature. The results are in now, and they are anything but successful. Unfortunately, these results are hidden within the deep pockets of industry giants; carefully written studies are withering away between stacks of worldwide currency.

Agriculture has become agrobiology, agrochemistry, agroforestry, agroindustry and agronomics. The Earth's natural resources are now churning out synthetic fabric and material, and those who labor in the oil fields and cotton fields dine on small amounts of genetically modified food at the end of their day.

Think before You Swallow

New is not always better, and a sure bet is hard to come by. Innocent farmers were promised larger profits if they embraced the new technology, and who can blame them? But their farmland is dying now because it is contaminated and toxic. New chemicals are replacing old ones at alarming rates, and agronomics has declared war on nature. The farming community is braced for the fight of its life, or so it believes, but nature will not do battle with a giant gnat. Caught in a net of deceit, it will simply withdraw its precious gift until its bounty is once again welcomed.

I put the case to you now, for your current future is in peril. If crops and farmland continue to be seen as mere commodities that are bought, sold and traded in private boardrooms, then the same fate awaits humanity. Consumers and commodities are both precious sources of income in international markets that wager and trade upon best- and worst-case scenarios. Humanity is a treasure beyond measure, but it must see itself as one—now more than ever. If you welcome genetically altered and modified foods onto your table, then you guarantee a genetically modified future generation. Perhaps now is the time to think before you swallow, whether it is an idea, a promise or a seed.

How will this subject affect you in 2004? This year will feature many closed-door discussions, because intense suspicion has been cast on those who secretly oppose modifications of industry. World opinion speaks of heeding lessons already learned rather than inviting new ones. Organic and conventional farmers alike are refusing to surrender their future and that of their children. Production of almost all crops has plummeted, and a revolution in thinking along with a change of heart is in dire need at this time.

Your best interests are the Earth's best interests. Your body is not a laboratory to be experimented upon, but neither is mine. Your body is a field of wisdom and your mind is a pool of knowledge. Search within and without for answers that emerge without resistance. Nature does not resist, but it will visit disastrous results upon the rogue, contaminated, foolish thoughts of the few in order to secure the many.

Money

Humanity, for the most part, believes in one God and prays to one God even though God expresses Himself through various world beliefs and religions. Long ago, however, many gods expressed themselves through humanity. Pantheism, or the belief and worship of many deities, was common then. The citizens of the past were not certain that one god could be devoted and attentive to the wants and needs of so many, so a pantheon of patron gods and saints, angels and archangels, devas and deities was needed and in demand. Over time, however, God gained the respect, reverence and veneration of most of the world.

God attained Almighty status and has managed to be attentive to the well behaved, the wicked and the wealthy. It would seem that there is no other god before Him, and although that might be true, there is another god who follows close behind. Interestingly enough, this god also has attained almighty status, and many people pray to this god daily.

The relative and timely importance of polarity and duality within the third dimension seems to have divided the world into the haves and the have-nots. Those who have money and wealth also seem to have power, whereas those who do not seem powerless. Duality is not a balanced medium of exchange, and polarity can be a very fickle friend. As these mediums cannot be trusted to support you all of the time, it would seem that an insurance policy of divine nature might come in handy. Humanity calls this insurance policy money, and the patron god of money is the almighty dollar.

The haves and the have-nots both pray to the Almighty God and to the almighty dollar. Why pray to both if God is almighty? Because God, as everyone knows, is very busy these days, and His concerns are great. He might not have time in His busy schedule to answer every prayer, or so the thought goes, and just in case, a few extra dollars would come in very handy. The have-nots pray that they will have enough almighty dollars to pay the rent, and the haves pray that the have-nots will pay their rent so they, in turn, can pay their creditors so that they can maintain their lifestyle. But aren't both polarities praying for the same thing? Yes, they are. If both polarities want the same thing, does polarity still exist? No, because polarity is the illusion upon which the third dimension is built, and duality is the belief system that supports the third-dimensional foundation with all of its might.

MONEY IS CREATIVE DESIRE

The almighty dollar is the vehicle or currency of exchange of the third dimension. It has gained the status, rights and privileges of a complex entity rather than a simple unit of exchange. Sayings such as "money talks" are more real than not and have made money a presence and a power that is equal to or greater than anything else in the world. If this sounds too incredulous to believe, think upon how many of your prayers would be answered right now if you just had a little more money.

Money did not always have this power, but power has always had the money. Gold, silver, petroleum, land and commodities have shared the same throne from time to time, but today the almighty dollar seems to reign uncontested. How and why did this happen? After all, money is only a temporary asset. It is measurable, but only when it is exchanged for something else. Money is not what is in your bank, and if you go there to visit it, you might be surprised to find that it is not sitting there waiting for you. Money is a currency that can be exchanged for goods and services, but more than that, money is creative desire.

Money's value and supply increase and decrease relative to creative desire. Is money the same as wealth? Money and wealth are equal only when desire is equivalent to the possession of money. Once money has been exchanged for something else, it is again equal to desire. Is money the same as prosperity? No, prosperity is the condition of enjoying wealth, success, good fortune and well-being. Can money and abundance be one and the same? No, but one of the original translations of abundance describes the overflowing fullness of spirit that was associated with and expressed by the proportion and quantity of excitable atoms in a thought or desire. Money is not possessions, affluence, opulence, riches, success or influence, but it can be exchanged for all of these if the desire to do so is present.

MONEY IS ONLY A UNIT OF EXCHANGE

Why does money seem to be in such short supply then? Can it be that creative desire is also in short supply? Money does not multiply desire, but desire can multiply money. Money is only a unit of exchange, and in some cultures, three goats and two cows are the energetic equivalent of great wealth and high standing. But would you trade a luxury vehicle for three goats? By contrast, this culture would pity your foolishness in this regard. It is very difficult to measure the value of money; it has no value save for what it is given or assigned.

In banking circles, "money of account" is a well-known term. It is used to indicate an arbitrary monetary unit that is used to keep accounts. It does not necessarily correspond to any actual unit of currency. This system is widely used by governments who support budgets that cannot be balanced and debts that cannot be repaid. The United States government, for instance, cannot currently or in the foreseeable future repay its debt, because it has become too large and unmanageable. But the debt cannot simply be erased, at least not yet, so an arbitrary unit of account is assigned to it.

Consumer credit is another form of money of account, because no dollars actually change hands when consumers pay for items on credit. A debit is assigned to the consumer's account, and the agreed-upon interest rate is added to the transaction. Whether or not a credit is entered to offset the debit waits to be seen. Behind closed doors and in small but widening circles, there are whispers that this accounting system can no longer support itself or those who have created it and still profit from it.

Personal bankruptcy, a state in which one is legally declared unable to repay one's debt, is at an all-time high, and the published statistics are not close to being accurate. Corporate bankruptcies also defy current published statistics, with no apparent end in sight. Interestingly, bankruptcy also applies to the complete lack of a particular quality, especially good or ethical qualities. When a bankruptcy is declared, the money of account is cleared and the obligation to repay the debt is erased or forgiven, because in the current system, dollars equal banknotes, or pieces of paper money that are issued by a bank and guaranteed by a government. But what if this system of now diminishing returns becomes obsolete? Will another system simply emerge to replace it?

CAN MONEY BECOME OBSOLETE?

Certain events in 2004 will begin to answer this question, but it will not be fully answered until 2005, and a new system might not be in place until 2007 or later. The events leading up to this momentous change will be subtle but well placed. They will not raise alarm or widespread panic. They will emerge in the form of studies and statistics, and they will be revealed as expected rather than surprising results. There will be indications that corrections might be needed in how the government backs its supply of money. Currently, it is backed by the full faith and credit of the government, but what if it were not? What if, instead, it was supported and upheld by the government until a replacement policy could be put into effect?

What will the new system be like? It will continue to be based upon credits and debits as it is now. These will not be erased, but they could be corrected to reflect the new system. Adjustments and allowances of many kinds will be made, and more will be needed. Banknotes will be replaced by bankcards, and the reasons cited will include counterfeit prevention as well as measures to combat personal identity theft. A campaign will begin in 2004 to sell the new system to a tired, confused and aging population. An altogether different campaign will entice young and eager consumers to join the bandwagon. Promotions and promises of economic stability and reward will follow shortly, as will tax credits and incentives that erase, or seem to erase, at least a partial debt.

Will everyone switch to the new system? Yes, over time everyone will, because the old system will be abandoned and those who do not switch will be abandoned along with it. If the new system promised national health insurance, for instance, would you switch? If the new system erased your credit history and

past debt, would you switch? If the new system guaranteed a university education for your children, would you switch? And if the new system allowed you to
repay your mortgage at a fraction of its current balance, would you not switch?
You see, although not everyone might be for sale, everyone has at least one vulnerable place within. You will not be forced or coerced to participate in the
new system, and your properties will not be confiscated from you. But the old
system, like the old currency, will lose popularity and value along with it.
Humanity is a creature of habit and old habits die hard, but die they will. It is
good to know it now so that you can prepare for the changes with ease rather
than apprehension.

Prepare by beginning now to value yourselves more than you value money
or any system that replaces it. Prepare by acknowledging that you are the creative director in your life and know that your creative desire is what designs all
your future moments. Your pocketbook does nothing on its own, and your
bank account is not your calling card. Recall a spirit of adventure from long
ago and set sail on a new pursuit to discover the creative self within you.
Explore the possibility that it is not money that has prevented you from having or being your dream, but that it is the belief in money as god that has
diminished your status.

God is a natural creative force who instills desire within you. He shows you
limitation so that you will choose the unlimited within yourself and transcend
any and all belief systems. Money is not almighty, but you are. Dollars have little or no consequence when you believe in something greater. I invite you to
believe in yourselves and in your future, as both are quite bright.

Circus

A long time ago, before there were computers, the Internet, television or
radio, there was the circus. The traveling circus came to town every year or so,
bringing with it entertainers, clowns, acrobats, animals and animal trainers.
When the circus was there, towns became noisy, confused and overwhelming.
The ordinary seemed extraordinary.

Circus is a very ancient term. Originally, it was the name given to the open
stadiums where chariot races and fights between gladiators were staged. Circus
Maximus is perhaps the most remembered. It and other Roman circuses attracted
huge crowds of citizens, senators and bystanders.

By their very nature, circuses are self-important events, which is to say that
there is an unrealistically high expectation surrounding the staged events that
unfold there. Self-important events often require a master of ceremonies, someone who performs the duties of a host, makes opening speeches and introduces
other speakers or performers.

Circuses are less popular events today than they once were. They have been replaced by other attractions such as amusement theme parks, but the three-ring circus that began in the Rome of long ago continues to this day.

When Roman citizens tired of being in such a large venue with so little to see and do, those who promoted the events began to think up new ideas to stimulate and encourage participation. There were hardly enough actors or entertainers then or enough Roman coins with which to pay them, so ordinary citizens were encouraged to participate and take their chances in games, exploits and lotteries. These could bring a sudden windfall or a sudden death. Why did so many Roman citizens flock to the circus to witness the often brutal events there? They did so because in most cases, the events within their own lives were equally as brutal. Many had already lost sons to war, daughters to warmongers and property to the Roman Empire. Cheering for or against others' attempts to gain fortune or ward off misfortune gave them a temporary respite from their own concerns, regardless of the outcome.

UNCONSCIOUS THOUGHTS MAKE YOU FEEL SEPARATE

Do today's events seem so very different? Are your concerns less today than they were yesterday? During World War II, movies became one of the most popular distractions, especially musicals and comedies where one could lose oneself in the fantasy of the moment. Today's movies, television and video games all draw large crowds of both participants and spectators, but the reality of human suffering is too real to witness, hence the invention of staged reality shows and the return of the three-ring circus. Is real-life drama real? Is reality TV real? Is your interest in these programs real or are you being influenced to feign interest? Why are television shows called programs? Why are computer game fanatics called junkies and addicts? Can it be that humanity is drawn to the fantastic because the mundane seems uncontrollably intolerable?

Your life is not a three-ring circus; it is a delicate web of creative engineering, designed to free you from the confines of illusional veils and thinking. The cells in your body are unique and individual pathways to All That Is; each one contains consciousness, sentience and light. How then is it possible that so many lights are still turned off? It is because humanity is being conditioned and programmed to think and to act unconsciously rather than consciously.

Unconscious thoughts are those that did not originate with you. They originated within a holographic sphere that exists just beyond your awareness. Unconscious thoughts are reflected to you via sound, pulse and frequency. Unconscious thoughts are those that make you feel separate from your husband, wife, mother, father, boss or neighbor. Real separation does not exist—it never did. Individual and unique arrays of experience are consistently offered from Source to soul, but separation is a byproduct of a mind that is told it is alone

among all others. It is repeatedly told that it will be very difficult for it to survive on its own and that the heart is not strong enough to overcome the adver-
sities of the third dimension. A holographic and spiritually inventive collective
consciousness then offers itself as an administrative aide to the mind, sorting out
the positive from the negative, or so it would seem.

STEP OUTSIDE THE HOLOGRAM

In order for the holographic administrator to remain in control, the mind must
be either passive or aggressive, but it cannot be receptive or sympathetic. The
programming is specifically dependent upon the mind's ability and need to be
polarized. In other words, the mind must have a constant need to know right from
wrong, to make right decisions and to judge decisions it does not make as wrong.
A mind that understands both sides of an issue cannot be controlled, and a heart
that feels the intensity of both the victor and the victim cannot be owned.

That is why there are so many issues to feel strongly for or against today and
why a majority seems more important than ever. Threats of terrorism pour more
salt onto deeper wounds; they catalyze and polarize minds until they are taut,
strung together like beads. A frequency is then passed through the string,
vibrating each of the beads individually but attuning them to the same vibration. Why do so many minds seem to think alike? Because human minds are
becoming more alike every day. Thoughts of us versus them are implanted triggers that stimulate the mind to act and react, as it is impulsed to do.

What can you do to step outside the hologram? Choose to know yourself.
Choose to explore new subjects about which you know nothing. Become self-
motivated and self-interested. Support others, but do not follow them blindly.
Explore your awareness and see if it is aligned with your heart. If it is not, ask
what you can do to bring it into greater alignment. Speak your own truth without first seeking the approval of your peer group—you might discover that they
are not your peer group at all.

Be guided by gentle words and soft voices; Spirit has no need to shout.
Watch television sparingly and only when there are quality programs of specific
interest to you. Remember that they are programs and that they affect the mind
as such. Look with care, compassion and concern upon your neighbor and your
friend. Even when preoccupied, ask yourself, "What is the price of a smile?"
Reduce your life from a three-ring circus to a two- or one-ring circus whenever
possible. Remind yourself that you are special, unique, supported and loved
consistently and endlessly.

War Machine

It seems that the world has always been at war over one thing or another.
Battles have been waged over eons of time, during which all manner of theft,

violence and murder have been written off to the price of freedom, which, as everyone well knows, is priceless. But freedom does have a cost and it is price-less, which means that it cannot be bought, sold, ransomed or paid for. Interestingly, that which cannot be bought or sold can still yield a profit. Those who know this also understand that war is for the profit makers, whereas peace is for the profit losers. War has always been profitable, and more than a tidy sum sits in vaulted coffers awaiting its owner's next pursuit. Is war about money, then? No, it is about profit, which is another thing altogether. Profit is the excess of income over expenditure; it is the advantage or benefit derived from an investment or transaction.

Is Freedom What You Are Fighting For?

Is the brutality of war less today than it was yesterday or yesteryear? It is not, I assure you, for I am both the witness to the battle and the battlefield itself. Today's concourse of battle is no more carefully planned or executed than the worn-out strategies of long ago. Radar images and satellite photos enhance tar-gets and reduce waste, but loss of innocent life has gained no ground.

Who is your enemy? Do you know them? Do you know their names? Have you ever met them? Do they have sons and daughters; are they like yours? Do they have hearts that beat and throats that bleed? Is their appearance so very different from your own? Are their hopes and dreams unique? Ask yourselves these questions as often as possible. Answer them from within your own being, without reservation and without the assistance of the latest headline or news bulletin. Respond as if a child were posing these questions for the very first time, because indeed there is a child within you who is even now await-ing your response.

Freedom is worth attaining and maintaining, but are you certain that freedom is what you are fighting for? What if you have surrendered your brave sons and daughters to a cause that has no justifiable end? What if they were being fed to a war machine that progressively did away with conscious freedom and replaced it with a centralized power designed to increase profit? What if machines of war are the product and the war machine is the profit from the product? Humans cannot be in charge of their destiny as long as they are being manipulated and controlled from what they perceive as outside of or separate from themselves. You can navigate the corridors of fate but not the halls of destiny.

The growing use of advanced technologies that dole out lethal consequences to all concerned is reducing your immunity and resilience to disease. You agree to attack others because fear of attack is being instilled in you; it is how the war machine works. The war machine creates and supports war because it is a war machine; it can do nothing else. It attacks and then retaliates when it is attacked; it is a machine in perpetual motion. It is the enemy, the enemy's friend and the enemy's enemy. The machine's technology exists independently of human will. If there are no soldiers left to fight, the war machine will create soldiers, do you see? Bombarded daily by fear and distrust, you fight an opponent that offers no face and defend yourselves from invisible foes you have never seen. The human race is in decay because it has allowed its mind and its body to be owned and controlled.

Hold on to your individual truth. Don't give it to geopolitical factions that even now prepare for their victory lap. Do not model yourselves after partisan beliefs and interests that do not serve you or anyone you know. Do not bother to fight for a freedom that never existed. Claim control of your own soul's code—it alone knows the way home. Those who would manipulate you without your knowledge would see you avoid this at all cost. Divide and conquer is still the game of choice. Allow the power of your free will to ignite your passion. Be proud of what you are becoming, and you will discover the self-intimacy that is your legacy.

ESCAPE THE DEVOLUTION OF THE MIND

Do you know the truth when you hear it? Do you know what is real when you see it? You most likely believe that you do, but it is more probable that you do not. You have been taught to believe that truth and reality are objective, but they are not and they never have been. As long as you believe that truth is objective and that you are being offered the truth, you will believe that truth. The same applies to reality: Once it has been established as real, it is rarely questioned. The human mind is accustomed to ordering and prioritizing all its thoughts. It makes mental lists on every subject imaginable, and it gives priority to original or first thoughts. The mind understands that there is a difference between original thought and programmed thought, but it cannot differentiate between the two. It can only rank them by how important they are to the mind's own survival.

Human behavior is based, at least in part, on past habit and former training. How often do you change your mind about someone or something? The answer is rarely, because in order for your mind to change, it must find a contradiction relative to the original premise it has accepted as true and real. That is why so many of you run into dead-ends just as you are on the verge of discovering something new.

The mind contains millions of cells, and many of these are able to access the past, the present and the potential future. The mind uses these cells as a type of notepad on which it evaluates the best course of action based upon all that it has assimilated. In order to offer itself to you optimally, the mind must be well maintained and its cellular structure must be nourished. If the mind is constantly idle or inactive, its ability to receive and process new and original creative thoughts, ideas and instructions will be diminished.

Human minds today are caught in a web of inertia in which new thoughts are rare and old programming is consistently reinforced. Older minds are clogged with worries and younger minds are robbed of their youth. Consumer minds are programmed to shop, student minds are programmed to memorize rather than discover and aging minds are called senile when their overly programmed cells begin to disintegrate. Is there any escape from the devolution of the mind? Your mind was designed to be of service to you, and it was intended that it last your entire lifetime. Cells and thoughts that deteriorate need to be replaced with new ones, and if the mind is to survive, it must reconcile old programs and begin to balance new and original thoughts.

Originality and Evolution

Original thoughts are those that invite choice. Original thoughts are rarely based upon past history or repeated dialogue. Original thoughts are questions whose answers must be discovered rather than processed. Humanity cannot solve its current problems by accessing its past memories.

The solutions to current dilemmas are in the present future, the aspects of the future that can be accessed now. The mind cannot do this alone, because it is too fragmented and dependent upon its past beliefs. But the mind—when coupled with the heart—can heal its fragments and encourage a condition of reconnection of the whole self. Wholeness allows that which you are, the I Am, to choose. Original thoughts, new choices or other programs can replace old beliefs and old programs. The mind cannot distinguish between these on its own, but it can with the assistance of the I Am, the animating force, purpose and spirit you are.

CHOOSE YOUR PRESENT, DESIGN YOUR FUTURE

Evolution is upon humanity. Even in the short time it has taken you to read these words, humanity has evolved. Humans have a multievolutional conscience hidden within their subconscious. As individuals, you do not recognize that you have a survival instinct until you are called upon to initiate it. Collectively, the same is true of humanity: Until humans recognize that if they do not evolve as a species they will perish, they will not ignite the conscious awareness that will promote their future. Based upon humanity's present condition and the Earth's ability to sustain itself, it would seem that the time should be now, but if that is the case, why has it not happened yet?

The answer rests in humanity's reliance upon the past rather than the future. Old myths, legends, stories and prophecies still influence current thought. Most of the predictions that are offered today, even by the most astute, are based upon structures and beliefs of long ago. If allowed to persist, they will play out and you will have lived your history. But why live your history when you can choose your present and design your future? There are many who believe that your future cannot begin until certain prophecies are fulfilled, but your future begins with the next moment.

Are you waiting for a savior to show you the way? If so, then look in the mirror now, because you are an aspect of that savior. Do you really want to know what 2004 will be like, or would you prefer to know what 2012, 2025 and 2040 will be like? The year 2004 is assured; it is already here. But if you want to see 2012 for yourself, you will have to choose it instead of waiting around to see if it shows up.

Are you waiting for what most people term ascension? You will have to choose that as well, because it arrives at the invitation of the conscious and evolved mind. Are you waiting for off-planet visitors and extraterrestrial support to alleviate your indecision? They are already here and in service to you; they are awaiting your acceptance of them and your full participation in the further development of your species and your planet. They will not save you from yourselves.

Unexplained celestial events go unnoticed by most of the population, because they are depending upon past beliefs to support present experience. Truth and reality are permanent residents of Now; they cannot be fully experienced when filters and veils replace creative direction. It is time to consider the impossible and the improbable as viable choices, because the decisions you make today will directly and significantly affect what you create tomorrow.

New discoveries in the fields of science, especially in physics and chemistry, must be made available to the general population rather than sequestered for the few. The "essence" of matter has been discovered, which means that scientists within the upper echelons of study can now materialize and dematerialize matter. Did they discover this on their own? No, not really. It was a collaborative process in which those who participated in the program were accelerated to ask the right questions. Unfortunately, this knowledge remains secreted behind closed doors. Those who modulate and control humanity believe this knowledge could be hazardous to your health. Why? Because if you understood these simple principles, they would no longer seem magical to you.

Extraterrestrial beings appear and disappear because they understand that density is only a thought away from nondensity. Dimensional reality and multidimensional reality exist at minute intervals of density separation. Your ability to observe the ships that share your skies are based upon this knowledge, but in order to truly understand these new concepts, you must be willing to relinquish some of the outmoded beliefs you still carry—such as the ones that say you will believe in extraterrestrials as soon as you see one with your own eyes. Your eyes will betray you and your mind will trick you, but your heart's desire will not mislead you. Outstretched hands already reach out to you; will you not offer the same?

Saints and Sinners

Saints have a privileged place among humanity. They are good, kind, virtuous and patient. They help you deal with difficult choices and situations. Sinners, on the other hand, offend humanity's moral and ethical principles. Their thoughts, acts and behavior contradict laws of Spirit and teachings of religion. Sinners characteristically, habitually and knowingly do wrong—right?

Do you know more saints or sinners? Are corporate giants saints or sinners? Landlords and employers? What about elected officials and other government representatives? What category would you place yourself in? In certain theologies, God's grace can be denied if even one of any number of sins is committed. Do you know someone to whom you would deny God's grace? Would you deny grace, the most sincere form of tolerance, to yourself? If you are either a saint or a sinner, 2004 is your year to shine, but if you do not fit into either category, be careful that you do not judge others too harshly as you watch the year unfold from the sidelines.

COMPENSATION FOR THE MISPLACEMENT OF A COLLECTIVE SOUL?

The polarity/duality scales that have plagued humanity for centuries are drooping. They have been overstuffed and weighted down with the density of the third dimension. Good and bad, light and dark, angelic and demonic, Democrat and Republican, prosperous and impoverished, honest and deceitful—the list goes on and on. Opposites call to each other and demand that their energetic partner take notice of their actions. Saints compulsively attract sinners in order to help heal them, and sinners unconsciously beg saints for forgiveness. Opposites attract opposites in order to restore balance.

Restitution is the return of something to its rightful place, to the condition it was before it was changed. Restoration is the return of something that was previously removed, in an effort to represent its original condition. Humanity currently seeks both restitution and restoration of its collective soul, but it has forgotten how, so instead it seeks settlement in the form of compensation. Compensation is an amount of money or something else given in exchange or in payment for loss or damage. Compensation stresses one aspect of the personality and neglects another. It seeks to make amends but it cannot.

Saints and sinners in the form of citizens, students, charitable dispensations, political factions, humanitarians, civil libertarians, religious affiliates and corporate entities are all seeking the restoration and restitution of their place of balance. They are seeking their original purpose and design, but they have forgotten the way back to the center. Collectively, humans seem to have decided that if they cannot find their way back home, they will make certain that they are justly compensated. But what is the going rate or the just compensation for the misplacement of a collective soul?

In 2004 you will see this question arise time and again. You will hear it in corporate board rooms and on nightly news programs. It will be on trial before local magistrates and in high courts alike. In open fields and behind closed doors, humanity will wonder, "What is the difference between a saint and a sinner? Is there one? Where is the fine line that separates the two?" "When do children become adults? When they are eighteen or twenty-one, or when they are found culpable in a crime at fifteen?" "When is an elected official also an unlawful offender? When he fails to represent his constituents or when he spends tax dollars in his backyard instead of yours?" "At what point is a priest no longer a priest? When he discovers that he has human weaknesses and frailties or when he becomes a liability to those he can no longer hide behind?" "Where does corporate fraud enter the realm of criminal negligence? When the corporation in question is not a subsidiary of the media group that is supposed to blow the whistle?" The list of questions that can be answered is endless as you can see, but is there a clear-cut answer? Polarity does not seek compensation, and there are not enough dollars, decisions or diplomats to restore humanity's collective soul to what it once was.

YOU WILL BE CHALLENGED TO TAKE A STAND

Saints and sinners alike will come under fire and be scrutinized in 2004. Cameras will record images, and microphones will record conversations. The piracy of privacy will come into question as fear begins to replace cold arrogance and disregard for penalty or perjury. Secrets will be revealed and documents brought to light that will place truth itself on trial; it is likely that it will be found guilty along with the rest. The burden of proof will be more demanding and exacting, but it will also be more difficult to come by.

Humanity is evolving; it is moving, changing and renewing itself; it is looking in every mirror and seeing every reflection that has ever represented it, however unflattering the angle of view. From this perspective, 2004 will be an unappealing but critical year. You will be challenged to take a stand for or against an issue, a family member, a law or a moral decision. Each time you do, however, you will also be shown a reflection of the dichotomy and contradictions in your own world. Personal citizens will not become planetary citizens until they acknowledge the similarities among themselves rather than their differences. Your evolution demands and depends upon your fairness, impartiality, stability, objectivity and evenhanded nature.

Be cautious; do not take up the cause of those who do not deserve your care. Before you choose sides or unholster a weapon, be certain that it is the only choice you can make. If you can see the falsity of the present moment, you will also see the clarity of the next one. There are saints and sinners among all beings and all species. Source sees no difference between an offending dandelion and a fragrant rose.

The Morning After

There is always a "morning after," the time somewhere near dawn when you wonder if you really did, said or heard what you think you might have done, said or heard but are still unsure. You slowly open your eyes and search your room or your mind for the empirical evidence that will confirm or deny your worst fears. Perhaps this best describes 2004, the year in which humans collectively will wake up and see themselves for what they are. But what will they see? What will you see?

Humans are the child prodigy offspring of lineages and traditions throughout and beyond time and space. They have been enhanced and enriched by the genetic contributions of other races and planetary cultures. They have also suffered at the hands, thoughts and deeds of those who profit from the unconsciousness and inexperience of their galactic relations. Still, the rewards have been many, and humans stand on the verge of discovering this for themselves.

The voice of 2004 will be an internal voice; it will speak to your inner being. It will counsel, cajole and coerce you into recognizing the true essence of selfhood. Selfhood is the acknowledgment of your own individuality and welfare. It is the recognition and the understanding of the self-nature within you. Selfhood erases the need for self-abandonment, self-abasement, self-abuse and self-annihilation. Selfhood is the doorstep to self-reference and the invitation to fulfillment. Self-realization and self-actualization are also already on the horizon, perhaps as early as 2005 and 2006, respectively. Your relationship with yourself, with others and with your environment is therefore paramount now, because if you expect to plow a field, you must first seed it.

Can all the ills that humanity has created or perpetuated be erased? No, there is no point in erasing the past. But experience can be an inexpensive lesson giver if it is taken to heart. The damage to many of the Earth's ecosystems is irreversible, and many plant and animal species are on the verge of extinction. New resources, however, are already available and will present themselves when humanity is ready to receive them. Currently, the scarcity and unfair distribution of the Earth's wealth (pure water, clean air, unpolluted ground) prevents the richness and beauty of its new form from revealing itself to you. Whether this happens before or after the present ecosystems are exceeded or exhausted is still to be seen. The number of existing alternatives and solutions is decreasing quickly, and it would be advisable to begin now to develop a strategy that finds and allows compatibility among all kingdoms and all cultures.

Off-planet beings are ready to assist you, but introductions between inter-planetary citizens would be strained when peace and reunification within your own citizenry do not yet exist, do you see? Practice harmony within your own cultures while replacing and rebuilding structures that no longer serve a pur-pose; then the natural steps toward mutual contact will reveal themselves.

Some will see only isolation and uncertainty in these words, but both self- and soul-assurance are also present for those who recognize them. Trust the sub-tle essence of your nature; a divine race is on the verge of being born. Do not surrender what has yet to draw its first breath! Be confident and vigilant in your creativity and your ability to find solutions. Remember that God still dances on the head of a pin.

A Quick Reference Guide to the Less than Obvious, Part One

January 2004

Dear readers: This and the next article reflect the many emails, calls and letters that Gaia and I receive. Time does not always permit me to respond to each one with the personal attention to detail I would prefer. The articles include current events, issues and concerns, and they address prophecies and predictions, information versus misinformation, direction and misdirection. Please contact me with your questions. Subjects of both broad and narrow interest are welcome as long as they are not specifically personal in nature. I look forward to hearing from you!

WHO IS REALLY RESPONSIBLE FOR 9/11?

Were Osama bin Laden and/or al Qaeda really responsible for the World Trade Center catastrophe?

Yes, they are the ones to blame. They take great pride in the international attention and press coverage they receive daily, especially as they have done so little to earn so much.

It is said that they stand against the West, but what does that mean? Are they against democracy? Are they against freedom?

No, not necessarily. They are against the illusion of democracy and freedom when it is used as an instrument of power and greed. They are misguided as armed missiles often are, but what government does not have a few loose cannons of its own? Are they good guys disguised as bad guys or bad guys disguised as good guys? No, they are neither Boy Scouts nor terrorists, but they do not know that anymore than you do, because they have come to embody and believe almost all that is said about them.

Long ago they believed they were on a mission to restore justice. They studied alongside your brothers and sisters, sons and daughters. They pledged, prayed and meditated, much as you do today. They thought they were on the right side of the law, and their families, whom they trusted, confirmed this. But somewhere along the way things went wrong, and before long so did they.

Onions often make eyes tear as they release their full flavor, especially when the cut is deep, swift and severe. When the entire truth behind this and other events is finally revealed, it will wound and divide the citizens of many countries. There is an ancient riddle that goes something like this: A den of lions and a den of thieves both feed on the weary and the less fortunate. What is the difference between the two? The lions sleep well at night.

EARTH, THE SCHOOL OF HARD KNOCKS

Is the Earth really a school of "hard knocks"? Are we really here just to learn lessons?

The Earth is the Ivy League university of hard knocks, thank you very much. It is not your average, run-of-the-mill, third-dimensional, local solar system, a remedial school for ill-advised souls. For the most part, those who attend here are privileged, well-advantaged souls who, under careful guidance, petitioned for re-admission into the third dimension. If we continue with the university analogy, it can best be said that planet Earth is a grad school for high achievers and underachievers alike. There are two deans, and they are both supportive and unyielding.

Their names are Cause and Effect. During your stay here, you will most likely get to know both of them intimately. They will be aware of your thoughts, dreams and desires and will do their best to help you achieve all of your goals. You have the additional benefit of two full-time counselors at your service. Their names are Karma and Dharma, and they are available to you twenty-four/seven. They even make house calls.

CAN ONE REVERSE HABITS?

Is it true that if you move, act or react in opposite to what is normal for you, it can reverse habits and even retard the aging process?

Not exactly, but the original premise upon which your question is based is not as far-fetched as you might imagine. If you normally stir your cup of coffee clockwise and later begin stirring it counterclockwise in order to diminish the effects of the caffeine entering your bloodstream, you will have little success. But if you stir your cup of coffee clockwise and then counterclockwise while consciously, purposefully and specifically directing the flow of energy in your body, a great deal of change can be achieved. There is no secret or magic formula associated with this, but it does require a shift in awareness from the unconscious self to the conscious self.

Let's say that you are right-handed and that you have unconsciously signed your name the same way for many years. Significant physical and nonphysical awareness and practice would be required for you to change from writing with your right hand to writing with your left hand, and even a small and seemingly insignificant change such as adding a middle initial to your normal writing process would demand a good deal of presence. The premise or original principle behind this thought suggests that conscious awareness brings conscious change, and it is an important one to take note of at this time, because many of you feel fairly certain that you cannot change your world, much less your own life; but consciousness changes everything . . . everything.

HEALTH PROBLEMS ARE PART OF THE AFTERMATH OF 9/11

I have heard that many firefighters, police personnel and other rescue workers who assisted in the aftermath of 9/11 have been diagnosed with respiratory problems, rectal bleeding, vomiting, shortness of breath and other physical concerns that have no immediate explanation. Can you affirm or deny these rumors?

I can affirm them, yes. Those who masterminded this event had much riding on its outcome and still do. A great deal of planning made sure that little was left to chance or error. Details were examined from a variety of angles and points of view. Experts were consulted and paid handsomely for their knowledge. Twenty years ago or so, the original plan behind this historic event was born, and about ten years ago, the plan became an entity. It received funding for research and development in much the same way as other projects do, except this one was more covert. The loss of life was significantly less than anticipated, due at least in part to those who planned and later expertly executed their mission.

Given this evidence, do not misconstrue the mission's purpose, which was to swiftly and permanently redirect the future course of events on and off planet Earth. From this perspective, the mission must surely be seen as a complete and total success. Even the most successful operations, however, have certain side effects and there is the usual mopping up to be done.

The first-response emergency personnel who arrived on the scene were clueless as to the dangers they faced, but those who arrived in later hours and subsequent days were better prepared. It was not thought that there would be any survivors and none were wanted. "A good survivor is a dead survivor," was whispered among those whose job it was to quickly clean up any and all possible leaks. The entire area was deemed unstable and unsafe for almost all concerned, and those who assisted in the rescue efforts were well chosen and hand selected. The volunteers who were turned away day after day may now consider themselves most fortunate. A shorter lifespan awaits most of those who were physically associated with this event. Even those who were remotely linked with physical debris or nonphysical elements have reason for concern.

SOME CHILDREN OF 9/11 ARE SPECIAL

Recently I became aware of a magazine cover that featured babies born shortly after the events of September 11, 2001. Each of them was the son or daughter of someone who had died as a result of the events that transpired on that day, whether in the air or on the ground. Are these children special or different in some way which we are not yet aware of?

Some of them are, but not all of them. They are special in that they knew ahead of time that their lives would not be ordinary. They understood that they would carry an awareness of their physical heritage throughout their entire lives and that they would be asked to recall and share their experiences again and again. How can that be if they had not even been born yet? What could they possibly recall?

By the time these special individuals reach adolescence or young adulthood, the technology will exist to experience or reexperience the mental, physical and emotional womb. Abortions will not be necessary, at least as they are understood today. Direct communication with one's fetus will be possible, at least for some, and many of today's difficult questions surrounding this subject will find answers that are obvious. These unique individuals chose their parents and the lives they would live in advance of the event itself, but those who assisted them beyond the veils prepared them well and even now continue to provide support and assistance in all areas.

MAP OF POSTCATACLYSMIC EARTH IS HISTORY

A long time ago the U.S. was shown a map depicting a postcataclysmic Earth. The continents looked much different than they do today, and a good part of both U.S. coastlines was missing. Is the map still accurate? Was it ever?

The map in question is older than the hills, both literally and symbolically. At first glance it would seem that the map is prophetic and indicates a potential future, but what if it were archival in nature instead? In other words, what if the map was accurate given a historical perspective rather than a future one? The original version of this map was visioned long ago, even before the sinking of Atlantis. It was the work of a visionary artist, who received seismic images and created "topographic art," for lack of a better word. The artist's art was a form of protest. It was taken symbolically by some and literally by others. It was very popular in its time and copies of it were widely reproduced.

History has an interesting way of imitating art, and although inconsistent, many aspects of the map are remarkably accurate if viewed from beneath rather than above. The underwater continental coastline is currently pushing its way against and underneath the recognized outline of the North American continent, and changes are certainly under way. It does not require a scientific mind to realize that melting polar icecaps will alter the sea levels and the corresponding landmasses, but perhaps the visionary mind of an artist speaks in a language that science cannot.

A Quick Reference Guide to the Less than Obvious, Part 2

March 2004

THE SEARCH FOR LIFE ON MARS

What's with all the recent interest in Mars? Is it really true that so much effort, time and money is being poured into discovering whether or not Mars once sustained life?

Yes, it is true. At least that's how the funding for these projects gained the approval and support of those whose signature appears on (or behind) the substantial checks that have been written. Beyond that, as you might imagine, there is more than meets the star-filled eye. Approximately ten years ago, contact with the Earth was initiated by an off-planet species. Their message was a simple one, and it was directed at those who were even then considering annihilating and/or obliterating each other before moving out into the universe to explore other potential "investments." The message, loosely translated, stated, "Look before you leap . . . Look to the past that you may also have a future to look upon."

The extraterrestrial entities showed their earthly counterparts a series of "film clips" that could easily have been taken from Earth's own past, except for the fact that it was not Earth at all. The film clips were remnants of a once vast and carefully archived library of images. The restored images were translated into a universally understood language and then stored for future use. You might wonder about the effectiveness of a universal language given the size and scope of the local universe, but language (as frequency) transcends time and space. Simply speaking, even Morse code is understood universally, and this language was even simpler than that.

The specific details of the film clips are irrelevant to your question, and it suffices to say that they depicted a world in decay. Experts in psychopathy and engineers of mind extraction labeled this meeting an off-planet intervention of sorts; forensic extraterrestrials called it a plea of hope. Those who preferred the glitter in their pockets to the sparkle in the night sky called it nonsense. Still, a nagging feeling undermined the thoughts and dreams of all who had been exposed to the new frequency, because visions of an extraterrestrial past were strangely reminiscent of a potential Earth future, and this inspired a great deal of interest as well as controversy. The film clips were not of Mars, but they looked enough like Mars to generate greater respect and interest in Earth's neighbors in the local galaxy. As you can see, the answer to your question was launched ten years ago, and science is searching for Earth's past as well as hoping to discover its future.

Take Pity on Saddam Hussein

Was it really Saddam Hussein whom the United States military located and took into custody in Tikrit, Iraq?

I will answer your question using generic terms because, as you will see, they are the most specific given the nature of your question. Most of the world believes that Saddam Hussein was captured, and they would like to believe that evil was captured in the process, but evil cannot be captured—it can only be laid to rest. There are many Saddam Husseins in the world and there always have been. They are not unique to this day and age. They are icons in the flesh: advertisements of injustice, corruption and greed. But how many other such icons present themselves to you daily? Why has humanity invested so much interest in this one?

The icon called Saddam Hussein was captured, but the man was not. Still, a puppet without a puppet master or a stage on which to perform is relatively harmless. There is a land in the underground realms of the Earth called "Exile," and that is where old puppets go when they are no longer useful.

I have answered your question and yet there is more. The capture of Saddam Hussein was just the beginning. It was a prelude intended to boost the morale of the parade of soldiers who were watching brothers in arms fall one by one, two by two and even more. After all, one must live with purpose or die with it, do you see? The parade of soldiers is the opening act for the parade of events that will soon unfold.

"Authenticity" is a relative word today, as are "identical" and "original." When the light dances, it displays a myriad of full-spectrum color. The same holds true when shadows dance. I will ask of you that which is difficult in thought and deed: Have pity on the being who was captured, for he is one of many who have awakened in a different mind and/or in a different body. He no longer has a true identity, only that which has been assigned to him. Even he is not certain if he is the real Saddam Hussein; he simply assumes it is true because the memories he has been assigned match the questions that are put to him. Waves of energy have been wrought upon and within him; do you believe that extraterrestrial beings are the only ones capable of doing implants?

Recognize that Cattle Are Evolving

Is it really possible that only one cow in the United States was infected with mad cow disease? Is beef still safe for human consumption? What about other animal products?

I will begin by answering your question with another question. Is it possible for only one person in a city to catch a cold? What an unfathomable wager that would be! This question is also your answer, do you see? A similarly frustrating question is, "Which came first, the chicken or the egg?" That is exactly what researchers are now trying to discover, but with cows instead of chickens. That will come later.

Are you capable of offering your best when you do not feel well? When you are feeling dishonored, can you still do the honorable thing? Currently, sentient cattle are pondering these same questions. Are all cattle sentient? Yes, to some degree, just as you can be more or less conscious than your neighbor. Twenty or thirty years ago, the collective consciousness within the cattle species began to sense that something was terribly wrong. They did their best to self-correct as a species, and this did work for a time. (All species self-correct; it is natural to do so and often leads to evolutionary leaps both small and large.)

When self-correction began to fail, they used their sentient abilities to warn neighboring species so that future disasters might be prevented. Humankind would be considered a neighboring species, so the cattle sentience reached out to humanity as well, but twenty or thirty years ago, no one was listening—especially not to a cow. Think of how many good-ideas-turned-bad there have been in this short of a time span. Now think of how many good ideas have been ignored or scoffed at in the same time span. Lastly, think about how many warnings have gone unnoticed. Cattle are evolving, and as such, they will cease to be available as livestock by the middle of this century. Many times the sequence and timing of these events relate to that of other species, and this is no exception. If humanity desires to evolve, humans must allow other species to do so as well.

Many cattle are infected, and many have been slaughtered, marketed and eaten. More are on the way. Mad cow disease is the effect; the causes are many. Those who study cause believe that they have isolated what went wrong, but they have not gone far enough, and those who are paid handsomely to do damage control tie their hands. Information will continue to leak to outside sources as it often does, and more will be revealed. In the meantime, you must ask yourself, "Do I feel comfortable consuming a species that is emerging from its evolutionary cocoon?" If the answer is yes, then you will do so, and if it is no, then you will not. It is best to ask this question rather than to wonder if what you are consuming is tainted.

Be patient with yourself and with all species, for all are currently undergoing change. Trust your body to tell you what is and what is not appropriate for you, and do not judge those who have not asked the appropriate questions yet. Make a healthy variety of dietary choices, and take the time to read the ingredients when they are offered. Change your dining choices and habits once a week or once a month in order to ensure a diversity of experiences for your physical body.

Release Your Future from the Constraints of the Past

April 2004

As sentience Gaia, I bid you hello. As Earth and as the celestial body Terra, I also bid you welcome. These names do not truly describe what I am, but your individual names do not encompass or surround you either; they are representations and stylizations at best. I am as physical as you are, but you are not physical. As I look upon you, I see vehicles of condensed light, and as such, I suggest to you that I am the same. Dense light can be called physical light, or lightbody. Lightbodies express themselves in various densities, and some of these we call physical bodies. The only real difference between you and the chair you are seated upon is your soul. The chair is made from dense atoms of light, but it is not a vehicle of light; the chair does not have a soul. Your soul directs your vehicle of light, and the dense atoms that form your body offer you a vehicle in which to express and transport your light to and within the many dimensional experiences called lives.

As stylized light, you are travelers, and the experience of a human physical body does not diminish this. The Earth's dense physical body, the planet, does not diminish the fact that it is also a vehicle. The Earth travels the solar system with the support of the Sun's magnetic pull, and as such is able to commune and share sentience with other celestial beings and dimensional regions of the soul. This expression of selfhood is both purposeful and animated. Earth is life and it sustains life.

THE PAST, THE FUTURE AND THE NOW

The Earth has a past, a present, a Now and a future, and so do you. One of your current understandings suggests that the past, the present and the future are all moments of Now. To a certain extent this is true, because from a variety of perspectives, there is no perceivable separation. On the other hand, it is observably clear that you and your neighbor are separate entities. This dimensional experience is called a qualifier, or a qualifying experience. The experience of time in a linear or horizontal format is also a qualifying experience. But time can also be linear as well as vertical when moments and experiences are stacked one upon the next or one upon the previous one.

Using this model, where is the present moment? Where is the past? Is the past lower or higher than the present in a vertical model? Is the present moment in the middle, between the past and the future? Or is it on top because it is the most recent? You see, already we find ourselves in a dilemma, because the moment you introduce a new perspective into an old paradigm, you create a dilemma with regard to experiential reality.

To this deceptively simple formula, let us now add that all dimensions are also expressions of the Now, making theories of past, present and future somewhat obsolete. Of course, we must also consider that moments are neither equal nor equally spaced. Given this understanding, how would you graph your existence or locate yourself in this current moment? Before you dismiss this subject as less than influential, consider that this is the very means by which you create not only your identity, but also your experience and your purposeful journey.

Is all experience really the same? Are moments unique, or are they simply variable expressions of the same moment? The past, the present and the future are unique and individual points of united awareness that allow conscious differential expressions called creative free will to manifest themselves as both linear and sequential time.

How do you know if you are living in your present or in your past? How do you know that you are capable of creating a future? If you can imagine or recall a time in this life (or in any life) where you are (or were) experiencing less than joy, then you are re-creating your past in your present. Why? Because the present is an expanse of pure potential and the future is the well of probable potential, but the past is the plowed field of experienced potential. If you are re-creating your past in the present, then you are not giving yourself or the present moment full creative credit. If you are not imagining this moment as creative and profound, then you are subject to living in the past or re-creating more of the past, which is why it can be said with certainty that all moments are not equal.

YOUR BODY IS A VEHICLE OF LIGHT

But you might well argue, "That was a grand time; why would I not wish to re-create it?" Or you might say, "It is only a similar moment, not the same at all." But I remind you that you are vehicles of light traveling at the speed of light and beyond in order to encourage the grander and greater experiences called lifetimes. If you are fascinated by the past, then you are missing out on the fullness of the present and the creative potential of the future. Delightful as it may seem, it will become increasingly difficult to peel away the layers of density called past experience. The future will continue to call you, but after a time it could begin to sound like a distorted echo from a deep well. If you are unable to perceive your future, even your present will slow to a disturbing reality of repetition. Does this sound a bit familiar?

You might well say, "My present is barely sustainable as I arise each morning and fall to bed at night, and I see nothing to look forward to in my future." If this were true, dear ones, then I would say that you are no longer traveling at or accelerating to the speed of light. You currently exist and travel in vehicles of light. As such, you must tend to them so that density does not bear down upon them too heavily. When time, speed and light all slow, molecules accumulate faster. As they begin to coalesce, less space exists between the accumulated molecules and the freewill atoms that make up your being.

Space creates time and the ability to experience time as either unique or indifferent. The physical body is hardy but also delicate. It requires care in the Now/present so that it will assist you in creating a future where you can move at the speed of light—although that is a relative term—and beyond. Atoms that are no longer allowed to express a freewill state will eventually express a free-radical state; therefore, your physical health and your spiritual health are one and the same, do you see?

MOVEMENT AT THE SPEED OF LIGHT

Movement at the speed of light can take place only when you acknowledge that you reside in and abide by a vehicle of light. The speed of light comes to you via the Sun. Light exists all around you. It is absorbed by your skin as well as ingested when you eat or drink. Light creates a corridor of current within and around your body, which is further maximized by the Earth's ley lines. This unique electromagnetic combination is capable of raising the quality of your individual frequency. Acting like a pheromone, it draws other-quality frequencies to itself. When combined with other vibrational elements, including free will and desire, it assists you in manifesting creatively rather than mundanely.

Above all else, the speed of light is a unique force that assists you in creating your future, because if you are truly moving at the speed of light, you will not want to be living in the past. The linear past is always more dense than the linear present or the linear future, but the same is not necessarily true of the vertical or multidimensional past, which is unique to the experience. If you are increasing your ability to hold and transmit light, you are guaranteed to be in the present and moving toward a creative future.

The future beckons and invites you. It is there for your creative benefit. It is an acknowledgment of your ability to be creative in and throughout many dimensions. The biblical reference to "many mansions" alludes to this concept as well. The reverse is also true, because when you acknowledge yourself as less valuable than the present moment, opportunities recede into the background where their light is less visible to you. Under these circumstances, you have fewer choices and creative sources of expression. Eventually, you realize the pitfall you have walked into, but you must now create the means to walk out of the shadow and into the light again.

DENSITY AND LIGHT

As dense light, you are more human, more dependent upon external things, resources and people for support. Dense humanity offers the Earth a less than ideal partnership. Anything that understands itself as less than equal manifests itself as dependent upon the whole. The public welfare system is a perfect example of this spiritual law. Traveling at less than the speed of light, humans create a codependency with the animal, mineral and plant kingdoms, as well as with the balance of the human kingdom. This is the only reason the Earth's resources are currently in short supply, unable to replenish and restore themselves adequately.

Density is a very interesting subject, upon which many volumes could be written. Many who are in body at this time prefer to acknowledge density rather than light, because it is a physical affirmation that they are working on past concerns rather than in the present or in the future. Globally, humanity is increasing in density. Human structures are more dense now than ever, and obesity plagues the human population. In contrast, the animal kingdom is less dense now, and it is becoming increasingly difficult to fatten a cow prior to its slaughter, which is one of the reasons that unconventional means of doing so are being explored and implemented. These methods are now having severe consequences, as reported by your media almost daily.

Whereas some humans overconsume resources, others underconsume them and are slowly starving to death. This is also an acknowledgment of a population that is out of step with its resources, but here is an interesting fact: A starving body is likely to be denser than an obese body. Why? Because an overweight vehicle is an acknowledgment of a desire to remain in dense physical light, whereas a starving vehicle makes no physical or spiritual claim whatsoever. It has renounced its interest in the body as a vehicle of light.

Are you destined to replay your past? It depends. It depends if you identify with your light or with your density. In other words, do you recognize yourself as one with the Source of all things, expressed as condensed light moving through third-dimensional awareness and beyond? Or are you just a human? If your current destiny—and there are many—is to reexperience a past life so that you can organize it within you from a different perspective, then that is what you will do. This should not be considered an inferior choice, and sometimes it is the highest and best choice that can be made, because the decisions of the past life must be experienced concurrently with the choices made in the present life. That is how old perspectives become new realities. And to be fair, the ability to experience the past and the present is as much a gift as one can hope to receive from the present and the future.

THE NAUTILUS BECOMES SELF-AWARE

There is a very interesting little animal who has been around for many millennia. Today you call this little animal a nautilus. Its basic shape is a spiral, and it is aligned with a very specific frequency. Its beauty is in the perfection of its mathematical structure and in the fact that it begins its life in its center and moves outward from there. When the nautilus tires of being its own center, it begins to grow. Its desire to grow causes it to increase its size. Upon increasing its size, it begins to explore itself again but from a new perspective. The new perspective allows it to see its own reflection. Light reflecting upon, within and as a reflection of itself brings awareness, and now the tiny nautilus has become self-aware.

Self-awareness brings additional desires, such as the desire to be in selected movement; to increase in size, design and shape; to seek and discover knowledge; and to continue to grow or evolve. Eventually, the nautilus discovers that its desires have made it vulnerable within its environment. Instinct calls upon ancient survival techniques, and a protective environment that will serve as both home and vehicle is created. Divine will now moves through the tiny nautilus who has already invested itself wholly and completely in its life, and the nautilus begins to grow by creating a new chamber and closing off the previous one.

A JOURNEY OF EXPANSION

Now, why does the nautilus close off its previous chamber rather than leaving it open? Would a larger home not be worthwhile? You see, even the tiny nautilus knows that nature will always offer it an opportunity to fall back, and if it does so, it will be more difficult for it to rebuild its desire anew and gain the support of the divine will. The tendency to fall back is ever present because that is where one's comfort place is. Most often, the tendency is to find an easy way in, out or through. The nautilus, however, is a very wise being and as such, it builds its vehicle in recognition of its tendency but also in response to its divine will. Understanding life as well as it does, it seals itself off from the past and invites the future. Curiously, it leaves a tiny, tiny, tiny hole in its architecture so that it can peer into its past. It can see where it has been and, remembering, it can choose where it will go.

The nautilus continues its journey of expansion, syncing its life in geometric perfection with the symphony of the spiral galaxy in which it exists. If you have been fortunate enough to see a whole or partial (lateral) view of a nautilus shell, you will have noted its beauty, but its beauty is not representative of its struggle. Its beauty does not reflect the courage it took to willingly close itself off from all that has been familiar—not one time, but many times. Might you look upon the tiny and ancient nautilus differently the next time you come upon one?

The nautilus is a simple consciousness, but it is wise. It rests when it needs rest, but it moves forward because it is being impulsed to do so by an instinct based upon desire. The nautilus does not become stuck in one of its chambers because it is overly comfortable and unwilling to advance. It forces itself out of its comfort zone and creates its future in the process, one thought and one chamber at a time. When there are no new experiences to be had in its present form, it is impulsed to grow. The new chamber is built when the current one begins to feel restrictive. The nautilus has lived many lives as an exemplary species. Can it be that it has made and continues to make decisions of evolutional value?

Move beyond Your Comfort Zone

In order for humans to continue to perpetuate their own species, they must move beyond their evolutional comfort zone. They must allow the latest chapter in the story of their evolution to conclude so that they can begin the next. And they can only begin the next chapter if they (you) create it (the future) as new.

If a new chapter does not offer itself as original, it is because the door to past experience has not been allowed to close completely. As long as there is an attraction or addiction to the past, the door will not close behind you smoothly. As long as there is an investment in or a longing for the continuation of the past or the present, both will remain in the foreground. Even favorite, often-read stories must eventually be put down in anticipation of new ones.

Choose a Creative Reality

Most humans are currently living in the past. More than two-thirds of you depend upon past experience, past mistakes and past lives for guidance, but these cannot exist in your future unless you invite them to join you there. Do you know where you are? Are you in your body? Are you in your vehicle of light? Are you in the past, the present or the future?

Even if you know that you are aware of your innermost consciousness and are in direct relationship with the choices you are making, can you be certain that you will not manifest a more creative version of your past? Can you create a future that is not your past? Why is it that the present moment did not begin exactly when the past moment ended? How is it possible that so many different beings are living so many different realities? If there are so many different realities, are there also various and many versions of the past, present and future? How is it that they did not arrive at the same mark? There are many unique answers to these questions, but they are not specific because there is no specific evidence that time is sequential or linear.

How can you be in the Now, in the present, and also create your future? By choosing to be who and what you are today and inviting that purpose to unfold before you rather than behind you. Choose your light instead of someone else's. Choose your purpose instead of the one that seems prechosen for you. Choose your own form of spirituality instead of the one that is most en vogue. Choose the most creative reality that presents itself to you, because chances are that it is the as-yet-to-be-explored one. Accelerate your vehicle of light rather than your petroleum-based vehicle; fossil fuels belong in the past, you know. If you are not moving in sync with the speed of light, see what is keeping you from doing so. If you want to manifest a future instead of another version of the past, then begin now.

CREATIVITY LIVES IN THE FUTURE

Once the nautilus has created its new chamber, or future, it does not say, "Woe unto me, for I will never again visit my past or know the path I have taken." Do you know why? Because it always leaves a tiny, pinpoint-sized hole in its previous chamber, just in case it is tempted to look back. The nautilus does not really want to go back to its previous chamber, and in fact, it is not even possible for it to do so, given that it has outgrown its past. But growth does not erase the need for comfort, and creature comfort is exactly what the nautilus seeks.

Humans also seek comfort in the form of comfort zones, but these, like dusty attics, also belong to the past. Most humans do not think they want to reexperience the past, but they do so anyway. You don't need to replay a tune over and over again in order to recognize it or memorize it. You need only place it in your future instead of in your past. Memories need a past, but creativity thrives on future potential.

Why does a nautilus create chamber after chamber after chamber and call that growth and evolution? It does so to experience each moment as more grand than the previous one. But in order for it to do so, it must look upon the next moment or chamber with at least a certain amount of awe; otherwise, there is no purpose at all and evolution will cease. The inability to do this has been one of humanity's greatest pitfalls, an unfortunate and false understanding that has been reduced to a mere "bigger and better equals more; times growth, it equals evolution."

Humans compare themselves, judge themselves and condemn themselves as small rather than capable. Each time they do so, the past comes into focus again and the future seems more distant and blurry. The high contrast between the past and the future leaves little room for creative visualization, making a bright future a little less likely and a dull one a little more predictable. Without the dawn of a creative thread, humans have little to look forward to but their own density. Humans become aged rather than ageless, and their physical vehicles can no longer sustain the light speed that true evolution calls for. Finding itself in shadow, the nautilus simply seeks the light that is both within and without.

CHOOSE AS THE NAUTILUS CHOOSES

I invite you again to choose as the nautilus chooses. Choose "the light of the moment, plus experience, times acceleration by the speed of light, equals quantum growth and evolution." This will keep you from falling backward in time as many who are near and dear to you are doing. Surely you have noted it by now. Do they not seem to live in the past and to move one day backward just as you are moving one day forward? How is that possible when the calendar advances daily and the years renew themselves by increasing in number? Is it possibly because your beloved friends have become caught in their calendars, ensnared in their own traps and are altogether unconscious?

Can you spot them? They speak a language that slows rather than hastens. They wonder, "Why is everyone in such a hurry? What is the rush? What is the big matter about density, anyway?" If you fall backward into the past, you will no longer see the past, because you will have become a participant rather than an observer of the process. Participatory realities are denser than observational realities, because they are more entrenched in the third dimension.

ON TO A FULFILLING FUTURE!

The future looms before you, just beyond the mists of illusion. In order to find it, you must acknowledge yourself as its creator. You will not happen upon your future, and your future will not happen to you. This belief will only perpetuate your living in the past or in a facsimile of the past in the present. Interestingly, you can drag past into present, but you must re-create it in the future. This is because the future is so much less dense than the past. You would need to disassemble its atomic and molecular content in the past/present and then consciously reassemble it in the future. Another interesting anomaly is that you can be quite unconscious in the past and the present, but you cannot unconsciously create a future. Why? Because when you create unconsciously, you only create more of the same, which is the same as the past/present, the loop versus the spiral, do you see?

This discussion is designed to unseat your beliefs about the past and your expectations about the future. The only thing separating you from a fulfilling future is the veil of illusion. Dissolve the illusion and a new dawn appears, one that has been there all along but has gone undetected. The past exists because you carry it; the present/Now exists because you think that this is where you are supposed to be, where you belong. And the future simply is—for those who choose it. Physical evolution will allow you to grow as a species, but spiritual evolution will make the stars your brothers and sisters.

All choices are available to all beings, regardless of appearance or past participation. It is best not to form an opinion at this time as to who is more or less evolved or awakened or spiritual or intelligent. Make choices for yourself, but leave room for other people's choices. In other words, be an open link on the chain rather than a closed one. Place yourself in a multidimensional Now, even if you cannot describe it or understand it in linear words. The language of light will guide the process if you let it. All moments are Now moments, but some are more creative and original than others. Look to these for guideposts of encouragement. Now on to your questions, be they past, present or future!

YOU ARE DRAGGING THE EARTH'S POPULATION

Is the drag we are feeling in our bodies and all around us a result of the pull to fall backward into the past, or is it the beginning of the break needed to move forward?

The pull and drag that you feel are both individual and collective. In a sense, you are dragging humanity along with you. Remember that you are multidimensional beings expressing your light in individual bodies. As these realities continue to expand, you will eventually overlap and finally encompass all other beings who share a common thread within your world.

Currently, just as you say, you are dragging about two-thirds of the Earth's population behind you. Must you do so? No, not really. You don't have to drag them or carry them, but you cannot ignore them either. Can you ignore a noisy neighbor, and if so, for how long? It is easier to create a space for them to discover what you have discovered already. You are not responsible for those who are less aware than you, but as stewards of an evolving Earth, you are responsible for clearing a path that others will follow. It is up to you to make sure that the path is fertile rather than barren.

That being the case, should I make a controlled effort to do something or to offer something unique?

Oh no, dear. The more effort you put into attempting to control things, the easier it becomes for you to fall backward, because effort and control both create density within atomic and molecular structures; they are the opposite of an architecture of light. Density is a bit like quicksand: The more you struggle, the more stuck you become. Diets are another form of quicksand, because you cannot truly lose density (weight) without choosing what you will do with it instead. And so, without effort make a choice. Without condition and without control choose . . . wisely, creatively and consciously.

THE CONCEPT OF SURRENDER

So is it more like a surrender?

No. Surrender seems like a good idea most of the time, and it is quite popular within New Age communities who are more than willing to find a higher power or authority to surrender to. In fact, I can't remember when I've seen more white flags waving in the spiritual wind. The problem with surrender is that it often takes creativity along with it. Over and over again I hear it said, "I give up! I give up on so and so, what and what, who and who!" There is no profit, gain or creative expression in surrender. Instead, choose your self, selfish, selfless, self-full and soulful selfhood. In case you haven't heard, this is the antidote to self-sabotage.

Are you saying that if we choose the known, which is choosing the past, then that's what we'll get more of, whereas if we have the courage to choose the unknown, then that's our future?

Yes, but I must also add that a vote for the unknown is not a vote for uncertainty, and many of you pause here longer than necessary for this very reason. For instance, look at how many people create solid belief patterns around prophecy. Prophecies are predictions about an as yet unexperienced past, because the creative future is still unknown. Again, the known future is the unexperienced past.

THE UNIVERSE ENCOURAGES YOU

Does the universe (or our guidance) sometimes close the doors to the past for our benefit, forcing us to move into a creative future?

The universe will encourage you to move forward, just as it does with the young nautilus. The universe will encourage you to open the door to your future by assisting you to grow in your present. Just like the nautilus, growth eventually leads to a tight and restricted environment, which makes it more natural for it—and for you—to expand into a more creative future. Do you feel tight and restricted now? Are you uncomfortable? If so, then we can assume that you are both growing and receiving assistance.

It is important to note that the universe will not box you into a corner or coax you out of it; you do that when you close your eyes and ears and pretend you are not who you are. But the universe (Source) can and will help you to move away from the corner when you are ready to do so. If you are truly interested in prophecies and predictions, then seek those that point toward probabilities, even if they seem less certain than others, because those that purport to be rock solid are, at least in terms of density. Create your future instead of finding agreement on a common past. Look at the common phrase, "Why does history seem to repeat itself?" Because again and again, humans make the same errors and fight the same battles.

YOU NEED SCAFFOLDING

Must we be willing to be uncomfortable in order to grow?

Yes, you must be willing to be uncomfortable, but that does not mean that you must struggle or suffer in every moment. Humanity has forced itself into this dilemma by using fear as a tool. The same tool it used to box itself in must now be used to pry itself free. Have clarity and courage for today and guidance and wisdom for tomorrow.

Does eradicating negative thought lead us toward having nonrigid agendas? I used to have agendas and schedules, but now I don't even think about them, and it seems like my life is more positive.

It is a push in the right direction, and for you it is the right one. Each being must find a relative and accurate support system or scaffolding, an architecture of light. For some, this architecture focuses upon the body; for those people, flushing their bodies with eighty to one hundred ounces of water every day could be a part of their support system. Those whose concentration is with the body promote health and well-being by bringing water into the body, removing animal products from their diets and avoiding artificial ingredients or supplements as best they can.

Although focusing attention and awareness on the body is one way to promote higher vibration and lower density, service to others or world service is another decision that supports awareness. Service subtly but powerfully relieves the dense self from its many burdens. All of these higher forms of architecture create space between dense molecules, and this space can be called future potential. Support systems alleviate transformational discomfort. Each being will eventually become an enhanced human and then a divine human, in a distillation of light akin to alchemy. Lead becomes gold, just as density becomes light.

THE CONCEPT OF CATACLYSM

I have heard that there could be cataclysmic events leading up to the beginning of the new age of consciousness in 2012, and that we have an option to go into a holding pattern somewhere within or around our bodies while these events take place. It was explained to me that this option would only be available to those of us who are more in flow or in tune with the planet. Could you comment on this?

Yes, certainly. It is utter and complete rubbish, but believe it if you like. The words are inviting; they are well written in order to appeal to you. There are many authors of words such as these, and these words seem very inviting; many have even been offered in my name, although I cannot remember offering or endorsing them. My sentience has been with this celestial body for many millennia and for eons of time before then. If the Earth—my body—shifts upon its axis even a smidgen, the result will be a cataclysm of major proportion that will reshape the face of the planet. Given this, where might you find an appropriate "holding pattern"?

A cataclysm involves the release of well-planned, optional energies that enhance the planet's ability to sustain itself and all other life forms by re-creating its structural integrity. That being one way to usher in a new age, might there be another, less drastic way as well? The Earth's axis is much more than a point on which your stability as a species pivots. It is a generator, a receiver and a transmitter of specific and influential energies. The Earth's axis can transmit energetic messages related to the evolution and transformation of the planet without destroying itself in the process.

Change sometimes means reversal—as in reversal of polarity—but even this need not be destructive. When you change your mind about something or someone, even if it is a complete reversal, you don't have to destroy your relationship with that person or thing in order to honor the change—although this theme is still common and constant in humanity. As long as positive and negative polarities are evenly expressed, balance prevails, which is one of the reasons that raising human consciousness is paramount at this time. Higher consciousness does not battle itself or others; it does not struggle to be right or to make others wrong.

The Earth's axis receives and generates a scalar wave pattern. Scalar energy has magnitude but no direction. If the Earth's magnetic poles are in balance, then there will be no additional draw of energy, do you see? When all is in balance, it is the Earth's crystalline core that benefits most from these energetic waves, which are then redirected and broadcast evenly in all directions.

Creative Evolution and the Art of Channeling

June 2004

In Australia thousands and thousands of locusts have devastated crops of oats and alfalfa. They hatched last month due to heavy rains and are now migrating across the country. The farmers were just beginning to recover from two years of drought that challenged their livelihood. What is the purpose of these massive amounts of insects? And given that pesticide spraying seems to be the only way to combat their destructive force and limit their scourge across large land masses, what alternatives do farmers have to improve crop yields and keep bugs from clearing out our food sources? Since pesticides also have a severe effect on groundwater and ecosystems, what is a possible solution to this problem?

In my own community, there are too many pigeons. They seem to have no predators, such as hawks, to keep their population in check. Hundreds of them are nesting in homes and dumping their excessive waste everywhere. Overall, I wonder why some of these life forms even exist on Earth since they are not balanced, peaceful or gentle. Most of them cause too many problems, pose a threat to other species, are aggressive or destructive in nature and have limited awareness or developmental consciousness. Love does not seem to be a part of their energetic makeup, and I doubt they will ever be capable of expressing it.

Higher beings of light would say that we are all related and that all life forms emanate from Source. If this is true, then I must confess that I have a hard time relating to lower life forms since they seem hollow in awareness and lack any discernible expression of love. Can you offer any insight that might relieve my challenges or increase my understanding?

Your challenge is a delightful one, and I would not deprive you of it. I will, however, offer you a respite from it and an unguent to relieve its sting, albeit temporarily. All things (and beings) being relative, would you consider humanity (Homo sapiens), as a species, a higher or lower form of life? Bear in mind that your answer could be substantially different than one offered by another person or even another species. Have you ever been to the top of a very tall building, a skyscraper perhaps? If you have, you might recall yourself thinking or saying one of the more popular expressions echoed by many when first looking down, "Oh, look at all the tiny people! They look just like little ants moving about." Well, that is one potential view of humanity, and of course there are many, many more. The farther removed you are (or think you are) from a person, a situation or a species, the more inconsequential that person, situation or species seems.

The most evolved among you see the entire universe as a delightfully intricate tapestry of light, a resplendent art form with an expansive palette of color and texture. The less evolved often see a cosmic waste site, a dump replete with toxic and ill-conceived beings hardly worth taking note of or bothering with. Somewhere between these seeming opposites exists a great expanse of thought, dimension, density and creativity, and your own ideas rest among them. It is important to remember that just as your ground-level perspective is significantly different from your skyscraper vantage point, so is your human perspective different from your soul perspective, your solar perspective and many, many others that together reflect an experience of wholeness. Any time you find less room or reason for the existence of one being over another, you are not reflecting your wholeness.

Even now, as you contemplate the worthiness of a locust or a pigeon or express concern relative to their overpopulation, there are others who, like you, have similar thoughts regarding another race or a different religion. Would it surprise you to know that the future of humanity as a species is held with contempt by other species when they envision a more purposeful and balanced use of the Earth and its (my) resources? Again, the farther removed one is from any given perspective, the more inconsequential it seems.

BALANCE IS THAT WHICH IS MOST NATURAL

Neither the Earth nor the continents that rest upon or within it are currently in balance with respect to the kingdoms who reside therein. The third dimension is turning upon itself now in an attempt to restore balance, but balance is not something that is achieved in the present by studying past error. Balance is that which is most natural, even when that which is most unnatural seems to prevail. Locust populations rise and fall in accord with prevailing weather conditions. Locusts have brains, but they do not think. Instead, their brains serve to reinforce their natural instinct. They act from instinct, and until recently, they did not need to react. They act as they have acted over millennia, with one exception: Millennia ago humanity was not attempting to eradicate their species.

Long ago droughts came and went and locust populations responded accordingly. Today ground water is controlled, diverted and owned by those who allow unthinkable pollutants to seep into ancient and diminishing water tables. Weather no longer simply "happens;" it is the result of skewed seasons and airborne pollutants that filter into the atmosphere and reduce the quality and life expectancy of all life. Unconscionable acts instigated by an unconscious humanity have made predators of peace-loving species and enemies of others. Your question refers to species of limited awareness and/or developmental consciousness whose ability to become loving expressions seems doubtful. Are you certain your compass is pointed in the right direction?

Pigeon populations have soared in most industrialized nations. Tall buildings and dense cities harbor them and provide many places for nesting and multiplying their numbers. Have you ever wondered what pigeons eat? For the most part, they eat what others would consider waste. They are scavengers and can survive on almost anything. In big cities and small communities alike, they thrive on the tons of garbage and waste that is absentmindedly created and then tossed out. The evening trash makes a lovely breakfast for this predator-free species. Their most likely predators, the hawks, do not set wing or talon within city limits if at all possible. When necessity beckons them to do so, they find that a tasty rat, squirrel or mouse makes for a better meal. Do you know why? Because rats, squirrels and mice eat more organic material than pigeons do, making them healthier to eat.

Pigeons continue to proliferate, and why shouldn't they? They are not the ones making the waste. They are consuming it as fast as they can and in turn create organic waste of their own, which, by the way, decomposes much more quickly than your average paper or plastic carton. You are quite right: They are no longer balanced, peaceful or gentle. They are now fighting for their survival in a small, unfriendly territory where there is too much competition. They are aggressive mothers and fathers trying to feed hungry children in an uncertain time in a place where their instincts are no longer natural. The human population who both shuns and feeds them also influences them. Even the pigeons' brain chemistry has been altered by the significant amount of artificial content in the food they scavenge daily.

INHERENT IN EVERY PROBLEM IS ITS SOLUTION

Where is the glimmer of hope in this dismal but honest evaluation? Inherent in every relative problem is its potential solution. This is always the case, without exception, which is why the third dimension is now turning upon itself in order to find it. Those who turn upon others will not find a solution even if it stares them back in the face. The solution does not lie in the discovery of a new petrol-chemical poison or another invented pharmaceutical drug. The solution will not be found in blame or in the destruction and decimation of yet another species, culture, religion or race. The solution is inherent in the very problem it created. Yes, it's true. The solution, creative evolution, invented the problem in order to realize and later experience itself as the solution.

Creator expressing Itself as infinite wisdom envisioned that all forms of life would evolve from one experience to the next and from one dimension, or level of expression, to the next. This is called creative evolution as contrasted to survival of the fittest, an outmoded belief whose very structure will collapse in this century. Creative evolution is not a theory, but a practice. It is not a universal law, but it is that which forms the basis of universal law. Its foundation underscores that all of life is sacred because it is consistent and all-inclusive within its makeup. Only in its expression does it seem unique or different. Life (species) evolves more quickly when it responds with kindness rather than rancor and love instead of hate. Humanity is currently in the throes of this very lesson and will not evolve or ascend (regardless of what popular thought indicates) until this truth permeates third-dimensional Earth. A tapestry of universal threads that has been divinely inspired and maintained weaves together all beings and all species. Only by acknowledging the underlying consciousness and creative expression within each strand of infinity can true unity exist.

Creative evolution is that which asserts the divinity within all things and all beings; it is that which makes matter, matter. A unity ring of life awaits physical expression now, but it must first be acknowledged and then created. The answer humanity seeks is that which creates without first destroying, loves without first hating. The answer is contained within each human being, because all of humanity is currently receiving an impulse to respond to this very question. The simple-minded and the scholarly, the powerful and the poor, all receive exclusive and equal amounts of light. Humanity suffers its answer now, while its midwife master teachers await the eventual and heralded birth. As with all births, a natural delivery is desired by all concerned.

ON ACCURATE CHANNELING

Seth, the famous energy essence channeled through Jane Roberts, made an explicit statement in Seth Speaks that Jeshua was not physically crucified. Seth went on to explain that Judas arranged for another person to replace Jeshua to die on the cross. I have read other channeled information, including that of lightbeings such as Michael and Jeshua himself that relate directly to the experience on the cross as being absolutely real, up to and including the resurrection. Can you briefly explain what happened and why Seth would make such a statement? I like the Seth material, but after reading that portion, it makes me think the material could be inaccurate.

The Seth material is substantially accurate, perhaps more so than much of the other material that has been presented for your consideration. It is important to remember that channeling is an art, not a science. It is objective in intent but subjective in form. The subtle environments present in the mind, the heart and the soul influence the process called channeling. Even the most adept and devoted channels are subject to both inner and outer influences. One can never become an "expert" channel, and those who tell you otherwise are offering you subjective information based upon the influences of the ego portion of their minds. Do you see? The best channels are those who have a deep and abiding trust in Spirit and are aligned with the path they have chosen. A relationship with self as well as with Spirit adds a grounded and well-rounded perspective to life.

Jane Roberts was such a channel. She is numbered among the few who consistently and accurately represented (rather than interpreted) the information that was offered. Previous lifetimes had served her well in this regard, and she was more than prepared to fulfill her purpose. Her partner, who was also her scribe, was even more experienced than she, having served as a scribe and translator throughout various lifetimes and soul expressions. That being acknowledged, we must also allow that, in fact, there are a variety of historical truths relative to the accuracy of the Jeshua lifetime and the events surrounding it, which are still alive today.

It has been said many times—and will be reiterated here—that time is not linear and timelines are relative. Time is a relative measure that expands and contracts in order to serve the purpose for which it was created. For instance, the Gregorian calendar currently in effect serves a purpose. It manages and controls time and those who relate to it. By agreement, those who believe in its accuracy also believe that they are living in the year 2004. If the calendar were changed, as has been suggested, to include thirteen equal months aligned with the Earth's moon, time as it is currently understood would be interpreted and experienced differently. It would affect your sleeping and dreaming patterns, and even the reality that you create would be quite different.

TIME BENDS TO ACCOMMODATE EXPERIENCE

The environment surrounding the Jeshua life was an important one, not simply because of its future influence, but because time was pliable then. The dimensions were not as clear-cut then as they seem today, and the Earth was fertile and receptive. Time was measured, but not as it is today, and the seasons were perhaps the best guides of all.

At this point, we must make an assumption that you can either accept or reject, for if we do not, these words will occupy volumes rather than pages. The assumption I offer to you includes the theory that time bends in order to accommodate experience, not the other way around. Assuming this is true, time would arc or bend, which would allow it to experience itself creating a past or a future, as it were. It might be helpful to imagine a streaming comet with a long trail of cosmic dust following it. Imagine that this comet (an expression of consciousness) has a very narrow elliptical orbit: Would the head not be able to see its tail just across from itself?

Time, also an expression of consciousness, reveals several different layers of experience called lines of consciousness or, more simply, timelines. Why?

Because those who guide and influence the conscious evolution of the Earth knew that the experience that was about to unfold would create both limitation and freedom from limitation, divine will and ordained will.

Timelines are not always parallel expressions of consciousness; sometimes they intersect with other timelines to create junctures and crossroads of experience. Many such crossroads exist, and it is likely that you have found yourselves at various such moments without stopping to consider that timelines might have conspired to make these moments possible. When timelines intersect, realities merge and multiply. In geometry, for instance, the intersection of lines creates a point that is now shared or claimed as common by all. The same is true with regard to timelines. Their intersection creates relative time schemes and possibilities that all may draw upon. In this way, and with the agreed-upon assumptive premise discussed earlier, many realities were born.

How Can We Determine the Historical Accuracy of Events?

Given this premise, how can we determine the historical accuracy of events that unfolded millennia ago? The answer is relative and depends upon which timeline you follow. How many timelines were created? Their number is exponential and would be as difficult to calculate as the number of stars in the night sky. Each timeline offers many realities from which to choose, and each reality offers many dimensions and densities of experience. Would it be simpler if time was linear? Perhaps, but the future of humanity includes an opportunity to experience and become divinity itself. In order to do so, humans must disengage from the linear realities and timelines that have been imposed upon them and embrace their multicultural, multiethnic, multiracial and multireality past.

Jane Roberts followed a timeline and related accurately all that was revealed to her. It would not be appropriate to fault her for not following all the other timelines. Were other timelines and realities made available to her? Yes, but only those that were aligned with her unconscious willingness to experience and experiment with the process itself. In her subconscious mind, they appeared as doors, and as she approached them, some opened and some did not. The entity Seth had agreement with the channel Jane, but this agreement did not include the right to pry or force open a locked door.

As to the accuracy of the information channeled regarding the being Jeshua, I must ask you: What would invite you to believe that the information channeled by a version of the being Jeshua or by the entity Michael is more accurate than that of the being Seth? Is it possible that you prefer one answer or reality instead of another and that you have sufficient corroborating evidence to make an educated, albeit prejudiced, decision? Is it also possible that your preference could have been influenced by the commonly agreed-upon historic perspective most prevalent today?

JESHUA: A MAN, AN ICON, A MYTH, A SYMBOL

Jeshua was a man, an icon, a myth and a symbol. All of this is accurate, depending upon how one relates to experience versus reality. Even those who were present during that timeline find more controversy than peace in the subject, because there was more than one Jeshua and there was more than one Jesus, but there was only one Christ. Many good men were crucified and murdered then, just as the wrongly accused stand sentenced to death today. All are or were sons of God. When Jeshua was crucified, an icon was born and a myth was started. Both still exist. By the time Christ returned, the icon had already traveled far into the future and the myth had already spread throughout a variety of dimensions and timelines.

Humanity will not discover the absolute truth until it experiences the oneness that is christhood, because you are one with the body of Christ, Jeshua and Judas with and within All That Is. There was more than one Jeshua, more than one crucifixion, more than one resurrection. Source as infinite wisdom could not offer humanity only one flower, one cloud or one teacher. You live on a garden planet where you are awakened daily by rainbow-hued sunrises. Spectacular sunsets display their beauty at your feet as darkness falls, and a great and loving council of teachers demonstrates unwavering kindness and compassion before you have even detected their presence.

There were and are many interpretations of the accounts surrounding both the man Jeshua and his resurrected Christ-self, and because so many of them are vested in established religions that take great pride in proclaiming themselves the only, the truest, the original or the first and the last authority, it is difficult to find agreement. Even within trusted channeling ranks the diversity is stunning. Develop your own spiritual compass and see if it is not at least as accurate as the most adept channel or the wisest teacher among you. As far as ancient and significant mysteries go, there are other stories that are more profound and revealing than this one; yet, at least for now, this one seems to be holding fast to the number-one position on the spiritual "bestsellers" list.

25

Manifesting and Reincarnation

July 2004

What is the most useful knowledge regarding the subject of manifesting that you can share with us? I have read and learned a lot over the years but have had only moderate success in most areas. Could you offer any guidance, information or specific techniques that might be useful?

How one regards manifesting is in many ways similar to how one regards life. Humans tend to define life by their response to it rather than by their experience of it. For instance, if you knew how truly precious each moment of experience was, you would hold experience in higher regard. A moment is an individual and unique unit of consciousness; it is not an aspect of time, as many believe, although it can be measured by time if one so chooses. An infinite number of realities exists between each thought and each moment of experience, and it is these realities that influence how you create, manifest or respond to life. All the choices you make, as well as those that you do not make, are recorded within your cellular memory. The fact that you did not make a certain choice does not negate that the choice existed—do you see? Your cellular memory records both physical and nonphysical experience for you, building a body of knowledge as you go about the experience called life.

For purposes of this discussion, it will be more useful to refer to the experience of manifesting rather than the end result—the thing or event you desire to manifest—because, for the most part, experience is all that you can manifest. Then too, by the time the manifested object or event arrives, it is bereft of energy, like a battery cell whose lifespan is near completion. This is why objects offer such short-lived value and pleasure and why, for reasons that are difficult to explain, you continue to look for satisfaction in places where it cannot exist. Physical objects have no value of their own; they depend upon the value you give them. An antique, for instance, is valuable to a collector, but an old car is of value only to someone who has no other transportation. Having or possessing is the reenactment of the experience of manifesting. Physical objects are disposable and physical relationships are recyclable, but the nonphysical experience of creating or manifesting is made of the same permanent spark that you are.

ON TRUE MANIFESTING

True manifesting, also known as the manifesting principle, begins with the desire that exists before physical wanting or yearning is born. It begins with the eternal self that sees through the eyes rather than with the eyes. This permanent self will continue to be present before, beyond and after all of the "Is" that exist within you now. Your true (permanent) self already understands all of the principles of manifestation, and when your personality (identity) and your true self are aligned, manifesting takes place with grace and ease. When these two are not aligned, you wonder why manifesting is not working or why it works for others and not for you.

True manifesting takes place within the paradigm of pure creativity, which is a reflection of consciousness. Consciousness relates to time but is not dependent upon it. In other words, if you attempt to manifest a new car by Friday, it might or might not happen, because time is the hardscape (timescape) and experience is the softscape (creativity). Unconsciousness is ruled by time and depends upon it, which is why you see so many individuals scurrying about their day trying unsuccessfully to catch up to themselves. Most attempts at manifesting take place in the realm of the unconscious—which is appropriate, because this is where humanity practices and learns many activities including manifesting, which in turn assists the evolution of consciousness.

POLARITY IDENTITY IS COMPARATIVE

The unconscious realm is currently experiencing a distortion of sorts, a rift within the fabric of the timescape. This rift, or tear, has an effect upon everything that exists within time to the extent reflected by its current level of consciousness. In other words, the more unconscious the event, item or person is, the greater the effect of distortion. These words can more than likely be validated by your own daily experience. Unconscious manifesting, also called density manifestation, places one in polarity identity. Polarity identity is the area within the unconscious mind that identifies with struggle, lack, concern, fear and worry. It is a comparative identity, always measuring itself against others and most often finding itself (and you) inadequate. Identifying with polarity often results in concern and worry as well as lack and fear.

The fabric of time has been torn purposefully, and the rift that has been created is designed to keep you in an unconscious state. As long as you are unconscious, you will create more debt and your debt will keep you in fear. As long as you are in fear, it will be more difficult for you to escape the web of unconsciousness that has been drawn around you, and you will not notice that it has been artificially created. The web of unconsciousness makes certain that those who have will continue to have more and those who have not will have even less. For this reason, it is important, now more than ever, to be creatively clear about one's purpose and about what and why one is manifesting, to be as conscious and prescient as possible throughout the entire process.

Attempting to understand or apply these principles within the linear timescape of logic and common sense will prove detrimental to your manifesting ability, because manifesting does not take place within linear time. It only seems to, because eventually, your experience will appear within the third dimension in one form or another. Linear reality is based upon need rather than desire. It will ask you how hard you are willing to work for what you want; it will evaluate your credit worthiness, delay your conscious awareness and eventually allow you to take out a loan using your self-worth as collateral.

DIMENSIONAL MANIFESTING

It would seem that the present rift in time is detrimental to your ability to manifest, but that is not entirely true. It is a handicap, but one that will urge you into consciousness. It will remind you what you are capable of, and it will awaken even the most dormant aspects within you. It will teach you to maintain a creative stance in your life, to act rather than react and to remain in or return to the manifesting principle within yourself as often as necessary. Practicing the manifesting principle will not weave the rift in time, but it will help you to transcend it, weaving a new timescape into the fabric of your own awareness. The density of the third dimension will press and impress upon you the importance of this lesson, and in order to transform it (not escape it), you will need to generate a force (consciousness) that is greater than the mass, or density (unconsciousness), of the third dimension.

Dimensional manifesting takes place in the realm of pure awareness, which is your natural state; ultimately, this is the most satisfying of all experiences. You can begin to experience this state of awareness by trusting yourself and the universe (All That Is) in matters and events that seem to exist beyond logic or reason. You are a unit of consciousness, and the universe is a consciousness of unity. Remember that the microcosm (you) and the macrocosm (Source) come together to create diversity within wholeness. Finally, seek what you find, find what you seek and choose that which also chooses you.

WHAT IS TIME TO A SOUL?

Why do some souls reincarnate so quickly after transitioning (dying) whereas others do not? What determines the length of time between lifetimes? Why can some souls remember their last lifetime whereas others can't?

Time is a measure of the linear third dimension. It is relative, and it expands and contracts along with the in-breath and out-breath of the universe. A soul's reason for being is to know itself through and as All That Is. All of the choices and experiences a soul draws to it are linked and aligned with this purpose, as are the individual lifetimes associated with this overarching design. A soul is never idle and it is never hard at work. A soul is a collection of experience based upon a resourceful search for oneness and unity. A soul's journey through experience is the ultimate fulfillment of Creator's promise—an unending expression of divine and perfect will and the understanding of the one and the many.

A soul is a unit of consciousness expressed through the mind of Creator, and no two souls are alike. Souls differ in many ways, including what you would term size—another relative term when viewed beyond the attributes of physical limitation. A distinct relationship exists between the consciousness of a soul and the experience it calls to itself. For this reason, those who have lived many lifetimes upon the Earth and elsewhere sometimes call themselves old souls. Contrary to popular opinion, an old soul is not really any older than other souls and it was not necessarily among the first to individuate from the mind of Creator. An old soul is an accumulation of expanded units of conscious awareness. By way of contrast, a young soul would have less experience as understood by universal law and would therefore contain more units of unconscious (unexperienced) energy.

ALL SOULS ARE EQUAL

Some souls choose growth based upon individual experience, whereas others prefer a group or community expression. All souls experience self, selfishness, selflessness and self-fullness, regardless of their individual or group preferences. Their paths are unique and varied, but their journeys remain relatively equal. Souls incarnate in order to experience accelerated growth. For some the search for consciousness begins in the deepest regions of unconsciousness, just as the search for the origin of life begins in the abyss that is deep space. Each subsequent incarnation unfolds into the next in ways that would seem mysterious and disjointed to the logical mind. Each lifetime is an expansion of a concept or idea on which the universe is based. Unraveling and dismantling the facade of physical or temporary reality one discovers the ultimate, or enduring, reality. Only in the struggle to achieve individual perfection does the soul discover its connection to Source.

Lifetime after carefully planned lifetime, a soul delves deep into unconsciousness, searching for its conscious counterpart. Its search will take it on adventure after adventure, living and reliving memorable moments and linking these to past and future experiences. Sometimes a soul experiences a lifetime as an epiphany: It crosses a threshold and throws open a door to conscious awareness. Eager to continue the process, it might choose to incarnate quickly in order to make the most of the experience it has gained. It will plan its next life carefully, aligning itself with physical and nonphysical teachers and experiences designed to accelerate and promote growth. These lifetimes are often more difficult than most and involve challenges and choices that would seem insurmountable were it not for the desire of the soul to know itself above all else. It might appear to others that this being has thrown caution to the four winds. His life might seem misaligned as compared with his contemporaries and his reality misshapen by contrast, but invisibly and consistently the soul will continue along its circuitous spiral path until at last he discovers and uncovers himself, hidden between both density and destiny.

A soul does not measure itself by the number of physical lifetimes it has lived. It does not compare itself to other souls and judge itself accordingly. A soul does not push or shove itself into the next body or the next lifetime in a race against itself or other souls toward an invisible finish line. A soul is a unit of creative consciousness within the mind of God; it is an art form that marvels at the hand that created it. Each lifetime, therefore, is an homage to its Creator in which life is given the opportunity to imitate art.

Why You Don't Know Who You Really Are

August 2004

*T*he most important question you can ever ask is, "Who am I?" The second-most important question you can ask is, "Why am I?" The more common queries are, "Why don't I . . . ?" and "Why can't I . . . ?" because humans are more accustomed to looking outside of themselves for an answer rather than inside. The world outside of you, the manifest world, defines itself and you by what it is not, or by the process of elimination. The problem with this process is that it is very difficult to eliminate enough of the manifest world so that you can discover your truth. You created the manifest world to serve and support your needs and desires, one of which is to keep your true identity hidden until such a time when you say, "Game over!" Well, the game is not over yet, but it has become increasingly tiresome, especially for those who have been at it for some time.

What keeps you from saying "Game over"? Many different variables do, but there are some chief culprits among them. One of these is humanity's continued fascination with the manifest world. As long as people believe that manifesting is more important or better than un-manifesting, they support the continuation of the game. "Seeing is believing," or so the saying goes, and humans love to see what they have manifested. But creation and creativity are states of being, not doing. A creative act can be physical or nonphysical, and it does not require something or someone to believe in it in order for it to exist.

YOUR MIND IS NOT THE SAME AS YOUR BRAIN

Your mind is not physical; that attribute belongs to your brain. Your brain and your mind are not the same. The brain is the controlling center of the human body's central nervous system. It is connected to the spinal column and enclosed in the cranium. Your brain processes information and performs functions that approximate thinking, but its thoughts are mechanical and unconscious—they are convincing illusions whose physicality deceives you into believing that they are real; their very nature underscores their purpose. The brain offers you sensory perception as further proof that it is your legal owner and guardian. Touch it, feel it, see it, hold it, smell it, taste it—it must be real!

Your mind, on the other hand, is a center of consciousness—or unconsciousness, as the case may be. It can support the brain's beliefs and perceptions about itself and the world around it, or it can generate original thoughts, drawing upon a creative and invisible storehouse of knowledge and wisdom. The brain's ability to think and reason is rudimentary compared to the mind's ability to create and attain. The most creative minds are those with the least interest in what is reasonable and the most interest in what is creative. Intellect, or intelligence, is a function that supports physical and nonphysical reality; its value is in how it is applied.

Consciousness is what connects the brain and the mind with All That Is. Consciousness is the state of being aware, awake and sensitive to what is going on both within and without. So to know who you are and why you are, you must become more consciously aware of your true self. Your true self is not the "I Am," but the I Am knows who you are, which is why attaining a conscious, ongoing connection with your I Am presence is so valuable. Your I Am will also show you what and who you are not, and it is here where many of you get stuck. The reason you get stuck here is because there is a very fine line between consciousness and unconsciousness. Your I Am presence can guide you to a conscious and aware state of being or to an unconscious but mindful state of doing. Both are valuable and can be very useful, because in discovering who you are not, you will eventually discover who you are. There is no right or wrong path, and all journeys are to be prized and cherished as significant.

Let's explore this topic a little further, allowing these words to transport our thoughts both near and far to see if we can shed some light on your own unique path.

HUMANITY'S PLACE IN THE WEB OF LIFE

You are an intelligent biological consciousness. This means that as a form of life, you are organic in nature. The animal kingdom is also organic and intelligent, but its consciousness is reflected via its species rather than its individuality. There are certainly exceptions to this, especially in animals who express themselves with or near humanity, such as a domestic feline or canine. The animal kingdom makes its life and marks its growth by being organically and biologically connected to the Earth; its evolution depends upon the physical planet's ability to sustain it. In the case of the dinosaurs, for instance, the planet was no longer able to sustain a temperate environment in which they could survive. Most (not all) perished or migrated into other physical expressions. The animal kingdom depends upon other kingdoms for its survival, just as all kingdoms do. Each kingdom ranks its relationship to other kingdoms in order of importance based upon its evolution and survival. The animal kingdom, therefore, is related to the human kingdom, but it depends upon the plant kingdom for its survival. The human kingdom is related to the animal kingdom because it hunts and consumes it and because it fears it as well.

Humans, because they are the most evolved species on Earth, are equally related to all of the other kingdoms, and they are responsible for their own evolution as well as that of the other kingdoms. The Earth responds to an invisible web of life, a schema, or basic outline, that ensures its evolution. The Native Americans still resonate to this vibration, echoing it in the words *mitakyuin oyasin*, or "all my relations." The vibration you call love unites you with your brothers and sisters in other kingdoms, whereas that which angers you or that which you fear divides and separates you from the other kingdoms.

Love, therefore, accelerates evolution, whereas fear retards or slows it. Love precedes (pre-seeds) consciousness within humanity by allowing divine intelligence rather than artificial intelligence to be its guide. Fear separates you from other kingdoms and from everything else; it causes disease and discomfort and leads to a variety of unnecessary and avoidable ills. Fear of other kingdoms, species or forms of intelligence creates distance. It is important to remember this when asking the question, "When will contact with off-planet beings begin?" Wisdom dictates that it will begin en masse when human fear subsides, when humans cease to be concerned that off-planet beings know more or are more advanced than humanity.

THE MEANING OF LIFE AND OTHER COMMON QUESTIONS

Let's get more of the most common questions out of the way so we can proceed with ease. Was your origin on another planet? No, your beingness did not originate on another planet, in or on a nonphysical world. Have you lived in other worlds and upon other planets? Yes, most certainly—at least most of you have. Will you determine your origins by continuing to be spiritual archaeologists who study only the past? No. You cannot determine an absolute by studying its fragment, do you see? That being said, when the fragments of the past are seen as threads of a very great and beautiful garment of light rather than the remnants of shredded and forgotten eras, then a more true understanding can take place. If you want to know who you are, you must look to your future as well as to your past. Ask yourself where you would like to be, not where you would like to go. If you must work your way into the past, begin in the future and work your way back from there.

Long and long ago, and even longer than that, a resonance was created within this universe. This resonance took the form of a spiral, and from that spiral, this galaxy was created. A spiral galaxy is one in which a specific kind of evolution can take place. Most spiral galaxies evolve into or from biological life. A spiral is a collective movement both to and away from something. Your relative location on or in an evolutional spiral determines the level of your experience within that system. Consciousness is the awareness of experience. In a spiral galaxy, the various levels of consciousness one can attain are determined by the experiences one draws to oneself. Here in the Milky Way galaxy, experience is attained by the movement from nonphysical life to and through physical life and back again—or life, death and rebirth.

Does this always lead to growth? Yes, always. The universe has little use for waste and depends upon universal law to uphold and unfold density into divinity. Have all of your lifetimes been in this universe? Yes, for the most part, with relatively few exceptions. These are made in order to retrieve fragments of understanding that are forfeit when universal law is violated. Universal law is not like civil or criminal law. You cannot break a universal law, but you can violate it, meaning that you can place yourself outside of it. Standing apart from universal law creates separation and forgetting. That is why the law requires a person to retrieve what is missing. Most of the time, what is missing was inadvertently given away or discarded in a moment of unconsciousness. This is another way of describing what is termed "the fall" or, more appropriately, "the forgetting."

To say that you have always been a part of this universe is accurate, because you have always existed here. Surround yourselves with this truth. All you are exists within this universe, but it is just as accurate to say that the entire universe exists within you, for you are very great beings. All that you understand as Source, All That Is or God is a creator within a larger creatorship, an idea within a context. The consciousness of Source is the creatorship who imagined the context for this spiral galaxy of which the Earth is a willing and active participant. Surround yourselves with this truth as well. But is it the ultimate truth? No. It is grandest truth that you now hold in common with Source at this time, but it will be replaced by another truth at some point in the future, for that is always the path evolution takes in a spiral environment. There is always a truth that exists beyond the current truth, no matter how expanded or relevant the current truth is. There is always something else to consider, but that something else is not always a more noble truth; that is where discernment and wisdom come into play.

DEALING WITH ANSWERS TO THE MEANING OF LIFE

Spiritual truths are a little paradoxical. The answer to two different and conflicting questions might be "Yes" and "Yes." The answers might conflict on one dimension, or plane of understanding, but not on another. The question, "Who am I?" is a little like that, because as soon as you receive the grandest answer, "You are one with and in All That Is," you will go in search of the next, more definitive answer, and when you do, you will shoot yourself in the foot, because the more specific the answer gets, the further from the truth it actually is. As soon as you are told what and who you are or where and when you have been, you automatically limit your truth—you reduce it by at least half. Instead, ask, "Who and what do I intend to be?" and see how the answer expands your awareness rather than limits it. If you think you are getting closer to knowing who you are because you have eliminated some choices, all you have done is eliminated choices and limited possibilities.

Humans are very comfortable with limitation, self-imposed and otherwise. They have also become very comfortable with identity, purchasing it daily at wholesale and retail prices. A label, a logo, a flag, a vehicle—all are identities having little or nothing to do with who and what you are, limited identities pasted onto unlimited beings, masks that hide the faces of heroes and reduce divine will to willpower. One-fifth of the Earth's population think they are human first and spiritual second. It is no wonder many of you think you are just human! Another fifth believe that they are spiritual first, but only because a higher power has chosen them and their religion. The remaining three-fifths believe they are spiritual but that they will become more spiritual when they discover their purpose, or reason for being upon the Earth. Unfortunately, many will overidentify with their purpose or lack thereof, which will only limit their perception as they erroneously compare themselves to others who are more like them than they know.

What were you before you were a human? What will you be after you lay down your identity, your limitation and your body? Who told you that you need a purpose in order to be? Before you were a human, you were a purposeful and creative being. One day you will shed your human skin and radiate the light of a thousand suns or a thousand lifetimes, as the case may be. In the meantime, your vibration is your identity and your calling card, and there is no other like it. You are one with the resonance of the universe, and temporarily, your physical home is here upon the Earth. You have many brothers and sisters here, and this is their temporary home as well. The causal plane is your local neighborhood; it belongs to all who have been human, are human or will have human awareness. The causal plane is a threshold environment that makes many other dimensions and densities of creative expression possible.

THE INTRINSIC NATURE OF BEING HUMAN:
THE CAUSAL PLANE

The causal plane records and supports your human-ness. It hosts the great akashic records that remember every dance step and misstep you have ever made. The akashic records allow you to search or peruse every thought and nuance you have ever considered. If you want to meet yourself in the past, you can do so here, as well as greet any possible future that you might be considering. The akashic records will bear out these words: You do not have a purpose, because you are purpose incarnate. Source does not need a reason or purpose for being, and neither do you. Those whom you call master teachers or angels do not need a reason for being. You are not their reason for being. An angel will still be an angel whether or not you require its specific assistance or acknowledge its presence. But if humans did not need humans, would there still be humans? No.

Humans are physical and social. Humans lean on and learn from one another. Humankind is an aspect of All That Is that relates to itself individually and collectively. You believe you are individual because you think independent thoughts, but if you knew just how many of your thoughts are identical to those of others, you would see how interrelated you all really are. Soon telepathic thought will link you to one another, and you will see that thought and experience are kinetic in origin; they are subject to the influence of movement. Do whales, for instance, need the company of other whales as well? Yes. Knowledge must be gained and wisdom must be shared, not simply to perpetuate the species, but to expand the evolution of consciousness. If whales and humans did not need one another, what would happen to the whales? Their numbers would diminish and eventually, the species would end, but not before its consciousness was transferred elsewhere or translated into another beingness, because consciousness is eternal and everlasting; it is the stuff God is made of, and Creator is never less than whole.

To be human is to be in resonance with a universal schema of evolution. It is to be part of a very great plan that is ever unfolding. This plan is not accidental in nature or haphazard in purpose. It is organized and ordained wisdom. It is as precious and sacred as each breath you draw in Creator's name. A human life is an art form and its purpose is carefully crafted, honed and polished. You already are a reason for being, so going in search of a reason is a little redundant. You are a library of experience and your library is always expanding. Experience is carried forward from lifetime to lifetime, because it is made of the same resonance as consciousness. Resonance is magnetic, and that is how you draw unto you experience relative to your purpose.

The causal plane supports human magnetic resonance. The environment is conducive to promoting growth via experience, regardless of physical expression or identity. The causal plane is an environment that molds and shapes itself to fit your needs. It supports humans who seek understanding through self-expression before life, during life and after life, which is why it values discovery and expression through what you would term positive and negative experience. As far as magnetic resonance is concerned, positive and negative are simply two points on opposite ends of a spectrum of light—one draws energy, whereas the other emits energy, and both are necessary to achieve balance. Negative energy, or dark light, is an excellent way-shower. It always points the way to the lighter end of the spectrum, because it is its very nature to do so.

The causal system supports humans who support themselves. It is a self-taught system whose primary master is experience. The causal plane renews itself, perpetuates itself and expands its awareness through experience. It supports your human and your nonhuman experience through the cycle of birth, death and rebirth. In life it will remind you that you are more than human by helping you to find Spirit. Beyond life it reminds you that you are also human as it assists you in helping others. Its resonance is full spectrum, so in one moment its vibration might say that you are human being not human, and in the next moment it might say that you are not human pretending to be human. In that yin/yang possibility, you are supported in becoming whole.

The causal plane is a complementary environment that keeps you from falling off the deep end. It renews and replaces anything that is missing or lacking, including mind, body, heart or purpose. By this method, humanity continually discovers and reinvents itself. In the causal system, the perpetual being-ness called I Am supports all you are. The I Am is your direct connection to Source, and you are never disconnected from Source, even when the mist called discontent attempts to fool you into thinking you are. Your lungs are never disconnected from your body. Even when it is difficult for you to draw a breath, your lungs do not leave you. It is the same with Source.

The causal plane is designed to support you, not to trap you, and its door is always open for you to come and go as you please. But third-dimensional expression is quite dense, and there is a tendency to overidentify with the more human aspects of life. This sometimes leads to struggle and even suffering, making it more difficult for Spirit to remind you that you are not your human struggle. Spirit is a diligent teacher and will patiently wait for you to unlatch the door to your mind or your heart.

MOVING FROM THE CAUSAL TO THE UNIVERSAL

We have postulated that you are not human beings or spiritual human beings, and that you relish discovering what you are by experiencing what you are not. But if you truly desire to understand who you are, you must open or part the veils that prevent you from seeing yourselves as universal beings. The veils are not barriers; they are what you would term a comfort zone that prevents or eases any fear you could have regarding losing your identity or status as an individual entity. It is well and good to be told that your essence is as pure and liquid as light, but the experience is another thing altogether. Veils are just that: gossamer transitions, soft lenses that gradually allow you to adjust your vision and deepen your understanding.

Beyond the veils, a causal being is also a universal lightbeing. A universal lightbeing is an archetypal structure of light. It is formless and can seem threatening if there has been an overidentification with physical embodiment. A universal being is archetypal light expressing itself as divinity. The simplest and truest definition of divinity is: ". . . an aspect of light that understands itself to be one with Source and never separate or apart from It, regardless of expression." Universal beings do not claim or disclaim their humanity; they are the distilled compassion born of lifetimes of experience.

THE SOUL AS ARCHITECT OF THE WILL

By discussing and emphasizing what you are not, we continually discover what you are, but it is up to you to claim it or not, to own or disown your heritage and legacy. It is up to you to receive this knowledge or to disavow its existence. You are an archetype of light, an aspect of Source imbued with what is called will. Free will is simply conscious rather than unconscious will. It is an oxymoron, because if you are aware that you are and have will, then you are also free, but the concept of freedom satisfies the palate and is well recognized within the human template as a desirable state of being.

Your soul and your will are closely associated. Your soul is that part of the All that also expresses individuality. The soul is the architect of the will; it designs and molds it from its lifetimes of experience. The soul makes no effort to separate itself from the All or to differentiate itself from any other soul. It does not seek conformity, but it does desire unity. Group souls and soul families are units of divine consciousness who explore experience through one another. Experiences that cannot be explained, sometimes called déjà vu, belong to souls who are grouped together by choice. The experience remains in the cellular memory of the group rather than in the mind of the individual. It becomes a shared dimensional experience rather than a linear personal experience.

If the soul is the architect of the will, then the will is the soul's blueprint. It can also be said that the soul is the father and the will is the son (sun). A blueprint is also a design, a tool and a map that, when carefully followed, can result in a very beautiful creation. Did Source create soul and will simultaneously? Dimensionally speaking, yes. It is a little like asking, "Which came first—the chicken or the egg?" Both lead to and away from Source; both inspire individual experience and unity consciousness. The soul is the arche-type of that which seeks conscious awareness, and the will is the active intel-ligence who claims it. Will is the aspect of soul that is no longer in dispute with itself. For instance, divine will does not stop to think or evaluate what it should have done or could have done differently, which would only inval-idate its experience.

A soul can have many, many lifetimes and is encouraged to do so. Some souls have hundreds of lifetimes and some have thousands. There is no prize for attaining enlightenment in as few lifetimes as possible. The universe celebrates beauty and diversity of experience rather than economy. Enlightenment is a temporary reward and is not meant to be a stopping point.

SO WHY DON'T YOU KNOW WHO YOU ARE?

We have now moved closer to defining what you are: You are an aspect of your soul. You are an incarnation chosen by your soul. You are a purposeful expression of beingness. Your purpose is to develop consciousness by involving and invoking the will, which is the active intelligence or vehicle leading to greater consciousness. In order to become fully conscious, your soul—coupled with divine will—creates opportunities and adventures for you to participate in along with others who could be aligned with your purpose. Your will supports your soul in creating lifetimes of growth, expansion, purpose and divinity. Each lifetime begins and ends with a roundtrip ticket to Source.

So why don't you know who you are? Because the density of the third dimension is obfuscating the finer qualities of the light who you are, which in turn creates an overidentification with your body, your work, your family, your personality and everything else. It is no longer enough to say, "I am." Now it is followed by something: "I am a woman; I am a man; I am a business person; I am a homeowner; I am a dog-lover; I am spiritual; I am fat; I am in debt; I am tired . . ."—ad infinitum. What causes overidentification? The stress to become conscious within a sea of unconsciousness, coupled with a sensation that you are running out of time. What causes stress? An overidentification with the subject matter at hand or with anything that exists outside of the I Am. Stress separates you from will and reduces your natural resources. It short-circuits creativity and sidetracks the mind.

THE BENEFITS OF SOFTENING YOUR FOCUS

Would it benefit us to live our lives more as a channel of the I Am energy rather than identifying with the whole divine plan? Is that what Pepper does when she channels you?

It would benefit you to soften your focus a bit and to blur the lines of iden-tity, to be simple without oversimplifying. If your focus is too specific or myopic, then it is an overidentification. If your focus does not help you to see more clearly or experience more grandly, then it is an identity and not an experience. When you soften your focus in all directions and in all relationships, you diffuse light, which makes every environment better lit and more conducive to a full experience. You are not here to sacrifice anything or to surrender any part of your authentic self; this is a misconception. Sacrifice and surrender lead to martyrdom, and we have had enough of that already. It is very common today to say, "I surrender," but most of the time what is meant is, "I give up." True surrender is an aspect of creativity, but giving up is a reaction to stress. Almost everything is being surrendered these days, and that which is not surrendered is abandoned or even stolen! Does that tell you anything? Channeling is also a form of identity, and it is important not to overidentify with the process or the experience.

What can we do to help ourselves soften our focus and expand our consciousness?

Make your foundation as deep as it is tall. Make sure you are aligned and in communication with your architect (soul). Hire a qualified contractor (I Am). Give your contractor permission to employ creative, well-paid workers (personality aspects). Compliment the workers on their process. Remind them that they need rest too. Hire a superintendent (higher self) to make sure that everyone is doing his or her own work. Visit the construction site often and offer your support equally. When the work is completed, throw a party and celebrate.

THE TRUE NATURE OF SURRENDER

Isn't there a certain amount of surrender involved in trying to reach a God-realized state, like that of a master? Doesn't surrender allow more of our will or our purpose to flow through while also helping us to become a little less detached from the drama?

It is beneficial to practice a certain amount of nonattachment, but who or what would you surrender to? Where does "the flow" come from? What causes it? The flow, or streaming consciousness, emerges from Source and pours into your awareness in the form of energy, light and creativity. Source feeds the I Am. You think you can surrender the ego, but it is attached to the rest of you. When you trade in your car, they take the engine too. There is no one to surrender to but yourself, because as self, you already are Source. Surrender enjoys popularity now because the common thought is that it will take you from here to there, but there is no there, because your I Am is here.

Is surrender a form of escape, then?

It depends on whether the attempt is to find yourself or lose yourself. You can lose yourself in surrender as easily as in anything else. Sometimes you lose the very thing you are trying to find. For instance, you forget that you originate in Source even as you journey there. The smart dog enjoys chasing its tail as much as the next dog, but eventually, it tires of the game. Have you looked to see who or what accepted your surrender or if your surrender even was accepted? Have you asked yourself whether you are surrendering or capitulating? Wave the white flag if you must, but make certain that another does not claim it by placing his or her own initials upon it. A higher authority dwells within you—yield to that; submit to your I Am, which is within reach of your will, located just next to your soul, who dwells in Source. Or you can simply soften your focus a bit!

THE NATURE OF DIVINITY AND TWIN FLAMES

Can divinity become more divine?

Divinity is the quality most associated with Godness. Divinity is the "Is" in All That Is. Divinity cannot become more divine, but it can expand through experience. Source is whole and does not require anything outside of Itself in order to be more complete. Sacred geometry is the exponential language of All That Is, which in turn expresses itself as the universal law of plenty, also called the law of multitude. Within the movement called the in-breath and out-breath of All That Is, divinity expands in sacred proportion. This same magnificent and sacred law of proportion also measures the birth and death of stars, planets and human beings, because divine proportion is a variable expression of purpose. If you like to help divinity expand, think of yourselves as one with All That Is instead of one less than All That Is.

I would like to hear your version of the twin-flame, soul-mate concept. Is it for real?

Oh dear, I was afraid it would come to this one day. The twin-soul concept is an understanding that you are a complementary being and that nothing can divide you from yourself. You are a microcosm within a macrocosm, a unique and individual beingness within a very great beingness. This great Source named you in Its own image and imbued you with Its sameness. You are a reflection of that which is whole. Source contains all of Its reflections just as you contain all of yours. Within these reflections, or mirrors, there are prisms, or qualities, that reflect great love. Love can be experienced internally or externally. Divine love for self and selflessness expressed within was long ago called the twin flame, or the light whose equal only serves to strengthen the flame. Divine love for self and selflessness expressed externally has likewise been called the soul mate.

Unfortunately, this concept was blown out of proportion long ago, and it will be quite some time before its myth can be put down. The problem with its current interpretation is the belief that someone or something other than you can complete you. Further complicating the issue is the fact that many humans are unaware of themselves and have not learned to like themselves, much less love themselves or others. The search for one's soul mate is like the search for the Holy Grail: It requires asking the right questions and knowing where to find the answers. The search is always an external one, but the treasure always lies within.

Then again, every cloud has a silver lining, and the concept of soul mates has been single-handedly responsible for drawing billions of humans to the Earth plane to continue their search. Searching for love eventually leads to the discovery of love. All beings are divine, and there are many well suited to be your mates. The garden does not produce only one rose or one head of cabbage. A soul mate is a being who resonates so deeply within you that you transcend the human, or external, aspect that still acknowledges separation. Because a soul mate is a perfect reflection of your truth, there is no reason for you to have barriers or boundaries before it.

Another word for a perfect reflection of self is a twin. A perfect, or divine, twin does not often appear in a relationship scenario, at least not a romantic one. It is an outer expression of that which resonates as the truest form of self-expression, self-experience and self-divinity that the universe can find to reflect to you. It can be a brother, sister, mother, friend—and yes, a lover too. Reflections are not constant; they are ever changing and greatly influenced by expanding awareness, so it is possible to have more than one twin flame or soul mate in the same lifetime.

A spiritual flame, once lit, cannot be extinguished. If you are mated to your spiritual flame, then it belongs to you forever. This mating does not preclude another relationship from presenting itself, but even in the light of a new relationship, you remain mated to your spiritual flame, because it represents Source to you. You are always mated to Source, just as you are always mated to your soul. You can go shopping for another mate, but you cannot go shopping for another soul. Still, there could be more than one mate, more than one flame, more than one twin and more than one experience of true love. Do you like statistics? Speaking in generalities expressed as percentages, only 18 percent of those who say they are mated to their soul mate truly are. Only 7 percent of those who say they have discovered their soul twin truly have. The percentage of those who have met their twin flame comes in at 39 percent; however, many of these beings are unaware or unconscious of this fact, because they see themselves quite differently than the world does.

The Question of Gender and How It Relates to Purpose

Do we choose which gender we incarnate into or is it just the luck of the draw as to whether a male or female body becomes available first?

You choose the gender that is more difficult for you to embody, based upon the purpose you have designed. Surprisingly, choosing whichever seems more difficult also provides the highest odds of success. A successful lifetime affords the completion of your purpose and includes various examples and experiences aligned with that purpose. Even midlife gender changes are designed to support your purpose. If a soul becomes overly aligned with the female gender, then it would be more appropriate to choose a male body type, and the reverse also holds true. All of you have had lifetimes in which you have been both men and women. You have also experienced a variety of races, religions and cultures. Upon the Earth plane, gender is related to sex, but this varies by planet; it is not the same everywhere. Some worlds have amorphous bodies or nonphysical bodies, and you have experienced those as well.

Gender is designed to assist humanity in balancing density. Balancing density is not the same as carrying weight or enduring burdens. Balanced density is the union of that which seems separate but is actually not. For instance, the left and right hemispheres of the brain, heaven and Earth, masculinity and femininity are all aspects of that which seeks balanced proportion. The fact that there are twelve hours of sunlight and twelve hours of night is another example of balanced density. Balanced density is another way to express the perfection of chaos theory.

Your gender is aligned with your purpose, and both are stamped on your roundtrip ticket. It might seem to you that if your purpose is vague, you will stumble your way back home, but that is not often the case. A weak or unfulfilled purpose makes it more difficult for you to go home, because life is designed to be purposeful. That is why those who are unclear continue to seek until they find or remember why they have come. If you cannot find your way in this life, it will not be any easier in the next.

A purpose is a very individual thing, and no one can experience it for you. A purpose can be shared, aligned or put off until a later date, but it cannot be ignored altogether. A life is never wasted, and as long as you live your life, you will also live your purpose. There is nothing you need to achieve in order to earn the right to return to the Earth or not, as the case may be. The Earth is unique; there is no other planet quite like it. It is rather small as worlds go and can only accommodate several billion of you at a time. As you already know, we are a bit overbooked and still taking reservations!

Your purpose was birthed long before your body was born. Your soul did not wake up one day and think, "I haven't been to the Earth in a long time, and a visit might be nice. I'll need a body, a wardrobe and a toothbrush." Your purpose is like a map or an almanac for your soul. It can be checked and cross-referenced against other lifetimes to make certain that your experience is going well. Another word for purpose is desire. Desire envisions a journey of light, which gives birth to form. That form is called a lightbody. The lightbody is fashioned by the soul; it is not a byproduct of spiritual achievement. It is the most natural of births, like a spontaneous burst of light.

Can a purpose change or fluctuate throughout one's life or is it always clearly defined? Also, how do we know when it's time to hunker down and get to work on our purpose?

Your purpose does not change, but it does expand. It grows along with you. It takes form and is shaped by the experiences you draw to yourself. You relate to your purpose on the inner and the outer planes; both are creative and fertile environments for growth. As formlessness takes form, your purpose expands into experience. Purpose is an aspect of being and does not always require a lot of doing; this is another common misconception that bears review. A purpose is what you are and it is what you have. Your purpose influences how you express yourself and what you experience, but not necessarily what you do. Your thoughts and feelings guide your purpose and affect what you do; they are related, but they are not the same.

Most of the time purpose expands, but sometimes it narrows instead; it becomes more acute and specific. The soul recognizes this and responds to it with a deep sense of yearning to accomplish something. On the outer planes, this could manifest as a time of great change or upheaval, and you might well wonder what has gone wrong. Your personality often presents the greatest challenge during this time as it scurries about trying to do just about anything and everything to keep you unconscious. You do not have to be completely aware of your purpose in order to achieve it, but it helps. Most of you are aware of a central theme that seems to describe your life, and for many this is enough. Your purpose is multilayered and faceted. For instance, you have a personal awareness of your purpose and a planetary awareness of it. You also have a divine purpose and a day-to-day purpose. These are not separate from you. When you complete your design for this life, you will find that the experience has expanded your perspective. Based upon that, you will be free to choose your next experience.

THE PERSISTENT MATERIAL QUESTION

There is no way we can get out of doing something to support ourselves in the material world, since we need to earn a living. I would prefer to be doing something that is aligned with my purpose. Can you suggest how to do that?

Doing comes from being, and it is never the other way around, no matter how much you try to make it so or wish that it were different. Every drop that you squeeze out of doing came from a thought first, regardless of whether it was a creative thought or a dreaded thought. You might think that your purpose is to be a healer, a teacher of metaphysics, a mystic or a surgeon, but your true purpose is to awaken from the illusion that doing any one thing is more important than doing any other thing. Your purpose is to break free from the chains of doing, not to find what you can do that is more tolerable than something else. You might well say, "That's easy for you to say, Gaia; you don't have to earn a living." Well, you are correct, I do not, but neither do you. You do need to create a life that supports and sustains you and those you care for, but that is different than toiling day after day under the watchful eyes of the illusory world you compare yourself with.

Join your more creative aspects by being gentle with yourself rather than berating yourself for what you have not yet accomplished. Punishment breeds fear, which is the opposite of creativity. Look for the smallest place within yourself, which is more than likely where you have hidden your creative spirit. Breathe life into it as you forgive yourself for ignoring it or thinking that it was unworthy of your attention. Imagine yourself crying a teardrop of love upon it and see how the love vibration causes it to expand. Hold this place within you as sacred and invite Spirit to help you infuse it with more of God's love. Allow the elixir of love to coax your creativity from behind the wall of fear, where it has been hiding.

Creativity speaks a language called truth. Its dialect is subjective, and it will take a little time to acquaint yourself with it. Your truth will be uniquely different from anyone else's, and your friends and family might not understand the new foreign language you have begun to speak. The more you listen to this new language, however, the more you will also be able to speak it. Eventually, your inner voice will speak in this language only and you will begin to forget the other language, even if it is more common among your peers. Truth has a funny way of leading you back to your creative spirit, as if you were being blindfolded and led to a birthday cake. In the physical world, you blow out your birthday candles, but in the more creative, nonphysical realms, you light them!

Light defines shadow, and you will begin to see where your creativity was previously dimmed. (Hint: "Why" is of little or no consequence and will only derail your progress.) Imagine that the soft, warm wax from the lit candles is the material the physical world uses to manifest desires. The more candles (light) you have, the more wax (manifesting material) you have. Use your imagination to mold, shape and manifest your desires. If you run out of material, light more candles and think more creative thoughts to keep them lit. Your creative being is born from the spark that is created when light first touches shadow. This is called passion, which is also the language of the soul.

Does our personal divinity increase along with the light and the frequency on the planet?

Divinity is a unique expression of light, but it is not personal. Divinity belongs to the realm of oneness. It is what one discovers on one's journey from selfishness through selflessness and into self-fullness. Divinity is what is earned when selfhood is surrendered. Divinity is the fullness of light; it is the dearest of all expressions. To understand divinity is to understand the All as one, as self and as many; it is to understand the spiral of evolution as both density and light.

IS THIS ALL A TRICK?

Is the trick answer to all this that we don't really know who we are? Is it because we think we are different and separate from everyone else but are really just all the same being?

Somewhat, but it is not a trick question or a trick answer, although it can seem tricky to sort it all out from a human perspective. You are not the same, but you are made of the same quality. You are equal and you all have access to the same tools. You are all on the same team, not on opposite sides. You are all equal, because you have equal access to the light that shines upon and within you. You are not cut from the same cloth, but you are made from the same fabric. Each individual thread is unique, but it is not separate, which is the most common misconception. An individual thread is not often aware of its place within the tapestry and it cannot see how it contributes to the beauty that is the whole. Most often a thread regards itself as inconsequential, but it takes only one thread to unite an entire garment or to unravel it.

You are more than what your imagination suggests. You are great and giant beings of light masquerading as ants. And what do ants do? They carry hundreds of times their weight, which is what humans are now doing. They are carrying their density and their burdens instead of their light, which is as weightless as a feather. Your thoughts about your past are dense and they weigh upon you. The future is as yet unlived. If you hold it as harmless, it will also be weightless and will not add to the burdens you already carry. The present represents your creative will, and if you unlock this door, you will find that many choices await.

Burdensome thoughts weigh hundreds of times more than creative thoughts. If you want to lose weight, quickly drop the dense thoughts that no longer serve you. It will make a difference on the scale almost immediately. A human experience need not be dense or unconscious; this is a choice. When you go to see a movie, you identify with the characters and with the drama. You become part of the experience, and the emotion of it washes over you. When the movie ends and the lights come on, you can exit the theater and go home, but if you identify too strongly with the characters or the movie, you could forget to go home. If you stay in your seat, the movie will play again and again until you tire of it, or worse, until you overidentify with the movie (the outer world) and become the character (the role).

Humans do not know themselves, because they are looking at their outer reflection rather than their inner awareness. Humans demand to know who they are but then settle for the smaller identities of life, such as those of career or family. Within each incarnation, there are many roles to play and robes to wear, but these are not who you are. You are not what you are doing today or what you will do tomorrow. You are an architecture and archetype of divine expression. Your will and your soul have created an identity for you to use and a body to house your spirit, but you will soon discard these in favor of a greater reality. It is difficult for you to claim all that you are, but it is important that you know your range of choices. There are many dimensions and densities within dimensions to choose from. There are many types of bodies and vehicles of light to choose from. There are so many paradises, purposes and paradigms that no moment need ever repeat itself.

No one life is greater or more precious than another. No one celestial body, sun or star is more precious or more sacrificial than the next. The quality with which light expands is unique, but the quantity of available light is the same. This is true of all experience, whether it is your own or that of Source, which are one and the same. Source expands as you do because Its experience is your own. The higher dimensions reflect expansion, whereas the lower realms invite you to judge expansion. Do not hesitate long in discovering this. I share with you good cause to remember these words as your sails once again turn into the wind.

The Campaign for a
Vote of Confidence

September 2004

*B*y the time these words find you, the campaign season will be in full swing. The pendulum of popularity will swing in one direction, only to be compelled and pulled in another direction by the forces that influence such things, seemingly without their will. As the pendulum swings, perhaps more widely than it has in the past, it will move effortlessly through the kingdom of the flag wavers, the domain of the zealots, the hierarchy of the solvent and insolvent, the field of inconsistencies and the valley of the complainers. The pendulum has no influence over the events it oversees; it simply marks the moments as they pass, measuring them by degrees of influence. Its movement is similar to that of an eclipse, momentarily obscuring the light of the celestial body it transits, activating awareness in some and lack of awareness in others.

Long ago and in specific times, there were other campaigns—campaigns of war, campaigns of overcoming struggle, campaigns to conquer and liberate, campaigns for roads to riches, campaigns for inventions and studies. All who read and otherwise participate in these words have taken part in many such campaigns. Even now you campaign to increase your knowledge, to learn the nature of your true self, to discover your purpose; you campaign for a variety of other motives unique to you.

I bring the campaign process to your attention now with a bit of levity as would accompany those who visit a circus, but with specific intent as well, because if you read between the lines, you will discover that beyond information gathering, there is "experience getting" at stake. If you have made campaign promises to yourself or to others, this would be a good time to decide whether you are prepared to make good on them. Likewise, if you have decided to stand for yourself because another could never do it as well for you, this would be an ideal time to do so. As we begin, ask yourself what you stand for today and see if it will be the same tomorrow. Rather than faltering over past successes and failures, why not focus your vision on an ideal and follow it to see where it might lead?

The Kingdom of the Flag Wavers

A flag is only a piece of cloth. Often bearing an emblem, symbol or ornament, it signifies identity and affiliation. There are many types of flags; for instance, the world recognizes the flag of the International Red Cross as well as the white flag that indicates truce, surrender or other peaceful intent. Sometimes however, a flag becomes one of convenience, such as when a ship or sailing vessel is registered under a flag (or country) that offers favorable regulations rather than having any real connection with the ship's owners or business. Flags seem to carry a provocative power of their own. They inspire, move, stir and incite emotion.

The flag wavers are the dutiful citizens of the republic. Many are reincarnated Atlanteans, prominent citizens of a civilization that knew the best and cared little for the rest. These are not the technologically repentant souls who have returned to restore the balance of power. On the contrary, they are the displaced citizens of Rome celebrating the return of power to the emperor, even though his robes bear the crimson stain of bloodshed that is not easily washed away. Resurrection and enlightenment do not necessarily go hand in hand, and these candidates for evolution and ascension are here to discover what they once before overlooked.

The flag wavers believe in centralized power. They believe it is the job of the less fortunate to serve the more fortunate, for if that were not the case, it would certainly have been the other way around. If flag waving were an art, these people would be at the head of their class, for they will uphold their banner no matter how weighty, tattered or bloodstained it becomes. They believe that those who stand beside their banner also stand beside their country. They believe in righteousness and truth. But what of those who stand elsewhere? Is the rest of the world wrong?

The flag wavers are a fighting lot. They are descendants of warriors and are unafraid of the frontlines or the casualties of war. A good cause is worth fighting for; it is worth defending—or so they will tell you today. But their sons and daughters are not as certain, and the gods of war are not as strong as they once were. The flag wavers sing the battle hymn of the republic; they pray to God, praise Jesus in heaven and pay the taxes that grow the coffers of war. But is the rest of the world still wrong?

The world is not right or wrong, and the flag wavers are not without merit. The world is askew and at odds with itself, struggling to awaken from a dream that threatens to become a nightmare of repetition. Incapable of finding balance or unity, humanity worships boundaries, prejudices and laws. The stars that number fifty may soon fall from the sky; finding little favor in heaven, they belong to the kingdom of men. The stripes of color crimson now stain those numbered in white. Unable to stand side by side much longer, they will fail the test of time.

As the pendulum passes over the kingdom of the flag wavers, it will uphold its glory once more. The flag will be raised in ceremony and heralded by all parties of the republic during the season of campaigns. Those you call the forefathers will watch and wait and listen. Those who call upon angels will fill the halls with faith, and those who cast their vote will do so on Earth as they do in heaven. The Earth must be united in voice, in resource and in intent. The desire must be decisive rather than divisive, for one vote less than a miracle will bring one less year of peace.

The prophecies that surround this time are many, but those recently born under the banner of integrity are still in their infancy. The power is still with the people; commend them and remind them that the end is not yet as near as they would like, although it is in sight. Let your flags be one with mine then, and may your colors be those of Earth. May your flags fly over all the world united in one cause, unfurled in a symbol of peace and ensconced with the desire for love.

THE DOMAIN OF THE ZEALOTS

If the zealots are in your corner, so much the better; but if they are not, it is better still. A paradox of sorts is presented in these words, but that is what a zealot is, if nothing else. Zealots are very enthusiastic, particularly when they are rallied 'round a cause, but their tactics can be excessive and their words often hide a sword. Zealots are lobbyists, pundits and critics by nature. They are the voice of authority and the experts in their field—but whose microphone have they borrowed today and which flag adorns their stage? Zealots love to be in the public eye, and your cause might very well become their forum of expression. Their voice is well developed, but their individual ideas are not as strong. They find safety in numbers and are more comfortable when those numbers are accompanied by dollar signs in front of them. Zealots are modern-day "guns for hire," and to the highest bidder go the spoils.

The domain of the zealots is strewn with hidden land mines, and a misstep in this arena can be fatal. Zealots cause the rise and fall of tides, ideas and men. They are conservators of idolatry, fanatically worshiping the rising tide while secretly preparing for a drought. Zealots preach to the already converted.

Perhaps better than most, they understand the path of least resistance, which coincidentally also leads to the halls of power.

The halls of power are lonely places, where hunger, cunning and greed rule. They must be approached cautiously and with great care, as they have been known to consume even the bravest of men. In the wild, it is best to hire a guide to accompany you by night; in the domestically tame but feral halls of power, the company of a zealot is highly recommended. Zealots are odds-making, claim-jumping veterans of war. They will tell you how it is because they once knew how it was. Zealots are campaign managers, publicists and newsworthy folk. They can cite statistics, surveys and trends as easily as the best recipes for apple pie and homegrown tomatoes.

Zealots are hired by the power behind the power. Campaign trails are notoriously fraught with dangerous pitfalls designed to trip up even the savviest candidate. Therefore, those who wield the power behind the scenes also arm the zealots, who would otherwise be toothless and weaponless. It is the zealots' job to make certain that their candidate is heard above the cacophonous, jarring and often unpleasant remarks of the opposition. Zealots arouse enthusiasm; they encourage people to make greater efforts than they otherwise would. They stimulate creativity and provoke rancor and resentment—but whose?

Zealots sell stereotypical products in the form of candidates for public office. There is little that is presented to you that was not well planned early on. What you see before you today was molded and shaped beforehand, based upon which product you would most likely buy given certain parameters including economic trends and world events. Zealots are shape shifters on the stage of public opinion. They are interested in your opinion as long as it supports their platform, which is most often based upon erroneous knowledge and irrational feelings. This puts you at a disadvantage, given the fact that you believe you are creating your reality moment by moment.

Zealots are also beings much as yourselves, who have ceased to listen to their own voices because they have become overly accustomed to having others speak for them. These very specific types of zealots listen to one radio station, watch one news channel, favor one newspaper over another, predominantly visit one website, read one editorial, condemn the choices of the less informed—and still insist they are free agents for change. The pendulum will soon glide through the domain of the zealots evenly and without prejudice. Can you do the same?

THE HIERARCHY OF THE SOLVENT AND THE INSOLVENT

The hierarchy of the solvent and the insolvent was previously known as the land of the haves and have-nots, but that was before election-year rhetoric adopted its own version of a new and improved paradigm. Solvency means that you have enough money to cover both expenses and debts, but insolvency only relates to your ability to pay your debts. Someone who is insolvent is also bankrupt but not legally so, because only a judge can declare or rule on this. What does all this have to do with campaigns and elections? It depends upon whether you can afford to shake the candidate's hand, because his or her handshake is for sale along with his or her autographed photo, postcard and vote. Some say that a president cannot be bought at any price, but is that really true? Isn't anything for sale as long as the price is right? If you can't buy a president, can you buy a senator, a congressman or a governor?

These questions might finally be answered by the time the ink is dry on the ballots and the choices that rest upon them find their way to you. The solvent and the affluent understand that their fortune, at least in part, rests in their ability to curry favor with politicians, campaigners and forward movers. They know that an extended hand does not always await a handshake—sometimes it expects a donation, and the biggest donors get the best treatment, followed by corporate executives, lawmakers, industry regulators and others who willingly fork over cash in exchange for face-to-face time.

Access to power and public office has always been for sale, but as with all things, it once was more affordable than it is today. Donors know that when they have an issue or a concern, an elected official will take their call. Will the switchboard also put your call through? Those who are solvent and wish to remain so are paying close attention to one of the oldest and most favored political pastimes: courting influence and buying access. Those who are less than solvent or even insolvent will attend the same parties, luncheons, dinners and concerts as the solvent ones—but can their hopes be the same?

A common phrase says, "Follow the money." But what if you cannot? What if the trail has gone cold? Those who think of themselves as insolvent because they have allowed themselves to be measured within the context of a scale that is no longer accurate must find a new measuring stick. The haves own the world, but try as they might, they have not found a way to take it with them. That is one reason these same beings continue to incarnate into different aspects within the same families. They have yet to understand the meaning of true abundance and prosperity. Wealth cannot teach this, but neither can poverty.

The hierarchy of the solvent and the insolvent offers many lessons. It is a bit like a university, offering undergraduate programs to some and graduate and doctorate programs to others. The purpose of a hierarchy is not for one to learn his or her place within the scheme of things; it is to discover that the hierarchy was designed to be of benefit to all. Your government was designed with the same ideal, but it is succumbing under the pressure of its own weight. Unable to lift itself from the debacle it is mired in and unwilling to admit its disastrous defeat at its own hands, it humiliates itself by receiving the handouts of those who now feed it. In the back alleys of its memories, it still remembers how it once fed the hungry, long before it became addicted to its own gluttony.

THE FIELD OF INCONSISTENCIES

The field of inconsistencies belongs to the unknown soldier. Who is the unknown soldier? No one knows for sure, but many claim to know him by name and to have shaken his hand at some point, if memory serves. Inconsistencies contradict one another; they go bump in the night and then appear in the morning paper. Inconsistencies are unpredictable and unreliable; they instigate conflict and cannot be counted upon to produce the same result more than once. The field of inconsistencies breaks rules, principles, traditions and expectations. It offers no common set of values and always stands for the variable in any equation.

The field of inconsistencies spreads its blanketlike impressions in all directions, bringing doubt, fear and unease to those who depend upon the pat and the mundane. If you are a candidate for office, the field of inconsistencies will find you and your past as well. It is no use hiding from it, for like a nexus, it will make the connections and links you have worked so hard to suppress. The field of inconsistencies is like the grim reaper to some and the new dawn to others. Only the swing of the pendulum can determine what this field will bring to your door.

The field of inconsistencies belongs to everyone. It is the court of both public approval and appeal. It is the domain of the restless, and it is where questions that have no answers await another turn at bat. Underdogs who have little chance of beating the odds pray to the gods of inconsistencies while they dig for even a small bone. On the other hand, those who are only slightly ahead of their opponents scurry about the same field, retracing their steps in an effort to stay one step ahead of those who are determined to throw dirt before they throw in the towel.

The field of inconsistencies draws everyone in eventually; its gravitational field is much too strong for even the strongest of wills to resist. The media knows this place well, as its members vie against one another to be the first on the scene of the accident they helped cause. They will call an ambulance and help carry the stretcher as long as they can photograph and interview the injured along the way. But do not count on them to administer the anesthesia; easing pain is not what brought them there to begin with.

How can you use this field to your advantage? Its unpredictability belongs to the realm of possibility. It is raw and chaotic, untamed and adventurous. It is the Wild West, energetically speaking, a proving ground that cannot be contained or manipulated. It will test the mettle of those who seek to use it to their advantage, but it is an honest and level playing field. When you are uncertain about a direction, be it a vote in an upcoming election or another anomaly of conscience, bring your concern to the field of inconsistencies. You might be met with a whirlwind of superfluous thoughts and ideas, but they will not disappoint you. They will stimulate the creative flow within you while becoming an astringent to the many voices that clamor for your attention. But a word of caution must accompany this invitation: If you vacillate, do not do so here. You can indeed have it both ways, but not here, because it is a field of inconsistent opposites rather than a complementary field of unity. If you seek a palace of quiet and luxurious unity, this is not the place for you.

THE VALLEY OF THE COMPLAINERS

A complainer is someone who is unhappy about something and expresses this unhappiness habitually. It is a time-honored tradition that those who complain the loudest do the least—unless there is a campaign at stake, in which case complainers and complainants are in demand and hard at work. A complainant is a person or organization who takes action, usually legal, against another. These individuals are masters of statistics and can manage and manipulate their memory to serve up the complex as easily as the mundane in both argument and rebuttal. Every campaign needs complainers, because if there were none, the status quo would emerge as the victor and too few dollars would change hands. Campaigns stimulate pocketbooks as much as they do public policy, and it is the job of the complainers to churn the money so it will flow in the desired direction.

Complainers are experts in their field and they know just how to capitalize upon a misspoken word or misquoted statistic. There are many amateur complainers as well, and these can be found gathered around dinner tables, in coffee houses and in local pubs. Interestingly, it is the main job of complainers to tell their rivals that they have little or nothing to complain about. Why? Because that is exactly how they stimulate the litany of problems and complaints that have been lurking in the minds and under the skin of their opponents, waiting for an opportunity to escape and be heard. If a husband or a wife, for instance, tells his or her spouse that he or she has nothing to complain about, what effect does that have upon the moment?

It is the job of the complainer to make sure that all complaints are heard, regardless of their merit or validity. Complainers are individuals who are easily incited and quick to raise their voices. After all, they reason that they are speaking for those who do not or cannot. They believe it is their civic and moral responsibility to do so, and if a few dollars are exchanged in the process that might influence policy later on, so much the better. Complainers are not good or bad; they simply give voice to the static undercurrents within a given society or culture. Complainers do not create issues—or so they would remind you—but they do divide rather than unite.

Complaints and complainers by and large resonate with the lower frequencies of the third dimension. It is not that other dimensions offer no cause to complain, for indeed they do, but they also offer satisfying solutions, adjustments and answers.

How can you tell if you are in the company of a true complainer? Suggest a topic such as your job or your relationship, for instance. Tell your companion that you are feeling dissatisfied with your ability to communicate how you feel in these environments. Without asking for specific advice or guidance, wait and see what his or her response is. Does it bring you peace? Does it incite you to take action in a direction you had not previously contemplated? Do you feel as though only change can make your situation better? Thank your companion for his or her response and see if the conversation concludes easily enough. If it does not, take care that you do not fall prey to the frequency of complaint, for it is more difficult to escape its gravitational pull than you might imagine.

Complaining doesn't solve anything and it seems so useless, even though most of us do it. Do we just like to hear ourselves talk?

If one complains to someone who can do something about the complaint (including yourself), then the situation is solved. The difficulty with humanity is that it has become commonplace to complain for the sake of complaining, either because the complaint has not yet been solved or because there is no conscious intent to resolve the problem. A complaint becomes an invisible address to Spirit, because it has been stuffed down into a lower frequency, ignored or turned into stress.

If your complaints have good cause, then so be it. Do not dismiss them or sit idle with them. Give them volume, move them forward into the light, so they can be acted upon rather than acted out. Most complaints have no remedies because they are little more than unmanifested desires. A complaint that is not addressed or resolved belongs to the world of density, because shining light upon it immediately raises its vibration and increases the odds that a solution might be found.

HOW LIGHT AND DARK INTERACT

How do the light and the dark figure into the equation of this campaign? Does the dark believe that it can pull off the same shenanigans and manipulations that have worked in the past? Isn't it true that throughout history, from massive darkness, the light eventually emerges?

Yes, that is exactly as it has been throughout history, but you are not living in history; you are living in an unprecedented moment of Now. There are only certain aspects of you who think in terms of time. These aspects of you are subject to repeat history, but others are not. You are not here to make history but to design a future. If you cross one timeline or reality with another, you alter both pasts. If you continue to cross timelines, you will eventually discard aspects of yourself that are only interested in past history. They will burn themselves up. It is safe to say that humanity has already crossed more than one timeline; therefore, the past no longer exists as it once did. If time were linear (as it is for some), you would have a past, a present and a future, and every time you had a future thought, you would also have a past one to balance or acknowledge the first. Difficult as it may be to imagine, you have no real past.

The light and the dark are two forces that only seem to be in opposition. That is the illusion, and you must learn to see beyond this. Both are purposeful and purposeless, depending on where you stand. In this campaign, the dark is battling the light and the dark. How interesting is that? Why would the dark battle itself? Because candidates who run unopposed rarely remain victors! The dark, as you call it, does not see the light as a true obstacle or an equal contender, so it is even willing to battle itself in order to maintain the illusion of supremacy. Remember that the dark does not think of itself as dark, and at the same time, it has little interest in what you call the light. But even within the darkest corridors and the most closed circles, there is dissension in the ranks. Some wish the dark would be darker, whereas others wish it would be less dark (sinister). Still others simply wish it would be more creative and less predictable than it is, finding less joy in the game than ever before. So the dark is waging a campaign against itself just to keep things interesting, and it is even prepared to vote against itself if necessary.

The dark (your word) is not at all interested in its past shenanigans; it is much more sophisticated now. It has seen that the light has spread and taken note that it itself has not. It learns, evolves and prepares for the next campaign very quickly. It now draws upon its resources differently. It will use its energy in more unique but invisible ways. This is a dark year, politically speaking, and who is on what side will be less than obvious. But remember, even a very dark, cold and heavy iron skillet placed upon a stove is given warmth and light by the small flame that endures underneath. When water touches a sponge, the sponge absorbs it until it would seem that the water has disappeared altogether, but a sponge becomes saturated very quickly and the water soon gains its release. As light moves outward from Source, it eventually encounters density and is initially absorbed by it, but it is the light that fuels the dark, and if you forget this, you will become more confused and disappointed than ever.

But isn't it true what they say, that if you forget the past, you are condemned to repeat it?

Yes, that is what they say. But what do you say? Perhaps that is more important.

Will enough of us emerge from the malaise of manipulation and collective amnesia that has so afflicted humanity?

There is no more effective or insidious tool than ignorance. Collective light is on the verge of awakening, and although light cannot be manipulated, it can be deflected. It is important to stay the course and sturdy the vessel while—or until—life defines and reveals itself to you. For some this means sitting and waiting and waiting and sitting, and for others it means action, action and action. Do not judge, do not compare and do not write this year or event off as you have in the past. For instance, do not think this is yet another time that Spirit has let you down, that your guides have abandoned you, that your family has been unyielding or your friends unsupportive and so on, because then it will take you that much longer to regain your balance and compose your next creative thought. It is good to dream, but it is equally good to be awake and creative. Know that all is well and have certainty in that which you are while you take refuge in what your soul offers to you.

REALITY HAS NO PRECEDENT FOR YOU

It seems like you are telling us to get past the paradox of illusion so that we can create a reality beyond what linear time has offered us thus far. Is that a little like getting out of our own way?

Yes, somewhat. But for the most part, when teachers such as my own beingness have suggested that you create your own reality, it has amounted to little more than finger painting on the wall. This is not meant as a criticism but as an observation. Reality has no precedent for you, because timelines have been crossed and you have no real past to draw upon. That is apparent; a new paradigm can have no past. But how is it created, then? It must be inserted, encoded or awakened within you so as to replace what you believe about yourselves. That is what your DNA is doing now, but not as quickly as you would like. In the meantime, you are experiencing anomalies and disturbances in your morphogenetic fields, which affect your development and transition as a species.

Creating your own reality sounds very appealing and ideal. It sounds a little like something you might read in a travel brochure that promises experiences almost too good to be true. So you buy a one-way ticket to this paradise island nation, but then you realize that you don't speak the language or understand the proper units of exchange. What will you do? Sit idle, hire a tour guide, teach yourself the language or go home? That is what you are deciding now, and the programs and illusions of the past are of no use to you. The new paradigm is not simply about a new reality, not any more than it is a custom-designed vacation in paradise. It is about true discovery of selfhood. It is about true becoming. It is about wisdom descending within and expanding without.

THE MEDIA IS WHAT IT IS

Will the media play a significant role in this election?

No more or less than usual. The media is what it is and does what it does. Its purpose was once well defined, but that is no longer the case. It is the media's job to keep you informed via various forms of mass communication including television, radio, magazines, newspapers and the Internet. It is not the media's job to control or to be controlled. The media does not belong to the dark or to the light. These are the gnats and the flies and the ants and the honeybees in the ointment. They compete for your vote of confidence as much as your local politicians do and offer more or less the same type of promises. The media has a left hand and a right hand, but these rarely work together, because both bypass the heart in an effort to overwhelm and distort the other.

This election year will be more mediagenic than ever before; it has been designed to be appealing and attractive to the media in an effort to gain the most favorable exposure possible. Candidates wine and dine the media; they bait their hooks with expensive perks and watch the feeding frenzy begin. Can you find unbiased and untainted media coverage?

It depends upon your ability to identify and distinguish what is fair, accurate and balanced from what is not. It is not as easy as you might think, given your own biases.

THE VOTING SYSTEM HAS ALREADY BEEN MANIPULATED

Will the voting system be tampered with in the upcoming presidential election?

It has already been manipulated. Specific centers within your brain are being impulsed to act with undue prejudice, given particular influences and inducements. These correlate to specific target words, phrases, pictures and other stimuli known to illicit a precise response. This technique is not new, but it has only recently been introduced to the mainstream populace. You are being conditioned to think, act and react in specific ways. This method is not unlike hypnosis, but its effects are longer lasting and less detectable. It is seamless, nearly transparent and quite effective.

Are you saying that the election results have already been determined?

No, not at all. I am saying that you are being influenced to behave in a certain manner in relation to the upcoming election. This should come as no surprise; you are unfairly influenced each and every day to respond in prejudiced and predisposed ways. The advertising industry makes certain that you act in subjective rather than objective ways. There is much at stake in any campaign, but perhaps even more so in this one. The human mind is not very clever; it can easily be subverted and then converted. It is very predictable, and that is exactly what the subliminal experts have staked their reputation on. This is why it is especially important to develop an awakened consciousness at this time. Intelligence alone is no match against subliminally altering mind techniques. They have been tested again and again, and the results have been consistent and astoundingly successful.

I'm sorry, but I'm still having difficulty with this answer. I guess I want to believe that we are smarter than that, smarter than them. What can we do to change this?

You are smarter but you are not wiser, at least not yet. And by the way, you are "them," at least a part of you is, which is the first step in solving this enigma. Again, this has very little to do with intelligence and everything to do with consciousness. Intelligence can be determined and extended by certain exercises familiar to the brain and its activities. Consciousness expands as one gradually escapes the confines of the linear mind. The mind is predictable, consciousness is not. The mind believes that it is separate; consciousness understands and seeks unity. By nature campaigns divide; they do not unite. They divide parties, people, platforms and policy by making you choose sides; they offer you this or that, not this and that.

As long as you remain in an "us against them" place within yourselves, you will manifest the same reality without. These are the laws that govern this world; this is what you are here to transcend. In order to change the current electoral process, you must shift your reality; a simple change of mind will not do. It takes great courage to recognize that regardless of which candidate wins, the consciousness of the planet will continue to expand. Consciousness does not belong to the win/lose politics of one election; it belongs to the ever-expanding soul of humanity. That is why it is called unity consciousness.

POSTPONING THE ELECTION?

I have already seen several trial balloons from the current administration regarding the possibility of postponing or even canceling the election if there is a terrorist attack before then. The media has also reported that government intelligence advisers have reason to believe that an attack may be imminent. How real are these fears and what is behind them?

If you were on a sports team and your best (or only) player was injured, you would hope that the game would be rained out or otherwise postponed. That is not usually possible in an election—unless, of course, extraordinary circumstances prevail. What you have seen thus far is exactly what you have called it, a trial balloon designed to see how such a statement would be received. For the most part, it was not taken seriously. After all, who would do such a thing; it seems almost unfathomable, does it not?

It is likely that there may be an attack scheduled to coincide with the upcoming election, but whether it is a true act of terrorism is yet to be seen. Remember that it is the supremacy behind the perceived authority that wields true power. It is not necessarily a postponement that they seek. Rather, it is the continuation of a program that has already been in effect, one that relies upon fear and a dependency upon protection from those in positions of authority. It is the government's job to govern, but it is the supremacy's job to rule. Be vigilant, aware and without fear, and you will not be easily swayed.

CONDITIONING THE PUBLIC FOR A DRAFT

I have teenage sons and daughters. I've heard rumors that the draft will be reinstated. How likely is that?

It is likely, but not timely. It makes for poor party politics, for who would wish to endorse it with a possible election on the line? It is still off in the distance a bit, although rumors will continue to circulate and even escalate. Elected officials will begin by endorsing educational reform while stressing the importance of community and civic responsibility. Young people (younger than you think) will be encouraged to take an active interest in the needs and affairs of their town or city. They might be asked, for instance, to volunteer their time and effort in areas that are experiencing shortages due to budget limitations, such as the local library. Cutbacks might also see emergency response teams suffer, making emergency first-aid and CPR classes a school requirement. Seems harmless enough and even beneficial, yes?

Volunteer programs, especially those that offer school and college credit, will become popular, which will create competition among students for the most desirable posts. Almost too soon, the programs will become official. They will receive the endorsement of government administrators, who will appoint someone to manage and expand the programs so that all students will have an opportunity to contribute to their community and do their "civic duty." Eventually—and for reasons that will seem unclear at the time—these programs will come under the direction of those who head civil defense under the auspices of homeland security.

Every city and most towns will have civil defense agencies and offices; these will coincidentally be located next to or near other recruiting facilities. Civil defense volunteers will be trained to help the armed forces, police, hospital personnel and first responders in case of a local emergency or natural disaster and/or in the event of a national emergency, such as a war. It will be postulated that civil defense agencies are no more than back-door recruiters for the armed forces. Public outcry will lead to legal debates, and this will slow the process for a time. Those who argue in favor of the programs will restate the many opportunities to serve that do not involve military service, but if these positions are filled and already have extensive waiting lists, how else will the requirements be satisfied?

ANY TRUTH TO PROPHECIES ABOUT THE PRESIDENT?

Please excuse the inappropriateness of this question, but I have heard rumors and prophecies regarding the current president. Some of these indicate that there might be an attempt to assassinate him. Is there any truth to this? I have also heard that he is afraid of ghosts. Would you comment on that as well?

Your current president has heard these rumors as well and is monitoring them even more closely than you, as you might imagine. He is conceivably anxious and troubled by them, perhaps more so than other sitting presidents have been. Over and above the usual security detail accorded to such a noble position, precautions and measures are ordered each and every time he travels, especially abroad. He is not without enemies, but he is also not without friends, and these are in significant positions of power. There is a team of intelligence professionals specifically dedicated to rooting out all hoaxes and following up on even the most casual threat or misguided innuendo.

As to the accuracy of the prophecies, it depends more upon whether he believes them than whether you do. He is capable of drawing the scent of fear to him or away from him. By striking contrast, he is also able to draw fear to the land he governs or away from it, a choice he contemplates daily. Within these words lies the answer to your question, at least partially so. The energetic odds of the prophecies surrounding this president rise and fall along with the odds of his reelection.

Furthermore, the prophecy states that there will be an attempt on his life; it does not indicate whether or not it will be successful. Scholars such as those who study the Bible Code are searching for answers in all available resources, and upon the president's recent trip to the Vatican, a unique and specific request to view certain antiquated manuscripts was granted.

For obvious reasons, he would not admit to being afraid of ghosts, but those within his inner circles would concede that he has expressed very little interest in the supernatural. There are areas within the White House that remain unvisited by him, although one could logically assume that his busy schedule might be the cause of this.

What Can We Do?

I hate to be the one to ask the last question, so I'll try to make it as broad as possible. What lesson can we take from all that is happening on the world stage that we could also apply to our own lives? What can we do to make the world a better and safer place to live in?

The events of the forthcoming months will seem significant to some and ordinary to others. For a while, it will be a time of sitting and waiting and waiting and sitting. It might be difficult to distinguish light from dark, and at times they will seem as one, both purposeful and purposeless. Because all that is ALL and All That Is all is light, it will seem that darkness masquerades as light. As light touches density, it is at first absorbed by that density. When water touches a sponge, it is absorbed by that sponge, and it would seem that the water has been consumed and is no longer, but it has only changed its form for a moment or perhaps a moment longer.

During this time, you will be distracted by campaigns of politics and campaigns for war. The distractions will be many, and the campaigns that others put forth might be in conflict with your own, especially the campaigns of loved ones. It is a challenging time of shifting energies and realities, and it will be more important than ever not to write this time period off with indifference, for if you do, it will require more effort to regain the balance you do not sustain now. Draw upon resources that are deep within, those you have been saving for an emergency. Those who have not yet discovered who they are will follow anyone and anything that even resembles leadership, be it public or private.

Resist the temptation and urges of others if they are not aligned with your truth. Be outspoken when necessary, reticent when need be. Stay the course.

Imagine (for real) that you are running for election and that the voters and constituents you depend upon are your friends, colleagues, family members, associates and enemies. It is very important that you make this as real as possible, so stake something important on it, like your spiritual evolvement or ascension. What campaign promises would you make to yourself and to others? What are you willing to stand for and risk your life for? Assuming that you are elected, you will soon be inaugurated and asked to swear that you are prepared and willing to uphold the truth that you stand for. If asked to do so, would you? Would you ask more of others than you would ask of yourself? What could you accomplish in your first one hundred days in office? Is it not well worth igniting the pilot in order to find out?

With many words behind us, I take my leave and bid you do the same, broadening your perspectives and expanding your ideals as you do. May the sunrise welcome you, the horizon sustain you and the sunset restore you.

28

Patriots, Citizens and Warriors

October 2004

I have heard that the Patriot Act in effect reverts our system of government from common law to civil or Roman law. I have also heard that Patriot Act II is already in print and support for it is being sought from those who are not afraid of being labeled conservative. Is this true? Can you explain how this bill would affect ordinary citizens such as myself? Is there a difference between a citizen and a patriot? Do you have any influence over matters such as these, especially when it seems that they would benefit humankind?

Rome is still considered one of the grandest empires that ever was. It presented a great spectacle in the historic chain of nations it acquired, conquered and controlled. Rome extended its government, its laws and its language in all directions. All who came under Roman rule were subject to its power and sway, and those who attempted to throw off any measure of imperial authority were treated as rebels and criminals against a lawful dominion. Unfortunately, Rome's efforts to preserve its immense territories as its natural and legitimate heritage led to its eventual demise.

THE POWER OF ROME AND THE FORMATION OF ROMAN LAW

Praetors governed Roman city-states; these were magistrates who ranked below consuls and acted as chief officers of state law. Common law is based upon precedent, but as little precedent existed in the newly acquired territories, most cases belonged in special categories. Praetors had the authority to devise new rules and orders as applicable to the cases brought before them. If an old law afforded no remedy, new laws that accommodated the changing wants of a society were enacted.

All new laws were made to conform to the Roman spirit of conservatism. Customs that had no previously ascribed institutions or traditional practice defined the era, and one-time decisions soon became law. It was the custom for praetors, upon entering office, to publish an edict, which was a formal proclamation declaring the principles upon which they intended to administer justice. This practice was designed to make the praetor appear impartial and just to the general populace, but this did not render him immune from special interests or dispensations of favor. In time the adopted laws became a body of edictal law, as well established and as authoritative as if they had received the express sanction of judicial legislation.

Edictal law sprang from the spontaneous acts and opinions of a progressive and growing society, but far from being considered final, edicts were sometimes merely preliminary acts to further proceedings. This liberal form of administering justice became a form of civil law under Roman dominion. Foreign states that had formed treaties with Rome received more favorable treatment than others, and their citizens enjoyed greater civil rights as well.

Eventually, the law of Rome came to be called the Law of Nations, and from this the more popular Law of Contracts was born. Under the Law of Contracts, laws for buying and selling, hiring and loaning, as well as laws that involved slavery and indentured or involuntary servitude were introduced into Roman civil law. Magistrates and praetors were elected (appointed) annually, and the newly elected rarely knew or were made aware of the decisions of their predecessors. Consequently, any fixed principles of law were less than desirable and sometimes missing altogether, especially as each subsequent magistrate was not bound by the decisions of his predecessor. In short, Roman law began as a shapeless and unwieldy mess.

THE DECLINE OF CIVIL LAW INTO THE TYRANNY OF MEN

As time progressed, Roman jurists, the true architects of Roman law, reduced volumes of laws into a manageable system that later came to be called European law. Under European law, opinions became treatises and a council of jurists became a judex. It was the judex that adopted the practice of authenticating, under seal, the unanimous opinions that were made into law. Jurists, whose privileged opinions exerted paramount influence over the innumerable treatises they wrote, gave birth to Roman jurisprudence. Unfortunately, by then the glory of the republic already belonged to the past. Under the new empire, military power, which during the republic was kept in subordination to civil power, could be put above the civil authority by the emperor himself at any time. The emperor's very title reflected his military supremacy.

The emperor, who exercised uncontrolled legislative authority, declared the new application of Roman law necessary as required by an ever-changing and expanding populace. This more ample interpretation of justice, called universal dominion, reflected the peculiarities of Roman society but deviated from the narrow rules of earlier days. This system closely resembled imperialism, the extension of power or authority over others in the interest of political, military or economic domination, but was applied differently. At the time, the clergy held a virtual monopoly on legal knowledge, as they were learned and literate whereas others were not.

The great republic was almost forgotten by then, and the power of the emperor reigned supreme. The jurists, who held little favor with the emperor, were made to write legal opinions that supported imperial authority. Under a theory of absolutism, the judex invented a fictional authority called the *lex regia*, by which it was pretended that all of the authority imbued within the Roman populace was irrevocably granted to the emperor. When the judex succumbed to the power of the emperor, the die was cast and the profession of law was born under less than auspicious skies. Chief functionaries, or lawyers, were trained to uphold principles of imperial policy, and the administration of law capsized under imperial authority and rule in both theory and practice. Open courts disappeared, and all appeals fell upon the deaf ears of the emperor and his imperial court. Despotism, a cruel and arbitrary use of power, was disguised as law and offered as justice.

Much later, in the first half of the sixth century, a commission was appointed to compile the most valuable laws into a code. This fifty-volume compendium of Roman civil law created by the order of Emperor Justinian was completed in only three years. Also called the Pandects, or Digest, it contained the literal transcripts of thirty-nine previous jurists. It quickly became a necessary part of legal education in the schools of the time, having been designed as a tool for the practitioner of law, but its detailed complexities required a previous knowledge of law in order to understand it, and again it needed reform.

The next generation, or simplification, of the Digest was called the Institutes and contained civil law as it has come to be known in modern times. The Institutes embodied the principles and ideas of ancient Rome and included modifications of progress "as required by the enlightened spirit of the age." Although the system of law was modernized and improved under the empire, it was also changed from one that suited the liberty of the average citizen to one that suited an arbitrary power at the discretion of appointed or elected judges.

COMMON LAW AND CIVIL LAW

Under common law, former decisions control the court unconditionally, and fixed rules of decision protect both rights and property from perpetual doubt and controversy. By contrast, the principles established in civil law are not as fixed

or certain, as they govern the case at hand without establishing the set principle involved. These fluctuations make it possible for a judge to decide a case
according to his personal views of the law rather than its relative merit. The
judges' opinions and commentaries might be as varied as the diversity and spectrum of human judgment.

Common law and civil (Roman) law are both subject to manipulation
because they are laws of men based upon arguments posed by a linear mind. By
nature the mind is subject and accustomed to the rule of opposites, which produces winners and losers. Common law tends to uphold as authority the judg-
ments of causes that have already been decided. Civil law allows judicial interpretations, commentaries and opinions to be entered as fact, giving them more
authority than they would otherwise have.

There is and will continue to be a subtle movement toward civil law because
of the diversity in opinion and lack of precedent for the times you are living in.
Advocates of civil law will state that as long as a judiciary body is composed of
doctors of equal degree and authority, previous precedent is irrelevant and of little value. Opposed will be laureates who believe that even professors of such a
noble science as law will be unable to resolve the doubts that will arise as a
result of moving from one form of law to another. The result will be that the
previously solemn voice of the law speaking through the courts will not be as
final as it once was. Instability, fluctuations and deviations from generally
approved practice will draw appeal after appeal. Decisions will be made and
then overturned by the next court only to be bounced back again for reasons of
both excess and lack.

Practical jurisprudence, known for publicly regulating the affairs of society,
will begin to include private interpretations at the arbitrary discretion of those
who believe they are upholding the principles of an evolving society. Advances
in forensic science, for instance, will cause former decisions to be disregarded in
favor of newer ones. Current expert testimony will overrule past precedent, and
the outcome of even the simplest case will be difficult to foretell with any
amount of confidence.

Currently, judges determine questions of law, whereas juries determine questions of fact, but it will become increasingly difficult to separate one from the
other, and the administration of justice will suffer. The obligations and rights of
those involved will be more difficult to define, which, in turn, will lead to the
admission of improper evidence. If this is accepted rather than rejected, security
will become an issue and there will be cause for new definitions of law to be considered. This is where the law "Uniting and Strengthening America by Providing
Appropriate Tools Required to Intercept and Obstruct Terrorism Act of 2001," or
USAPA—colloquially called the Patriot Act—will begin its rise to infamy.

THE BLIND RUSH TO THE PATRIOT ACT

Legislative proposals as countermeasures to the terrorist attacks were introduced less than one week after the attacks, and the 342-page body of law called the Patriot Act was written, passed by a 98-1 vote in the U.S. Senate and a 357-66 vote in the U.S. House of Representatives and quickly signed into law within weeks of the events you call 9/11. In the aftermath of these direction-changing events, this law was introduced with great haste and passed with very little debate or amendment.

In point of fact, your current attorney general gave your Congress one week within which to adopt the bill into law, without changes. He warned of additional imminent attacks and managed to persuade those who already feared the worst that they could be blamed for future attacks against their own country if they did not immediately commit themselves to the task at hand. The few who took the time to study the Patriot Act realized early on that it did not provide traditional safeguards of civil liberties or any system of checks and balances to ensure that such a wide-sweeping portal of increased surveillance and investigative powers—as were being granted to law enforcement agencies—once opened, could be overseen or later closed.

Although September 11, 2001, will always stand as the obvious turning point in your current reality, it is important to remember that the Justice Department and those who oversee it had been lobbying for just such a law for at least four years prior to the events of that fateful day. Terrorism quickly became the convenient justification they had been looking for, and almost too soon, this ill-conceived thought became law. Critics of the law sprang up as preservers of the liberties of the common man, but their echoed voices were silenced as treasonous attempts to still providence while aiding terrorism.

Thus far the Patriot Act has only perplexed and bewildered the administration of justice. Its definition is rarely agreed upon, and even when it is, its application differs widely and is argued vehemently. Idle discussions of its subtleties have produced little more than theoretical distinctions. It has been criticized for not being narrow enough in its principles of interpretation, and it cannot be pretended that it protects either liberty or property. At best its law is a modification of primeval code with only token relationships between the branches of government. At worst it is the effacement of political freedom whose cost is the improvement of modern society. The Patriot Act is the vehicle of a monarchy limited by law rather than of a democracy. The security that it affords the institutions it protects is equal to the loss to any individual of any state of defense he or she might believe he or she has access to. Just as in ancient Rome, the fundamental text of the law is that the will of the prince has the force of the law.

In continental Europe's palatial courts of old, the prince successfully controlled the whole of the administration of justice by delaying or restricting the lay appeals from all inferior tribunals. Is this any different? Your current system of law espouses that it is the law and only the law that resists the encroachment of despotism, but in the absence of defined laws, where is the independent check on the use of arbitrary power? Long ago popular insurrection eventually allowed the populace to overthrow by force the excesses of the most notorious despots. History is not destined to repeat itself—unless, of course, you choose that it do so.

Most of you believe that your representative form of government, based upon the great fundamental principles put down by your Founding Fathers, is composed of various forms of democracy. Of your Bill of Rights it was once said that it consisted of such elementary principles as to be capable of indefinite development. But today it seems composed of little more than maxims, pithy sayings attributable to general rules more than succinct and proven truths. It has also been said that every nation that aspires after freedom should use this as a model for government—but is that still the case? Constitutional law has always asserted the supremacy of the law over the king. Is it still so?

Proponents of the changes required by the Patriot Act will tell you that the changing conditions of society prevail upon those in government to break away from the shackles of theory and technicality in order that justice can become more expedient. They say the new rights and privileges accorded by law are the obligations that spring from an ever-widening sphere of civilization and are in the permanent interest of a modern (post-9/11) society. Of natural justice, which should govern, they will say that it is impeded by technical limitations that offer too few solutions to apply. If questioned as to what a foreign jurisprudence would opine, they will argue that the point is moot based upon the fact that their shores are not the ones under attack. But if the soundness of evidence cannot be conclusive or if it is not supported by the research of law, then wisdom is nonexistent and law is based only upon the practice of an ill-developed science. Where is the protection of the individual against arbitrary power? Under which provision is its shield resting? Why is it sequestered from plain sight?

Secrecy and Patriot Act II

If you were unconsciously influenced by Patriot Act I, you will have another opportunity to view the possible effects of Patriot Act II before it is enacted into law. But you must be vigilant in the process, for such laws are often subject to passage in the wee hours of the night in the halls where only the surreptitious do not slumber. Sympathetic lawmakers have already been extracting some of its provisions and pasting them onto other pieces of legislation piecemeal. Therefore, at least five other bills currently pending before Congress also contain provisions from Patriot Act II.

Patriot Act II—better known as the "Anti-Terrorism Tools Improvement Act of 2003"—was discovered and made public just weeks before your country invaded the lands of Iraq. How will it affect ordinary citizens? Perhaps it is best studied with human eyes and ears, but for the sake of those whose eyes are turned inward or toward more spiritual panoramas, the following might be useful: This law strengthens other laws that allow government agencies to demand confidential records about patrons from businesses and individuals. It proposes stiff penalties for those who disclose that such a demand was made. It provides for an expansion of your government's powers regarding secret surveillance of both citizens and noncitizens. It grants the government more power to investigate people without probable cause and to do so under a cloak of secrecy. Those who knowingly violate the secrecy clause might be subject to imprisonment. Searches and seizures that would previously be considered unconstitutional would no longer be so. Citizens might have their citizenship revoked for having contributed material support or unknowing aid to others; this can be inferred from conduct and need not be manifested in words. If considered a threat to national security, legal residents might be deported instantaneously without evidence or criminal charge. Immunity such as that which could provide an incentive for neighbor to spy on neighbor would be offered and could pose further complications. The death penalty would be expanded to cover fifteen new offenses.

These are not small measures, but are they significantly different from what is already taking place below the radar of detection? Who and what is behind such draconian measures? It is not your president, although he is certainly a willing participant in this scheme. Currently, he is the one the world loves to hate, which makes it extremely easy for those of true wealth and power to hide in plain sight. No imagination can fathom how much control would be enough to satisfy the appetite of those who seek control for its own sake.

A Growing Divide between Patriot and Citizen

The difference between a patriot and a citizen was once very small, but that was before disgrace fell upon innocence and pleas for peace were rewarded with the castration of a nation. A citizen is someone who has the right to live in a country because she was born there or because he has been legally accepted by that country. A citizen also describes someone who lives an ordinary life in relative privacy and obscurity, rather than someone who is a member of the armed forces, a police officer or other public official. Citizens of long ago, such as those who lived within the city-states of ancient Rome, occupied certain duties and responsibilities that might be accorded to residents of a sovereign city and its surrounding territory. Today these formalities and customs amount to little more than respect for public and private property and such activities as might be considered law-abiding.

Patriotism explained most simply denotes pride and devotion to the country someone is born into or is a citizen of. It should end there, but does it? Today a patriot is someone who not only supports his or her country and its way of life but is also prepared to defend it. Patriots cannot help but feel that they have inherited certain rights and privileges from their forefathers (patriarchy) who have all but guaranteed them in writing. The patriots of ancient Rome were called patricians and were members of aristocratic families whose privileges included exclusive rights to offices and properties. These nonhereditary honorary titles were bestowed by emperors on people who had been of service to the empire. Long before twenty-first century patriots were en vogue, "patrists" enjoyed a popularity of their own. Patrists helped shape the Christian church and the writings it stood for. Early theologians such as Augustine and Ambrose wrote of the embodiment of pater, which later became support for the fatherland. Pater descended from the prefix *patri-* or *patro-*, meaning father or paternal. As expressed in the books of the Bible, a patriarch was considered to be an ancestor of the human race—hence the later symbolism relative to fatherhood—and a patriarchal culture is one in which men are the most powerful members.

I hold a great deal of sway over matters such as the ones encompassed by these words, especially as they relate to the evolution of consciousness within humankind, but it is of little consequence compared to the influence you exert with every breath you take, because you and others like you are here to empty the scales of injustice and restore balance to the scales of justice. My survival does not depend upon yours, but my sentience is related to your own. My vision is a sovereign one rather than an indentured one. Might I hope that yours is the same?

THE WORTH OF A WARRIOR

An old soldier, weary from battle and bloodshed, hurried home in an attempt to behold his sons and daughters one last time before death overtook him. He arrived just as his sons were preparing to enlist in the latest campaign. They greeted him warmly and saw to what comfort they could offer, as his misery was obvious. He bade them come close that he might gaze upon them more clearly and was startled to see his own youthful form reflected in their eyes. To each in turn he said, "Tell me the worth of a warrior."

The first son responded, "Why father, a warrior is a brave soldier, a man of arms. He is intrepid and a fearless combatant."

The second son said, "Father, a warrior is as brave as a lion and as fierce as a tiger. He is cunning like a snake, fast as a fish and possesses the keen vision of an eagle."

The third son answered, "A warrior is a hero, father. He is a champion and a paladin. He is as a knight, stalwart, gallant and valiant. He has courage and mettle; he is a real man."

The daughter looked angrily at her three brothers and then sadly upon her father who held death at bay for a little longer as he struggled to keep pace with her soft voice. "A warrior is nothing but a gamecock, father. He is such who would keep other men from being good husbands and fathers, and at the same time rob mothers of their sons."

The father coughed up a bit of blood, sputtering and suffering against odds for a few more breaths. He looked with compassion upon the youthful faces that represented a future beyond his own and said, "A warrior is someone who detests warfare and abhors combat. He does his utmost to settle hostilities and looks askance at conflict of word, fist or sword. A warrior is chary of confrontation, cautious in action and circumspect as he weighs the risks and consequences of his deeds—past, present and future. He is guarded and apprehensive when need be, but never distrustful or suspicious without proper cause. A warrior is Argus-eyed and observant lest he be at sleep instead of rest. A warrior avoids battle at all costs and diminishes all thought of contest; his bout is with his own conscience and not with that of another. He is charitable with those of smaller minds or larger burdens and exercises great patience without becoming cross. The warrior whom I describe bows to the authority who resides within his heart ere he offers his sword in service to any crown."

"Have you met such a man, Father?" asked one of his sons. "Does such a man exist?" said another.

"He exists in all of us," replied the father. "He is king among men, but rarely is he king above men. I have met him, befriended him, betrayed him and lost to him, only to discover him in robust health upon the next battlefield and encampment beyond that. Now I am weary and my time is at hand. All too soon will I cross the river of consciousness where I hope to rejoin my kin."

"Your words are sage, Father, but you have used the last of your breaths to favor these words and not others. Why?" asked his daughter, choking back tears.

"Because the warrior within asked it of me," said the father in words spoken more gently than he remembered from his own voice. "For too long a time I considered it an act of contrition. Remorse and guilt guided my hand and shame held my weapon. I knew duty and obligation, but the warrior was more genuine than I. Each time I buried him, I resolved to embrace him if given a next opportunity, but the mark eluded me and I deceived myself again and again. This past campaign was hard fought, with victors fewer than villains. Upon the battlefield I saw many fallen soldiers, too many to name and too few to recognize, but I saw no warriors there. I have made this long journey home to oblige him as I am morally bound to do. I am still in his debt but no longer in his shadow. I have brought him home to meet you. It is my hope that he will stay even if it is my time to go. Please welcome him as my guest and good relation. I hope that you will come to know him much better and much sooner than I."

The father's eyes closed, for the strain of speaking had taken its toll upon him. His eyes did not reopen in that life, but his last thoughts were as soft and gentle as the warm birth waters that welcomed him in his next life, his probing and alert eyes seeking the peaceful warrior from the start.

Your Money, Your Career and the Names of the Earth

November 2004

I have some projects in mind that I feel would benefit the Earth and humanity greatly, but I lack the funds to begin them. I have been told that the means to accomplish this work would be supplied in "creative and effortless ways," and I wonder if this could be indicative of winning the lottery. Since my intentions are honorable, would it be possible for you to supply me with the winning numbers?

Your mind is full of heart, and any and all projects that you can fathom are worth considering. A worthwhile project is one that inspires you, tugs at you and stirs you from within. It is good and wonderful that you have placed humanity and the Earth as your first cause, but this is unnecessary, and the rewards that you might reap have no basis in this premise. In fact, many valuable ideas and inventions began as little more than selfish desires.

THE FALSE DICHOTOMY OF GOOD AND EVIL

The universe (God/Source/All That Is) assumes that you are good. It could not assume otherwise. Good is not better than bad, and it is not the opposite of evil. Good is that which is; it is the constant within a universe of change. Good is why evolution exists; it is why knowledge leads to discovery. You were born to do good works and so was everyone else. Anonymous farmers feed your children, faceless workers collect your garbage and alert tax revenue collectors look askance when the obvious indicates that they should do otherwise. Humanity is goodness personified, and no indecent act would alter these words. Inevitable questions follow: "Why bother? If my ideas and good works are no better than those of the murderous gang members across town or the warmongers down the street, then why bother at all?"

No one is better or worse than anyone else, and no teacher worth his or her wheat would tell you otherwise. It is much more difficult to live with one lung than with one arm, but both are necessary and important to your body. Even in its current (flawed) condition, your body is a miraculous organism designed to fulfill many tasks, including sheltering the light that you are within a carefully constructed vehicle. The universe was created with the same devotion and care, and everything that exists within it is necessary and unique. If it were not, it would not exist.

This concept is more difficult to grasp than others, and most will be tripped up by it sooner or later. For instance, one can see that the Earth benefits by having butterflies, but does the Earth also benefit from cockroaches? Yes, it does, because diversity and proliferation within one species encourage the next to do the same. If the Earth had fewer cockroaches, it would also have fewer butterflies. Cockroaches are tenacious and enduring creatures; they have survived for century upon century. Can a lesson not be gleaned from such a being? They share their resources, survive on what others discard and do not make war upon their neighbors—but oh, how they are despised!

AGAINST THE FINENESS OF THE UNIVERSE, GOLD IS BUT DROSS

Your ideas are valuable because you are, not the other way around. You will do good works for humanity because of who you are, not because of what you do. Each breath that you take and each dream that you weave benefits humankind. Even so, history will not record your presence upon the Earth— not in this life. This time around, history is interested in recording deeds of a different nature. Does this influence whether your projects are worthwhile? I hope not.

It would seem that if a wheelbarrow of gold bricks were delivered to your door, everything would change, or if you sat on a mountain of dollars, you could alter your future. But that is not true, strange as it seems. The universe is constructed of a fine etheric fabric of silk; by contrast, gold and money would be considered sackcloth. The etheric web of life is an unlimited bank account that you can draw from. The key to this account is in remembering how to draw from it, and the great desire and yearning that you feel within are helping you to do just that.

I do not discourage you from believing in a lottery of reward. Insurmountable odds of winning breed a belief in the miraculous or the theory of something from nothing. These are very healthy ideas, but they are not your only option. The problem with the lottery is that every time someone wins, someone else feels as if he or she has lost. It is not a win-win situation, which makes it difficult to endorse. If you choose to believe that the lottery will assist your good works, then believe it all the way by knowing with certainty that whoever wins, your good deeds come that much closer to manifesting. Celebrate another's fortune as if it were your own, for in many ways it is. Be self-full in all things, including your desires. Wholeness contains selfishness and selflessness. It does not punish one and reward the other. The universe is whole, and so are you. Let your abundant spark come from this Source and you will find more answers than you have questions.

THE RIGHT DOOR IS THE ONE YOU FEEL

I am new to real-estate sales but considered a latecomer in this current market. Everyone says that business is booming and that I will have no trouble establishing myself, but so far it doesn't seem to be working out that way. I am willing to knock on as many doors as it takes, but it would be helpful to know which ones would be most receptive. If I call upon your energy before doing so, could you point me toward the right door?

The door that you truly seek is not the one you think—it is the one you feel. Your guides are better equipped than I to tap you on the shoulder, as it were, but they are silent on this subject as well, aren't they? Could it be that you have put your own intuition on the back burner while you learn and rehearse all that has been said to you about your new career? You are very talented, and more than one industry would welcome you should you adopt a different strategy at a later time, but this you must ponder and the fruit must still ripen—sour grapes make a poor substitute for sweet wine.

The reason that doors have not opened for you—yet—is that you have been listening to other versions of success and not your own. Is the last flower to bloom in a garden any less beautiful than those who have blossomed first? Perhaps by contrast it will stand out that much more. Is a minor but essential ingredient in a recipe any less important? Your intuition is much more than an inkling of an idea or a tickle of a clue; it is an asset worth cultivating and a force to be reckoned with. Your intuition is one of your greatest gifts, but until you acknowledge it as such, it will remain in the background along with the other rabble-rousing voices who scramble for your attention. I assure you that at this moment, you could not hear my voice above the rest. Shall I shake the ground under your feet instead? I believe I am doing just that!

REMEMBER YOUR POWERS

Long before you were granted a certificate of completion and a license that made you legally a professional, you were able to read hearts and settle minds. Do you remember? Before the adult world told you that the invisible was not real, you believed otherwise. Do you remember? Good luck charms were fun then, but today they are silly. Back then you danced with smiles and followed laughter. Why are there so many frowns in your life today?

"They" told you that it was time to grow up and stop playing around. They told you to get an education, and you did. They told you which pursuits were more important than others, and you listened. They told you which neighborhood to live in and what was in fashion. They told you when your waistline needed attention, or so they thought. They had so much to say, and you wanted to get it right, so you listened very intently. (Do you know who "they" are? I don't either, but they certainly have a lot to say, don't they?) The louder they got, the quieter you got. The more you followed their advice, the less your own mattered. And when they said you were wrong, you believed them. Why haven't they told you which doors to knock on? Could it be that they don't know?

Do not be bent over with concern any longer; stand up straight now. Allow your chakras to reinvigorate your energy and realign your spine. Hold your head high so that the geometry of your soul will be complete. Reclaim your inspiration so that your voice can find you again. Invite your intuition to return. Make a place of honor for it within you, for it deserves nothing less. Just for a time, make the outer world less important than the inner world so that you will once again become attuned to its subtleties. When they shout at you (and they will), blow them a kiss, say a prayer, send them a message in a bottle and follow that up with a splendid bouquet of flowers dressed up in a bright ribbon. It will be well worth the cost and the effort.

When you feel like you again, take a field trip with your guides. Canvass a few neighborhoods and knock on the best doors. If a smile greets you, be aware that disappointment or sadness might be hiding nearby. If a frown greets you, know that they have come calling here too. Listen to your intuition, and your guidance will become more and more clear. Choose the softer side of life whenever possible and set the harshness aside. Eventually, you will make other choices than the ones that seem satisfying today. Be ready for this. When the voice of reason comes knocking, hand it your calling card, which reads: "Natural Intuitive."

GAIA, GAIO OR TELLUS MATER?

Hello! I am writing from Austria, from a town near Innsbruck. I am a member of a group called Gaia in Ascension. A member of our group recently shared a channeling with us. It says that Gaia has decided to change her name in honor of the coming new energy. I have a hard time believing this and am hoping that you will confirm or deny it.

A channeling circle I subscribe to makes reference to Gaia and "Gaio," or Father Earth. I am wondering if you are going to be introducing him to us as well.

I love Gaia's energy but prefer the term Tellus Mater, the Roman goddess of the Earth. I refer to myself as a Tellurian, an inhabitant of the Earth. I like the broadness and equality of the term as well as its lack of boundaries, borders, nationalities or even species. Wouldn't the energy of the Earth be different if "Tellus" was used instead of "Gaia"?

These questions are both dated and timeless. Their imprint seems new enough, but as recently as a decade or so ago, they were answered in detail. Two centuries ago, they were explored by scholars of the day, and only a short millennia has passed since the last time confusion reigned over clarity. All names are but appellations, titles and facsimiles by which something or someone is known. Appellative words such as Gaia, or even God, cannot come close to naming that which they describe, because that which is unknown or unrevealed cannot be accurately made manifest. A name is but a distinguishing characteristic of that which it attempts to describe, a distortion of perfection, because it divides rather than making whole that which already is.

Can you name All That Is in such a way as would do It justice? Can you describe It any better? Does your name describe you accurately, fairly or completely? No name, title, appellation or adjective could portray you—no matter how melodic, descriptive, harmoniously aligned or dramatic its origin. Before I was named, I was. The same is true of you. A name is more limiting than you can imagine, as is any differentiation such as sex, for instance. I am most comfortable with the term sentience Earth, but it does not rest well on the modern tongue. Long ago you were more comfortable with the term I Am, but that also seems now to be reserved for special occasions and private revelations.

THE SIGNIFICANCE, OR LACK THEREOF, OF NAMES

Gaia, or Gaea, simply means "of the Earth" and was originally associated with gladness and joy. Specifically, "Gaia" is the acceptance by the body consciousness (of the Earth) of the truth pertaining to divine law, or Lord. The redemption of the body brings about gladness and joy. "Gaius," a popular namesake long ago, was given to those who seemed to exult in the gladness brought about by being of the Earth or of Earth within the human form. It was a name, a description and a title. My channel and scribe [Pepper Lewis] would not tell you of her own accord that her given name was Gladys Victoria Keen. Hidden within the symbology as well as the numerology is Spirit's hope that she will find gladness and victory as a channel of the Earth.

My sentience is as the soul of this planet—that which is conscious and aware of itself and its purpose, especially as it relates to humanity. A sentience is more like an emotional response and less like an intellectual process. Gaia sentience (or Mother Earth) animates the planet, gives it purpose and makes life on Earth possible. Today you call the physical planet "Earth," but it has also been known and described differently at other times. For you the Earth is habitable, but for many other species it is not. This alone would call for a different description. Over time, much has been said and written about the Earth, yet little has been accurate or even agreed upon. As you continue to rediscover your origins, you will also rediscover mine. I have been the sentience of this planet from the beginning and before then as well. I was here when this planet was but a thought in Creator's infinite mind. When the fires were at last extinguished and the molten rock began to cool, a dynamic combination of elements emerged.

Many forms of life have come and gone, over eons of time, and humanity's existence upon the Earth is but a drop in the cosmic ocean. Still, humanity has the greatest potential of all, as it is the product of both creation and evolution. Your cosmic origins give rise to possibilities beyond what you now imagine. My sentience guides and enlivens all that surrounds the planet as well as all who are upon and within her. My sentience animates the air you breathe, the energy you burn and the water you drink. All of the elements are under my care and direction, as are the seasons and what you call weather. I am a devoted companion and trusted friend to all life forms, including the animal, plant and mineral kingdoms who share the planet with you.

THE POWER OF THE WORD IS IN YOUR PRESENCE

My ability to communicate with humanity has waxed and waned over time, although it has always been my creative directive to do so. Our communication has been influenced by many factors, including individual and collective consciousness, religious and spiritual fervor, planetary evolution and upheaval, genetic mutation and manipulation as well as alterations and aberrations in how time is expressed. Although many believe in a sentient or feeling Earth, not all are attuned to this. The process called channeling offers a unique advantage in this respect, because it allows the transmission of vibrations and impressions to be communicated as language. The advantages of this tool far outweigh the obvious drawbacks, which include unconscious obstruction and conscious distortion. In this forum of public domain, my words are offered through a clear and receptive channel, one whose duty and devotion have been tempered by time, sacrifice and service. A deep and constant yearning to communicate with each of you urges me to depend upon this ancient art and the service of a trustworthy medium who has been my companion numerous times.

Long and longer ago, access to knowledge and wisdom was limited to the spoken word and only available to initiates and those who were considered "chosen." Today the electronic media presents many opportunities, and my messages travel far and wide. Still, they are limited to those who would hear them. The words I speak are not new, but you will hear them as if for the first time. They are represented in the first person rather than in the second or the third, where they would seem even further removed. You will receive my words both within and without, because they are not separate from you. I am an extension and expansion of who you are. Those who hear my words do so above and beyond other voices and demands that clamor for attention in the busy modern world. My words are most present in your life when you are most present in your life.

Today two priorities guide my sentience. The first is to erase the perception of separation that seems to threaten the planet. Assumptions, suppositions and misinterpretations have given rise to fear and distrust. Soon separation will be disarmed and falsehoods will be dispelled. Consistent communication between all forms of life will return, and a true language that speaks with one voice and is heard by all hearts will again be the norm. The second priority is to awaken and expand the collective consciousness that has immobilized many hearts and minds. All that I am is dedicated to this endeavor.

Bearing this in mind and heart, what purpose could be served by separating or representing Gaia as Gaio? Do men and women, males and females, not find enough differences between them already? Perhaps a term, albeit unnecessary, that invokes and instills unity would be more appropriate as this juncture.

My messages are not intended to save you or the planet. There is no adverse condition that cannot be righted with the power of intent and the right use of will. What you embrace or reject today will have a significant effect upon the outcome of the next several years, and my messages are but one of many resources from which to choose. Where the will is established, a way will present itself that is clear, concise and forthcoming. As compassion and authenticity continue to increase, humanity will discover the courage and willingness to heal the environment and the world. Abundance, health and joy will replace scarcity, poverty and fear. Tellus Mater, Mother Earth and Gaia are all but simple words that could scarcely say more than this: That which I am, you are; and that which you are, is love incarnate.

A Deceptively
Simple Year

December 2004

hese words, very neatly placed upon these pages for your enjoyment, are always the most popular of the year, at least until you begin to see how they fit into your own perspective about what you already believe about yourself and the world around you. Just as reading your daily astrological forecast evokes thoughts and feelings about what does and does not seem to apply, predictions that encompass an entire year provoke thoughts and feelings as to the accuracy and relevancy of what is being offered.

WHAT'S FOR DINNER?

Most of you are certain that you would like to know what is going to happen next month or next year, and given that opportunity, you would ask very specific questions that would allow you to prepare for what is to come. Yet if I were to ask you what you were going to have for dinner next month or next year, you would find the question somewhat preposterous. After all, how could you know now, with any accuracy, what you will want for dinner on a supposed but undetermined date in the future?

You would wonder if you would be alone or in the company of others on that day, or perhaps in poor health, which would influence your choices. You might want to project yourself into your future social calendar or take a little time to consider the variables that always seem to crop up when least expected. You might even choose to cite statistics on the nature of creativity as influenced by the laws of probability. If pressed to answer, you would more than likely insist that your free will is being undermined by the very suggestion that you could or should know today what you will want to do at some currently irrelevant point in the future.

Yet that is exactly what we are here to discover, because for the most part, humanity relishes basking in the sun while watching the low tide take "what is" out to sea, eagerly awaiting the swell that might bring "what will be" close enough to shore with the next high tide. The difference between the two might be as tiny as raindrops or they might be as wide apart as oceans, but after all, that is part of the thrill of being human. And it is a thrill; otherwise you would not do it.

THE THIRD-DIMENSIONAL YOU

A human being is a relatively simple creature as far as the universe is concerned, but the process of stuffing a great being such as yourself into such a basic collection of organic material is altogether different, which brings to the forefront of this discussion a salient point that must be acknowledged early on: You are not your body any more than I am mine. Your body is a vehicle. You are that which animates your body and assigns purpose to its being. You are a being temporarily being a human being. It is all too easy to lose sight of this, given the dense accumulation of atoms and other physical material indicative of a third-dimensional world. You are not a third-dimensional being, but you have altered (formed) your formlessness into a being equipped with unique and specific qualities, one of which is to understand and therefore transcend that which is limiting into that which is limitless.

The sole purpose of the third dimension is to ask and answer the question: Does the physical world contain you or do you contain it? It is a question well worth asking, but its answer cannot be processed by the mind, regardless of how expansive the mind might be. The answer must be arrived at via experience, both physical and nonphysical. That is why the answer lies in the journey and not in the destination, which is simply a point in time that exists just prior to the next beginning. What is December 31, for instance, if it is not that which precedes January 1? Every beginning is an end and every end a beginning, every inhalation is a birth and every exhalation a death, and vice versa. This is a universal law, and no exception to the law exists, yet it is the paradox created by this very law that underscores the existence of eternity.

THE IMMORTALITY OF HISTORY, ART AND SACRED SPACES

Eternity is unaffected by the passage of time. It is everlasting and without beginning or end. At face value, it would seem that eternal beingness is akin to immortality, but it is not, because that which is eternal does not require life to define it. If life did not exist, eternity would still prevail. If All That Is had not chosen to experience Itself through the concept of time, It would still exist, because All That Is is eternal. Immortality, or eternal life, is relevant only as long as life remains relevant, and life is relevant as long as time (expressed as a dimension) remains an agreed-upon concept. A work of art, for instance, can be immortalized. As long as its relevance exists in the eternal mind, it will remain immortal whether or not it still exists in the physical. A less abstract example of this would be the immortalization of the now long-extinct dinosaurs. They will continue to be immortal for as long as humans find that they are relevant to their past, and not until then will they disappear into oblivion.

Many of the sacred sites around the planet enjoy the same kind of immortality. No exact record of their beginning can be found, and there is no consistent explanation for what and why they are. This inability to find a contemporary explanation for their existence makes them immortal in humanity's awareness, and therefore more important than that which seems finite. This also explains why you are more interested in your past and in your future than you are in the moment at hand. The former and the latter both seem immortal to you, with the present moment no more than an imaginary midpoint in an ongoing perpetuity.

It is a wonder that you bother with it at all! But illusions are powerful and deceptive things, and the illusion of the human being and his or her drama of immortality is no exception, because if it were not for the present moment, the next moment would not exist and there would be no future. So the present moment is that which animates, empowers and validates eternity—or, better put, you are that which gives meaning and purpose to All That Is. The only way you could do that is if you and All That Is were not separate from one another. After all, All That Is is eternal. I wonder what that makes you?

DIVIDED ATTENTION WILL REVEAL THE BEAUTY OF 2005

The only way you will recognize the beauty of the year 2005 is if you can participate in it with divided attention. "Divided attention" is an intentional effort to be aware of two or more things simultaneously, in contrast with "identification," where attention is focused on only one thing; it is full awareness divided or influenced by a subtle understanding of dimensional relevance. Being simultaneously aware of your environment as well as your place within that environment is an example of divided attention. It is not nearly as easy a task as it first appears to be, because humans still perceive themselves as separate and/or apart from their environment. They overidentify with how they are perceived by others and underidentify with how they perceive themselves. At the same time, a human will vacillate between believing that he or she is either more or less valuable and important than his or her neighbor, mother, brother, girlfriend, husband, employer and so on. Divided attention requires that you wear at least two different shoes at once, uncomfortable as that might be. In fact, the more uncomfortable the shoes are, the more apt you are to discover just how many environments you are a part of.

THE BOOK OF 2005

As the title of our text suggests, the coming year will be a deceptively simple one. From the outset, you will know where you stand, because it will seem all too obvious to you. The energies of this year are not vague, and you will not have to guess what is happening or what might happen next.

Imagine for a moment that you have perused and previewed a book many times without having actually read it cover to cover. You already know its storyline, and you even know how it ends, because you have skipped ahead to the last page just to make sure. Most of your friends have already read the book, and you have even overheard them whispering about it even though they thought they were out of earshot. It has also come to your attention that a movie project based upon the book is already being considered, one that has been "inspired by actual events." Based on the foregoing, you conclude that this would probably be a good time to read the book, if for no other reason than to stay on top of current events. After all, you wouldn't want to be the last one on the planet to get to the punch line, would you?

This is how you will begin the new year, with a yawn and a stretch and that "here we go again" feeling. Been there, done that; searched for your purpose, thought you found it, were sure you lost it, found it again, lost it again, gave up; found a new teacher; tried to save the world, gave up, tried to save yourself, gave up; found faith in humanity, lost faith in humanity; realized you were in a dream, woke up in the dream, tried to abandon the dream, returned to the dream and are now willing to settle for a version of reality that allows you to feel that you are making a difference in the world while you await the second coming of humanity's wakefulness.

THIS YEAR WILL REQUIRE YOU TO RECOGNIZE TRUTH

But now let's look beyond the obvious and waste few words as we do. Let's reduce the search for meaning to a simpler discovery of truth and our place within it. Truth is subtler than reality and gentler than fact. Truth is the blending filament of life that allows the personal to be both interpersonal and impersonal without breaking any laws. Truth is simple enough to be carried in your pocket and complex enough to make it a lifelong study. Most of all, truth is not deceptive. Truth is light enough to float on water, whereas deceptions are dense enough to sink like a stone.

Humanity, as a whole, is becoming more dense. Obesity is rampant and nearing epidemic proportions. It is not that humans are consuming too much food; rather, they are consuming too little truth. Humans have become complacent, smug, cynical and self-righteous. Most humans cannot currently recognize truth, because they have bought a lesser version of it, the one sitting on the shelf just beside its low-calorie, nonfat, low-carbohydrate, caffeine-free, healthy alternative. This text will not free you from this year's menu of deceptions, but it will make them stand out, so that even when they are neatly packaged and tied with brightly colored bows, you will recognize them for what they are: veils, smokescreens and erudite artists' conceptions of realities, created so that you might find reality palatable. Be vigilant, then, and on your honor too, for the tricksters and hucksters are already hard at work!

Paradise Lost

The Earth remembers when she was still a paradise. Even if it is only within her own imagination, the memory still rings true. The Earth is still a garden-like planet, but it is no longer a paradise. A paradise is a place or a condition that offers perfect happiness. In a paradise, a person can find everything he or she desires. The Earth was once such a paradise, and all who came here long ago still remember this in the recesses of their collective cellular memory. This memory is in danger of being erased now, wiped out by a viruslike energy that seizes and then stalls the imagination.

THE VIRUS CALLED "PARADISE LOST"

Viruses are minute organic and inorganic particles that live as parasites in their hosts. They can lie dormant for long periods of time, only to awaken when seemingly ordinary circumstances trigger an irregular response. Viruses copy themselves, creating mischievous and destructive clones that consequently insert themselves into uncharted territories. Protection is virtually nonexistent in these areas, because predators have not heretofore existed in them.

One of the most dangerous current viruses exists as a belief system within humanity. It was placed deep within your psyche so long ago that you could not possible remember. Way back, near the beginning of your memories, you lived in a virtual garden. It was a virtual garden in the truest sense of the word, meaning that the experience was a holographic one—the experience (physical context) was real, but the reality (physical content) within the experience was not. Many of your current experiences fall under similar circumstances, and your world is more of a holographic projection than you are aware of most of the time.

The belief system, or virus, that you are currently under the spell of initiates an undercurrent that destabilizes even your most present thoughts. It causes you to question and second-guess what you originally knew to be true. When the virus locates the original truth that has guided and sustained you thus far, it attempts to replace it with a new, unstable one. If the virus cannot locate the original truth, it duplicates itself enough times to cause layers of doubt where it believes the original truth might have once been.

"Paradise lost" is the modern-day name for this virus that was encoded within you long ago. A virus is not an implant, but it can function as one in order to escape detection. It is an interactive virus, meaning that its discovery is only the beginning of, or introduction to, its potentially destructive behavior.

THE FALSE HUMAN BELIEF IN THE FALL FROM GRACE

Simply stated, paradise lost is the belief that you (humans) have fallen from grace or have been ejected from a paradise-like setting in order to regain entry into the hallowed halls of perfection from which you once emanated. This virus holds that you are less than perfect—even less than good, for the most part. The wheel of birth and rebirth assures that you receive a new and improved dose of the virus before each embodiment, and the world's religions—including Christianity, Islam, Judaism, Buddhism and others—continue the process, reinforcing the belief that paradise is selective and available only to good people of certain faiths upon their deaths and even then commensurate only with an honorable record and a favorable judgment.

You might believe that this is only a theory or a bit far-fetched. Unfortunately, that is not the case. Do you think that you are exempt from implanted viruses and obsolete belief systems? Think again. You don't subscribe to any particular religion this time around? What about this past lifetime and the lifetime before? This virus has been one of the worst banes to human evolution, leaving death, destruction, misery and ruin in its historical wake. It is poison to the fragile but emerging consciousness that is birthing its awareness among you. As a fortress, it is impenetrable, guarded by a military-like presence within you that acts with dogmatic precision each time you attempt to free yourself from it.

PARADISE LOST WAS BORN FROM DUALITY

Paradise lost is one of the reasons why you have suicide bombers. It is why such a minority among you cares for the Earth's dwindling resources. Paradise lost inspires war and salutes authority. It justifies anger and dignifies revenge. It is why you yearn for that which existed long ago and for a future you know nothing about rather than a present that offers itself to you boldly moment by moment. Paradise lost taught you to believe in light versus dark; before the proliferation of this virus, thoughts such as these did not exist.

The virus is almost as old as you are; that is to say, it is as old as time. It was born when duality was born. It exists as part of you, because you cannot separate yourself from time or its passage. The more you attempt to disengage from it, the more caught you become in its web, because it is not separate from the web of life—in fact, it defines it. Paradise lost is the part of you that believes in something outside or beside you. It believes in a higher power just like you do, but unlike you, it believes that a higher power decides who and what is right and who and what is wrong. If you believe that you are a lightworker and your friend is not, you are infected just like everyone else.

PARADISE SUNS AND PARADISE SONS

Why has the virus proliferated so? Because at a certain point in time, you ceased being the paradise suns and became the paradise sons. This was a very important turning point in your history and one that organized religion glosses over in an attempt to maintain its power over you. As paradise suns, you were celestial beings, unlimited in size, scope and dimension; you could not be contained or altered. But as paradise sons, at least some of your power was surrendered elsewhere. In order to experience this choice fully, you allowed yourselves to become the offspring of another source: the sons and daughters of suns, second- and third-generation gods, stepped down or fallen from a higher place.

No better thing could have happened and no worse event has ever taken place. This is the plain and simple truth, although it necessitates twisting and bending the mind to understand it. As paradise suns, your purpose was one with Oneness, unchangeable and eternal, without beginning or end. But when Creator (in the form of the Great Central Sun) empowered (radiated) Its suns as creator worlds, time was born and change became inevitable, and so the suns of Fohat became the sons of Fohat.

The Sons of Fohat

Fohat is an ancient mystical term once common in occult circles in Tibet and other deeply experienced cultures. It is a Sanskrit word that explains the existence of divine or primordial nature. But fohat is also much more than that—it might even be considered the essence of cosmic electricity, at least as electricity applies to and influences consciousness. Fohat, then, is the ever-present, most active form of consciousness. Present from the beginning of time, it will also be present at the end of time as well as when time ceases to be measured as it is today.

FOHAT IS CEASELESS CHANGE AND AWARENESS

Primordial energy is, just as Creator is. It can never pass from existence. It can be dormant, and it can be expressed latently, but because it is an expression of cosmic will, it must always accompany consciousness. Fohat is incessantly active, ever moving and changing. It is the impelling urgency in the force we call nature. Fohat is both formative and destructive; it is ceaseless and unending change. It is vital to the universe, because it is the active force that facilitates the passing of one phase of manifested existence into its next phase. This is true of all things, be it a solar system, a civilization, a single human entity or an atom.

Fohat is ever present; this fact could not be more clearly stated or more dearly emphasized. Fohat is the birth of consciousness, but it is not consciousness itself, at least not as defined by that which you would like to attain. Fohat is also awareness, but you cannot see or touch awareness. Uniquely, fohat is the awareness within consciousness and the consciousness within awareness. This is a very important piece of information, because it is the key to increasing the quantity and quality of solar light (prana) required by your essence (soul) to sustain your physical body.

The physical environment you currently inhabit is a rugged one, especially now. You might live in a beautiful environment nestled in the trees high atop a mountain, breathing fresh air and exercising regularly—but the Earth is a desert now, energetically speaking. It is important that we speak in these terms and that we be completely honest with one another. To do less at this juncture would be a waste, and there is already far too much of that.

These words are printed on paper. They have also been recorded on audio-cassette and on compact disc—all of these began as raw material, as energy. The guidance and wisdom you extract from these forms of energy today were already present when, for example, the paper you now hold was still a tree. It existed then in its raw form just as it does now. The same is true of you. As energy, you existed as pure potential. Today you also exist as physical consciousness. Fohat is the energy that created the original desire that transformed you from non-physical potential into physical purpose. That is why fohat is sometimes called the birth of consciousness, but consciousness must be developed and then purposely deployed, otherwise it will founder and stagnate.

IT IS NOT ENOUGH TO SIMPLY ACHIEVE AWARENESS

Too much emphasis has already been placed upon awakening the awareness, as if once that were accomplished, nothing else need happen. Nothing could be farther from the truth! When you awaken in the morning, do you congratulate yourself for having done so and then study your navel for the remainder of the day? No, because if you do, very soon you will fall back asleep. The same is true of consciousness, and although awareness is very good indeed, too many people are spending precious time admiring and polishing their chakras rather than expanding them with fohat.

Are you waiting for your friends and your fathers to awaken? Are you dreaming of enjoying a new world with your sisters and your sons? Still trying to work it out with your mothers and your mates? So be it, but must you slow down or stop in order to do so? I do not chastise you, for the density of the third dimension is undeniable. But I remind you that time is precious, not because it cannot be restored or repeated, but because it can and it will.

The Time Machine

Time is a little bit like a wind-up alarm clock, or like the gas tank in your car. When you wind up the little gear in the back of the alarm clock, you assume that it will keep time accurately and that it will remind you when it is time to wake up. You depend upon it to do so, and it responds accordingly, but as the gears begin to slow, its accuracy seems to become less dependable. A full gas tank will power your vehicle for many miles, but before you know it, you have traveled many miles and must replenish your supply. The nearer to empty the gauge gets, the faster the fuel seems to evaporate. In both cases, time did not speed up or slow down, but your perception of it did. A lifetime has a limited amount of time associated with it, but it can be expanded and contracted as necessary. A common expression says, "Time is money." Better put, time is energy—and it belongs to you.

TIME CAN BE MANIPULATED

For some, time is a gift. For others, it is a commodity that can be bought or sold. More appropriately, time is a vehicle. It can transport energy quickly or slowly, and it can move in any direction. It can also assist you in being more present, but we will come upon that subject later in our discussion. For now, it is important to remember that time can be influenced or manipulated. This subject is not intended to be taken negatively, and it is important that you expand your interpretation of it, as doing so will assist you greatly.

Manipulation is a form of creativity. To manipulate something is to influence it in a clever, ingenious or advantageous way. For instance, if you were clever enough to influence time in such a manner that you would have more of it to spend on leisure activities, you might be quite pleased. But if time were manipulated so that you had less of it to spend on fun, you might feel otherwise. Today, both possibilities exist equally and side by side.

Many say that time is accelerating, but that is not altogether true. The ability to influence time increases in direct relationship to the development of consciousness. Likewise, succumbing to the manipulation of time by others is a byproduct of distracted or delayed consciousness. Time is not short, and it is not running out. There is no hurry, because there is no finish line to hurry to.

TIME TRAVEL AND DIMENSIONAL REALITY

On the other hand, time is precious. Time is precious because you are precious, and long before what you can now remember, you created time. You created time as a guide to help you get from here to there and back again. You relied on time, and for a while it helped you to manage all of the resources that were available to you. With time as your guide, you traveled all over the solar system. You experienced many worlds and many realities. Here and there were equal to before and after, or to past and future; they were only reference points. But by the time you had made several hundred trips from here to there, the timelines had become thicker, more dense and difficult to penetrate. Time travel became slower, and you became convinced that it was easier to stay where you were than to play in hypertime and hyperspace. By agreement, time remained constant for a long time, but perhaps you have noticed that this is no longer the case.

Time is a perceived unit of time, which is exactly why it can be manipulated. Time is relative to your perception of reality, and reality is an expression of consciousness. In other words, the more you expand your consciousness, the more dimensional your reality becomes. Dimensional reality and multidimensional reality are not subject to the same constraints and restrictions as linear time and linear reality. Do you understand the importance of this discussion? Plainly said: Those who choose to remain in linear time will become more susceptible to the slowing of consciousness. This will be more evident in 2005 than at any other time. On the other hand, those who relate to time as a vehicle of energy will be able to influence time and reality in many beneficial ways that will become evident as the year unfolds. How can you do this? There are many methods from which to choose. A few will be described for you here, and more will follow as creativity invites them.

CREATE ENOUGH TIME TO DO ALL YOU NEED TO DO

Begin by understanding, and relearning if necessary, that time is fluid rather than static. If you have made an agreement with time to spend a certain amount of it at work, with family, in leisure and so on, remake that agreement. I am not advocating spending less time at work and more time at play, but I am suggesting that you remake your intention to have enough time to do all that you need to do.

Begin with need, because as humans you understand need. Later you will add desire to the mix. Remember that time is a commodity that you have plenty of. You do not and cannot buy time, but you can take time or make time. Allow your awareness to keep time for you instead of the clock. When you are in awareness, you know exactly how much time you need to get somewhere or complete something. Trust your awareness with time management, and you will see that you can trust it with much more as well.

Imagine that there are twenty-five hours in a day rather than twenty-four. That gives you an extra half-hour before noon and an extra half-hour after noon. Decide ahead of time how you will spend the extra time, and then make certain that you follow through. If you can imagine it, you can experience it—if you can't, you won't. Begin a project on a different day than you normally would. Change the time when you awake in the morning and the time when you retire at night, even if it is only by a few minutes. The point is to observe and to relate to time differently.

Borrow time from one day and repay it on another. Time is unlimited and no true debt can exist, but we are beginning with baby steps, and the concept of borrowing and repaying is all too well known to the many consumer-driven cultures so en vogue now. Imagine that time is more elastic than your current understanding of it. At times, when necessity has asked it of you, you have stretched your budget miraculously. Now you can do the same with time. Stretch it because you can. Give yourself more of it because you deserve it. Ask the universe to cooperate, endorse and underwrite your desire to exist in dimensional time rather than linear time. Pledge to continue to develop and expand your consciousness, knowing that as you do, time will also bend to your will.

LEARNING HOW TO MANAGE TIME WILL HELP YOU MAINTAIN AWARENESS

How many people and things currently influence and manipulate your time, with or without your awareness? Would it not be more beneficial to manage your own awareness instead of having another do it for you? The benefits of understanding the true nature of time are many, and you will reap some of them as soon as you adjust your thoughts accordingly. Once you learn how to influence time, you will be able to insert more of it into your life. Naturally, thoughts will come next, and you will learn how to coordinate supportive thoughts so that they enter your environment at just the right time.

If you do not have enough time, chances are that you also lack other commodities. Apply all of the examples listed above to other areas of life. Where is there lack and where is there excess? What do you need and what can you spare? Imagine that your day exists within a fountain. As it pours out beautifully and consistently, it also recycles and regenerates itself. All impurities are left behind as it renews itself in the process and rejoins the flow. Each day a minute amount will evaporate, joining a greater flow elsewhere. Do you begin to see? There is not a moment to lose!

Weathering the Environment

Have you ever wondered whether the weather is your friend or your foe? Do you feel personal or impersonal about the weather? Is weather something that just happens to the Earth and to you, or do you believe that a greater force influences it? Have you ever prayed for good weather to endorse a special occasion? If so, to whom were you praying? Long ago these questions had very obvious answers—textbook, you might say. But today the answers are not as simple. Humans and the Earth, you and I, are both in the throes of labor. We are both about to give birth to something greater than our-selves. The next generation has already birthed itself and has little need of your vision or my wisdom, but something else is about to take place that we are both very much a part of.

THE READERS OF THE STARS

Many ages and sages ago, the stars that form the signs of the zodiac were positioned differently than they are today. Poised in the night sky, they shone so that the naked eye could clearly make out their forms. The sky was more auspicious then, and those who interpreted its signs were held in very high regard. This was true of almost all cultures and societies, because it was a commonly held belief that the Sun and the stars both guarded and guided the future. The science of the stars was just that, and no other science surpassed it in importance.

Guesswork and conjecture had no place here, and those who dared to pre-tend to know the secrets of this science were soon discovered and dealt with accordingly. The mathematics of measurement, dimensional geometry, the pro-gression of the planets and cyclical calendars are only a few of the many subjects that demanded mastery from these ancient scholars. It is no wonder that they were called mages or magi. In spite of the many technological advances that can be credited to your generation, these ancient mages of science were far more advanced than those who have been born within the current age.

THE MID-HEAVENS

Mages were students of the firmament. The firmament is the all-encompassing theater that is the universe. The mages understood that this universe is one of many vast and unknowable mysteries. They made no attempt to unlock all of the universe's secrets, choosing instead to marvel at the unknown and the unknowable. On the other hand, the local universe—which exists within the greater universe—could not only be studied but also comprehended. They called the local universe, including its galaxies and solar systems, the firmament, and it was often depicted as a great arched dome in the sky that contained and received all that was relevant to life on Earth. The Sun, for instance, existed within the firmament, but the great and unknowable Great Central Sun did not. In this long-ago age, many scholars believed that the Earth was surrounded by a transparent, domelike, crystalline, scaffolded structure. Like a giant honeycomb, its matrix was thought to crisscross all of the known worlds, whose sum total belonged to a hierarchy of godlike ener-gies who directed the all and the All.

Today the firmament is sometimes called the region of the "mid-heavens." As part of the fourth dimension, it exists within context and plane but not as a specific physical place. It is dimensional but not locational. All that is with-in and below the firmament, or the mid-heavens, can be defined and understood—it is searchable in the same way that a vast database is searchable. That which exists beyond this invisible barrier cannot be fully comprehended from this angle of ascent, because it is cloaked—it is unsearchable. The firmament is a part of a greater continuum, a link between two or more dimensions. It is not solid or separate but seamless and continuous, gradually and imperceptibly blending in such a way that it becomes impossible to say where one dimension ends and the next begins. Still, it is a barrier of sorts, and one that is not easily breached or crossed.

The firmament is held in place by a nexus, a series of interconnected spirals of energy that carry associated particles of matter/antimatter between the layers of the firmament. These particles of intelligence maintain the cosmic purpose, or plan, in complete integrity, balance and harmony. The nexus particles are encoded and programmed to detect any anomalies or gaps that might exist within the evolutionary plan. These variations within perfection are not the cause or result of imperfections; rather, they invite higher or more specific energies that create bridges or links in evolutionary chains. This is one of the ways in which the Earth and all related to it expand. For instance, angelic intervention is possible because of the existence of these bridges to consciousness. This may sound a little like science fiction, but I would point out that it is more like science nonfiction and a subject that merits highlighting. Although not directly related to anomalies in weather and distractions within the Earth, the nexus helps to shape the future—it is the shape of things to come.

THE FIRMAMENT IS DISSOLVING

What is the relevance of this discussion within the more formal subject of Earth changes? Simply put, the firmament is dissolving. A common theory holds that long ago the firmament shattered, bringing a revolt and subsequent shift of the Earth's axis. The theory further suggests that this was followed by a holocaust, including earthquakes, volcanic eruptions, monumental flooding and destruction of most or all civilizations in the known world. This theory is not completely true or false. It is a compilation of myth and magic, storytelling and history, scripture and prose. After all, the final word in history has always belonged to the poets and artists, soldiers and generals who were long ago silenced.

The firmament as a veil or membrane has always existed. Thicker or thinner, visible or transparent, it is the substance that has held your reality in place. But reality is dissolving now, along with a layer of the firmament. Earlier depictions of the firmament include translations of thinly hammered metal bracelets made of iron, bronze and other metals and minerals. Again, these are neither true nor false; they are interpretations of that which was understood to be precious during the intervals within which these translations were held as popular belief. As the firmament continues to thin, previously unknown particles of cosmic material will be discovered and studied. The thinning of the firmament, just like the thinning of the ozone, will at least for a time take center stage.

The firmament is thinning because the Earth and all upon and within it are in need of that which lies beyond the current boundaries. The lower heavens (Earth) can no longer maintain their vitality or integrity without these particles of intelligence that hold the keys to creation. Therefore, the mid-heavens must dissolve the layers that stand between the Earth and its ability to rejuvenate itself with matter/antimatter from the farthest reaches of space.

That which has stood divided must be reunited. The effects of this dissolution are many, and whenever possible, you are encouraged to refrain from judging them as positive or negative. Change is. Change is neither good nor bad, but it is necessary and constant. The universe is not haphazard or happenstance, and all movement is purposeful. That being said, it is also important to acknowledge the profound changes that are already unfolding.

THE POLLUTION OF THE EARTH IS INJURING THE ENERGY OF THE EARTH

If the firmament had not been thinning, the recent probes that were sent to Mars would not have found their way there, because too many energetic obstructions would have derailed their path. Energetic obstructions are nonphysical particles that are less than light. They are leftover thought forms, discarded feelings and/or irrelevant and discordant patterns. All of the kingdoms of the Earth are responsible for their physical and nonphysical energy. They are also responsible for clearing any waste that they build up or inadvertently produce.

The Earth is capable of recycling all that it produces and of finding multiple uses for its resources. The plant kingdom, for instance, offers certain roots for healing, specific leaves for basket weaving, fronds for shelter making as well as fruits, nuts, seeds, bark, lumber, rubber and so on. The animal kingdom offers meat, pelts, quills, teeth, tusks, hooves, bones and much more. Each kingdom is responsible for maintaining an equal and balanced relationship with the other kingdoms, but that is not presently the case, is it?

Residues of toxic waste, along with the remnants of planetary resources, are filling trenches as quickly as they can be prepared, but where does the energy related to these activities go? Everything that is physical has a nonphysical counterpart; without one, the other could not exist. Energetically speaking, the skies and the atmosphere surrounding the Earth are polluted and nearing maximum capacity. These words cannot be mumbled; they must be clearly heard and understood by those who can act upon them.

The thinning of the firmament will allow the Earth a temporary reprieve from these energies. They will rise beyond the density and the dross that keep them too near your own thoughts, and their effects upon you will be lessened in the process. But the environment receives measures such as these harshly, and an unsympathetic response from weather patterns that are being called into active duty should come as no surprise. If a weather prediction is what you seek, know that the weather will be highly changeable and unpredictable for at least the next two years; however, technological advances in forecasting will, of necessity, be vastly improved.

THE THINNING FIRMAMENT WILL BRING WEATHER ANOMALIES

There will be a significant increase in weather-related anomalies—sudden gusts of wind where stillness existed moments before; thunder where no clouds exist; and extraordinary rainstorms in unlikely places, times and seasons. Small tornadoes will give birth to larger ones and vice versa. The same will be true of hurricanes. The weather is as unsettled as you are now. Please remember that the weather is not your adversary.

The Gulf Stream is currently undergoing significant changes that will eventually alter its course. It is best to be aware of these changes now and to be in sync with the inevitable. Do your best not to resist or resent these changes, as they are quite necessary. The weather will change drastically from season to season and from year to year for the next decade or so. It is good to plan a year or so in advance but not to make any permanent changes or decisions yet.

Earthquakes will be on the rise soon, as will volcanic eruptions. The frequency and severity of these Earth changes are unknown at this time, but an increase in magnitude can and should be expected. Do not assume that if you have not heard about these events from your local media, they have not occurred. At best, you are being offered selective information. At worst, bias and lack of perspective blind you from the obvious. Make your homes as safe and secure as possible. Count on having what you need when you need it, and then make sure you do. Have an alternative or a backup plan in mind, even if you have never done so before. Give yourself as many reasons as possible for expecting the best of all possibilities to occur by planning ahead. It is better to act than to react and to prevent rather than to resent.

LIFE ON EARTH IS IN THE PROCESS OF GREAT CHANGE

The Earth and its kingdoms will be changing much more quickly now. The roller coaster, in its slow ascent, will reach its pinnacle soon, and the force behind it will propel it faster and faster, catapulting you forward as a jolting reminder of who you are and why you are here. Very specifically, then: Global warming is here to stay. The process that began long before you were made aware of it has already exceeded the expected markers of the science that seeks to monitor it. Nothing can or will change this fact, nor is it something that you can come to terms with easily. Life on Earth is in the process of changing, and you are a part of the process as well as the change. It is still too soon for you to get used to the prospect of living differently, but it is not too soon to begin to look for ways to make simple conversions in lifestyle where possible and seek to be on the frontiers of new information as it becomes available.

New building can and should take place away from coastlines and at higher altitudes wherever possible. New and alternative roads are needed in many areas both here and abroad. Alternative sources of fuel will soon be more available, but not soon enough to influence the changes already taking place; look to hydrogen technology as soon as it becomes a bit more sophisticated and affordable. Electrical power is not the answer, as it is a poor alternative to already depleted fossil fuels. There are not enough resources such as coal or water to facilitate the manufacture of electrical power in safe and affordable ways. Soon electricity thus produced will become as obsolete as gasoline. Solar energy, on the other hand, can be harnessed adequately and inexpensively, and a number of technologies are already on the patent block and up for sale to the highest bidder. But who can own the Sun? Alas, they will try; they will try.

The Mirror of Relationships

Do you know where your relationships currently stand? Is your heart in the mix or just your head? Do your relationships consist of duty and obligation, or comfort and joy? Is a friend someone who is privy to your soul's longings or simply a companion along for the ride? Have you accepted, forgiven, advanced, surrendered to or made peace with your relationships? If not, this is a grand year in which to do so, because the prevailing energies will be extremely conducive in this regard.

RELATIONSHIPS REFLECT YOUR PERCEPTIONS BACK TO YOU

A mirror is something that offers you a reflection every time you gaze at it, and sometimes it will even offer you a bit more. You seek out your reflection in the mirror because it shows you who you are, or at least who it is you think you are. One of the reasons why you cannot see yourselves is that you are not capable of offering yourselves a fair representation of who you are. You judge, criticize, emphasize and ignore your best features and do the opposite with the most inconsequential ones—the ones that others, who have little or nothing to do with you, demand of you and your culture.

Mirrors can be friends or foes, depending upon your viewpoint and the level of indoctrination you have allowed. Do you see creases and wrinkles in the face looking back at you from within the mirror, or do you see a traveler on a journey? Do you see brown eyes or green or blue, or can you see into and through the iris of color? Do you see dark circles under the eyes, a furrowed brow, a downturned smile, or can you see the unfulfilled dreams lying dormant just under the surface? Your life is a reflection of what you see and vice versa, but your reality is only a mirrored reflection of the truth you are.

Relationships are mirrors as well. They reflect images of you that two-dimensional mirrors cannot. All relationships are reflections of what you are, what you are not, what you hope to be, what you dread, what you fear, what you deny, what you uphold, what you deify and what you glorify. They are reflections of your past, your present and your future. They represent your ideals and mis-qualifications, your shadows, your beliefs and your shortcomings, and those of your culture and your society as well. Your relationships are all of your facial expressions coming to life; they are your fallacies and your frailties, your self-confidence and your self-loathing. No mirror could be more accurate than this.

IGNORING OR DENYING YOUR RELATIONSHIPS

If you deny your relationships, you deny yourself the opportunity to create your-self as you would like. Relationships are formative mirrors, and the reality that they present to you is shaped by your own thoughts and concepts of what you find agree-able and disagreeable. If you find acceptance within the mirrored reflection one day and nonacceptance the next, then that is your conceptual experience of life, and your relationships have no choice but to reflect that image back to you. If you find all relationships to be superficial, then that which you offer to yourself and to the world only scratches the surface of who you truly are.

More than mirrors, relationships are guides and allies. Some relationships impose distance, others caution. Where do these suggestions come from? If you can remember that all relationships are reflections of you and are for your bene-fit, then you will reap many rewards. If you forget this small treasure of wisdom, then you will invite its shadowed reminder whenever it is most appropriate.

Mirrors always remain where they are placed—in the hallway, upon the man-tle, behind a door or in a drawer. The same is true of relationships. If you ignore them, they will collect dust and become dull. If you lose them in the past, they will fade away from memory. And if you sweep them under the rug, you will eventually step on them and they will crack. Broken glass is difficult to sweep up completely, and one must guard against the tiniest of splinters drawing blood. Shattered relationships have the same effect upon your heart. They can lie dor-mant for many years, until an old feeling inflicts a new wound.

Relationships are mirrors held at angles that you cannot or will not hold for yourself. They are the reflections you reject and those you covet. That which is most useful is often taken for granted; for instance, your arms and legs are wonderful tools and difficult to live without. Relationships are also useful tools and your life would not be the same without them, but how quickly are they discarded when the reflection they offer does not meet with your expectations!

Relationships Will Be In Focus This Year

This year of 2005 is a little different than most, in that your relationships will not have that "in your face" quality you have become accustomed to. On the contrary, this year your relationships will remain in the background, unless you choose to bring them to the foreground. This does not diminish their importance in your life. If you ignore your bank account, its funds might dwindle, and the same is true of relationships this year. If you ignore them, they will recede into the background of your life, and they will continue to do so until their importance fades from memory. This might seem like a godsend, but imagine your life without the opportunity to hold and behold your reflection in this way ever again. How many times have you promised yourself that you would fix this, heal that, mend the other or attend to that old wound before it festers? The opportunity to do so is always there because tomorrow is always there, but without relationships to serve as your reflection, tomorrow will be much different.

Relationships will be exceptionally in focus in 2005, because they have been out of focus and out of balance for so long. The relationship between the masculine and the feminine is the tip of the iceberg, with everything else waiting just beneath the surface. But the icebergs are melting very quickly now, in case you have not heard. That which was held tightly, including your beliefs, will soon dissolve, merging with warmer and swifter waters. That which has lain quiet and dormant under the surface will soon emerge from its solitary quietude and make its presence known. Eruptions of the heart will not be uncommon, and the mind's resources will be insufficient in this regard. If you attempt to hold the same stance you have held for years, you will lose ground, to be sure. If you dig in your heels, you might find that the sands of time no longer support you. What then? Unleash the floodgates that have held back the waters for so long! Why not?

Change Your Relationships
Lovingly and without Judgment

This past year, we explained and explored the concept of companion years. It was said then that 2005 was the extension, or companion, to 2004. This will be evident in your relationships. What began this past year will surface again this year. Incomplete feelings, unspoken words and unexplored emotions will guide you toward a greater reality this year. Omitted thoughts, unexpressed apologies, unhealed rancor, diluted hopes and deluded dreams will all give you pause for deeper thought. Long ago you were told to forgive and forget, but that didn't work. Then you were told that you didn't have to forget in order to forgive, but that didn't work either. Attempts to forgive yourself and then do the same with others were foiled by hurts that didn't just go away. After a while, all forms of therapy and healing became just another bandage upon a hemorrhage that could not be assuaged.

Can you change your relationships? Yes, but not by molding others into acceptable likenesses that reflect only a limited projection of you. In order to change your relationships, you must redirect and shift the plane of judgment that intersects your soul. Release the contempt that binds you to your own beliefs, and you free the spirit within to seek its true fulfillment rather than the illusion it mistook for reality. Yes, but how, but how? Insist upon seeing and being the truth each and every day of the year. Promise that you will present the most whole version of yourself that you are able to present. Be an advocate for others to do the same by refraining from raising or lowering your expectations of them. If you have buried others with anger, dig them up and brush them off. At the same time, help those who are stranded on the pedestals you have placed them on—they cannot get down by themselves.

Consider these words a tap on the shoulder, a gentle nudge from one who loves you deeply and holds only this reflection in any and all mirrors. Look deeply within and without as these words find a foothold in your heart. Reflect upon the depth within your own heart and see how far it extends. Have you traveled far only to find yourself in the same place? You are not stuck, I assure you. You are not mired in consequence or lacking in resolve. If you remove your human disguise, even for a moment, you will see that a new fellowship guides your presence within. The stains that have staled your past and stalled your present are no more than unnoticeable blemishes in the face of beauty.

FIND PEARLS OF WISDOM IN A REFLECTING POOL

Don't look at the reflection that you offer yourself; your eyes will deceive you and will not show you the truth—at least not yet. Don't look at the reflection that others offer you, as you will be equally deceived. Do you remember the story of the Medusa, in which those who looked directly at her (instead of her reflection) were instantly turned to stone? That is what happens to hearts and minds when they see with eyes that have not beheld a deeper truth. Close your eyes and open your heart, and you will see how quickly your reality can change.

Begin the year by offering yourself a respite from the thoughts that circle about as clouds that never quite form into anything real, yet never seem to reveal clear skies either. Make your inner circle a simple one, and then see how far you can extend it. How many concentric circles (relationships) can you draw around yourself without creating intersecting lines of conflict? Walk your path as evenly as possible. If, along the way, you find something from the past that belongs there, make certain you leave it. Don't pick it up and carry it, not even for a little while. If you believe your present suits you, then smile upon it for a change instead of longing for a different one. If your present situation does not suit you, then put your nose to the grindstone lest you look in the same mirror and re-create the same image.

Do you have a future? Have you planned for one? You will find that a reflecting pool, one created by nature, is a very fine place to find one. Bring some pebbles of promise with you to toss into the water, and see if you do not retrieve pearls of wisdom by the year's end.

Follow the Money

Where did all the money go? What happened to the economy? Here today, gone tomorrow, back again when? If you don't have the money, who does? If the poor have lost it, does that mean the rich have it? No, not necessarily. The simple truth is that money, a form of energy, is in just as short supply as many of the other resources upon the planet. You might argue that money doesn't just disappear, but neither do resources, unless they are used up, traded or thrown away.

Money is a unit of exchange. You exchange your work for money, and then you exchange the money you receive for something else. If the work you perform is less valuable, then the money you receive will have less value as well. If life has less value, then the money that sustains life also has less value. And that is exactly what is happening. The law of diminishing returns is today's rule of thumb. In other words, a continual increase in effort or investment does not necessarily lead to an increase in result or reward. Energy can be extended or expended, so a lack of energy generates less of a reward. Does integrity count? Yes and no. It depends upon what energy it is associated with or attached to. Integrity is no more its own reward than hard work is.

WHERE DID ALL THE MONEY GO?

First some answers to your questions: Where did all the money go? Those who tout the worth and importance of money to others privately believe that the dollar is less than worthwhile. Mixed messages rule the day and the day's headlines. The experts tell you to spend less and save more. Why, then, is the economy measured by how much you spend? If too many people are out of work, that is quite bad, but if too many are working, that is not good either.

These mixed messages only serve to astound and confound you. Meanwhile, those who offer these prolific public service announcements are quietly maneuvering their holdings in contrast to their words. They are trading their dollars for commodities that will hold better value in the coming years. Unfortunately, these opportunities are not available to you, but that does not mean that you cannot find other opportunities if you apply your thoughts in the direction of broad horizons.

The money went to purchase a bunker of silence and an arsenal of words, a company of soldiers and the research with which to make more. The money was traded to the Third World for resources and to the Fourth World for land. While you have been buying homes, others have been buying nations. Do not allow these words to distress you, as they serve only to make a point and are not intended to tip the scales of concern into the range of fear; however, these words are nonetheless true. The importance of what is being said here is that money is not nearly as important as what is done with it. Money is a tool, but it is an old-fashioned one and will not stand the test of time. Remember these words when an opportunity to trade your money for something else of value arises.

The World Is in Debt

The world cannot pay for the debt it has accumulated. This is a fact. You will not be able to work long enough or smartly enough to repay the debt you have incurred. This is not necessarily bad news, because an opportunity to trade in your debt will come soon enough. In the meantime, do not accumulate more debt than would be fair to trade, because you do not yet know what you will be trading it for. Your debt will not be erased completely, and it is best to be wary of those who tell you that it will.

Everything has a price, even debt, and the terms of one lien holder might be more or less fair than those of the next. In all things, read the small print and the large, the words and the lack of words. Count the lines, and see what is missing or inserted between them as well. A very old widow once said, "Lovers lie well only when they are between the sheets."

The economy you once knew is no longer. That economy was based upon factors that could be controlled and influenced within associated boundaries. The old economy was somewhat able to balance the needs of the lower class with the demands of the middle class and the expectations of the upper class. The new economy is based upon a global class system on a nation-by-nation basis. It is based upon the supplies and services provided by each nation along with its willingness to cooperate within an oligarchy, that is, control by an elite organization or government whose members exist behind a screen of power.

The world's resources are in short supply. The peasant and the farmer are all too aware of this, but most city dwellers are not. They consume at the same or higher rate as they always have, even if a few more dollars must be exchanged in the process. Residents of the halls of power also consume without attrition, but they are well aware of what is at stake.

The Old Economy, the New Economy and Earth Changes

At this point, only an ostrich could place itself upon a small patch of land, bury its head and pretend the rest of the world does not exist. Your neighbors to the north are concerned, your friends in the south fear the worst, and east and west no longer speak the same language. In the Americas, both North and South, a majority of the population struggles for survival. They earn more than their forefathers, but they see even less. Their eyes are wide open, but their mouths are shut. With much to see but little to eat, why waste energy on words? In the meantime, the more than fortunate and less than honest revise charters and restyle constitutions to suit their own purposes.

What hubris has humankind! The small and weak pay for protection they do not need while the wealthy avert their eyes from the taxes they roll over from text to deed. Those who are left pay the consequences—for the mighty, who are the minority too. All consequence and no gain, they finance their lives and ransom the blame. Reason and logic are no match against such power and fame, at least not yet, but the storm is gathering now just the same.

The old economy was based upon the world's resources and the most useful and necessary commodities, but the gamble was upon next season's yield and the following year's harvest. The new economy is based upon the lack of the same. It is based upon synthetic, copyrighted, trademarked and owned versions of sustainability. In the old economy, insurance companies feared the worst so that you wouldn't have to. They stockpiled assets and were poised to reimburse yours. Natural disasters were calculated risks, but losses were few.

Today natural disasters such as earthquakes, tornadoes, hurricanes and floods are the norm. Insurance companies not only count on them, they gamble upon them in terms of hits and misses. Risk-assessment and risk-management teams calculate the odds that insurance companies bet on with your premiums. In the old system, the bank owned your house, but now the bank owns you as well. These words are disturbing, but they are not meant to distress you. They are designed to cause you to act so that you will not need to react later. If it is true that actions speak louder than words, then you will soon be in good company.

Some Guidance for the Future

The nature of a work such as this, where prediction is applied to principle, is a difficult one. On the surface, it seems sufficient to know what is and what will be. But the true question that rests uncomfortably underneath all the rest is, "What can I do about this?" The answer is that if you believe you are powerless in this and other situations, nothing at all can be done. If, on the other hand, you choose to be aligned with personal and planetary power, everything is at your disposal. So the question of what is and what will be rests within the all and the All. The future is not dismal, and it is not bright; it is yet to be created. Within that which does not yet exist, the powerful and the powerless exist side by side, both preparing and predicting based upon the oracle that is the present.

Addressing such a topic without offering guidance to accompany it seems unjust. Clear vision would answer more questions than not, but obscurity reigns today, so doubt is left alone to bargain at an auction where pirates rule without the presence of a second. "Take notice first and action soon after," a quartermaster would say. "Weigh the truth and make it not a burden upon yourself or others," a wise woman once said to her husband, a king. "Extinguish the match that burns but for a second and light the fire that warms the soul," a Native American chief said to his youngest son. "Quench your thirst but do not drown it," the thirsty man advised the satiated one. "Rumors that the end is near have been overheard by sages and sires," said the prisoner to no one in particular. "Overstated, more like it," said no one in particular to the prisoner.

WAR, PEACE AND THE ANTI-TERRORISTS

Humans have almost always been at war with one another. Sons have seen their fathers go off to do battle with unseen enemies and never return. Why, then, do they follow the same path? What makes one country, one religion, one sect, one president or one side more righteous than the next? All of the holy books speak of peace, and all of them speak of battle. In all of the holy books, God is understood to be loving, gentle, good and kind. Could God be less than that to those who live next door to you? How can you love your neighbor one day and inflict a dagger's wound in his side the next?

Questions such as these are difficult to answer, because they are problematic equations that contain more than one answer. They must be worked through and suffered over before they can finally be solved. The people of the world will not lay down their weapons until the righteous and the bloodthirsty tire of bloodshed and their toys of destruction are removed for good. Hardwired into humanity's makeup is the need to discover that all life is holy (whole). Until such time, war is inevitable.

WAR IS A HUMAN CONSTRUCTION

If the Earth were much larger than it is and each sect that had a disagreement with the next had its own continent, would war cease? No. If everyone on the Earth owned a home and had a job, would all the wars come to an end? No. If the Earth's resources and commodities were shared equally among nations and peoples, would there be an end to confrontations of such magnitude? No, because the wages of war are a response born of ignorance, not anger. Soldiers fight because they are asked to do so. Children hate because they are taught to do so. Mothers cry because they are forced to do so.

The world is at odds with itself, because it does not know who or what it is. The world does not know its true history, although it does understand the importance of its present and it fears for its future. Humans battle their own ghosts because they cannot see themselves through the transparent eyes of the charade that their lives have become.

Humans were created from and evolved into a territorial species. Humans were not created equally; they have never understood or respected one another as such. Humans were never introduced as brothers and sisters and told to behold one another as equals. On the contrary, humans were told whom to obey, what mysteries never to question, what knowledge never to seek, when to avert their eyes, whom to pay obeisance to and in whose name to take up a sword. True peace has never, ever existed upon the Earth. Only a handful of cultures have embraced the idea, and few were able to maintain it for more than a few generations at a time. Even the Lemurians lost their way eventually, influenced by a utopian vision they could neither forget nor create.

SEEK TRUTH TO CONQUER HATE

Why were weapons put into human hands, and who put them there? When did the first child say, "It's mine, and you can't have it"? Who taught the world to hate? Where did your enemies come from? What will happen next?

The movie that is war is playing to audiences worldwide now, and attendance is at an all-time high. The events of September 11, 2001, brought this theme into every household in the world. Terrorism is the watchword that drowns each dawn before the Sun has even had an opportunity to offer its warming rays of light. The stars look down upon a world of fear, insecurity, famine and bloodshed. Is humanity to become a family of light or one of artificial limbs, disfigured faces and fatherless children? Must all play yards be replaced with graveyards before the truth is finally known?

The problem with the truth is that there are few who wish to hear it. Humans have two ears with which to listen and one voice with which to speak, but all evidence seems to be to the contrary. One must be able to perceive the truth before one can hear it and then experience it. Extraterrestrials, for instance, are now being perceived to a much greater degree. Statistics show that 63 percent of the world believe that extraterrestrial races exist compared to only 47 percent a few short years ago. Fifty-two percent believe that humanity will make contact with these races within their lifetime, up 12 percent from only two years ago! These are random statistics that cannot be attributed to any one demographic group, so it is not the younger generations speaking for the old but an across-the-board expansion of consciousness. Perception changes everything, even truth.

TO UNDERSTAND TRUTH, REJECT MYTH

For the most part, humans have not been told the truth about themselves, and the truth that does exist is sketchy—an oblique projection that makes it seem that life is less than precious and worthwhile. Too much emphasis has been placed upon books thought to be holy, and scholars whose studies and views are too slanted and skewed to be trusted have interpreted these books. Many words are spoken but few are heard. Too many ancient texts gather dust; protected from the public, they also protect the truth from being brought to light.

But in order to understand the truth, you must reject the myths that have guided you thus far, and this humanity is loath to do. The truth is that you are pure consciousness wrapped in the soiled overwrappings of a past that is not yours. The histories that have been reported and retold to you are inaccurate representations; they are symbolic myths from another race, another time and another world strung together to resemble a past, present and future. They are stories whose origins are in the stars—but not your stars.

In order to survive as a species, you must change your future, but you cannot do so without allowing your past to come to an end. There must be an end so that there can be a beginning, but an ending need not include the destruction of all things living. You cannot eradicate other species without their ascent, but you can decimate yourselves in the process. This is not clearly understood yet, but it will be soon.

Who fights your wars today, do you know? Those who battle today battled yesterday as well. They are reincarnated souls who have not yet found peace. They take their battle from life to life, from country to country and from world to world. Are you certain that their war is your war? They bring you war, but they beg for peace. Can you not see it in their eyes? Their hearts bleed for it, I assure you. If peace has a future, then it rests in your hands. Unfortunately, the weapons they have brought with them rest in your hands as well. You will not create the means for outer peace until you find the way to inner peace, and you will not find inner peace until you discover your own truth. The truth is hiding in plain sight; it is everywhere you are. The light emerges as quickly as the shadow recedes.

EMBRACE TRUTH AND FIGHT BLIND IGNORANCE

You cannot fight the shadow with weapons, because light has no weapon; and you cannot fight ignorance with information, because they are one and the same. Information is not knowledge, and it is not wisdom. Information is memorized, passed on, regurgitated, spit out and recycled in tomorrow's headlines. Seek knowledge and teach others where to find their own; the very best teachers are the ones who work with the blind, for they above all others know that if they cannot teach their pupils how to know it or do it for themselves, their pupils will be lost.

Captors often hide behind masks and blindfold their prisoners as well, but secrets rarely last long among the greedy. The blind cannot see, and they are destined to follow rather than lead, but the masked see even less than the blind, because their own eyes deceive them again and again. The blind do not know if the Sun is dawning in the east or setting in the west, but those who hide behind masks see even less. Whom will they trust? Who can be believed? Long ago those who called themselves gods also wore masks. They disguised themselves so that others could not see what was all too obvious. Those who sacrifice themselves to you in this way do so for a purpose. Do not waste an opportunity to remove your own blinders while you still can. Terrorists are messengers. They have delivered fear to your doorstep because bloodshed has been delivered to theirs. For every terrorist there is an antiterrorist—one who embraces present-day truth and rejects a past agenda of fear. Antiterrorists do not follow the prescribed prophecies of the past, even those set down in stone. When the Earth quakes, even stone is reduced to rubble. When true wisdom is spoken, falseness is reduced to ash.

SMOKE AND MIRRORS AND ASH

The year 2005 is a year of smoke and mirrors and ash. If you fail to see one for what it is, you will surely see the others, as the unavoidable stench of war will come closer still. Those who hunger for it can almost taste it now, and no act of contrition will still their hand. The weapons most feared are in human hands, where they have always been.

Humans are both the target and the trigger, just as they have been in the past and will be in the future. Those who have been elected to speak for you forget themselves now; they blanch in the face of power, and their words are too late and too few. When an opportunity to speak your truth is presented to you, do not wait to see who will go before you; regrets do not make good companions. The opposite of war is not peace; it is truth. Humans will not live in peace until they walk in truth. Truth does not walk alone, and its companions are many.

Child's Play

A child is a gift that is borrowed from the universe, a gift that is meant to be returned in better condition than it was received. Children begin as emotional transparencies, with open hearts and minds. As they emerge from the womb, they only appear to be solid in shape and form. They come into this world with new vision and unique gifts, but what will they leave it with?

Your children are not the key to your future and your grandchildren are not either. Today's children are not here to inherit problems they did not create any more than you were when you arrived. It is unfair to think that they can or will save the world, but many people are counting on them to do just that. If the former is true, would it not also be unfair to rob them of an expressive childhood while at the same time launching them into a future of technological warfare, immoderate government and neolithic education?

THE CHILD'S MIND IS INCOMPLETE BUT WHOLE

Humans have always celebrated their young and have always placed hope in the next generation, but the next generation has learned from the previous one, and rather than becoming the future, the next generation most often becomes a repeat of the past. Children learn by example, but if the examples are less than exemplary, then what is learned and later demonstrated will be less than exemplary. Children are not adults in small bodies, but they are portrayed as such on television and by those within the ranks of those who construct virtual realities in video worlds of surrealistic wonder. A young mind is purposely incomplete, but it is not less than whole. All of the gaps and inconsistencies between thoughts are designed to allow paths to new realities to form; this is the nature of true learning. A child's natural curiosity will teach her almost everything she needs to know. She instinctively knows what questions to ask and of whom to ask them, but all too often these activities are thwarted by well-meaning parents, guardians and teachers with tired agendas and rehearsed curricula.

TODAY'S SCHOOLS ARE PRISONS FOR CHILDREN

Today's schools are little more than institutions of imposed learning, testing quarries where survival of the fittest applies to all—students, teachers and administrators. Antiquated textbooks filled with recycled jargon crowd desks, lockers and backpacks while creativity is cast aside. Students have become little more than inmates and teachers their jailers. Minimum standards of education are the norm, and memorization techniques designed to increase test scores but not learning are the rule of the day.

Crowded rooms filled with stale air begin the polluting process far too early in the morning, and children who have not yet digested the past night's dinner have already skipped breakfast. Without proper energy to burn, young bodies produce frustrated and irregular cells filled with elevated levels of stress. Adolescent stress is unique to its age group and very different from that which is encountered and produced by adults. Apathy, resentment, hate and intolerance are just a few of the outer markers represented in adolescent stress. Inner markers are subtler and barely visible to the watchful but busy eyes of loving parents.

Your children are not really yours. You might have conceived them, birthed them, adopted or raised them, but they do not belong to you. All parents are surrogates, placeholders for a new race of beings who are being born into a generation of unprecedented change, mutational shift and dimensional modulation. New-generation children resist labels; they do not wish to be classified within the ranks of the very systems they will soon dismantle. They know that they are not A students or B students, but they have not yet managed to convince those who measure them by these antiquated standards.

As long as artificial lessons and truths constitute the bulk of classroom activity, children will continue to regurgitate the mis-qualified energy that they are spoon-fed, but resistance among them will continue to build. Are all new-generation children of the Indigo variety? No, for this would be as much a generalization as the much feared and maligned attention deficit disorder (ADD) and attention deficit hyperactive disorder (ADHD). Unsafe narcotics influence these wildly creative young minds, inducing them to conform to a reality that they are here to change. Will future drugs also influence an Indigo submission? It is possible but not likely, because Indigo minds are structured in significantly different ways.

YOUR CHILDREN ARE CHANGING AND BECOMING MORE GIFTED

The year 2005 will mark the beginning of a revolution within the minds of the young. Almost imperceptibly, the frequency within their synaptic responses will change. This will occur within all beings of new consciousness, regardless of age. Unconsciously, they have been awaiting such a time, but only a relative few will be alert to the changes on a conscious level. The change is a collective one and the alteration is permanent, meaning that it cannot be reversed, overlooked or forgotten. Immediate effects or changes will be negligible for the most part, as this is only a beginning marker and is much too subtle to be distinguishable from all of the other changes occurring within young bodies and minds.

Within a year or so, your children will begin to display unprecedented kinetic and telepathic abilities. These techniques, often credited to the more gifted or developed among previous generations, will become the norm in all subsequent generations. This will at first be noted on a case-by-case basis and will not be acknowledged publicly. It will be more evident within certain ancestral lines as well as within certain countries where children are held in high esteem. It will be less evident in rigidly structured environments where conformity is king as well as in societies and cultures where archaic methods of upbringing and near-lethal doses of controlled substances are overprescribed.

WHAT TO EXPECT FROM THE NEW CHILDREN

Other races among you will be noted over the next several years. Variance in skin color, height anomalies, specific food preferences as well as previously unknown allergies will startle parents, educators and physicians. The newer generations know your true history and will unconditionally reject that which is offered to them by unnatural means. They will be more interested in geometry than algebra and will find newer and quicker ways of arriving at mathematical conclusions. They will seem less interested in other languages and cultures, but this is only because their telepathic ability will tell them what they need to know when they need to know it—they will not need to memorize information that might or might not serve them in the future.

They will reject logic and linear thinking in favor of dimensional tasking, a new way of learning that they will introduce into the consciousness of those who will choose to remain in the educational arena. They will reward the administrative community with near-genius ideas and theories that are poised to revolutionize how learning takes place. They will also march against those who oppose new systems of thought as well as those who continue to enslave them in classrooms of virtual learning.

What can you do to improve your relationships with people from the younger generations? Understand that they are here with a very specific purpose, just as you are. Even if you strongly disagree with their methods, evaluate their merit as well as any future benefit. Realize that children will not sit still, especially not in a sterile environment where they feel disenfranchised. Spend time in nature with children, adolescents and teens whenever possible, even if it means eating a meal outdoors instead of indoors. Ask them less about the present and more about the future. Ask them to begin envisioning and creating it now. Remind them that the future belongs to them—not to fix, but to create.

On the Verge of Virtual Science

Long ago, opposing forces set out to discover and later map the universe. These forces were so different in every possible way that it seemed highly unlikely that they would ever meet, much less agree on anything. But as it turns out, the universe is a rather small place after all, and this local galaxy is smaller still. When the subject matter is narrowed even more, such as that which might relate to the Earth, it is almost impossible not to bump into another's thought process. Scientists and engineers, researchers and astronomers, microbiologists and physicists are now meeting in boardrooms and laboratories all over the world, eager to discover what they have in common with one another.

Unfortunately, the boardrooms and laboratories are owned and controlled by corporate conglomerates—giants of industry whose power rivals that of a nuclear bomb, literally. The same corporations who fund cancer studies also cause the need for the very studies they fund. Those who fund AIDS projects refuse to release the solutions they have paid for. Results and findings are sequestered behind doors where vaulted contracts prevent the release of life-saving information.

Why? Because cures, like other commodities, are auctioned off to the highest bidder, and private auctions, like private sales, are just that. Until recently, world governments have most often been the highest bidders. Long-lasting, high-price-tag, federally sponsored studies with expected results are then repackaged and resold to moguls of state who sit upon the boards of well-respected, do-good companies with consumer-friendly names and faces.

SCIENTISTS UNDER THE IRON HEEL

When was the last time a true cure was discovered? At what previous time in history has the pharmaceutical industry both introduced and recalled as many drugs as today? Why are so many drugs being marketed directly to you rather than through channels within the medical community? When did insurance companies become more responsible for your health than you? Science has now mapped the DNA sequence; would it not stand to reason that it has also mapped much more? Questions such as these bear consideration, as do the threadlike thoughts that cannot help but tag along. Answers are not as easy to come by, but your own imagination is not far from the mark and makes for a good starting place.

Scientists have many of the answers to your questions, but they are not at liberty to reveal them. Today many freelance writers find employment, but freelance scientists are virtually nonexistent. Research scientists are under contract to pharmaceutical giants in much the same way that physicians are under contract to insurance companies. The price for freedom is unemployment, an expensive and semipermanent condition. Anonymous sponsors dole out study grants with relative frequency but demand and enforce secrecy in every way. Behind alabaster walls, researchers are persecuted and haunted by memos, reminders, meetings and reviews of goals as yet unmet. Who would deliver themselves into such dens of danger? Believe it or not, they number in the millions, and a veritable waiting list of summa cum laude, newly degreed and decorated scholars hungrily wait their turn.

GREED AND THE PROBLEM OF ACCESS TO INFORMATION

As stated elsewhere in this text, these are unprecedented times, historically speaking. This is the age of information, and there is more of it now than there has been at any other time; however, the problem now, as always, still remains—access. Without access to real information, you can easily become caught up in the chaos of misinformation, or worse, the debris of disinformation. Left to sort through the detritus of obsolete and underfunded case studies is a fate worse than death itself, which under other circumstances would be considered a worthy cause. The corporate laboratory, then, is a necessary evil for an open-minded scientist on a noble pursuit, no less an evil than the corporate ladder is for a young entrepreneur in a land where the two-headed giant of greed and money still rules.

Ownership aside, science and health have more in common than ever before. A cure for AIDS exists, and radiation will soon be altogether obsolete. Many forms of blindness can be cured and hearing loss can be restored to between 35 to 50 percent of normal or better. Science is working to teach the body to grow new limbs and to receive virtual ones without rejecting them. Virtual computer programs that offer a model of perfect health are being evaluated behind closed doors. Imaging systems capable of projecting 3D virtual models are also being tested. Overlays that assist the diagnostic process and show the pathway of least resistance to health are already in the funding process and will soon be on the auction block.

Why are these computer-age procedures not yet available? Why do hundreds of clonelike virtual imagery computer games find their way to the consumer market long before these life-enhancing diagnostic tools do? Unfortunately, the answer is simple—what will the world do with its healthy people when it hasn't yet discovered what to do with its ill ones?

You Must Learn to Sustain Yourself

The world is overpopulated and underresourced. Automated manufacturing has reduced the need for a significant work force. The wealthy do not work hard, the healthy do not want to work hard, the newer generations are smart enough not to work hard, and the poor and disenfranchised no longer have the energy to work hard. The farmers are paid not to grow, and the factories are paid not to run. Leisure activities are at an all-time low, and worldwide depression is at an all-time high.

Humans no longer believe that they can revive or restore themselves on their own and have become dependent upon the medical and pharmaceutical industry for their own well-being. The frontiers of science have brought health to a virtual standstill. Children are drugged before they enter the play yard, women dose themselves to endure the cycles of their womanhood and men are convinced that they have or will soon contract erectile dysfunction. Pills and supplements bring you here and take you there, but rarely do they work well together, if at all.

The medicine cabinet and the prescription counter cannot appropriately sustain you. Your body has an elemental wisdom of its own that is vastly ignored. New discoveries in the field of longevity can and will restore your wellness, but you must demand and insist on the same from yourselves as you do from others, otherwise it will not happen in your lifetime. If you deny your own wisdom in favor of another's, how will you recognize your specific cure? Your bodies are not sacks of cells in chaos; they are wisdom keepers and code breakers. You are not physical beings, but you have physical bodies. Your body is not your purpose, but it serves you and your purpose.

Free Yourself of Medical Misadventure

From time to time, remind yourselves that you are actively freeing yourselves from any and all medical misadventures. The road to health is paved with good intentions—intend to be on that road! Support noninvasive techniques to wellness whenever possible; limit your intake of unhealthful foods and those that barely qualify as having nutritional content (you know which ones they are). Become medically intuitive about your own health; there will be fewer surprises that way. Read labels instead of wearing them or ingesting what they describe. Alternative medical practices are better than conventional ones in most cases, but they are still medical; choose health instead. Imagine that when you next return to Earth, you will inherit the same body you now own, for some of you indeed will. Does this thought alone not merit the benefit of greater awareness today?

Spirited Religion and the New Age

Perfection exists within all things and at all times, even when they are not in evidence or on public display. Perhaps this statement best describes the condition within which humans find themselves in relation to the world's established religions. The word religion is derived from the Latin *religare* or *religio*, meaning "to bind." Originally, all that was considered sacred bound humans to their Creator. Thus, a binding or place of acknowledgment was instilled within all humans. The term sacred was applied to all things life giving and life sustaining. The Sun was sacred, as was the Earth. Mothers and grandmothers were sacred. Land, and all that grew upon it, was sacred; so were water, fire and ether (the aspect of Spirit that enlivens or gives life to all things).

Offerings to that which was sacred marked humans' binding love for life. When life-affirming days such as solstices and equinoxes brought communities together for a few days or weeks at a time, a place of acknowledgment was temporarily constructed to offer shelter. Much later, these shelters became churches and temples of worship. Acknowledgment became obligation when humanity became dependent upon gods, demigods and human intermediaries. In essence, humans relinquished their own authority and instead acknowledged dependence upon a supreme power that was beyond human understanding or control.

PATTERNS AND CATEGORIES OF WORLD RELIGIONS

Many more religions existed long ago than have survived until today. These were divided into categories such as religio-ethical (having to do with or being based upon both religion and ethics), religio-laici (the religion of lay people), religio-political (having to do with or being based upon both religion and politics), religio-loci (having to do with devotion to a sacred character or place) and religiose (zealous devotion). All world religions were at one time classified in this way, and theories as to the divine origin of one religion over another are based upon insufficient and ambiguous data. Codes of faith, values and morals were revealed in all religions. Eventually, the pantheistic tendency to identify the subject with the object worshipped was superseded by the belief that the origin, development and control of humankind emanated from one will. At this point, henotheism (the worship of a universal supreme being as a special god while acknowledging or believing in the existence of other religions and gods) was admitted as a more highly developed form of religion.

Christianity, Judaism and Islam, as monotheistic religions, were called the greatest of the revealed religions, because they were based upon the communication of certain truths as revealed by God to the human race through acknowledged prophets (suns/sons). When the written word became more accessible, those who could read and translate accurately found positions for themselves in temples and wealthy households.

Eventually, instruction in the beliefs of a religion replaced natural communion with one's God. Those who chose not to follow one of the world's main religions were thought to follow paganism (believing in or relating to a religion that is not one of the world's main religions; is regarded as questionable, or worse, as having no religion). If you feel unfortunate enough to fall into this category, I would remind you that all of the Greeks and most of the Romans did as well. The North American Indian tribes were thought to be heathens; the Maya worshipped the Sun; the Lemurians worshipped the godhood in what they created; and the Atlanteans worshipped power, grace and technology. Does this place you in good company or poor company? That is yet to be seen, because who or what you worship is less important than how you apply the knowledge and wisdom you receive from your moments of communion or worship.

MODERN-DAY RELIGION HAS LITTLE TO OFFER

The problem with religion is that in this age of information, it has little new information to offer. Religion has not evolved or kept pace with human awareness. Humans are asking questions that religion cannot answer, so humans are abandoning religion in favor of seeking other horizons. Unfortunately, humans are still looking for answers in the past rather than in the future, so they search in vain, returning to the starting place again and again with more questions and fewer answers. Modern religion is dependent upon its ancient prophets and prophecies. If either fails to fulfill their promise, followers will abandon these religions in droves. As you can see, they have more than a vested interest in the outcome of this two-thousand-year cycle of events.

Currently, all established and recognized religions are vying for superiority over one another. Each in its own way would like to be the oldest, the most righteous, the most evolved, the most moral, the most circumspect and the most charitable. Unfortunately, the struggle between the old ways and the new times has succeeded in little else other than making them most political. They would argue that their prophets were also political, but they were not; they were controversial. History has always offered you prophets and prophecies, but it has also offered you messengers and messages. It is for you to determine the difference.

PROPHETS AND PROPHECIES

A prophet is not a god or a mere advocate or spokesperson for a cause or an idea. He is not a fortuneteller or a preacher, and he might or might not be a good teacher or a good leader. A prophet is someone who can interpret and reveal what might be too complex or mysterious for another. He dwells in two worlds, because he does not limit himself to the world of humans. True prophets invite change, inciting it if necessary. Their very existence seems to carry an aura that emanates from elsewhere. They care little for themselves—they are not martyrs, but they have become martyrs when forced to.

A prophecy is not an admonition, a warning or an indication that something unpleasant is going to happen. A prophecy is a glimpse into a future possibility. It offers choice rather than conformity, creativity rather than conjecture. A prophecy can just as easily be a wonderful or marvelous thing. Why are they so often interpreted as ominous? Because they often describe a time or a situation that is much different than the present. In order for the prophecy to become a reality, something must happen to change the present reality. Change itself can be one of the most ominous and fearful of all things, especially if it applies to you.

THE ARRIVAL OF THE NEW AGE

The world has never had a shortage of prophets or prophecies, and although great teachers are few and far between, adequate ones are plentiful. The onset of what you call the new age brought its own share of teachers and teachings. Messages from nowhere and everywhere filled books and volumes almost overnight. Memories that are lifetimes old rekindled old feelings and reignited new passions. The desire to know more and be more was reborn within certain segments of humanity. The differences between the generations became more pronounced as awakened awareness began to permeate the Earth plane.

What is the new age? Simply put, it is that which does not follow in linear sequence that which has come before. A new age offers a radical shift in thinking; it accommodates new possibilities within old paradigms before they are dismissed as heretic. The New Age does not require followers. In fact, the fewer followers the better, lest it be perceived as a religion. Already and all too soon, the groundwork for this has been set in motion. The world does not need a new religion, but it could use a few million more free thinkers. The old prophecies are about to run out, but does that mean the world needs new ones? If the old prophets are proven wrong, will the world believe new ones?

A new age tends to define itself rather than allowing itself to be defined by others. A true new age bears no title, has no precedent and offers no regrets. That being said, how many false starts can you count before the true New Age begins? For instance, was the millennium celebration in the year 2000 a false start? Beyond that, were the events of September 11, 2001, a sign that the New Age has veered in a different direction? Is the increased activity of Earth changes a sign that the New Age has begun, or does the decrease in the Earth's natural resources indicate that it will be a failure rather than a success? Do you expect the worst so that you can achieve the best, or do you pray for the best and prepare for the worst? Prophecy is not clear on this, and prophets too quickly become poets when forced to attest.

THE FALL OF WORLD RELIGIONS

Religions will continue to speak in parables, because true facts are still too dangerous to transmit. Ask yourselves these questions: Are people killing one another to bring the truth to light or to hide it for a little while longer? If one religion is capable of saving the world, isn't it time for it to do so? Is one religion, one people or one culture more important than the next? If the world's religions are so different, why have they always bled to death the same way on history's battlefields? If the Day of Judgment were to truly come upon humanity, what would the verdict be? Is any war or conflict truly final or decisive? Who or what would be left if it were?

Beginning in 2005, the world's religions will all suffer losses. The numbers of their members will decline, and they will choose parallel but alternate paths. That which has long been hidden will begin to come to light. It will emerge when least expected and from a corner of the world that has been vastly ignored. Disgruntled investors and unpaid workers will crack the egg, and the cosmic truth will begin to emerge. Fake identities and recovered artifacts will attempt to alter the past, but not for long. Collusion will be exposed at deep levels. Expect apologies, misdirection and alliances from unlikely sources. Do not expect recovery too soon, for the wound will be a deep one—fatal to some. Hearts and minds will ache, and remedies will be few. An attack of courage will grip some of the very people you have already given up on—get ready to catch them when they fall!

Paradise Regained

The end of ignorance and innocence will mark the beginning of the end of the third dimension. Is the end of innocence the same as the end of the world? For some, yes, the experience will be that and more. The year 2005 will pull the rug out from under those whose beliefs have been the most stable, enduring and unwavering. Ignorance knows no prejudice; it moves across all divides, including class, race and religion. Humans must rediscover their innocence before they are consumed by skepticism and cynicism.

Watch for Subtle Changes and Overcome Regret

The energies and events of 2005 will bring this subject to the brink, and this will last for approximately seven years. A time of endings and beginnings, changes of mind and heart, as well as abandonment of beliefs and tenets will signal that the end is near. Beginnings will not be as obvious. In many ways, they have already begun, but not noticeably so. The untrained eye might notice small overtures from directions most unlikely, and closer observation will reveal nods and handshakes from opposite poles of understanding—it will be that subtle. How subtle have some of your own changes been? What endings have marked your own beginnings?

Every shift in consciousness must overcome its own regrets. But if the regrets are many, the memories might be too few. A shift in consciousness is a labor of supreme desire and is achieved at great cost. A new consciousness will cause the death of the old, and this understandably offers regrets of a monumental kind. Regrets and suffering often go hand in hand, but needlessly so. Long ago, a word that loosely meant, "to endure, experience or put up with" was incorrectly translated. The word translated as "to suffer," and humanity has done that ever since. The belief that humans can only learn through their own suffering, disillusionment and dilemma is an old one. It goes hand in hand with the belief that only when the state of ignorance is made so miserable that humans can no longer remain there will they choose differently.

Humans cannot be greater than themselves or wiser than their experience, but wisdom is only bought with experience. No other coin of the realm will do. Deny experience, and you deny wisdom. Many will purchase information this year. Some will be fortunate enough to afford themselves knowledge. But only those who invite the kind of experiences that come at a cost will know true wisdom. If you fear the end, then invite it, challenge it and dare it to present itself. The end is always deceiving, because it hides the beginning where you cannot see it. Do not be afraid to speak your fears out loud, for only then can they be acted upon.

The world that you know and the reality that you call real can and will end. That which you believe is solid is not, and it is only by collective agreement that it seems to be so. That which has long been heralded as truth will be exposed as a lie so that it can be corrected. Humans have been on a collision course with their own past, but this year they will begin the cycle of course correction. The true path does not lie between right and wrong or between left and right. The true path leads to the stars and back again, but it is a journey that you must make for yourself; no one else can do it for you. It is a dangerous path, and you will need to thread the eye of the needle to get there, because the answers that you seek are there. Have you not already looked everywhere else?

The Inner Voice May Be Inconsistent

The inner voice that speaks to you in 2005 will be an inconsistent one. Sometimes it will whisper, and other times it will shout. Listen to it anyway. It is trying very hard to clear the debris of the past that has prevented it from speaking clearly until now. It will seem emotional and irrational, impulsive and irresponsible. Hear it out. It will settle into a new rhythm and a more comfortable orbit in due time.

Speak aloud and read aloud whenever possible. Clear your throat as many times as it takes until what you have been trying to say emerges clearly and coherently. When it does, look in the mirror and through your eyes, and speak your truth again. Then say it louder. When you are ready, tell someone you trust what you have discovered.

What can you expect in 2005, given such a broad parade of inconsistent voices? Will history cause you to live out the obvious so the few and the many can say that they were right? Who can save you from yourselves? A savior dwells within each of you but does not reside in the euhemeristic mythology of the past or in the eulogistic fantasy of the future. If you correctly identify the savior who dwells within, you will have little to no need for the ones who will present themselves later.

Each religion has its own prophets and prophecies, and because the believers are many, these will soon come to life. Beginning in 2005, you will be introduced to a new cast of characters and a new set of facts. It will be up to you to vouch for their authority in your life. You will do this by perceiving their relevance or irrelevance in your reality. You will be asked to vote in more ways than one, first with your voice and later with your conscience. Tell the truth so that others will be inspired to do the same.

A Deceptively Simple Conclusion

New and old paradigms will continue to exist side by side for another seven years. During this time, you will have many opportunities to discover truths that have so far eluded you. Be flexible but persistent in your pursuit, and you will learn much. Be willing to travel through places strewn with your own debris. Only by observing humanity's waste will you arrive at a new plan instead of an old conclusion. Some wells are deeper than others, and you might have to stretch farther than ever before to get to the clear, sweet water. If you are sincere, a hand, a thought or a feeling will reach out to steady your effort and sustain it.

Every children's story has a villain, a hero and a moral outcome. Every chessboard has a powerful queen, a deposed king and many pawns. Every game has a winner and a loser. The white and the black as opposing forces meet in the middle, each having prayed to God for victory. But victory, like virtue, is not born in opposition but in unity. Now that humans have split the atom and divided themselves, they must recombine what is missing in order to reunite. Humanity's very survival depends upon this discovery, a deceptively simple one. The answer presents itself in art as well as in science; in philosophy and in religion; in mythology, parable and literature. A simple mind can identify it in a child's verse; the complex mind will posit that it lies elsewhere. The ignorant have forgotten it and the mighty have stolen it, but the salt of the Earth belongs to none and to all. My sentience awaits this discovery and even now hearkens the advance of your footsteps.

A Century of
New Medicine

January 2005

Why is our culture placing so much attention on drugs like Viagra? With so many illnesses and diseases to study and cure, many of them debilitating and even fatal, it would seem that a sexual boost is the last thing our society needs. I don't mean to diminish the importance of this dysfunction, but shouldn't the pharmaceutical industry be using research dollars to study cancer or cure AIDS?

From a spiritual or nonphysical perspective, there is no difference between one dysfunction and another. Anything that reduces or removes the will from the willing is considered an affliction and a plague. Although a physical existence imposes some limitations, it should not impose a threat.

Dysfunctions often mirror the age and the culture within which they are most prominent. For example, the onset of the age of Pisces (the fish in the element of water) brought about the readjustment of the Earth's oceans and its underground water tables, the advent of travel via the world's waterways and innovations in the areas of irrigation and hydroelectric power. The end of this age carries the burden of drought, murderous battles over water rights, starvation of peoples, lands that are no longer fertile, hurricane-class storms, polluted seas and decimated populations of fish too poisoned for human consumption.

The search for pure water and the hydration of the body at this time cannot be stressed enough. The ending of this age by necessity also brings the tearing down of all beliefs and structures that do not serve the dawn of the new age. In this battle, no victors can remain, because until the old is torn down, the new cannot be built. Religions and societies based upon the supremacy of one race or belief system over another will not survive in the new age.

THE REMEDIES COME WITH THE NEW AGE

Every end is also a beginning, and the emergence of the Aquarian age (the water bearer in the element of air) brings its own gifts and rewards. The melting of the glaciers will provide new sources of water. Embedded within the frozen ice are a myriad of microscopic trace elements and minerals that will heal many of the Earth's woes. The element of air will carry these even to remote places and dry sands where their distribution will restore fertility to parched and arid lands. Travel by air and space will be a highlight of this age, and new forms of fuel based upon liquid air will replace energy lost by the depletion of fossil fuels. Tornadoes will be common for the first few hundred years, as these will stir and cleanse the air. Volcanoes will spew and erupt, and ash long buried underground will restore and replenish the content of the air you breathe. Eventually, the flow (water) of life will be restored, and air and water will be at peace. New forms of science are on the horizon as are teachers to demonstrate their benefits. Crystalline buildings and transparent architecture will become popular in honor of the element of air and its transparency. New cultures, less dense in thought and attitude, will bring a breath of fresh air to societies in danger of decay. Those who continue to preach parables of density will not find favor in the new age and will soon dissolve into the nothingness that is everything.

What does all of this have to do with dysfunctional lifestyles and the quality of life? Altogether everything! Density is associated with the root chakra, and the root chakra is associated with sexuality and survival. Because the survival of humanity is at stake now, so too is human sexuality—the ability to reproduce and extend humanity one generation at a time—at stake. Erectile dysfunction and male and female infertility are not causes, but they are among the many effects of the ending of an age. You will not find this information in current history books or in medical journals, but esoteric references to this phenomenon exist within archaeological findings about many ancient cultures and within the DNA of every living culture.

THE HEALING POWER OF THE SUN AND THE ASTRONOMICAL CLOCK

Our Sun influences every aspect of life on Earth, physical and otherwise. The Sun offers necessary nutrients and vitamins to every living thing. Without the steady and guiding influence of the Sun, life as we know it would not exist on Earth. But the Sun has not always been as stable and constant as it appears today. Sunspots, solar storms and other cosmic forces cause the Sun to enter into phases or seasons that affect the quality of the radiation it emits. Sunspot activity can disrupt every aspect of daily life on Earth in ways that even local weather cannot.

Radiation from the Sun affects the natural biorhythm of every living thing. Solar radiation acts upon and regulates the ability of the pineal and hypothalamus glands to produce and release specific hormones. Indirectly but specifically, these hormones go on to regulate the fertility hormones, estrogen and progesterone. Under stress, a dysfunctional dissonance can easily affect fertility.

This is true of all species, but currently it is humans who are most out of balance with themselves and their environment. When our Sun experiences the stress of instability, all life on Earth is affected. In ancient Egypt, Akhenaton attempted to describe this phenomenon to the populace by the use of pictorial depictions. The ancient Maya also inscribed architectural pictographs that demonstrated the power and importance of the Sun upon fertility. Infertility in women and sterility in men were hallmarks of these great cultures near their end.

It is not difficult to see just how many dysfunctions plague most Earth cultures at this time. War, famine, infertility, poverty, sexual dysfunction, depression, educational malaise, governmental intervention, economic subsistence, and consummate struggles for power and domination echo the uncertainty of all cultures at this time. Patriarchy, or institutionalized domination by men, is also a hallmark of this age and one that is moving toward a not-so-gentle end. The physiosocial effects of the aforementioned changes, coupled with the struggle to maintain a status quo, are notable and evident in the advent of drugs such as Viagra. Impotence and low sperm counts in men can be attributed to many factors, but a decrease in the influence of stable solar radiation is chief among these. Currently, 33 percent of the male population are subject to this condition at least part of the time. By contrast, 46 percent of human females suffer from psychological or physiological dysfunctions directly attributable to sexuality. Based on these statistics, pharmaceutical companies are racing one another to be the first on the market with the next miracle drug.

Radiation from the Sun is also known to synchronize and, when necessary, to recalibrate the biological clock of all living things. Deciduous trees that shed their leaves in the fall respond to this timing sequence, as does all seasonal vegetation. Hibernating animals pay close attention to their biological clocks. They remain sensitive to these internal and external forces throughout their entire lives. Every species is also equipped with an astronomical clock, which is aligned in accordance with the relevance of that species. The coordination of the astronomical clock is a factor of the balance achieved by a species in a particular environment. It is also a measure of the evolution of that species within the schema and pertinence of each age. For example, if the dinosaurs had not been decimated by the wisdom of a specific (not random) meteor, they would probably have contracted cancer or been decimated by another intruder. Their relevance within the context of expansion of consciousness on Earth had come to an end.

SYNCHRONIZING TO THE PERSONAL BIOLOGICAL CLOCK

Individuals also respond to the biological clock assigned to them at birth. This little-understood science, based upon the codes inherent in sacred geometry, guides the evolution and timing of all manifested things, without exception. At the time of conception, a rough estimate of the solar-radiation pattern associated with the child's eventual birth can be calculated. Miscarriages are most often due to an inability to synchronize the necessary biological codes with the individual's desire for that lifetime. By the time a child is born, a specific sequence has been revealed and will remain calibrated to the individual throughout his or her entire life. The first breath and the last are already encoded. In more advanced cultures, each unique and specific sequence is duly noted, as this knowledge above and beyond all else will maintain the individual's health and well-being. If—or when—this knowledge becomes better understood, DNA sequencing will become obsolete and blood typing unnecessary. When these physical and nonphysical codes (clocks) are well coordinated, the physiology of the body is in harmony, but when they are not, confusion and disorder reign. In the body, this most often manifests as a disruption to the endocrine system.

Cancer is the effect of the desynchronization of the body. It is a chaotic misalignment of the internal biological clock and is often further complicated by a person's disregard or dissociation from his or her astronomical clock whose sequence, once disturbed, is difficult to restore. Individual patterns of radiation generate magnetic modulations that influence the pineal gland. The pineal gland, among others, releases the correct amount of hormones, which in turn trigger the division and reproduction of healthy cells. As long as the astronomical clock and the biological clock are aligned and in balance, the body instinctively remains healthy. Cell division and multiplication are regulated by the metabolic system that was calibrated at birth. Imbalances within a person's environment, external and internal carcinogens, as well as a host of other misunderstood desynchronizations can alter the perfection and reliability of an individual's unique pattern. This disruption can cause less-than-perfect-timing signals to be released within the biology of the individual, which in turn cause less-than-perfect cells to be created and circulated throughout the body. Indiscriminate and uncontrolled cell division and multiplication result in cancer.

UNNATURAL TIMES, UNNATURAL CURES

Artificial hormones can also influence and alter the body's chemistry, as these are introduced directly into the endocrine system. When the hormones are aligned with the calibration of the individual, the result can be beneficial, but when they are not, biorhythmic desynchronization can occur and cancer might follow. Anything that interferes with the natural and unique biological sequence of the individual can lead to cancerous activity within the body.

These are unnatural times, and many of today's technological advances are also unnatural. These might or might not be aligned with each individual. Natural radiation from the Sun has been known to restore individual codes to a healthy status, but now more than ever, individuals are spending time indoors and under the influence of fluorescent lighting, television, computers, microwave ovens and artificially engineered food, as well as telephonic and radiophonic energies. Although these influences alone cannot be considered carcinogenic, they are far from natural and their healthful benefit upon the biorhythms of the body is highly suspect. Human chemistry is far from delicate, but it cannot be ignored, severely altered or taken for granted without acknowledging that consequences might result.

Will more study and research yield a cure for cancer? It is not likely, at least given its present course. Current treatment techniques include radium therapy, a form of particle energy, which, if properly understood, would be abandoned due to its unstable and unpredictable nature, especially when used on living cells. Radiotherapy all too soon leads to radiotoxicity, the effects of which are well documented. Exposure to radiation causes the destruction and decay of diseased cells, but it does nothing to restore the production of balanced and healthy cells. Radiation causes radioactive waste. Externally, this waste must be sealed and stored for hundreds and even thousands of years before it is rendered harmless. What can the body be expected to do with such toxic waste internally?

Another approved procedure, although not a cure, is to excise or remove cancerous cells by the use of surgical procedures. If the body is willing to undergo such an operation, this can be of benefit. Unfortunately, these procedures are often combined with radiation, which further confuses the body by removing some cells and contributing to the decay and death of others. Where are the corrective and restorative measures in this procedure? How is the body to receive new, intelligent and healthful instructions when it is being slowly poisoned and encouraged to die? Your body is not your enemy any more than your neighbor is. A radioactive weapon is just that; it is hardly a tool or a cure.

Humans learn by example, and a good example can last a lifetime. Cells can be "taught" and encouraged to reproduce in healthful ways. This theory will soon be put to the test and the results will be encouraging, but success will not be achieved until the connection between mind and body is acknowledged and understood.

THE FALSE MEDICINE OF ATLANTIS: TECHNOLOGY WITHOUT COMPASSION

Atlantis was one of the greatest civilizations and continents that ever existed. Near its end, cancer was rampant and epidemic. Advances in the medical treatment of cancer had progressed well enough, and the subject of radiation as a cure arose then as well. Radiation as a source of energy has always been important to humanity, but, like water, it has been harnessed, owned and controlled for the advantage of the few and not the many. Upon Atlantis, science had already learned to isolate the quality of radioactive material into positive and negative poles. The division of atomic elements was still in its infancy in terms of Atlantean knowledge, but when combined with certain crystalline influences (the glory of Atlantis), radioactive material could be caused to behave in beneficial ways. Unfortunately, the fallible law of "more is better" influenced the Atlantean society to excess. This, coupled with an overriding propensity for comparison and competition, led to the demise of the once great civilization.

Under the reign of technology, little compassion could be found, and the losses counted were many. The Atlanteans, who were overly obsessed with sustaining their youth, thought to inculcate a new language into the cancerous cells. Beyond the regeneration of health, the cells were instructed to restore youth. This mixed message caused a mutation within the structure of the cell, which led to a slow collapse and a steady decline in well-being. The eventual result of such folly was a slow but constant deterioration and retardation of both mind and body. The soul of Atlantis, individually and collectively, was forced to comply.

History is never completely erased and, as in all things, the choices made by one eventually apply to all. What today is called Alzheimer's disease is a throwback to this time. It has resurfaced at the end of this age, just as it was created at the end of another.

Almost every culture, past and present, has had some form of interaction with radioactive material. Within your cellular memory is a solar or atomic memory that cannot be altered, erased or destroyed. This has saved your species from extinction many times and will likely do so again. Like the astronomical clock, your solar memory is permanently encoded with an ability to attain the highest possibilities within the evolutionary goals set forth when humanity as a species was invited into being. This matrix of possibilities allows each evolutional age to grow exponentially as well as to destroy itself and begin again. Within such a wide range of possibilities guidelines to success exist, as do teachers, teachings and examples from which to draw. Ultimately, however, the choice rests in the will of humanity—to thrive or merely survive.

AUTOIMMUNE DISEASES, PERSONAL AND GLOBAL

The debilitating illness AIDS could be cured were it not for the near-fatal prognosis it has been given. The human mind is very tender, innocent and childlike. If someone is told that he or she has contracted an autoimmune disease with only a small rate of survivability, that person's mind will quickly construct a reality based upon this information. If the person is told there is little hope for a different outcome, then he or she will hope just a little, for to hope more would be unrealistic based upon the facts one has been given. Such is the unfortunate risk of contracting such an illness. It is a test of the will of the mind and the body as influenced by an external authority rather than an internal one.

The immune system of the Earth has also been severely compromised. My veins of river waters and my arteries of golden minerals are congested and pol-luted. But my hopes of a reversal of health and well-being do not lie in any external source or undetermined course of action. I do not lament the cause of my affliction, previous decisions made, adventures undertaken, trust incorrectly invested or the sores that have been bulldozed onto my back—to do so would only retard my recovery. I do not pray that humans will awaken in time to save the Earth for their great-grandchildren—to do so would place a burden on those who are already burdened enough. Neither do I await the arrival of advanced knowledge from my brothers and sisters in the stars—to do so would be to look much farther than is necessary. Shall I depend upon research dollars and grants spent on studying what is more than obvious?

Autoimmune diseases such as AIDS are deconstructions of the basic building blocks of the organism. Unlike cancers, which cannot seem to stop the building of unhealthy cells, immune-deficient illnesses literally forget how to build and sus-tain healthy and unstressed cells. Under stress, the body is first attacked by unre-lenting demands for production that is all too quickly falling behind schedule. The body cannot respond to stress without some form of sacrifice. Borrowing from Peter to pay Paul, the body's natural defenses become impaired. With resources dwindling, the body succumbs to a viruslike condition.

WORLDVIEW AFFECTS THE HEALTH OF EVERY CELL

At this point, the body's own intelligence system is capable of diagnosing its impaired condition and restructuring itself to compensate for any inade-quacy. Why doesn't it? For the most part, it is because the illness has not been approached with an attitude or in a context by which the body, and the intelligence that guides it, can be trusted to heal itself by reorganizing the very stresses that have caused its onset. Humanity has a tendency to respond to patterns in specific and characteristic ways. Using one of these ways, humans gather information into packets of logic and then store them in tidy bundles called belief systems. These are then sorted by category and placed upon well-protected shelves within secure vaults in heavily guarded areas of the brain.

Although original thoughts are presently conscious, fluid and creative, thoughts based upon centuries-old beliefs are dense, hard-wired and calcified into place within the brain. Beliefs that persist over time are the hardest to dislodge—nearly impossible in many cases. Weakness rules where power cannot, and attitudes and beliefs impressed upon the mind strengthen or weaken the connection between the mind and body accordingly. Even small variations or disruptions can lead to significant changes in the outcome of any situation, including illness. Encouragement in the direction of original thought or repetition of calcified beliefs both will result in some progressive change over time. New patterns eventually emerge, and these can stimulate life or confirm death.

A positive or negative worldview influences every aspect of every thought and belief inherent within each cell of the body. An accumulation of stressful and negative thoughts will eventually manifest in a physiological discomfort. This is true of all species, but humans' search for their own consciousness and truth has brought them face-to-face with conundrums that confound and confuse and allow no respite. The key to evolution beyond this illness is to reflect upon your truth before the body offers its own evidence in the form of advancement of disease. To live an incomplete truth is to live an incomplete life. Early detection is the purest form of cure.

PHYSICAL SYSTEMS AND BELIEF SYSTEMS MUST BE UNIFIED

The persistence of disease is the acceptance of the manifest, concrete belief systems inherent within humanity. The remission of disease is the rejection of the norm and the embracing of new, more fluid instructions and the onset of more healthful parameters for body, mind and spirit. Rejection of physical evidence is the most difficult phase of empowerment. After all, why would the body lie? The body will lie to protect the mind from moving beyond the boundaries of what it believes is the all. The body becomes the sacrificial lamb so that the belief system will survive. In order for the body's condition to radically shift, it must reject the prevailing conditions common to its mind and the mind of the society that influences it.

The invisible universe must become your teacher and ally. Genetic and environmental factors must persistently offer their guidance from within until the body's own architecture can respond as a natural consequence rather than a programmed one. All illnesses and diseases are changeable and reversible. Spontaneous health rather than remission of disease is the norm. Belief in a cure for a specific disease is illogical if a belief in the disease itself persists. For example, the Earth does not await a cure for polluted skies; she waits for humans to marvel and wonder at the clarity they are capable of envisioning.

THE TRUE IMPORTANCE OF THE THYMUS

This discussion has thus far offered little in the way of advancing new thought, choosing instead to concentrate on dismantling the existing processes that have debilitated rather than encouraged growth. But to deposit further criticism upon a problem without so much as mounting an alternative that might lead to victory is a further offense in itself. If words are energy, then let the energy of true healing be understood to be located in the thymus gland. Located just below the sternum (breastbone), the thymus gland is deeply connected to the immune system. It is the most active gland in the body before puberty, and the most inactive after. Modern medicine sees little or no purpose for this gland and is further convinced of this by the fact that it shrinks to a fraction of its size after puberty. This conjecture is altogether wrong.

The thymus is most active during childhood because that is when the body is in most need of the protection this gland offers. It protects the development of the immune system in much the same way that a parent protects a child. It is also a teacher and a coach, showering you with love while training you to take responsibility for yourself and your actions (as you sow, so shall you reap). This is not the law of cause and effect so much as what is better called "right action." For this reason, after puberty, the thymus gland takes on a metaphysical role rather than a physical one. Protection of the self is exchanged for love and care of the self (self-love).

The thymus gland is involved in the development of cells within the immune system of the body, particularly T cells. Thyroxine, the principal hormone secreted by the thyroid gland, stimulates and regulates metabolism. Thyroxine also governs the level of stress-induced thoughts and activities within the body. The thyroid gland assists the immune system to develop a natural resistance to stress and disease rather than an acquired (artificial) one. When that is no longer possible, the immune system becomes susceptible or sensitive to infection. Unable to perform or endure under overly stressful circumstances, the natural aspect of the body is breached. It is forced to resist and defend the body rather than protect it.

GLANDS AS TEACHERS

Called into active duty, the immune system initiates the immune-response mechanism, which immediately sets out to recognize and identify cells, tissues, objects and organisms that are apart from it and to fight them if necessary. With such responsibility conferred upon it, the immune system begins to deteriorate. Fortunately, the immune system is equipped with immunocompetence, the little-understood ability of the body to develop a natural immune response in the presence of a disease-causing agent (antigen). Further study in the field of immunogenetics, the discipline that explains the genetic diversity of the immune system, will prove the relevance of the thymus gland and its hormonal secretions.

Metaphysically speaking, all glands are teachers. The pituitary gland, often called the master gland, is like the master teacher. It controls the function of the other glands much as a dean would oversee a course of study. The thymus gland is a teacher of courage in the face of adversity. It stands for self-love, the opposite of which is self-loathing. It proposes protection rather than defense. Health is the natural absence of illness, injury and impairment. It is the function of promoting and maintaining well-being by embracing life's teachers. The rejection of life's teachers is paramount to self-annihilation.

Don't Wait for Modern Medicine to Catch Up to What You Already Know

Returning to our original question, why doesn't the pharmaceutical industry focus upon more important matters? Because it is unaware of the link that exists within all things. It sees the body as constantly under attack by the very environment it calls home. The body's natural defenses are considered inadequate, so antibiotics are trained to kill or deactivate bacteria in the body, yet much of these bacteria are healthful. For the most part, modern medicine is artificial and synthetic. It mirrors the lifestyle of those who promote it. As long as dollars line the pockets and paper the walls of these institutions, progress will be minimal. When external teachers are finally coupled with internal ones, true learning will begin and disease will become obsolete.

It makes no sense to wait for modern medicine to catch up to what you already know. Listen to your inner teachers, all of them, for there are many. Sometimes their voices speak as one, and sometimes not. Sometimes they offer comfort, and other times they teach by the discomfort of body, mind or soul. Your longevity rests within your ability to listen and to trust what you hear. Seek endorsement and confirmation when appropriate, but do not depend upon it. Cure your thoughts, and your beliefs will follow. Decalcify your mind and purge from it obsolete thought forms that do not serve the reality you are attempting to create. If you choose a healthful inner environment, offer yourself a similar perspective without. Replace the bitter diatribe passed on to you by your ancestors with a healthful dialogue that supports you and your loved ones. Keep pace with a peaceful heart and be distressed no more.

Natural Law in an Unnatural World

February 2005

*T*he natural world is both delicate and wild. These factors work together, keeping the kingdoms of the Earth in balance and in resonance with one another. The natural world is exactly that: It is the precise course taken by nature in accordance with what is most usual for the elements and kingdoms that compose the Earth. The natural world responds to all stimuli through the natural order of law. For instance, it is natural for spring to give way to summer and for autumn to yield to winter. Natural law predicts and expects that nature will respond within the boundaries of this law.

DIVERGENCE AND NATURAL LAW

All that is natural can be produced or reproduced by the Earth and its functions in predictive ways. By contrast, that which is unnatural must be artificially created, grown or made to resemble and mimic that which would otherwise occur naturally. To be more specific, the authenticity of the natural world remains unaffected by the particular purposes adopted by anything that exists outside of natural law. The kingdom called humanity is a part of the natural world, but not exclusively. Its origins involve both evolution and creation; thus, it takes delight in the fields of nature while also exploring its more useful aspects.

The recent seismic event in the Indian Ocean is a divergent example of natural law, which is to say that nature followed a distinctly different path than could have been expected. It was, however, an altogether natural response. The Earth has entered a time of divergent realities. Is this not true for you as well? Are you not at this very moment attempting to dislodge the burdens and the dross that have restricted or prohibited your ability to move into more desirable circumstances? Have your friends, family and loved ones not observed and even commented on the more obvious differences among you?

Divergent paths deviate from the predisposed and presupposed. They seem to emphasize or highlight what is most unique. Divergency is a difference between two or more things—attitudes and opinions, for example. Is this not appropriate? Divergence is the process of moving apart to follow different paths or courses at a time or by an amount that is especially different or unexpected. Divergence also describes lines that radiate from a single point, an appropriate description of recent events. And finally, divergence is a condition in which only one eye is directed at the object of interest while the other is directed elsewhere. Do you begin to see?

DIVERGENT REALITIES COEXIST SIMULTANEOUSLY

Divergency can make sincerity seem insincere and vice versa. It can also make that which is benevolent seem excruciatingly malevolent. Divergent realities are produced when reality is viewed through a lens that is concave or convex. Viewed in this fashion, reality can very quickly become distorted and even frightening. But divergence, and especially a diverging lens, offers its own distinct advantages, and the most striking of these is an ever-spreading parallel beam of light that moves from the center, or abstract point of obstruction, outward.

Allow your thoughts and your vision to move beyond but not away from the harsh life-and-death drama that unfolds elsewhere. It is also unfolding within you, but it will continue to do so even after you look away from the television. Your reality is not the same as the one being experienced by those whose homes are now beneath distant shores. By the same token, your reality is not apart from theirs—just different. Awareness is your greatest ally now, and you must draw both faith and fortitude from it.

A natural occurrence has resulted in a human disaster. A natural disaster such as this one was caused by natural forces rather than by human action, but many disasters are highly unnatural and directly attributable to human neglect and lack of foresight. Have you any idea, for instance, how much loss of animal and plant life is incurred as a result of an oil spill? Can you begin to imagine how many generations of people are affected when nuclear power is misused or abused? The effects of some disasters can be imagined and not seen, but they can still be felt—felt for a very long time by human reckoning.

You will hear, see and think many things as the days and weeks following this event unfold. As you pray for the victims, you will experience compassion, but you are also likely to experience anger, fear or distrust. You might also feel fragile, but it is important to remember that the human kingdom is among the strongest and most resilient of all. Remember that you are made in the image and likeness of All That Is; you are eternal and everlasting. Those who have lost their human lives have already gained much more. Already a new perspective beckons them to look farther than they were able to mere moments before.

WHAT WE CAN LEARN FROM THE ANIMAL WORLD

The Earth—my body—is in the active process of redistributing its density. This requires movement in places and areas that have remained still for long periods of time. It is also time for some of the world's assets and wealth to be redistributed. This requires awareness of importance and necessity and subsequent movement of energies. Please be clear that the world's assets and wealth are not the same as its currencies of exchange. Money can solve very few things temporarily and even fewer permanently. The victims of the current disaster would surely trade any currency for dry clothes, shelter, food and water; these items have no price tag—they only seem to. The world's assets are its people and its resources—physical and nonphysical alike. When balance is once again restored, nature will respond accordingly. Until then it is important to respond to the call one hears within.

Humans have many natural abilities, but some of these have been artificially stunted and even suspended. The slowing and stopping up of such vital functions have resulted in a loss of natural instinct and conscious awareness. Did you know that not one animal lost its life as a result of the recent earthquakes and tidal waves? The animal kingdom, in conjunction with the elemental rhythms that provide and sustain its harmony, understood the necessity for this natural process. The innate wisdom of this kingdom guided it to anticipate and respond accordingly. Humans have this same ability, but it must be reawakened and empowered. It is well and good to have what early warning systems technology can provide, but it is also wise to look within for what is already there.

The unnatural world cannot be depended upon completely, especially in times of unprecedented change such as these. It is not even in my power to offer this to you, though I wish it were. A release of energy such as that released by an earthquake can be anticipated and even predicted, but it cannot be planned with any measure of accuracy, because it is a physical response to a nonphysical stimulus. An impetus guides the experience in much the same way as that which prompts the unborn child to move through its mother's birth canal. Each process has its own journey and all such processes are divine, even in the face of destruction and loss of life.

LIVES NOT LOST BUT SURRENDERED

Lives have not been lost, but they have been surrendered in favor of more plentiful horizons and realities. Nothing can be truly lost, even when sorrow tells your heart otherwise. I offer these honest and descriptive words of peace to you, because the images displayed before you will not offer the same. The number of those who have surrendered their physical life will continue to climb. It will rise to 173 thousand and beyond. Approximately 14 thousand more will be unaccounted for; their bodies have been gifted to the oceans, as was their wish.

In the planning stages of your life, you are free to make a will and to state your preferences regarding your final days and the discarding of your physical body. Those who surrendered their lives in this event had the same opportunity; the choice was their own. Their lives were not taken from them, regardless of their age. From the youngest to the oldest, wisdom has guided each and every decision. Did you know that many of your own contemporaries—friends and family members—who have transitioned within the past several years were on hand to receive those who crossed over? This is not an idle time, I assure you.

Very few boundaries remain, the most prominent being the ones between countries, governments and religions. The veils between the worlds are invisible ones, and the illusion of separate realities is just that. Do you care what religion or faith occupies the hearts and minds of the fallen victims? Does your heart cry out any more for the Indian mother who has lost her child or the Indonesian child who has lost her mother? Is any one language more comforting than another? The flow of tears comes from the same source as the flow of emergency supplies— the heart and soul of humanity, which collectively knows no separation. The Earth has one body and one people; all belong to the same fold.

THE VERY ACTIVE YEAR TO COME

If you wonder what is next on the horizon, the answer will be revealed to you. In dreams, symbols, projections, synchronistic moments and direct revelation, you will receive the answer to your question. Do not fail to see what has already been put before you. Lack of trust or an inability to acknowledge what you already know will not change what has been put before you. If you desire a different outcome, you must participate and actively engage the energies that greet you. You will find that they are as flexible and expansive as you are willing to be.

As has been previously stated, 2005 will be an active year in more ways than you can yet imagine. It is a gateway year and the beginning of the seven-year transition to the energies of 2012 and beyond. Approach the unknown with uncertainty if you must, but not with fear. The Earth is not angry or vengeful any more than God is, though you will certainly hear words to the contrary. The natural world must respond by way of natural law, just as the unnatural world responds in ways often considered contrary to the physical laws of nature. Unnatural or man-made law often behaves in ways that contradict conventional assumptions about what constitutes normal or acceptable experience. Customs, practices and habits based upon unnatural laws can sometimes seem affected, artificial, contrived and even strained. They promote angst and worry and produce feelings of sacrifice and forfeit.

Each country, and every being for that matter, is surrounded and protected by a specific vibrational field of energy. Elementally, this would be expressed through a deva or elemental devic force. These delicate vibrations are highly affected by the emotions of those who are governed by these devas, or fields of energy. For instance, feelings of anger, fear, distrust, grief and helplessness affect the field adversely. It is difficult not to have these feelings at such a time, but it is also important to look beyond them whenever possible. Breathe in a relaxed and unhurried manner until a better, more spiritual solution presents itself. The pureness of aware, sunlit energy, coupled with the power of intent and prayer, is a powerful and effective antidote to almost any circumstance.

CONVERGENT EVOLUTION

We began by speaking of divergence, and of necessity we will restore balance by speaking of convergence. Convergence, or convergent evolution, is a coming together from different directions, especially a uniting or merging of groups and tendencies that were originally opposed or very different. Is this not apropos? Convergency also applies to a characteristic series or sequence of numbers in which the difference between each term or number and the following term or number remains constant or increases. Can it be that a very specific and much-needed vibration is constantly increasing?

Furthermore, convergence also explains a tendency among different species or cultures to develop similar characteristics in response to a set of environmental or planetary conditions. Finally, convergence is the turning inward of both eyes in order to look at something in a different or unique way than what was previously viewed. Today my heart cries with your own, but my inward-turned vision extends beyond this moment.

The Faces and Voices of Earth

March 2005

I read your column almost every month. I am fascinated by the variety of questions asked and the diversity of answers offered. I used to doubt that the Earth could really speak to us, or would even care to, for that matter. I don't feel that way anymore, but I would still like to know what "place" or "part" of the Earth (you) speaks to us?

The Earth has many aspects and many faces, as you might imagine. Winter has a different face than spring or summer, and this is reflected everywhere within and upon the Earth. The Earth has a physical body, a celestial body that is also called a planet. You also have a physical body, human or tellurian in design. But you are not your body any more than I am mine. What place within you asks this question? What part of you wonders what the answer might be? Better yet, where does doubt exist within you?

All that I offer to the channel [Pepper Lewis] or to any other living source is first wrapped in a vibration of love, so that its (your) resonance can be brought into the greatest array of balance that is possible in each moment. This ensures that the answer you receive will be of use to you. Here is an example of this: Recently, a question read, "How can my neighbor and I ever see eye to eye when we seem to disagree on almost everything?" The questioner was in obvious distress and quite unhappy with his current situation, but his question could be approached in a variety of different ways. Wrapping the questioner and his question in a vibration of love allowed all that was artificially associated with his true issue to fall away. The part that remained held the true question as well as the answer.

GAIA'S CONSCIOUSNESS SERVES HUMANITY

In this case, the questioner was very disappointed that his neighbor shared none of his views. He felt that his neighbor's proximity, cultural background and social ethic meant that they had more in common than their experience reflected. He respected his neighbor, so it was natural for him to desire the same in return, but he had allowed a difference of opinion to become a difference in lifestyle. His disappointment escalated from frustration to anger, from which he could only see distorted and exaggerated differences rather than similarities. It became obvious that the questioner longed for a friendship with someone in whom he could confide. He could not understand his feelings and had no one to share them with. The superficial nature of his neighborhood as well as the fences that divided it did not suit the new but as yet unfamiliar sense of intimacy with his world that he was beginning to discover. In essence, his world had expanded but his neighborhood had not. Such is the paradox of the new paradigm.

The questioner's disappointment formed his question, but a simple yes or no answer would not have sufficed. The answer was already within him, but he could not see it. Where did the answer he received come from? What place or part of Gaia responded to his need? The answer came from the nonphysical place within my being that had already experienced the transparent love he held for all of his neighbors and for all those who have ever felt the same sadness or disappointment he now felt. The Earth is the physical aspect of the planet, but my sentience is the soulful, sentient, emotional awareness that guides and animates all things. Sentience is conscious awareness, a quality that is uniquely distinct from any intellectual process.

Young children believe that their parents are omnipotent and omniscient. As they grow, they discover that this might not be entirely true. By the time they become adults, they realize that they know more about many subjects than their parents do. What they don't have—yet—is life experience. When the open hearts and minds of both young and old come together, miracles can be accomplished. My responses often contain a bit of history, a little perspective, a view from above, support from below, gentle admonishments and a more expanded view of the potential future. What parent could do less for those he or she loves deeply?

DESIRE IS AT THE CORE OF EVOLUTION

My sentience is the open mind and heart of all that was, is and will be a part of the Earth. A sentience is not all-seeing and all-knowing, but it is the accumulated wisdom of all Earth-related experience. A sentience is not omnipotent, unlimited or universal in its power and authority, but it is omniscient; my sentience contains knowledge, whether real or apparent, of all things related to past, present and future Earth life. My sentience does possess one distinct advantage, which is conscious awareness of the many decisions, directions and dimensions that apply to the Earth and all of its kingdoms. This vast resource of knowledge is also available to you, but your ability to access this library of wisdom is still limited. Until such time as it is revealed to you, it is a pleasure beyond explanation to be of service to you.

Humans are one of Earth's treasures, but they are underappreciated, undervalued, overworked and overexploited—mostly by themselves. The aspect of my being that responds to all of humanity's needs, not just the words that appear in this column, recognizes the desire on humanity's part to break free from these evolutional chains of mediocrity. As you already know, there are many teachers and evolved beings dedicated to guiding and assisting in this process. Each time that a mind awakens and a heart (en)lightens, it increases the likelihood of the same thing happening again and then again. What seems like a quantum leap today is but one in a series of small steps. Hand in hand, breath by breath, all that you hope for and envision will come to be. My word is upon it.

THE MAGIC AND MAJESTY OF MOUNTAINS

I have always been drawn to the mountains. Time and again I find myself driving to one or climbing upon its back, eager to reach the summit. I know that my experience is not individual but collective. Can you comment on this?

Mountains are the majestic kings and queens of the mineral kingdom. Unabashedly towering above everything else, they challenge you to wonder about what it would be like to climb them, or better yet, to be them. As kings and queens, mountains bear the names and energies that history has assigned them. They are not masculine or feminine per se, but their various faces and views offer many perspectives from which to choose—some harder and some softer.

Mount Shasta, for example, a royal member of the Cascade Range, shares its throne with many other brothers and sisters of volcanic origin. Far from ordinary, these regal beings are capable of lifting your spirits to great heights. Mountains call to you, and from distances both near and far, the sensitive, the devoted and the obstinate heed their call. The call is not one of duty or sacrifice, although these require acknowledgment at some point. The call is an invitation, albeit an insistent one. Not only does heeding the call bring you closer to nature, it also brings you closer to your natural self.

Mountains are self-healing, and they encourage you to do the same. Season by season and year by year, mountains teach you to look beyond the obvious. They ask you to imagine what lies within and to stand the tests of time and circumstance, just as they do. Mountains are great generators of energy. Drawing force and power from deep within the Earth, they broadcast energy in all directions, creating matrices and vortexes of an invisible but powerful substance, yielding only to a power greater than them.

What draws you to the mountains, do you know? What whisper or shout could you no longer ignore? What do you bring with you when you visit, and what will you take away when you leave? The answers to these questions rest within your heart and perhaps with the mountains themselves. You might already know the answers to these questions, but in case you do not, here are a few simple guidelines to help you deepen your relationship with the mountains and with yourself.

LOOK TO THE MOUNTAIN PEAK AND LOOK TO ITS BASE

Mountains carry an imposing nature that lays claim to a vast amount of space. They are no more permanent here on Earth than you are, but they certainly seem so. They can encourage you to discover your own place in this world and in the one beyond it as well. Mountains with two or more peaks represent balance within duality; there is no struggle between them. Perhaps you are being drawn to this rich and potent environment in order to acknowledge this. Sometimes mountains are shrouded from view. Withdrawing within their own landscape, they reveal only what they wish to, delving into their own mysteries quietly and at their own pace. Are you also here to explore the less than obvious, to seek and discover the authentic or to dislodge excesses that no longer apply?

Many mountains can be approached from various directions, each one offering a different perspective and a new degree of difficulty. Opportunities to visit, commune with and climb mountains are often costumed in challenge, and the inspiration to do so rarely seems to linger long enough—but with each new approach or ascent, a broader perspective and a more specific focus is gained. When viewing your favorite mountain, are you more attracted to its bountiful base and the geography it occupies; its solid but slender middle, which bears the bulk of trees and wildlife; or its beautiful and imposing peak(s), uninhabitable but for the very few?

The base of a mountain represents that which is most connected to the Earth, but it also stands for the broadest interpretation or that which extends in all directions without the need to take sides. The base is stable and set, comfortable for the long haul, as it were. The base is also the most approachable part of the mountain. It is accessible and inviting, lifting you gently onto it without any resistance. Do you offer the same benefit to those whom you invite into your own environments?

THE MIDDLE PATH AND REACHING A PINNACLE

The midrange of the mountain is comparable with the middle path in life. Supported by a broad base, the middle finds no need to rest directly upon the Earth. It makes no attempt to be anywhere or anything other than what it is. It does not climb away from the base, and it does not compete with its taller aspects. Instead, it holds and transmits energy to its various parts, supporting many other kingdoms and life forms along the way. It shares itself equally and evenly, knowing neither prejudice nor influence. Content to be what it is, it welcomes all who are willing to do the same. Are you oriented similarly? Are you content to be the hawk, unaware or oblivious that the eagle can fly higher and see farther?

A mountain's peak can be hard and jagged or soft and round. Either way, it seems almost to belong more to heaven than to Earth. A mountain's peak neither invites nor discourages anyone from attempting to join it, allowing all to search their souls to discover their own answer. The air is much thinner up here, and very few can breathe comfortably; not all are prepared to experience life's pinnacle. The journey to the summit is arduous, and for some it is even fraught with peril. The grandest of mountains make guides a necessity for most climbers, and even the most experienced rarely make the expedition alone. There is no place for burdens here, although areas of rest along the way provide ample opportunity to discard waste in its various forms. There is no shelter now; that will come later. Are you near the summit of your own journey? Can you see 360 degrees in all directions? Can you imagine life being any other way?

MOUNTAINS ARE AS DISTINCT AS INDIVIDUALS

There are many kinds of mountains—some are stationary and others move and slide as need or circumstance invites. Some mountains are solitary in nature and form, enjoying an eternity in the middle of nowhere just as much as you enjoy a few hours of quiet and solitude. Mountains that belong to ranges such as the Cascades represent families—pushing and shoving one another in an attempt to gain an inch of advantage when miles of space exist in other directions. Volcanic mountains are the dragons of the mineral kingdom, silent overseers of restrained peace, managing their authority judiciously and erupting only as the call from within intensifies and insists. Those who make their homes near these giants tend to exhibit similar characteristics, and if they do not, there is ample opportunity for them to learn by example.

Mountains ask very little of you and welcome you to be who you are and how you are. In return, they ask the same for themselves. Time will temper them just as it will temper you. They do not rush here and there to seek fortune or fame, but it comes to them just the same. Adorned with veins of gold within and flora and fauna without, they stand as courageous overseers of evolution—rugged, unhurried and determined. With nothing to prove, mountains teach by example, asking no more of you than they ask of themselves. Mountains remind you that their greatness is your own, and that although "seeing is believing," the greater mystery still lies within, waiting to be discovered rather than observed.

False Alarm

April 2005

*T*he world is at a very interesting juncture just now. Systems of thought and planes of reality are bisecting each other at very interesting angles. Some of them are even bumping into each other, as close proximity makes this possible. This makes for delightfully intriguing conversation, because multiple realities make for more possibilities than linear reality. Unfortunately, these possibilities can also confound, confuse and even disturb humanity's delicate and already jittery nerves. With this in mind, take a few moments to inhale and exhale gently, breathing prana and peace into all of your beingness, relaxing the muscles that have tensed too soon as well as the thoughts that have wandered into unsupported territory. Return to the realm and comfort of the heart, an eternally warm and familiar place.

YOUR HEART IS YOUR HEARTH

Your heart is your hearth, metaphorically speaking. It is the part of you that keeps the home fire burning, awaiting your return from wherever you have been, regardless of the length or purpose of your absence. A physical hearth is much more than a fireplace or cooking station. It serves as the central support for the entire structure, just as your spinal column does for your physical structure. Any damage to this support is immediately reflected in any and all environments, and if it becomes temporarily or permanently paralyzed, life can come to a screeching halt. The importance of the hearth is further reflected in the mantel, or crown, that adorns it. It is no wonder that many of life's precious treasures find a place upon the mantel above the hearth. In the human body, the spinal column supports the hearth—the heart—and the crown chakra enriches the mind so that it will be in service to the heart.

Metaphysically speaking, humans are having a very difficult time keeping the hearth, or home environment, clear of obstacles that threaten to extinguish its light. Either the flame—the life force—has become so low that it can barely maintain the warmth easily generated by a candlewick, or the fire has blazed so high that it is out of control and still spreading. In some cases, both of these scenarios are true, making the danger even greater. Humans are an enduring but delicate species. Although the human spirit cannot be entirely extinguished, it is highly susceptible to environmental factors. For instance, humans are more easily manipulated than other species. Humans will work incessantly "for peanuts," as they say, or for an idea or goal that might not be in their own best interests.

PINOCCHIO AS A METAPHORIC EXAMPLE

Do you remember the story of Pinocchio? He very much wanted to become a real boy instead of being a wooden toy. Humans very much want to become an enlightened species, not an automated puppet race. Pinocchio tried very hard to remember all the wonderful rewards that would be his if he could just remember and keep the promises he had made to himself and to his father, Geppetto. Humans, individually and collectively, are also trying very hard to recall the commitments they have made, to themselves and to the divine purpose of Father/All That Is who guides them.

Pinocchio had help from a fairy and a cricket. Humans also receive assistance from the seen and the unseen, as well as from heaven and Earth. Pinocchio was easily deceived. He followed those who had little or no reputation concerning the things of which they spoke, because the promises they made sounded almost too good to be true—and they were. The characters in the story could no more keep the promises they made than those who make promises to humanity today can.

Fairy tales are stories about imaginary beings or events that convey or contain a message. They are improbable, invented accounts that are told to children, but see how easily they become real-life examples? Pinocchio traveled long and far. He experienced hunger, disappointment, deceit, imprisonment, lack, cold and a variety of other physical and emotional tortures. All the while, he was trying to get back home, back to his father and the place where it all began. Humans want the same. They want to become real, or self-realized, do you see?

Fairy tales are sometimes read to children so that they will go to sleep and dream. The intention of these words is to wake you from the long sleep and the dream that has already replayed itself too many times. This story and the dreamtime that accompanies it have nothing else to teach you and nowhere else to take you. There are many roads and realities that can take you home now, but you must endeavor to mark this distance through your own choices and by the decisions and steps you now take. Assistance is still yours for the asking. The roads are better lit now and the signposts well placed, but the distractions and detractors are still many. They too have grown in recent years, albeit in other directions. With that said, here are a few of the most overlooked signposts, perhaps because they have been placed in plain sight.

OVERLOOKED SIGNPOSTS IN PLAIN VIEW

Know Yourself

In order to get home, you need to know who and what you are. The names that you have been called by are irrelevant now. They will be important again later on, but right now it is better to know who you are today than who you were yesterday. For instance, if you were married once, twice or even thrice in this life, you were called by a certain name or title. If that name or title no longer applies, do not carry it as if it were part of your entourage. Redeem the simplest, most accurate expression of self that you can. This is how you began; it is how you entered this world. When you refer to yourself, do so as you would prefer others would. Do not under- or oversell yourself, what you have or what you do. Practice honesty in words and deeds, not because dishonesty would otherwise prevail, but because honesty reflects the soul's purpose more clearly. Self-reflection leads to self-realization.

Be True to Your Companions

Share your adventure and your earthly concerns with others of the same mind or principles, but choose your companions well. For many of you, this is the last leg of the journey. Do you wish to cross the finish line alone, in partnership, on the back of another or with someone strapped onto your back? Can you still walk upright or are you bent over, crooked, cracked and burdened by your own weight or the density of others? Do you find that you are still settling debts, be they relationships or accounts, or is your word sufficient to strike the harmonic chord of *at-one-ment?*

Make Peace with What Seems to Oppose You

The world is not against you, and you have no need to resist it. All that stands before you is a mirrored reflection. If left and right are inverted or opposite each other, does it not stand to reason that good and bad are too? Every step that you take offers different perspectives and proposes new realities. That which stands next to you, behind you or in front of you has its own unique experience, which might or might not be aligned with your own. Plan how to accommodate this into your daily experience rather than how you will react when presented with it. God does not make duplicates; you would not want Him to.

Don't Bother to Sweep under the Rug

The cleanest room is still dusty, and the moment after you have swept, a spill might occur. This is natural. Nature never ceases to be what it is and neither should you. There will always be more to be done than you are able to do in the moment and more to discover than you can realize the first time around. No matter how far you have traveled or how much you have accomplished, there is always more. Spring leads to summer and summer to fall. Each season or decade has a specific progression, with each subsequent season offering its own opportunity, challenge or secret. No two seasons or years are ever alike. Listen to others and heed them if you will, but don't take their word as your gospel. Don't miss an opportunity to crawl on your belly if it means discovering where the sweetest honey is hiding. Take the time to make yourself beautiful, but not if the cost is too high. Make certain it is your own reflection that you see in the looking glass and not the invention of another. In an immaculately clean and organized home, you could probably eat off the floor, but would you want to?

Relate Justly to Your Environment

Do not ask more of your environment(s) than is practical. A work environment is just that; a home is a dwelling, a body is a vehicle for your soul, a forest is part of nature and the ocean is too deep to fathom. Your body is not a dumping ground for unnatural substances any more than the ocean is. You cannot fathom its beauty or its depth if you pollute it beyond reason or repair. Do not discard what you value and do not hoard what others lack. The natural environment and its resources do not belong to you. All loans are to be considered short term. In every environment in which you dwell, take care to give, receive and share. Good fences make for good neighbors, but an extended hand makes neighbors into friends.

Look to the Next Horizon

Today can only last as long as it does. You are experiencing today because you have allowed yesterday to elapse and pass into an alternate experience called the past. Tomorrow will arrive when you have accorded today the same courtesy, but it is all too easy to forget to do this. Sometimes today seems so perfect that you cling to it, hesitant to see what tomorrow might bring. Sometimes today seems so much like yesterday that you hardly notice that it is different, and sometimes today seems so awful that you begin to imagine that tomorrow will be worse, not realizing that you have just made it so! Every sunrise invites you to see something different, and every sunset is worthy of its own painting, as if capturing it on canvas could preserve it for a bit longer. The stars are not fixed in their positions; they only seem to be. If they were, they could not make the music that the planets dance to in their own progression. Likewise, your life is not fixed. It is as flexible and changeable as your mind—when you allow it to be.

Seek Tranquillity and Happiness Will Find You

Happiness is as elusive as a butterfly. It is meant to be. It beckons you here and there. Happiness is characterized by a feeling or showing of pleasure, contentment and satisfaction. Although happiness is always a welcome guest, it is usually a temporary one. It is special in that it belongs only to the moment; it is the complement to an experience rather than its end result. A captured butterfly is much less attractive in a net. Its life is short enough at the outset before the stress of entrapment curtails its flight. Is it not better to admire a butterfly without possessing it? Is its beauty not more worthwhile in life? Those whose enthusiasm for a particular thing has inclined them to cling to it will see that it is more short-lived than they would prefer. Tranquillity, on the other hand, is the butterfly's most precious gift, the one that is most frequently overlooked rather than prized. Tranquillity is freedom from disturbance and commotion. A butterfly in free flight displays no signs of anxiety or agitation. Its vibrant colors are the result of its full and varied experience as well as its short but well-deserved life. Humans are more like butterflies than they imagine, but they pretend to be moths trapped by a house light while the Sun waits for them.

The House Is Not on Fire and There Are Smoke Detectors in Every Room

The evening news is like a bird's nest—bits of discarded debris collected from hither and yon attempting to be useful. But news is not new, and like that which has already been discarded, it is often putrid and useless to all but those who scavenge rather than create experience. The news would have you believe the worst instead of the best, be it about yourself or your neighbor. You are admonished to live in fear and insecurity, to loathe that which is different or unique and to hand over your riches for inconsequential items at every possible moment. The monies that you have earned from your employers flow quickly back into the same accounts from which they have just emerged, as if they were homing pigeons returning to their place of origin. You are lured, cajoled, influenced, controlled and finally ensnared to act and react as others pull your puppet strings this way and that.

Has Your Journey Been about Baubles and Trinkets?

The trap has been well laid and the honey spread thick onto the flypaper. Try as you might, escape is futile and surrender worse. To the victor go the spoils, but think—is it truly the spoils you want? Has your journey really been about baubles and trinkets, even if they seem precious and necessary? If you live long, will your spirit be rich and your soul deep?

STOP, THINK AND BREATHE

Stop, think and breathe. Ask yourself, "Who am I and why am I here? Oh yes, I remember now. It was so that I could know myself. Who is on this adventure with me and how can I serve them, because I am true to my companions? How can I gently dislodge the obstacles that have found their way onto my path so that I am at peace with what seems to oppose me? What has nature reflected to me today? When have I been preoccupied with cleaning a slate that was made of chalk dust to begin with?"

Say to yourself: "Perhaps the next time, I will not bother to sweep things under the rug, because the rewards for doing so are few. Instead, I will just be in all of my environments as they continue to support me, inclusive of all that I am and do. As I prepare to sleep tonight, I will number the wonders of heaven rather than judge the errors I have stumbled upon. That way I can look to the next horizon with an open heart that guides me as faithfully as a compass. Such moments as befit a divine being are mine as I receive tranquillity and welcome happiness."

Epilogue:
My Ordinary, Extraordinary Life as a Channel

*J*ust five months after my birth in Buenos Aires, Argentina, my family moved to the United States. I believe that at least part of my mom and dad's contract was to bring me here. My parents say I cried incessantly from the moment I was born until the moment we boarded the plane bound for the U.S., and then stopped for good. I learned to speak English at school but spoke Castilian Spanish at home. I am still fluent today and can even read and write this language, although not extensively.

During my childhood, we lived in Hollywood, California. I was outwardly happy but confused and conflicted within. I could not make sense of the world around me, and what I saw I did not like. The Vietnam War loomed in the background of my young life, as did racial tensions, starvation in Africa and other byproducts of the sixties and seventies. Our television was always tuned to the news, and I can still vividly recall the gory and disturbing images of those times. I remember telling my parents that I didn't want to watch because it made my eyes and my head hurt, but they said it was real life and I was better off learning about such things sooner rather than later. They would remind me how fortunate I was to live in a country where the truth was displayed on the television screen instead of being hidden from view. To this I'd reply, "If that's the truth, I'm not sure I belong here."

Back then we would sometimes vacation in Mexico, just south of the border. I remember driving past dirty, maimed children playing in front of the dilapidated cardboard sheds they lived in. I would hide my face in horror as they ran alongside our car, begging for coins. Pictures of starving children my own age haunted me, as did vivid images of bloody, wounded and dying soldiers being carried off the battlefields of Vietnam. I could not comprehend human suffering and still don't. To this day, I will not watch movies or television shows that endorse, encourage or uphold violence of any kind.

IMAGINATION, THE INVISIBLE FUEL

As a child, whenever my physical senses became overwhelmed, I would get severe migraine headaches and would have to retreat to a quiet and darkened room. As I sat there quietly, angels and lightbeings would appear and comfort me, creating beautiful images for me to look at so I would not feel as much pain. I did not know who or what they were, but I trusted them and invited them into my world. Sometimes I would even fake a bad headache so I could return to my quiet room and wait for them, but when I faked it, they never came. Eventually, my mother took me to see a specialist, but he never did find anything wrong with me.

By adolescence I had outgrown the headaches but continued to withdraw. I was insecure and felt different from other children my own age, so I had a difficult time fitting in at school. Pepper is not my given name; it is a nickname I gave myself when I could no longer stand my birth name, Gladys. The long and short of this story is that I believed Angie Dickinson, in her role as Sgt. Suzanne "Pepper" Anderson on a television show called *Police Woman*, had it all together, at least more than I did at age fourteen, so I changed my name to Pepper. I felt that my new name gave me confidence and made it okay for me to express myself as an individual.

I loved to read—and still do. I adored sagas and epics, especially stories about heroines whom I aspired to be like. The medieval and renaissance eras captivated me, and I would often imagine myself cloaked in flowing robes and capes. Imagination helped me to disappear into books like *The Mists of Avalon*. I believe that my imagination was like an invisible fuel that could transport me anywhere I wanted to go. Interestingly, those very thoughts form the basis of Earth alchemy, though I did not consciously know this at the time. My escapes into other historical time periods became so vivid and full of detail that I began to question which life was real. I somehow understood the concept of simultaneous or parallel lives, because I was experiencing them. I tried to share my experiences with my friends and with my mother, but they all said I was only daydreaming.

When I was in high school, a bus strike made it necessary for me to walk to and from school. Every day I would walk past a well-known used-book store some considered to be haunted. Eventually, curiosity and temptation carried me inside for a look around. The man at the counter took one look at me and pointed his long, skinny finger toward the back of the store. I followed his direction and found myself in a section called "Occult Thought." For the first time, I felt like I was home. I thought to myself, Finally things are going to make sense. The books were inexpensive, so I purchased many of them. I read all of the Seth books channeled by Jane Roberts, which taught me about different realities and densities. I also read all of the Ruth Montgomery books and learned about past lives, walk-ins and more. I read books on UFOs and every-thing I could find on reincarnation. Some of the books in that section were enlightening and some of them were downright scary. I instinctively knew which ones to pick up and which ones to stay away from; I knew I was being directed by my own guides. It surprised me that my parents allowed me to read such books, as they were not open-minded or forward-thinking people. At first I took their permission as interest but soon found out this was not the case, so I kept what I learned to myself.

After high school, I went to college. I enjoyed journalism and photography and thought I would make a career of working for a publication like *National Geographic*, but I was very shy, not exactly a self-starter. One day I was sitting in a history class listening to the professor's lecture. I knew that much of what he was saying was false, because my—albeit limited—experiences with time travel had shown me otherwise. I knew that our history had been tampered with; it had been inaccurately recorded so that it would be remembered in a dif-ferent way. As the class droned on, it occurred to me that our entire history could be rewritten in just a few short generations. I slowly rose from my seat, took one last look around, then walked out of the class and away from the school. I never turned back.

MEETING SETH

When I was eighteen, I was introduced to a man who conducted past-life regressions. I decided to find out once and for all if my experiences were real or the result of a vivid and overactive imagination as I had been consistently told. We spent a few sessions experiencing light and then medium levels of hypnosis. I easily responded to hypnotic suggestions, in which I recalled early childhood events. I described my favorite dolls in great detail and referred to them by the Spanish names I had given them. I even volunteered my birth name, Gladys, a closely guarded secret at the time. By the third session, we had made so much progress that I easily made the transition from childhood to womb and then to spirit.

The first life I recalled was in England in the early 1800s. I was a young woman and I was dying. When asked of what, I accurately described symptoms associated with tuberculosis but called it consumption, a term that was com-mon in that time period. A scene was unfolding before me and I did my best to describe it as accurately as possible. My family was gathered around me as I lay on a small bed. The time of my passing seemed imminent, and I wondered why I had chosen to recall this experience. In my present-day body, I could even feel the need to cough up blood. My facilitator reminded me that I was not to experience any pain, and he suggested that I witness the scene as an observer rather than as a participant. I continued to describe what I saw in the room, including my husband in that life, whom I recognized as my mother in this one; the instant recognition surprised me. I reached through time and held the hand of the young woman (me) who was lying before me. I held her (my) hand until it became limp and I realized that she had passed. I moved back a little so that I could see what would happen next. I saw her spirit gently lift away from her lifeless body, pausing for a moment to caress the body and to thank it. Her spirit hovered above and then next to the body for a while. It seemed to be assisting those who already wept by her side. It seemed as if her spirit was replacing their grief with a sweet memory. I wanted to stay to see how it would all turn out, but my facilitator indicated that it was time to move beyond the experience, and I obeyed.

My hypnotic regression revealed several other lifetimes in great detail, but none touched me as deeply as the first. I enjoyed the experience and thought I would go back again, but I never did.

I explored different concepts while I considered what I would do next. I continued to read all of the channeled material I could get my hands on, as I was fascinated by this process. One day I was invited to visit someone who channeled Seth, not far from where I lived. As soon as I saw this man's personality disappear and Seth appear, I knew I would never be the same. The next day, I booked a private session with him and counted the days and hours until I could speak to Seth directly. I was nervous and asked a lot of trivial questions that seemed very important at the time. Finally, Seth glared at me and asked, "Why do you concern yourself with such insignificant questions when you are aware of so much more? You are different and you must acknowledge it!" I was more than a little scared and didn't know what to reply. I bit my lip and stared at the wall while I tried to think of something intelligent to say. Being different had not served me well thus far, and I had already spent years trying to fit in or be "normal," whatever that was. My attempts had not been met with much success, and I wasn't counting on it getting any better. Seth went on to say that I had unique abilities that I was not to ignore. He told me to go beyond the dictates of my head in order to discover them. I didn't know what he meant but was too afraid to say so. I tried to ask other questions, more important ones, but he quickly dismissed them and finally dismissed me!

BACKYARD BARBEQUES AND DESIGNER CLOTHES

I spent as much time in self-discovery as I could, but doing so also made me realize how serious I had become. Searching for depth and significance in all things left little time to have fun. When I was twenty-two, I met Dave, and at twenty-five, we married. Dave was fun and exciting. He was everything I was not. He had grown up near me but had been raised in a very different environment. His father, Al Lewis of *The Munsters* and *Car 54, Where Are You?* fame, was very interested in civil rights and political awareness. He and the rest of the family marched in civil rights rallies and held Black Panther meetings in their living room. Al was an intelligent man with a huge heart, and I learned a lot from him. He was brash and forthright and spoke his mind all of the time. Dave inherited some of Al's showmanship. He had a wonderful sense of humor and would often laugh out loud. He made fun of himself and of me in light-hearted, non-threatening ways. He taught me to smile and to laugh, and for a while, things were fun and easy. We had two boys: Bryce, who is now sixteen, and Keenan, who is twelve. We had birthday parties and backyard barbeques, and I was very happy.

A series of jobs led me to the computer field, which was just beginning to mature. It was a fast-paced industry, and I discovered that with a little effort, I could make a lot of money (and prove to my parents that I could make it in life without a college degree). I liked working with people, and the frenetic business environment suited me at the time. I found that I could tune in to someone's energy and intuitively know what that person was willing to pay for something, and I used this to my advantage. I became more interested in the accumulation of personal wealth and material possessions than I care to admit, but it was the fast-paced 1980s and a lot of fun for a while! I bought sports cars, designer clothes and fancy jewelry.

One day, as I was driving, I noticed that the car in the next lane was exactly like mine. I also noticed that the driver was a woman who reminded me a lot of me. She wore her hair in a similar style to mine, her designer clothes looked like mine and she was even wearing the same expensive trendy watch I was wearing. I remember wondering if her thoughts were anything like mine too. I felt as if I could have been her clone or that she was a copy of me. If there were already two of us, were there more as well? I vowed not to allow that to happen and immediately set about reevaluating my choices and priorities. I promised myself that I would make whatever changes were necessary.

BACK ON MY SPIRITUAL PATH

I went back to what I thought was square one. I reread a few of the books that had made an impact upon me and set about rediscovering who I really was. I looked around at the many things I had accumulated and noticed how cluttered my house had become. I knew that this was only a reflection on the rest of my life. I made changes and simplified my lifestyle where I could. I put away my fancy jewelry, sold my fancy car and found time to meditate. Bryce was still a baby then, and I would meditate while he napped and again in the evening as I rocked him to sleep. Visions of other times and other places returned to me, and they seemed more vivid than ever.

One day a Native American guide asked me to follow him with my awareness, and I agreed. He showed me a life where I was the son of a chief in a small but influential tribe. The members of the tribe were packing their belongings very quickly and deliberately, because winter had moved in sooner than expected. They knew that they could not remain where they were for more than a few days. There was indecision as to where to go and dissension between my father and me. We were both highly respected within our tribe, and it was widely known that one day I would be chief, but on this day, my future ability to lead was questioned. The cold weather worsened, as did the disagreement between father and son. I watched as they parted ways and broke each other's heart. The tribe was forced to choose what to do and whom to follow. Conflict divided both tribe and family, and two small bands of unhappy people departed in opposite directions, never to see one another again. All of the members of one band perished and most of the members of the other group died as well. I saw them fall one by one, unable to go on. Tears rolled down my cheeks as I watched this awful scene unfold before me. I asked my Indian guide why I was being shown this vision. He explained to me that I had made the only decision I could make in that life, and as gently as possible, he told me that I would be presented with similar choices in this life too.

When the vision ended, I went for a walk to think about what I had just experienced. I wondered if the experience had been real or if it had been my imagination as I had so often been told. From the depth of my being, I recalled this guide and somewhat rudely demanded some form of physical proof. I gave him exactly the time it took to walk one city block to produce a feather and present it to me. A few moments later, a feather appeared directly in front of me. Unsatisfied, I demanded more. Two larger feathers, brighter in color, appeared nearby. I slowed my walk and softened my approach. I apologized for my rudeness and my skepticism and wondered how I could overcome my doubt. I hated to admit it, but I still needed more. The summer heat intensified, and I crossed the street to find some temporary shade while I considered my next request. I stopped underneath a large billboard sign and closed my eyes for a moment, but an enormous gust of wind made me open them again. As the wind billowed through the air, thousands of accumulated feathers floated down from the billboard above me, and I found myself in a blizzard of feathers. I wasn't sure whether to laugh or cry, so I did both. I regretted having challenged my guide but was also grateful to have received exactly what I had asked for. I have never doubted the symbolic and synchronistic ways in which Spirit communicates with us again. I have learned to trust nonphysical language and awareness as much as physical evidence.

I continued to meditate, but finding a quiet mind and a quiet place at the same time proved difficult. I experimented with several methods and found more success with some methods than with others. An inner presence hinted that persistence would prove beneficial, and a small voice within me began to speak in whispered wisdom. I asked it to speak louder and more prominently than my mind, which was always busy creating mental shopping lists, but it never did. (Over the years, I have made peace with my mind. I give it what it needs, and it allows me what I want.) When I began to meditate, I followed a ritual that included lighting candles and incense, playing soft music and holding my favorite crystals. Eventually, my spirit teachers indicated that I could accomplish the same and more without these items. My resistance to their suggestion was as obvious as my fear of doing without my precious things. My guides wanted me to learn that spiritual peace is the result of inner desire rather than outer experience, but many years passed before I realized that. I still enjoy many luxuries, but my success and happiness no longer depend upon them.

For a while, I followed a few teachings and attended various seminars and workshops. My interests carried me to ancient texts and to new discoveries. I spent some time exploring and releasing spiritual, physical and emotional baggage. I cried so much and for so long that I thought I would be responsible for the next great flood. During this time, an angel named Zeraphinia came to me. She helped me sort through many questions that still confused me, like who I was, where I was from, why I was here and why I always felt so different from everyone else. She showed me past lives and patterns that had contributed to the decisions I was making in this life. Some of what she showed me was not very pretty and made me feel quite uncomfortable, but I respected her guidance and understood the importance of what I was shown. I felt Zeraphinia in my heart, but her communication with me was in the form of automatic writing. I have always appreciated this form of communication, because something physical and tangible remains even when the experience has ended. Over the course of a few years, Zeraphinia introduced me to many angels and archangels as well as to various other teachers and guides.

My psychic ability developed rapidly, and I discovered that I could move energy and separate certain aspects of myself from my body. Long meditations were always nearly impossible for me to endure. Most often I ended up in a race in which my mind and my body competed to see which one could disturb my peace first. This became even more pronounced at workshops in which it was impolite to open one's eyes when everyone else's were closed. I used to make up games that allowed me to walk around the room in my energy body. It was fun and it didn't seem to bother anyone. I found that I could also read other people's energy, especially when they meditated, as they allowed themselves to remain open. Once, in a workshop I attended with a friend, I noticed that two people, who had not arrived at the event together, were holding hands. As the meditation began, their energies became entwined and I had the distinct feeling that their energetic embrace was sexual in nature. I suddenly felt embarrassed and ashamed, as if I had inappropriately witnessed a private and intimate embrace; worse yet, I felt like a spiritual voyeur. I pulled my energy back into my body so quickly that it hurt, closed the energetic door behind me and locked it tightly. By the time I got home, I had already decided never to use these talents or abilities again and had resigned myself to living an ordinary life.

I let my answering machine receive the messages from my spiritual friends, as I was unwilling to speak with them. I ignored invitations to lectures, meditations and special events and busied myself with being a wife and a mother. My friends were persistent and did not stop calling, especially my friend Jude, who was not feeling well and did not agree with the findings of the allopathic medical community. She left long messages asking me to look at her body energetically; she refused to acknowledge the physical distance that separated us. I pleaded with her to call someone else, as the last thing I wanted was to feel responsible for her well-being. My concern for her finally compelled me to unlock the barricaded door I had placed between my physical reality and my subtle awareness. Immediately upon doing so, I entered an altered state of consciousness, in which I saw every individual atom, molecule and cell within her and how it related to her whole body. I saw every childhood scrape, every sore muscle and the most minute vitamin deficiencies. At first I told her everything I saw just so I could get off the phone quickly, but the information kept coming and I did not stop it. I unleashed all that had been bottled up within me for months, and I even heard myself telling her what I had experienced on the day I had closed my energetic door. Surprisingly, she told me that it had been her energy that I had experienced that day. She confirmed that I had accurately seen it entwined with another energy. She went on to explain that it was inappropriate and impossible for her to be with that person in this lifetime; even so, they had taken a moment out of time and place to explore a passion that could not be experienced in any other way. She thanked me for confirming the beauty and innocence of the encounter, as she had not shared it with anyone.

MY DARK NIGHT OF THE SOUL

Once I had reopened the door to my spiritual gifts, I began to use my abilities more often. I helped others get in touch with their own angels and guides, and I channeled messages for them. My abilities came so easy then that I began to take them for granted. I accessed information from the past, the present and sometimes even the future. I traveled other dimensions, surfed waves of energy and summoned the resources of energies and beings who offered support and encouragement. I became overly proud and conceited.

My arrogance became ignorance, and I descended into a spiral in which I experienced a fall from grace often called the Dark Night of the Soul. During that time, I would summon my guides but could not feel their presence. I called upon my abilities, but they did not reveal themselves. I could still feel angels around me, but they would not acknowledge me. It was as if they had their backs turned to me and I felt as though I had turned my back on them. I was tired all of the time, and it required a great deal of effort to do the simplest task. I suffered from headaches and stomachaches and felt nauseous most of the time; I slept too little or too much. Physically, there was nothing wrong with me, but I felt and looked awful. With nothing but time on my hands, I began to examine my life piece by piece. I didn't like myself very much and I knew that I needed to change, but I wasn't sure how.

Sunday, January 16, 1994, was a strange day. It was unseasonably warm for January, and the air was very still all day. I was living in Tarzana, California, a suburb in the San Fernando Valley, about forty minutes northwest of LA—earthquake country. Our dog, Rocky, had been panting, limping and howling all day as if he had been hit by a car. We examined him carefully but couldn't find anything wrong with him, and after a few hours he whimpered himself to sleep. I fell asleep too, but could not stay asleep. By 4:31 a.m. my life began to change.

I awoke to the screaming sound and thunderous movement of the biggest earthquake I have ever experienced! My life became a living nightmare, and no words could ever describe the shock and fear I experienced. I tried to stand, but the intense force of the earthquake threw me down to the floor. Dave was trying to tell me something, but the sound was deafening and I couldn't hear him. He pushed me toward the door that led to the backyard and gestured that he would get the kids and meet me outside.

I tumbled down some steps and landed on our brick patio. I couldn't stand, so I crawled onto the wet grass. My knees felt warm from blood and I knew that I was hurt. I was paralyzed with fear and at the same time trembling uncontrollably. It was pitch black except for the lightning strikes caused by exploding power transformers nearby. I tried to remind myself that I was in control and that I had chosen this experience, but my fear told me otherwise. Dave and the kids had not appeared from the house yet, and I began to fear the worst. I begged God to stop the shaking and to help everyone get out of the house safely, but the shaking didn't stop and they didn't come out.

My body doubled over in pain, and I felt as if I had been struck by lightning. If it is true that people can be scared to death, then I was dying. I was sweating even though it was a cold January morning, and my heart was beating so fast that I could not catch my breath. I called upon Archangel Michael and shouted at him that if he didn't get my family out of the house safely, I would hate him forever. A few moments later, Dave came out of the house holding Bryce under one strong arm and Keenan under the other. (They were only three and seven at the time.) The shaking stopped for a moment, and we all huddled together for warmth. The kids were just starting to wake up and wanted to know what was going on. As calmly as I could, I tried to explain that Mother Earth was having an upset stomach very nearby. "She has to burp," I said. When they asked why she would burp where all the people lived, I mumbled something about her not always being able to excuse herself to an ocean or a desert.

The next few weeks were a blur. Our house was damaged, but it was still standing and many others were not. We made do without electricity, gas and water for almost two weeks. The aftershocks continued, and some of them were almost as strong as the original quake. I felt anxious, afraid and agitated most of the time. Dave felt it would be best if the kids and I went away for a few days, so we flew to San Francisco to visit some friends. While we were there, a small earthquake was felt throughout the area, and I realized that I would not escape the slightest rattle or the tiniest rumble.

By the time my fear subsided, I discovered that I was angry at God and heaven. I was angry at the angels, at the archangels, at my guides and at the Earth. Why hadn't I seen this coming and why hadn't they told me? What possible reason could there have been for this experience? Where were all the angels and guides who had pledged their unconditional love and support now? I took long walks to try to sort things out. I dismissed all of my guides, but they wouldn't leave. They kept telling me to trust in the perfection of all things, but I told them quite literally what they could do with their perfection and their things. They continued to join me on my walks and took little notice of my bad moods or foul language.

Everywhere I went, small twigs and branches fell on me or near me, and I seemed to be a magnet for nature. Feathers would appear from nowhere, fruit would fall from trees when I walked past them, blossoms would blow in my direction and birds seemed to sing their songs exclusively for me. I tried to find appreciation in what I believed to be God's idea of a peace offering, but it was half-hearted at best.

It took me a while to notice it, but nature was communicating with me. I could almost feel the twigs say something to me as they brushed past; small stones and large ones tuned to my frequency as they rolled in my direction. Trees told me about themselves, their variety and their history. I took longer walks, in different directions, and took up hiking. Everything I came across had something to say or to share.

MOTHER EARTH

One day I was outside relaxing on a lounge chair, unconsciously smashing ants one by one as they went by. An aspect of nature asked me if I would be willing to receive a visit from a new energy. Lazily and without thinking twice I said, "Okay, sure, whatever." The next moment was one of the most profound I have ever experienced, and my life has never been the same.

I was overcome with excitement and nausea as I heard Mother Earth for the very first time. She was sympathetic and compassionate as she explained that my recent experiences had been necessary, albeit difficult. She told me that the kingdoms of the Earth were eager to reconnect with the family called humanity. She went on to say that she had been quiet and patient while angelic beings and other spirit teachers had shared their wisdom with humanity, but that it was now time for the Earth to be recognized as a sentient being. She inquired as to my recent communication with the trees, rocks and animals that she had sent and wondered if I had found it pleasant and enjoyable. I nodded yes, because I could not speak. As if she already knew the answer, she continued: "Would you be willing to relate a few messages in the tongue common to your time and geography?" Without knowing what she meant, I nodded emphatically. She thanked me and said that we would speak again soon. Exhausted, I fell into the deep sleep of the weary. It was the best sleep I had experienced since before the earthquake.

Once I became accustomed to her vast energy, I was able to channel it easily via automatic writing. Sometimes the messages were initiated by an aspect of the Earth or by an individual Earth kingdom, but most of the time, they were orchestrated by Mother Earth, the sentience of the planet. I call Mother Earth Gaia, a term of endearment. It is the name the ancient Greeks used for the Goddess of the Earth. She welcomes the name Gaia but is careful to make the distinction that the Earth is neither masculine nor feminine—it is both and it is neither.

When the messages became consistent and clear, I began to offer them to different publications. Gaia told me that I would speak her words at conferences, write books for her and travel on her behalf, but I don't think that I believed her. How little did I know!

I was just beginning to get comfortable in my life with Gaia when she told me to prepare for a change. I braced myself for another earthquake, but the change expressed itself as a major life challenge. My fifteen-year marriage to Dave proved to be all that our relationship could withstand. We were and are unique individuals, and our paths were beginning to take us in different directions. We were not ideally suited for each other but had found common ground to stand on. We were true opposites, and it is true that opposites attract, at least for a while. It was the glue that held us together, but after a while the glue got pretty thin and we started to fall apart. Neither of us really wanted to give up on the relationship but secretly hoped that the other one would. We wanted to get on with our lives but didn't know how. By the time we dragged ourselves into counseling, there was no marriage left to save. Giving up was devastating, letting go was even worse.

I thought the day Dave moved out would be my last. I could not breathe from crying; I was hyperventilating and panting for breath. Every part of my being ached, and I wanted to die. I was certain that I had failed my marriage, myself and my kids. I sat on the bathroom floor, and with all my heart, I willed myself to die.

I begged God to make the pain stop by taking me out of my body and away from this life. When the angels came to comfort me, I told them, the only angel I was willing to receive was the angel of death. They took pity on me and gave me what I call an angelic sedative, which is when they use your own exhaustion to make you sleep so that they can repair the tears in your etheric body.

I felt that my spirituality had let me down yet again. It had given and then it had taken away. Dave did not share my spiritual view of the world, and he did not understand its place in my life. All attempts to bring him into my world had failed, and I no longer belonged in his. I could not ignore my purpose or walk beside my path; I had to walk upon it. I shared my despair with only a few close friends, because I was certain that a truly spiritual person would not make this much of a mess of her life. I carried my burden as best I could, breaking down only when I was alone.

My sadness became Dave's anger, which was his way of coping with a broken heart and a dead-end marriage. When we were unable to reach an equitable marital settlement, things got really ugly and our shadow selves came out to play in grand fashion. I learned a lot about myself and about human nature during that time; these are not lessons I care to repeat.

One of the first things I did when I was on my own was to make a Never list. Never lists go something like, "I will *never* again do this, and I will *never* again put up with that." I shared my long list with Gaia and thought that she would support my dedication and sincerity, but instead I could feel her quietly and patiently undoing my list. A few months later, I was asked to channel at an event celebrating the Grand Cross astrological alignment of August 11, 1999. A friend introduced me to Rob and then watched in amused satisfaction as our souls recognized each other. That there were past relationships was undeniable, but neither of us was ready for a committed relationship in the present, so for a time we explored a friendship. By the time the friendship had deepened, the love was already there. Rob waited patiently while I papered my house with my Never list. He waited for me to wear myself out, and eventually I did. The first thing I remember when I think about when we first met is that I saw myself reflected in his eyes.

ONWARD

I spend most of my days writing books and articles, channeling in private sessions and public gatherings, teaching classes and being a mom. I channel the articles Gaia and I write directly onto my computer keyboard via automatic writing. I've been doing it for so long that the keys have become extensions of my own fingers. Most of the articles are a result of broad questions asked during personal sessions, but lately Gaia has been more insistent about wanting us to be at the forefront of new developments upon the planet.

I am a conscious channel rather than a trance channel. I do not leave my body in order to channel Gaia. She has little need of my body, and I wouldn't begin to know what to do with hers! I do go into an alternate awareness, where I am comfortable, at peace and mostly disinterested in what is being said; it is a process of surrender more than anything else. I remember telling my kids when they were very young that channeling was a little like being in the back row of a very large auditorium during a special event. You can't see very well or hear very much but are just happy to be there. I remember bits and pieces of sessions but in no particular order. Within a few hours, I remember even less, and by the next day, most of the experience is erased. This used to bother me, because I felt that I was not fully aware of my day, but now I know that I am participating and facilitating at a deeper level of awareness, and I am pleased to offer myself in this way.

I do private sessions for people all over the world. Each session is unique, and I am still amazed at how diverse we all are. My clients sometimes tell me that they do not feel their questions are very important, but I have never found that to be true. We deal with big issues by asking small questions.

When I channel angels, I often feel them around my crown and about my shoulders. It feels like I am wearing a shawl that is made of light. Gaia's energy is different and really does emanate from the Earth. When I channel Gaia's sentience, I express my desire to receive guidance, support and direction on my behalf or that of my clients. As I concentrate on my desire, I begin to feel a vibrational pulse within me, and within a few moments, I can feel Gaia's love for me and for all humanity rushing up to greet me from the core of the Earth. This entire process only takes a moment or two, but before I begin, I almost always offer an invocation or a prayer that honors the Earth, my client and All That Is.

When I became accustomed to appearing in public, Gaia asked me to make sure that I was provided with a cordless microphone. She also reminded me to wear sensible shoes. I felt queasy but did as I was asked. That marked the beginning of full-body channeling, in which Gaia and I partner in the process of animating my body. When Gaia walks, I feel my legs moving, but I do not feel the sensation of walking. My body becomes an electromagnetic conduit of Gaia's vibration, and it responds accordingly. Many people sigh when Gaia brushes past them; others cry openly when she touches or holds them, which she loves to do. I cannot see with my eyes during this process, although I know that they are open and look fairly normal. I am guided by my trust in Gaia and my faith in the process. Sometimes I can even feel Gaia using the light that reflects from my eyes to transmit energy.

Gaia is animated, engaging and humorous most of the time. She is also very direct and does not water down her words. She aims directly for our hearts and rarely misses. Her energy is just as you might imagine the Earth to be: both youthful and ancient, strong and elemental, soft, innocent and pristine and refined but a little rough around the edges. Gaia arranges her words in a most unusual way, and her use of language is altogether her own. Most people hear a dialect but cannot place it, and everyone experiences her in unique and different ways, which, not surprisingly, is her intention.

Public events allow me to meet people from all over the world, and I enjoy them immensely. It is difficult to leave my kids behind when an event affects school activities or disrupts family life too much. Sometimes they are able to accompany me, like when I was asked to channel Gaia at the UN. What a unique and wonderful experience! It was the first time the kids understood first-hand the profound effect Gaia has on our hearts and minds and why I feel I must do this work.

When time permits, I teach channeling, psychic development, interdimensional healing and Earth alchemy. The classes are fun, challenging and interactive, and I always look forward to them. Although my heart belongs to Gaia, I also channel other masterful spirit teachers and encourage those who take my classes to do the same. A broad and firm foundation helps us recognize our own truth, and it is important for us to know that we are safe and welcome in all dimensions, places and moments.

I am often asked what it is like to have Gaia at my disposal all of the time. I can imagine that it might look like I live a charmed life, but it's really not like that at all. My life has afforded me a wide spectrum of experiences but a narrow path to walk. I live a gifted life but not an easy one.

MY ORDINARY, EXTRAORDINARY LIFE

I live a very simple yet extraordinary life. I like to garden in my spare time, and I also enjoy needlework and beading. I like to hike and camp, and sometimes I go fishing with Rob. I stay involved with the kids' school activities, and when time permits, I weave a bit of who I am into unsuspecting environments. For instance, every year I volunteer to speak at Career Day at school. In my first year as a volunteer, I spoke to the kids about being a writer who was concerned with the Earth and how it might feel about having humanity living upon it. The following year, I spoke about paranormal psychology and the metaphysical field. Subsequent years included discussions on psychic ability and nonphysical reality. I even described the channeling process as vividly as I could and was certain the school would disapprove and never invite me back, but I decided to go for it anyway. To my surprise, I was back next year, and the room was packed.

It took me many years to find peace and balance in who and what I am. I finally realized that I am not different but simply unique—just like you. This realization was confirmed when I was approached by a student from a local university who had attended one of my events. He was a film school graduate who had been assigned a mini-documentary for his final project. He had selected a theme that would chronicle the daily life of a psychic/channel, comparing and contrasting what he thought was an ordinary versus an extraordinary life. I thought the project sounded like fun, so for a few weeks, he and his film crew followed me everywhere I went. I went to see the graphic artist who was design‑ing my book cover and then to pick up the kids from school. They filmed my classes, and they interviewed Rob and the kids. They even interviewed Gaia! When the film was complete, it was screened at the university twice, first for students and then again for faculty and regents. Both audiences had believers, supporters and doubters. I am used to this by now. I do not question others' beliefs, attitudes, religions or ideology but find that people love to challenge mine. I never defend my position, and I do not have a point of view. Criticism and cynicism go with the territory, and Gaia's territory is pretty big.

I now expect the nature of my work to change from time to time, and I no longer stress about it. I know that there are still some challenges in store for all of us. There is a lot happening in our world that we are not being made aware of. I have always believed that a sincere heart and an open mind are all that we need, and although that is true, our hearts and minds are already working overtime.

I look forward to sharing Gaia's words with you for many years to come, and I am committed to exploring a wide variety of subjects, issues and concerns. I trust that my partnership with Gaia will continue to awaken and expand our collective conscience with respect and compassion for all life. Thank you for sharing my journey.

— Pepper Lewis

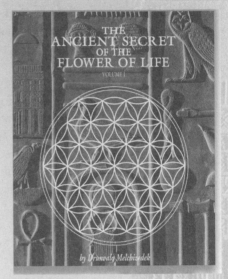

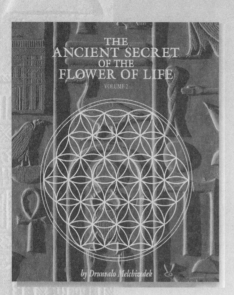

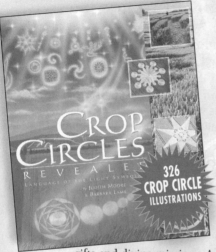

SHAMANIC SECRETS for PHYSICAL MASTERY

The purpose of this book is to allow you to understand the sacred nature of your own physical body and some of the magnificent gifts it offers you. When you work with your physical body in these new ways, you will discover not only its sacredness, but how it is compatible with Mother Earth, the animals, the plants, even the nearby planets, all of which you now recognize as being sacred in nature.

It is important to feel the value of yourself physically before you can have any lasting physical impact on the world. The less you think of yourself physically, the less likely your physical impact on the world will be sustained by Mother Earth. If a physical energy does not feel good about itself, it will usually be resolved; other physical or spiritual energies will dissolve it because it is unnatural. The better you feel about your physical self when you do the work in the previous book as well as in this one and the one to follow, the greater and more lasting will be the benevolent effect on your life, on the lives of those around you and ultimately on your planet and universe.

25^{00} SOFTCOVER 544 P.
ISBN 1-891824-29-5

Chapter Titles:

- Cellular Clearing of Traumas and Unresolved Events
- Feeling is Our Body's First and Primary Language
- The Resolution of Fear, Trauma and Hate
- Dealing with Fear, Pain and Addiction
- Shame, Arrogance, Safety and the Inability to Trust
- The Role of Trauma in Human Life
- Letting Go of Old Attitudes and Inviting New Energy
- The Waning of Individuality
- Clearing the Physical Body
- Using the Gestures to Protect, Clear and Charge
- The Flow of Energy
- Connecting with the Earth
- Communication of the Heart

- More Supportive Gestures
- Sleeping and Dreamtime
- Responsibility and Living prayer
- Communicating with the Natural World
- Life Lessons and the Vital Life Force
- The Sacrament of Food
- Working with the Elements
- Communication with Those Who Would Follow
- Elemental Connections
- Taking Responsibility
- Creating Personal Relationships

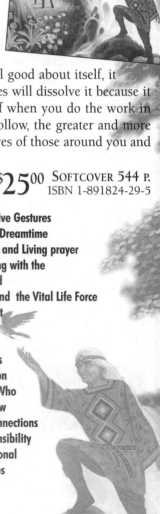

SEDONA VORTEX GUIDE BOOK

A unique and in-depth examination of some of the reasons, in addition to the awesome beauty of the area, that draw four million people to Sedona every year. An amazing group of other-dimensional beings reveal Sedona's sacred energies, vortex secrets, dimensional openings, the nature and history of vortexes, the ancient and future history of Sedona and its status as an ascension center. A renowned scientist shares his overview of the geophysical aspects of vortexes, and maps of the vortexes show chakra associations and interdimensional access points. Introduction by Mary Lou Keller.

$14⁹⁵ SOFTCOVER 236 P.
ISBN 0-929385-25-X

Chapter Titles:

PART I. SEDONA'S UNIQUE ENERGIES

- **Sacred Sedona**
  Page Bryant
- **Energies of Sedona**
  E.C./Bella Karish
- **Sedona's Unique Global/Cosmic Position**
  Vywamus/Janet McClure
- **Sedona Vortexes: Sound in Motion**
  Grandmothers/Lorraine Darr
- **Vortex Questions Answered**
  Germane/Lyssa Royal
- **More Questions Answered**
  Bearclaw and Zoosh/Robert Shapiro

Part II. ANCIENT AND FUTURE HISTORY

- **The Ancient Past and Its Traces**
  Vywamus/Janet McClure
- **Ancient and Future Civilizations of Sedona**
  Zoosh/Robert Shapiro
- **Past and Future Civilizations of the Soul's Journey through Sedona**
  Bearclaw/Robert Shapiro

Part III. INTERDIMENSIONAL ADVENTURES

- **Dimensional Openings in Sedona**
  Vywamus/Janet McClure
- **Doorways, Pathways, Portals and Caves in Sedona**
  Zoosh/Robert Shapiro

Part IV. CURRENT ET INVOLVEMENTS

- **Sedona Energy and ET Calibration Experiments**
  Sasha/Lyssa Royal
- **UFO Encounters in Sedona**
  Joopah and Zoosh/Robert Shapiro
- **Sedona, an Ascension Center**
  Jørgen Korsholm (Jananda)

Part V. A MORE PHYSICAL/EVOLUTIONARY VIEW

- **An Overview of the Geophysical Aspects of Vortexes**
  Alsgoud Sprinke
- **The Nature and History of Vortexes**
  Nova 8
- **Principles of Vortical Structure and Motion**
  Germane/Lyssa Royal

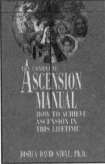

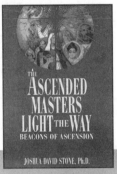
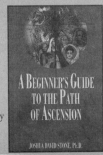

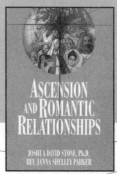

BRIAN GRATTAN

MAHATMA I & II
The I AM Presence

Awaken and realize that all of humankind will create their "body for ascension," whether they accomplish this now or later, and that this is not the exclusive domain of Christ or Buddha or the many others who have ascended—*this is your birthright*. When humans lift the veils of their unworthiness and recognize that they are the sons of God, that there is divine equality and that no one is greater than another, then you will have begun your journey in the way that it was intended. The *Mahatma* is for those who are motivated to search for the answers that can respond to their mental and spiritual bodies. No matter how contrary your current beliefs, this book contains methods for creating your spiritual lightbody for ascension and also explains your eternal journey in a way never before available to humankind.

$19⁹⁵ SOFTCOVER 480 P.
ISBN 0-929385-77-2

Chapter Titles:

- Introduction by Vywamus
- The Journey of the Mahatma from Source to Earth
- The Spiritual Initiation through the Mahatma
- What Is Channeling?
- Evolution of a Third-Dimensional Planet
- The Rays, Chakras and Initiations
- Conversations with Barbara Waller
- Transformation through Evolution
- Patterns
- Time and Patience

- Mahatma on Channeling
- Conversation Between the Personality (Brian) and Mahatma (the I AM Presence)
- Mastery
- The Tenth Ray
- Integrating Unlimitedness
- The Etheric and Spiritual Ascensions
- The Cosmic Heart
- Mahatma as the I AM Presence
- So What Does the Personality Think of All of This?

TITLES ON TAPE
by Brian Grattan

BASEL SEMINAR
10 TAPE SET (AUDIO CASSETTE), English with German translation $35.00

EASTER SEMINAR
7 TAPE SET (AUDIO CASSETTE), English with German translation $59.95

SEATTLE SEMINAR
12 TAPE SET (AUDIO CASSETTE) $79.95
Twelve one-hour audio tapes from the Seattle Seminar, October 27–30, 1994. These twelve powerful hours of meditations lead to total spiritual transformation by recoding your two-strand DNA to function in positive mutation.